TUCKETT B

Model T Ford Specialist

We are a family firm of dedicated enthusiasts who offer a friendly personal welcome to clients wishing to buy or sell Model T Ford vehicles or spares.

Visitors are always welcome, even if only to look through our range of stock.

We carry out courses on many Model T aspects including driving and maintenance.

Our rural location allows safe, scenic drives without the pressures of other traffic.

A comprehensive stock of parts (both new and used) is always available and you are welcome to browse. We also have an extensive library of books.

Our workshops are extensively equipped with all specialist tools to carry out any work on Model Ts.

Valuations and quotations are always available.
Advice is only a telephone call away.

MARSTONFIELDS, NORTH MARSTON, BUCKINGHAM, BUCKS MK18 3PG
Telephone: +44 (0) 1296 670500 / 07000 Model T (66 33 58)
Mobile: 07860 818818   Fax: +44 (0) 1296 670730
E-mail: modelt.ford@virgin.net   Website: www.modeltford.co.uk

MILLER'S

collectors
cars

Bonhams ^1793

WORLD LEADERS

With approximately 30 collectors' motor car sales per year throughout Europe and overseas, the Bonhams team puts the most authoritative connoisseurs in the automotive market at your disposal. Our regional offices and network of national and international representatives work together to give each auction the maximum marketing, publicity and exposure to the collectors' car market world-wide.

If you are considering selling your veteran, vintage or collectors' motor car, motorcycle or automobilia please contact:

Motor Cars
Tim Schofield, Marcus Ross,
Richard Gauntlett,
James Knight
or Malcolm Barber
020 7313 3176
020 7313 3170 fax

or Stewart Skilbeck
01757 638 894 tel/fax
email: cars@bonhams.com

Automobilia, Toys & Models
Toby Wilson
020 7313 3147
020 7313 2701 fax
email: automobilia@bonhams.com

Motorcycles
Ben Walker
020 7313 3139
0207 313 3170 fax
email: motorcycles@bonhams.com

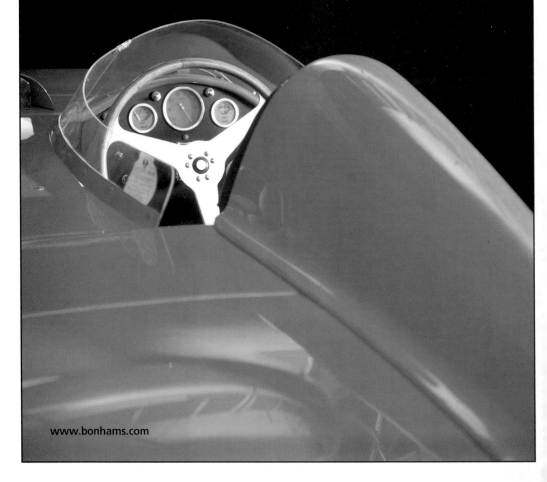

www.bonhams.com

collectors cars

GENERAL EDITOR
Mick Walker

FOREWORD
James May

MILLER'S COLLECTORS CARS PRICE GUIDE 2005/6

Created and designed by
Miller's Publications
The Cellars, High Street
Tenterden, Kent TN30 6BN
Telephone: 01580 766411
Fax: 01580 766100

General Editor: Mick Walker
Project Co-ordinator & Designer: Philip Hannath
Editorial Co-ordinator: Deborah Wanstall
Editorial Assistants: Melissa Hall, Joanna Hill, Maureen Horner
Advertisement Designer: Simon Cook
Jacket Design: Colin Goody
Advertising Executive: Emma Gillingham
Advertising Administrator & Co-ordinator: Melinda Williams
Production Assistants: June Barling, Ethne Tragett
Additional Photography: Simon Clay, Stephen Everest, Ferret Fotographics,
Charles Leith, Eric Newboult, Doug Nye, Robin Saker

First published in Great Britain in 2004
by Miller's, a division of Mitchell Beazley,
imprints of Octopus Publishing Group Ltd,
2–4 Heron Quays, London E14 4JP

© 2004 Octopus Publishing Group Ltd

A CIP catalogue record for this book is
available from the British Library

ISBN 1 84000 961 6

While every care has been exercised in the
compilation of this guide, neither the
authors nor publishers accept any liability
for any financial or other loss incurred
by reliance placed on the information contained in
Miller's Collectors Cars Price Guide 2005/6

Illustrations and film output by 1.13, Whitstable, Kent
Printed and bound by Toppan Printing Co (HK) Ltd, China

Front cover illustration:

1960 MGA coupe MKII
Photograph © Octopus Publishing Group

Contents

Acknowledgments

The publishers would like to acknowledge the great assistance given by our consultants:

Malcolm Barber
Montpelier Street, Knightsbridge,
London SW7 1HH
Tel: 020 7393 3900

Tom Falconer
Claremont Corvette, Snodland, Kent ME6 5NA

**Mark Hamilton
& Simon Hope**
H&H Classic Auctions Ltd, Whitegate Farm,
Hatton Lane, Hatton, Cheshire WA4 4BZ
Tel: 01925 730630

Simon Johnson
Military Vehicle Trust, 7 Carter Fold, Mellor,
Lancs BB2 7ER

Brian Page
Classic Assessments, Stonechat House,
Moorymead Close, Watton-at-Stone,
Herts SG14 3HF

**Mike Penn CEI,
Tech Eng ITE, Mairso**
Haynes Motor Museum, Sparkford,
Nr Yeovil, Somerset BA22 7LH

Mike Smith
Chiltern House, Ashendon, Aylesbury,
Bucks HP18 0HB

Neil Tuckett
Marstonfields, North Marston,
Bucks MK18 3PG

Peter W. Card BSc
Bonhams, 65 Lots Road, Chelsea,
London SW10 1HH

We would also like to extend our thanks to all auction houses, their press offices, and dealers who have assisted us in the production of this book, along with the organisers and press offices of the following events:

Beaulieu September Autojumble & Automart

Goodwood Festival of Speed

Rétromobile, Paris

Silverstone Historic Tribute

The War & Peace Show

London Classic Car Show

How to use this book

I t is our aim to make the guide easy to use. Marques are listed alphabetically and then chronologically. Military & Police Vehicles, Racing & Rallying, Replica, Kit & Reproduction Cars, Restoration Projects, Taxis and Children's Cars are located after the marques, towards the end of the book. In the Automobilia section, objects are grouped alphabetically by type. If you cannot find what you are looking for, please consult the index on page 268.

JAGUAR 101

Jaguar (British 1927–)

1948 Jaguar Mk IV 2½ Litre Drophead Coupé, 2663cc, 6-cylinder engine, fully restored 1988–89, finished in red, red leather interior, concours condition.
£26,100–31,000 / €39,000–47,000 / $48,000–57,000 ⚒ BB(S)

Miller's Milestones

Jaguar XK120/140/150 (1948–61)
Price Range: £6,000–65,000 / €8,900–96,000 / $10,6000–114,000
When Jaguar's XK120 arrived in 1948, it looked like an unbeatable package. The company's boss, William Lyons, was responsible for styling this superb roadster, which would have sold on its handsome lines alone. But the XK120 was not just about style, there was substance under the bonnet in the shape of a brand-new, twin-camshaft, straight-six engine displacing 3442cc. This classic power unit would survive well into the 1990s, powering everything from Le Mans winning cars to armoured vehicles and even fire engines. The first few hundred cars (built between 1948 and 1949) sported aluminium bodies, and today these are the most valuable of all the XK models. With a super-smooth 160bhp on tap, they were capable of 120mph, hence the '120' monicker. For a short time, the new Jaguar was the world's fastest series-production car.

Jaguar was totally overwhelmed by the massive demand for the car, which had been intended only as a limited-production model. As a result, the company tooled up for volume production with a steel body for 1950.
From then on, there was no looking back. A fixed-head coupé was launched in 1951, while a roomier drophead coupé arrived for 1953. A large percentage of production was exported to North America.
For 1954, Jaguar released the XK140, which had larger bumpers and, more usefully, rack-and-pinion steering. This was followed by the XK150 for 1957. Essentially, this was based on the original chassis, but it had all-new body panels. Concerns over lack of braking performance on previous models were addressed by fitting Dunlop discs to all four wheels, and with the arrival of the 3.8 litre 'S' version in 1959, power rose to an impressive 265bhp, giving a top speed of 135mph.

1951 Jaguar XK120 Coupé, 3442cc, 6-cylinder engine, left-hand drive, replica C-Type cylinder head, servo-assisted front disc brakes, Borrani wire wheels, finished in metallic green, green leather interior, concours condition.
£55,000–66,000 / €83,000–99,000
$102,000–122,000 ⚒ B(Kn)

1952 Jaguar XK120 Coupé, 3442cc, double-overhead-camshaft 6-cylinder engine.
£15,200–18,200 / €22,500–26,900
$26,800–32,000 ⚒ COYS

JAGUAR Model	ENGINE cc/cyl	DATES	CONDITION 1	2	3
SSI	2054/6	1932–33	£35,000	£18,000	£12,000
SSI	2252/6	1932–33	£22,000+	£17,000	£13,500
SSII	1052/6	1932–33	£18,000	£15,000	£11,000
SSI	2663/6	1934	£26,000	£22,000	£15,000
SSII	1608/4	1934	£18,000	£15,000	£12,000
SS90	2663/6	1935	£60,000+	–	–
SS100 (3.4)	3485/6	1938–39	£90,000+	–	–
SS100 (2.6)	2663/6	1936–39	£90,000+	–	–
Value dependent on body style, completeness and originality, particularly original chassis to body.

Source Code
refers to the 'Key to Illustrations' on page 251 that lists the details of where the item was sourced. Advertisers are also indicated on this page. The ⚒ icon indicates the item was sold at auction. The ⊞ icon indicates the item originated from a dealer. The 🚗 icon indicates the item belonged to a member of a car club; see Directory of Car Clubs on page 255.

Miller's Milestones
highlights particular models providing technical details, outlining important historic events and the effect they have had on the car industry.

Caption
provides a brief description of the vehicle or item, and could include comments on its history, mileage, any restoration work carried out and current condition.

Price Guide
these are based on actual prices realized. Remember that Miller's is a price guide not a price list and prices are affected by many variables such as location, condition, desirability and so on. Don't forget that if you are selling, it is quite likely you will be offered less than the price range. Price ranges for items sold at auction tend to include the buyer's premium and VAT if applicable. The exchange rate used in this edition is 1.48 for € and 1.76 for $.

Price Boxes
give the value of a particular model, dependent on condition and are compiled by our team of experts, car clubs and private collectors.
Condition 1 refers to a vehicle in top class condition, but not concours d'élégance standard, either fully restored or in very good original condition.
Condition 2 refers to a good, clean roadworthy vehicle, both mechanically and bodily sound.
Condition 3 refers to a runner, but in need of attention, probably to both bodywork and mechanics. It must have a current MOT.
Restoration projects are vehicles that fail to make the Condition 3 grading.

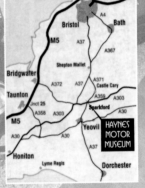

Foreword

I am an unashamed classic car fantasist, so I can honestly claim that *Miller's Collectors Cars Price Guide* is one of my favourite books. As a chap, I obviously prefer to conduct most of my research in the smallest room of the house, so to begin with I can vouch for its compactness. For assembling a fantasy garage on an imagined budget, it is worth a whole pile of magazines and is much more manageable.

However, there is more to it than that. For a start, Miller's deals with real cars that have been sold in the real world, so is much more authoritative than some of the rather arbitrary price guides featured in the classic car press, reliance on which can lead to disappointment.

Secondly, there's plenty of background reading to guide you through the potentially terrifying process of choosing a car that you will probably cherish for many years: marque histories, chronologies, tips on buying at auction – in fact everything to encourage and inspire that giant leap from idle day-dreaming to actually buying a piece of motoring history. It's worked for me several times, most recently uniting me with a Bentley T2 saloon.

All of which reminds me – I've been meaning to mug up on 1970s V8 Aston Martins, and this, as I am sure you will also find, is a good place to start.

James May

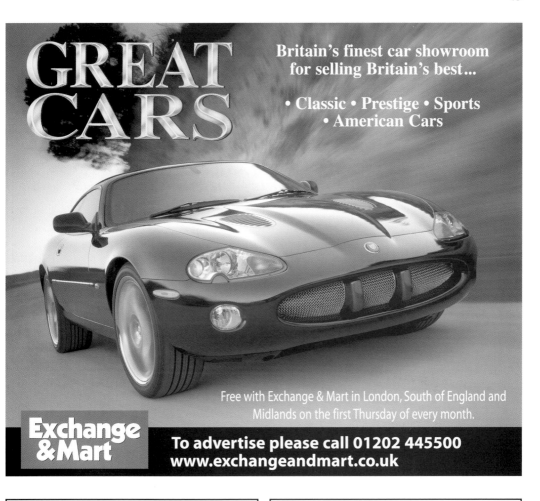
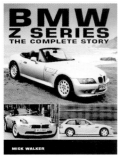

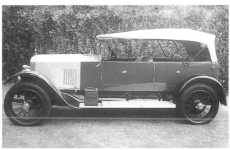

The State of the Market

Over the last year the marketplace has been stable during a period when financial investments have proved volatile as a result of the Iraq war. However, exceptional items of quality and rarity, that combine both condition and provenance, have moved strongly forwards.

In the collector cars auction world Bonhams and Christie's have remained key players, the former choosing the Goodwood Festival of Speed, Goodwood Revival, the National Motor Museum in Hampshire and Olympia, London as venues for their prime sales. International sales venues have included the Retromobile in Paris and Pebble Beach, California for Christie's and Monaco, Gstaad, the Geneva Salon and Quail Lodge, California for Bonhams. In the provinces active players have been H&H at Buxton, Cheffins in the East of England, Lambert & Foster in Kent and Barons at Sandown Park. In May H&H ventured into the metropolis, only to return to Buxton for future sales.

Under new management for 2004, the London to Brighton Veteran Car Run is attracting renewed interest. During the year there has been significant movement in prices of cars eligible for the run, with seemingly endless demand for the better-known marques, such as the 1901 De Dion Bouton which sold at Bonhams in December for a record-breaking £42,000 / €62,000 / $74,000. In the same sale a 1902 Panhard Levassor realized a new benchmark at £87,300 / €129,000 / $154,000, and at H&H in May a newly restored 1899 Panhard-Levassor Wagonnette achieved £107,500 / €252,000 / $189,000. In contrast, cars produced between 1905 and 1918 look excellent value for money: a 1909 Sears Roebuck buggy sold for £8,165 / €12,100 / $14,400 at Coys in June, a rare 1906 S.H.E.W. Double Phaeton, in need of restoration, realized £12,600 / €18,600 / $22,200 at Cheffins in the same month and a 1909 Wolseley-Siddeley 12/16hp Tourer sold for £19,550 / €28,900 / $34,000 at Bonhams in February.

Cars from museums will always command a premium when offered on the open market. Bonhams sale of duplicate vehicles from the British Motor Industry Heritage Trust collection at Gaydon in June proved this point, when a 1910 Austin 18/24hp Endcliffe Tourer achieved a staggering £91,700 / €136,000 / $161,000, trebling a low estimate, while in the same sale a 1995 Rover Maestro Clubman achieved £7,475 / €11,000 / $13,200. At the Beaulieu Autojumble sale in September, a 1937 Wolseley Super Six, formerly Lord Nuffield's car and previously on display in the National Motor Museum, doubled mid-estimate at £28,750 / €43,000 / $51,000. 'Barn discoveries' continue to amaze with Christie's sale of a 1927 Austro-Daimler 3 Litre – an ex Ards TT car – achieving £362,750 / €537,000 / $638,000 in London in March this year, over five times the price guide. Both Cheffins and H&H have achieved exceptional results during the year with 'barn discovery' pre-war Rolls-Royces – always a strong market.

The sports car market continues to flourish; Austin Healeys moved into positive territory during the year with good examples of Healey 3000 Mark IIIs fetching around £24,000–26,000 / €36,000–38,000 / $42,000–67,000 and 100/4's around £13,000–16,000 / €19,200–23,700 / $23,000–28,200 – an upward movement of about 15 per cent during the year. Jaguar E-Types remain in demand although restoration projects generally fail to excite bidders because of high restoration costs. The XJS V12 remains the bargain-basement Jaguar. The top price during the year was achieved by Barons for a 1989 Convertible at £11,276 / €16,700 / $19,800. Competition provenance will always up the bidding and at Christie's a 1960 Aston Martin DB4 GT – the 1961 Le Mans test car with racing history – sold in Paris for £441,045 / €653,000 / $776,000 against a going rate of £300,000–350,000 / €444,000–518,000 / $528,000–616,000.

Quality will always win out and Christie's 1939 Delage D8/120 Cabriolet, a 1999 Pebble Beach winner, achieved an estimate-breaking £393,900 / €583,000 / $693,000 in the USA, and at the Nurburgring in August a Bonhams one-owner 1972 Ferrari 365 GTS/4 Daytona achieved £257,394 / €381,000 / $453,000.

An emerging market in 'recent-day-supercar-classics' was tested by the major auction houses during the year. Christie's London achieved £731,250 / €108,000 / $129,000 for a 1998 McLaren F1, Bonhams at the Nurburgring took £582,746 / €863,000 / $103,000 for a 1997 Mercedes CLK GTR, and £459,238 / €680,000 / $808,000 for a 1998 Porsche 911 GT1 in Monaco in May. More recently a hushed hall in Monaco saw yet another new market emerging when Bonhams sold the 2000 Ferrari F1/2000 Formula 1 racing single seater, ex-Michael Schumacher, Grand Prix-winning car for £951,753 / €1,408,000 / $1,675,000.

So what of the future? With interest rates nudging gently upwards and predicted to rise further, the next year may see more quality cars coming to the market as owners find other homes for their money. Although no-one expects the car market to follow the property market in quite the same way as it did in 1988 to 1989, some upward adjustment may be expected at the top end to reflect the general increase in the domestic housing market, which now leaves top cars looking relatively inexpensive by comparison. The message of course remains that buyers should select their cars according to their enthusiasm and ignore the investment aspect. Rises in the marketplace will then only please and falls will not disappoint. **Malcolm Barber**

Planning of Restoration Projects

With such a buoyant classic car scene, the enthusiast has plenty to choose from. However, if you have set your sights on a car that is rare and expensive, things may prove more difficult.

Right from the start, it is vital to realize that restoring a car takes time, patience, equipment, knowledge and last, but not least, money. Without sufficient funds no one, no matter how enthusiastic, will be able to meet the demands of a full restoration. Set a limit on how much you intend spending (including the price of the vehicle) and consider how you are going to raise the money. If you intend borrowing, shop around for the the best deal.

Another early requirement is to assess your ability to carry out the task in hand. Everyone is different: some may have virtually no skills at all, just enthusiasm, while others may be qualified engineers. In addition, a person's level of expertise will often vary from task to task, which should be taken into consideration. An important decision, therefore, is to separate the jobs you can carry out yourself from those that will have to be entrusted to others.

One way of reducing reliance on others – and keeping costs to a minimum – is to accept a lower standard of restoration. For example, it is better to complete an enjoyable, usable car that is reliable, but does not possess an immaculate factory-like finish, than to put yourself deeply into debt with all the heartache this can bring. Know your abilities, both mechanical and financial, and stay within them.

A secure and weatherproof place to work is essential. It should be heated and well-lit, and provide enough room to work without constantly having to move things.

If you are thinking of sharing a workshop with another enthusiast, make sure that you both get on – the last thing you want is to be forced to move out half-way through the task.

Your workshop should have a solidly constructed bench, a ramp and/or pit so that you can reach the underside of the car, and shelves and cupboards for storing spare parts, tools, equipment and consumables. Other important pieces of equipment are an engine hoist, an engine stand and a sturdy vice mounted to the bench.

A successful restoration will be one where the under-bonnet area is as clean as the outside of the car; something that is not always appreciated by someone undertaking a restoration for the first time.

Hand tools are best hung on a board – this beats having to constantly hunt through a tool box. Files should be stored separately to avoid damage and to ensure that any metal particles are contained.

The most widely used tools are spanners and, like any other tool, it is essential to go for quality. My own favourites are the combination type – open at one end with a ring at the other. Sockets and open-ended spanners also have their part to play, but do not be tempted to use an adjustable spanner. It will never fit as well as the correct size

Will your restoration be up to the standard of this superb 1929 Bentley 4½ litre Blower?

of spanner and may slip, either rounding the nut or causing injury.

Other essentials are Philips (cross-head) and conventional screwdrivers in a selection of sizes. You may also need a set of allen (hex) keys. In addition to the various hand tools, you will require an electric drill and accessories, including a flexible shaft if you want to carry out porting work and a polishing buff.

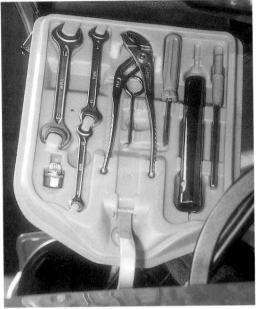

A full 'as supplied' factory tool kit is often overlooked when carrying out a restoration.

Next comes the more expensive and specialized items, such as a lathe, welding equipment and a hydraulic press. These, together with any specific factory tools, will allow a much wider range of work to be carried out 'in house', but you will need to learn how to use them.

Every successful restoration needs a work plan – without one, you will find the task a frustrating experience, which may eventually cause you to abandon the project. First, you have to decide whether you are going to tackle the complete car as a whole, or break it down into major parts, attempting only one task at a time and making sure this is completed before starting the next job.

As you strip down the various components, document everything carefully with notes, sketches and photographs. Always tag items so that they can be identified later on. Make sure that fragile items are given proper protection. Pay particular attention to electrical wiring, connections and equipment, comparing them to a standard factory wiring diagram. If they differ, find out why. Nothing is worse than attempting to sort out the electrics after everything else has been completed.

Plan ahead by sourcing spare parts, and collect as much data as possible on your particular model (including a workshop manual if available). Joining the appropriate owners' club can be invaluable in this respect.

Before beginning the actual restoration, examine every item to establish if it can still be used or needs replacing. Mark parts as necessary. For example, 'fully serviceable', 'repairable', 'scrap', 'needs painting', 'needs replating', etc. Some parts may have to be repaired simply because no replacements are available. In other cases, new components will have to be made, which can prove extremely expensive.

Patience is essential. Keep at the task, but never go faster than is practical. Rushing a job will only cause problems, such as snapped bolts and skinned knuckles.

If you plan to carry out the restoration over a long period, or if the work is not carried out in a workshop that is heated all the time, you will need to coat many of the parts in oil, grease or some other preservative. It is important, however, that rubber parts are kept well clear of these fluids, which would cause them to perish.

Good luck with your project!

Mick Walker

A restored BMW 328. In production from 1937 to 1940 this legendary car was considered the best Roadster of its time. In total only 464 cars were manufactured.

AC (British 1908–98)

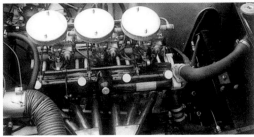

1954 AC Aceca Bristol Coupé, 1971cc, Bristol 6-cylinder engine, 130bhp, top speed 120mph, completely restored over 5 years at a cost of over £30,000 / €44,000 / $53,000.
£31,000–37,000 / €46,000–55,000
$55,000–66,000 ➤ B(Kn)
This car was the Aceca prototype and works demonstrator. Some time later, it was sold to World Land Speed Record holder Sir Donald Campbell, who became one of the first AC owners to have his car factory converted to Aceca Bristol specification.

1959 AC Ace Bristol, 1971cc, 6-cylinder engine, left-hand drive.
£46,000–55,000 / €68,000–81,000
$81,000–97,000 ➤ B(Mon)

1957 AC Ace Bristol, 1971cc, left-hand drive, restored at a cost of £57,000 / €84,000 / $100,000.
£64,000–77,000 / €95,500–114,500
$113,500–136,000 ➤ COYS
The Ace's origins lie in a racing design built by John Tojeiro in 1950. This consisted of a lightweight chassis, high-performance Bristol 2 litre engine and a pretty but spartan, functional aluminium body based loosely on the Ferrari 166 MM Barchetta. During its production life, the Ace was available with AC, Bristol and Ford engines. However, it was the Bristol engine, along with the car's elegant bodywork, that has made the Ace one of the all-time classic cars. The Ace was also a very successful racing car, and in no place was this more evident than in the USA. An AC Ace Bristol won the SCCA's E production class championship in 1957, 1958 and 1959. To try to give the Aces some competition, the SCCA moved them up a class in 1960, but to no avail; an Ace-Bristol won that class also. In desperation, the Aces were put into a higher class still, the C production category, but Pierre Mion and his Ace won that too!

1962 AC Aceca Coupé, 1971cc, factory-fitted with second fuel pump and fuel line from tank, bumpers, screen washers, heater and demister, extensively restored 1996, finished in metallic green, dark green interior.
£21,000–25,200 / €31,000–37,000
$37,000–44,000 ➤ H&H

AC Model	ENGINE cc/cyl	DATES	CONDITION 1	2	3
Sociable	636/1	1907–12	£14,000	£9,000	£6,000
12/24 (Anzani)	1498/4	1919–27	£14,000	£11,500	£7,500
16/40	1991/6	1920–28	£18,000	£15,000	£11,000
16/60 Drophead/Saloon	1991/6	1937–40	£24,000	£21,000	£15,500
16/70 Sports Tourer	1991/6	1937–40	£35,000	£26,000	£18,000
16/80 Competition 2-Seater	1991/6	1937–40	£55,000	£45,000	£35,000

1969 AC 428 Frua Convertible, 7014cc, Ford V8 engine, wire wheels.
£24,700–29,600 / €36,000–43,000
$43,000–52,000 ⚒ H&H

Following the fruitful collaboration with Carroll Shelby, which had resulted in the hugely successful Shelby AC Cobras, AC Cars went back into the Grand Tourer business. The AC 428, launched in 1966, was a very high-speed tourer indeed, available as either a fixed-head or drophead coupé. The 428 was built on a lengthened Cobra chassis with a 7104cc Ford V8 and Frua-built body. With breathtaking acceleration and 142mph top speed, the 428 offered a more exclusive alternative to the Aston Martin DB6 and Chrysler V8-engined Jensen Interceptor. However, body supply from Frua proved to be sporadic due to Italian labour relations, US Ford engines did not arrive when expected and large-engined motor cars became unfashionable due to the 1973–74 fuel crisis. By the time 428 production was axed, just 51 convertibles and 29 fixed-heads had been produced.

1997 AC Ace Supercharged Roadster, Ford Mustang V8 engine.
£24,200–29,000 / €35,800–43,000
$42,600–51,100 ⚒ B(Kn)

The acquisition of the rights to the AC name by Autokraft in 1982 led to the development of several prototypes of a next-generation AC to take the place of the venerable Cobra, a process that led to the introduction of a new Ace at the 1993 Motor Show. Aimed squarely at the Mercedes-Benz SL market, the new Ace was priced accordingly. A thoroughly modern sports car in every way, the Ace featured a stainless-steel chassis and was powered by the latest Ford Mustang V8 engine producing around 265bhp. The curvacious aluminium body rivalled the original Ace's for looks and was well equipped with an electric hood, air conditioning and heated seats. Autokraft's demise in 1996 seriously disrupted Ace production, and although the company was reconstituted as AC Cars Group Ltd, only a few more Aces were made before production finally ceased in the late 1990s.

AC Model	ENGINE cc/cyl	DATES	CONDITION 1	2	3
2 Litre	1991/6	1947–55	£7,000	£4,000	£1,500
Buckland	1991/6	1949–54	£9,000	£5,500	£2,500
Ace	1991/6	1953–63	£30,000+	£25,000	£18,000
Ace Bristol	1971/6	1954–63	£45,000+	£30,000	£20,000
Ace 2.6	1553/6	1961–62	£38,000	£32,000	£29,000
Aceca	1991/6	1954–63	£21,000	£12,000	£9,000
Aceca Bristol	1971/6	1956–63	£28,000	£18,000	£12,000
Greyhound Bristol	1971/6	1961–63	£16,000	£12,000	£8,000
Cobra Mk II 289	4735/8	1963–64	£90,000	£80,000	£60,000
Cobra Mk III 427	6998/8	1965–67	£135,000	£100,000	£80,000
Cobra Mk IV	5340/8	1987–92	£45,000	£38,000	£28,000
428 Frua	7014/8	1967–73	£19,000	£15,000	£10,000
428 Frua Convertible	7014/8	1967–73	£30,000	£20,000	£16,000
3000ME	2994/6	1976–84	£12,000	£7,000	£6,000

Racing history for Cobra will put the price at £100,000–120,000+.

AJS *(British 1927–33)*

◀ **1930 AJS Two-Seater with Dickey,** 1018cc, side-valve 4-cylinder engine, aluminium bodywork.
£8,700–10,400 / €12,900–15,400
$15,300–18,300 ⚒ CGC

More widely known for its excellent motorcycles, AJS started producing four-wheeled commercial vehicles in 1927. Perhaps in response to Austin's continued success with the Seven, belatedly jumped on the light-car bandwagon with its own Nine. The aim was for a very high-quality vehicle that perhaps owed a little more to the Clyno Nine than any other model. The car used a four-cylinder Coventry Climax engine and employed the best materials available. Unfortunately for AJS its efforts to provide quality came at a price that was too high for many, and it misjudged the market. The parent firm collapsed in 1931 and was taken over by Willys-Overland-Crossley.

Alfa Romeo *(Italian 1910–)*

Alfa (Anonima Lombardo Fabbrica Automobili) was founded in 1910 from the ashes of the failed Societa Italiana Automobili Darracq which had been formed in February 1906 to manufacture French Darracq vehicles.

Alfa's first cars were based on Darracq models, but it soon began producing much different and certainly better ones. Well built and powerful, these were designed by the former Bianchi and Fiat engineer Giuseppe Merosi.

Before 1914, Alfa progressed well on both production and racing fronts, but it was during WWI that the Romeo connection came about. Nicola Romeo was a manufacturer of mining equipment, but during the war, his company made portable compressors. In 1915, Romeo took over Alfa's Portello factory to build agricultural machinery and aero engines. Then in 1918 Romeo absorbed Alfa, and when the conflict was over the company returned to building cars which henceforth were marketed as Alfa Romeos.

Enzo Ferrari ran the Alfa Romeo race team during much of the inter-war period. Successes under his leadership were huge and helped establish Alfa Romeo as the premier Italian sporting marque.

Ferrari had recruited Vittorio Jano to design the race cars, but he also designed some superb road cars. These began in 1927 with a six-cylinder overhead-camshaft 1500 tourer and a 1750 version of the same car, followed by 1500 and 1700 twin cam-models. In 1931, Jano designed a 2.3 litre supercharged straight-eight (known as the 8C); that year it won the first of four consecutive Le Mans 24-hour consecutive races.

However 1931 also saw financial problems rear their head and in 1933 the company was taken over by the newly founded and government backed Istituto Reconstuzione Industriale.

Prior to Jano leaving to join Lancia in 1938, he designed the 6C (a 2.3 litre twin-cam six) in 1934.

This was subsequently further developed after WWII.

However, the company's postwar rebirth was truly remarkable. Even before Alfa's production road cars made a return to the market in 1947, the race cars were cleaning up. The Tipo 158 Alfetta and its derivative, the Tipo 159, totally dominated the immediate post-war GP racing scene. They scored in excess of 25 victories and won the first two official World Driver's Championships, but following this, Alfa retired from Grand Prix racing.

In the early 1950s, Alfa had entered the mass-production market with a four-cylinder 1900. In 1954, the company introduced the 1300 double-overhead-camshaft four cylinder Giulietta. This was built in a wide range of versions in both two- and four-door bodyshells, by Bertone, Pininfarina and Zagato. In 1962, a larger, more powerful Giulia made its debut. There was also a 2000 four and a 2600 six.

Expansion saw a new plant open at Arese, near Milan, in 1963, and the first car built there was the Giulia Sprint GT, which arrived in September 1963. In 1969, production at Arese exceeded 100,000 for the first time.

Next came the front-wheel-drive Alfasud, which entered production in 1972.

The Alfasud proved popular and ran alongside the Alfetta (1972), the Giulietta (1976), the sporting GTV6 (1979) and the unsuccessful luxury 6 model. A new small car, the 33, debuted in 1983. The Alfasud line ended in 1984, the final cars being Ti versions.

Although the Alfasud had seemed a success, in commerical terms it had proved a disaster. Because of constant strikes, it was later revealed that every Alfasud built had lost money. This also meant that by the mid-1980s the entire Alfa Romeo company was in serious trouble. Eventually it was only saved thanks to a take-over by Fiat.

c1932 Alfa Romeo 6C 1750 4th Series Gran Sport Spider, coachwork by Zagato, 1752cc, 6-cylinder engine, 85bhp at 4,400rpm, 4-speed manual gearbox, semi-eliptic leaf springs, adjustable shock absorbers.
£230,000–276,000 / €341,000–410,000 / $406,000–487,000 ✗ COYS
In 1929, Alfa Romeo announced the 6C 1750 in Turismo, Sport and Gran Sport specifications, all with normally aspirated engines. Soon after, the ultimate supercharged Super Sport and Gran Sport models appeared, rapid machines capable of 100mph and vivid acceleration, as demonstrated by Nuvolari and Guidotti's win in the 1930 Mille Miglia.

ALFA ROMEO Model	ENGINE cc/cyl	DATES	CONDITION 1	2	3
24hp	4084/4	1910–11	£25,000	£16,000	£12,000
12hp	2413/4	1910–11	£18,000	£11,000	£8,000
40–60	6028/4	1913–15	£32,000	£24,000	£14,000
RL/RLSS	2916/6	1921–22	£40,000	£24,000	£14,000
RM	1944/4	1924–25	£28,000	£17,000	£13,000
6C 1500	1487/6	1927–28	£50,000*	£20,000+	£10,000+
6C 1750	1752/6	1923–33	£150,000+	£100,000+	–
6C 1900	1917/6	1933	£18,000	£15,000	£12,000
6C 2300	2309/6	1934	£30,000+	£18,000	£15,000
6C 2500 SS Cabriolet/Spider	2443/6	1939–45	£100,000	£50,000	£40,000
6C 2500 SS Coupé	2443/6	1939–45	£60,000	£40,000	£30,000
8C 2300 Monza/Short Chassis	2300/8	1931–34	£1,500,000+	£600,000+	–
8C 2900	2900/8	1935–39	£1,500,000+	£1,000,000	–

Value is dependent on sporting history, body style and engine type.
*The high price of this model is dependent on whether it is 1500 supercharged/twin overhead cam, and with or without a racing history. Look for 6C 1750 Gran Sport Zagato Supercharged, £200,000+.

c1932 Alfa Romeo 8C 2300 Spider Corsa, 2336cc, 8-cylinder engine.
£560,000–672,000 / €829,000–994,000 / $985,500–1,182,500 ➤ B(Kn)
This car no longer has its original engine because at one time it was dismantled so that its components could be sold separately – they were worth more as secondhand spares than an assembled car – how times have changed!

> A known continuous history can add value to and enhance the enjoyment of a car.

1954 Alfa Romeo 1900 Super Sprint Coupé, 1975cc, double-overhead-camshaft 4-cylinder engine, 115bhp at 5,000rpm, left-hand drive, fully restored in the USA.
£31,000–37,000 / €46,000–55,000
$55,000–66,000 ➤ B(Mon)
The 1900 was the first Alfa to feature unitary construction. The first cars arrived in 1950 in four-door saloon form with an 1884cc engine producing 90bhp. This was followed by a cabriolet and coupé, both with the 100bhp engine of the 1900Ti sports saloon. They were upgraded for 1954 with a 1975cc engine and five-speed gearbox.

1956 Alfa Romeo 1900 Super Berlina, 1975cc, double-overhead-camshaft 4-cylinder engine, 90bhp at 4,800rpm, excellent condition.
£10,200–12,200 / €15,100–18,100
$18,000–21,500 ➤ H&H
A total of 192,917 four-door Berlina sports saloon models were manufactured between 1955 and 1962.

▶ **1961 Alfa Romeo Spider 2000 Veloce**, coachwork by Touring, 1975cc, double-overhead-camshaft 4-cylinder engine, 5-speed gearbox.
£9,000–10,800 / €13,300–16,000
$15,800–19,000 ➤ COYS
The 2000 Spider was launched in 1958, using practically the same engine and running gear as the Berlina Coupé, but with a tuned engine and convertible monocoque bodywork designed by Touring of Milan. The four-cylinder engine had the same displacement as the Berlina, but produced 115bhp at 5,900rpm, as opposed to the coupé's 105bhp at 5,300rpm. The result was a top speed of 109mph, as opposed to the Berlina's 99mph.

1964 Alfa Romeo 1600 Giulia Spider, 1570cc, double-overhead-camshaft inline 4-cylinder engine, 92bhp at 6,200rpm, 5-speed gearbox, completely original, with factory applied stickers on door shuts, original tyres, unused spare, finished in red, black interior trim.
£14,000–16,500 / € 20,700–24,400 $24,600–29,000 ⚒ H&H

1968 Alfa Romeo Duetto 1750 Spider Veloce, 1779cc, double-overhead-camshaft 4-cylinder engine, 5-speed gearbox, 4-wheel disc brakes, top speed 120mph.
£7,200–8,600 / € 10,700–12,700 / $12,700–15,100 ⚒ CGC
The Spider was based on a shortened version of the Giulia 105-series platform. The 'Duetto' nickname was the result of an Italian postal competition.

▶ **1971 Alfa Romeo 1600 Junior,** 1570cc, double-overhead-camshaft 4-cylinder engine, 109bhp at 6,000rpm, 5-speed gearbox, top speed 120mph.
£8,800–10,500 / € 13,000–15,500 $15,500–18,500 ⚒ COYS

1965 Alfa Romeo Giulia Sprint Speciale, 1570cc, double-overhead-camshaft 4-cylinder engine, 112bhp at 6,500rpm, 5-speed gearbox, top speed 125mph.
£13,000–15,500 / € 19,200–22,900 $23,000–27,300 ⚒ H&H
The Bertone penned Sprint Speciale version of the Giulietta appeared in 1957. With streamlined bodywork, the SS styling bore a marked resemblance to some of the Italian marque's earlier competition designs, particularly the Disco Volante sports racer and the futuristic BAT 9 show car. The last few SS Giuliettas, of which only 1,366 were made, were equipped with front disc brakes, and these became standard on the 1962 replacement Giulia, with its larger 1570cc engine and five-speed gearbox. A Sprint Speciale version of the Giulia with this same uprated mechanical specification was also available.

ALFA ROMEO Model	ENGINE cc/cyl	DATES	CONDITION 1	2	3
2000 Spider	1974/4	1958–61	£14,000+	£9,000+	£4,000
2600 Sprint	2584/6	1962–66	£11,000	£7,500	£4,000
2600 Spider	2584/6	1962–65	£13,000+	£8,000	£5,000
Giulietta Sprint	1290/4	1955–62	£10,000	£6,000	£3,000
Giulietta Spider	1290/4	1956–62	£12,000	£6,000	£4,000
Giulia Saloon	1570/4	1962–72	£5,000	£3,000	£1,500
Giulia Sprint (rhd)	1570/4	1962–68	£10,500	£6,000	£2,000
Giulia Spider (rhd)	1570/4	1962–65	£11,000+	£8,000	£4,000
Giulia SS	1570/4	1962–66	£16,000+	£11,000+	£5,000
GT 1300 Junior	1290/4	1966–77	£7,000	£5,500	£2,000
Giulia Sprint GT	1570/4	1962–68	£7,500+	£5,000	£2,000
1600GT Junior	1570/4	1972–75	£7,000	£4,000	£2,000
1750/2000 Berlina	1779/ 1962/4	1967–77	£4,000	£2,000	£1,000
1750GTV	1779/4	1967–72	£7,000	£6,000	£2,000
2000GTV	1962/4	1971–77	£6,500+	£4,000+	£2,000
1600/1750 (Duetto)	1570/ 1779/4	1966–67	£10,000	£7,500	£5,000
1750/2000 Spider (Kamm)	1779/ 1962/4	1967–78	£9,000	£6,000	£3,000
Montreal	2593/8	1970–77	£9,000	£8,000	£5,000
Junior Zagato 1300	1290/4	1968–74	£7,000	£5,000	£3,000
Junior Zagato 1600	1570/4	1968–74	£8,000	£6,000	£4,000
Alfetta GT/GTV (chrome)	1962/4	1972–86	£4,000	£2,500	£1,000
Alfasud	1186/ 1490/4	1972–83	£2,000+	£1,000	£500
Alfasud ti	1186/ 1490/4	1974–81	£2,500	£1,200	£900
Alfasud Sprint	1284/ 1490/4	1976–85	£3,000	£2,000	£1,000
GTV6	2492/6	1981–	£4,000	£2,500	£1,000

Watch for Zagato coachwork on early coupé models – very desirable.

◄ **1973 Alfa Romeo Giulia Super,** 1290cc, double-overhead-camshaft 4-cylinder engine, 89bhp at 6,000rpm, 5-speed gearbox, top speed 100mph, 1 owner from new, original, unrestored.
£2,500–3,000 / €3,700–4,400 / $4,400–5,300 ⋌CGC

1975 Alfa Romeo Montreal, coachwork by Bertone, 2598cc, double-overhead-camshaft V8 engine, fuel injection, electronic ignition, 5-speed gearbox.
£6,700–8,000 / €9,900–11,800 / $11,800–14,000 ⋌COYS
The Montreal made its debut at the Montreal Expo during the 1967 World Fair. Initially it was fitted with Alfa's ubiquitous four-cylinder twin-cam engine, in this case a 1779cc unit, but by the time the Montreal was launched for limited production at the 1970 Geneva show, this had been changed for an all-new V8. Developed from the engine of the successful Tipo 33 sports racer, this represented a departure in engine design for Alfa Romeo. With a capacity of 2598cc, the V8 featured twin overhead camshafts per bank and produced 200bhp at 6,500rpm. This provided strong performance, with a 137mph maximum speed and 0–60mph in just 7.6 seconds. Under the Bertone designed 2+2 coupé coachwork, the floorpan was derived from the Giulia Sprint GT and sported independent coil-spring front suspension, a coil-sprung rear axle, limited-slip differential and ventilated disc brakes. Inside, the seats had built-in adjustable headrests, vacuum operated headlamp stoneguards were another unusual feature. Production ended in 1977 after a total run of 3,925, the vast majority in left-hand-drive form.

1976 Alfa Romeo 2000 Spider Veloce, 1962cc, double-overhead-camshaft 4-cylinder engine, 132bhp at 5,500rpm, 5-speed gearbox, top speed 113mph.
£3,000–3,600 / €4,400–5,300 / $5,300–6,300 ⋌H&H
The mechanical specification of the 2000 Spider Veloce was identical to that of the coupé version, although it had a slightly shorter wheelbase and 51 instead of 53 litre fuel tank.

1983 Alfa Romeo Alfetta 2000 GTV, 1962cc, double-overhead-camshaft 4-cylinder engine, 5-speed gearbox, finished in metallic grey, tan velour interior.
£1,400–1,600 / €2,000–2,350 / $2,450–2,800 ⋌B(Kn)
Introduced in 1972, the Alfetta saloon combined a new body shape with initially the 1.8 litre version of Alfa's familiar twin-cam four. Independent front suspension and a de Dion rear axle were features (the latter incorporating a combined gearbox/final drive) as well as disc brakes all-round. The Alfetta family was extended in 1976 with the arrival of a Giugiaro styled coupé, the GT, which was followed by the GT 1.6 and 2000 GTV.

1989 Alfa Romeo 2000 Spider S3, 1962cc, double-overhead-camshaft 4-cylinder engine, 5-speed gearbox, converted to right-hand drive, finished in metallic grey, beige interior, tonneau cover, unrestored.
£3,000–3,600 / €4,450–5,300 / $5,300–6,300 ⋌BARO

Allard *(British 1937–59, 1981–)*

ALLARD Model	ENGINE cc/cyl	DATES	CONDITION 1	2	3
K/K2/L/M/M2X	3622/8	1947–54	£18,500+	£12,000	£8,000
K3	var/8	1953–54	£24,000	£15,000	£11,000
P1	3622/8	1949–52	£19,500	£13,000	£8,000
P2	3622/8	1952–54	£22,000	£18,000	£11,500
J2/J2X	var/8	1950–54	£70,000+	£50,000	£35,000
Palm Beach	1508/4, 2262/6	1952–55	£12,000	£10,000	£5,500
Palm Beach II	2252/ 3442/6	1956–60	£25,000+	£20,000	£11,000

Allen *(American 1895–1900)*

◄ **c1899 Allen Runabout,** 7.5hp, Aster air-cooled single-cylinder engine, coupled chain final drive, infinitely-variable friction-disc transmission; steering by tiller, believed to be sole surviving example.
**£23,000–27,600 / €34,000–40,000
$40,000–48,000 ➚ B(Kn)**
G. Edgar Allen was a New York carriage builder who is thought to have been actively involved in automobile manufacture from around 1895 to 1900. No records exist, however, and the number of vehicles produced must have been very small. Indeed, this car may be his very first, since it bears the number '101'. It was acquired by Sir Stirling Moss in July 1989 and displayed at the Brooklands Museum since 1990.

Alvis *(British 1920–67)*

T. G. John was the man behind the Alvis marque. He had set up his own engineering firm in Coventry during 1919, and later that year, he was approached by the engineer G. P. H. de Freville with a design for a 1.5 litre four-cylinder engine. This became the Alvis 10/30 when it was placed in production in 1920.

Although expensive, Alvis cars soon gained a reputation for quality engineering and production rose from 120 cars in 1920 to 733 by 1922.

In 1923, one of the most famous of all Alvis cars made its debut, the 12/50. This featured a 1496cc (sports) or 1598cc (touring) overhead-valve four cylinder engine. The 12/50 helped put Alvis firmly on the map by winning the 1923 Brooklands 200-mile race.

During the 1930s, Alvis turned out a maximum of 20 chassis a week. Bodies came from coachbuilders such as Charlesworth and Vanden Plas for the larger-engined cars (Speed 20 and Speed 25) and Cross and Ellis, Holbrook and Mulliner for the smaller four-cylinder cars (Firebird, Firefly and 12/70).

The Speed 20 had been introduced in 1931, and in 1934, it received two notable innovations. One was independent front suspension, the other, a first on a British car, was an all-synchromesh gearbox.

By 1939, Alvis had diversified into building aero engines and armoured cars; car production was halted for the duration of WWII.

Car production resumed in 1946 with the new TA14. This was based upon the pre-war 12/70 and

was offered with either saloon (Mulliner) or coupé (Tickford) coachwork. A total of 3,311 were built, plus a further 100 of the controversially styled TB14 roadster. In 1950, it was replaced by the 3 litre 21 series. These cars were manufactured until October 1954, when Mulliner was absorbed by Standard, which no longer wished to supply bodies to Alvis.

While searching for a replacement for its coachwork supplier, Alvis temporarily halted car production. Another important revenue earner was its range of military vehicles. These included the Saracen armoured troop carrier, Salamander fire tender and Saladin armoured car.

Car production resumed in 1958, following an agreement with coachbuilder Park Ward. The result were attractive two-door saloon and convertible models designed by Swiss stylist Graber on the 3 litre chassis. With very few changes, these continued until late 1967.

Alvis was acquired by Rover in 1965, and a prototype mid-engined sports car powered by the 3.5 litre Rover V8 was constructed. However, Rover was swallowed up by British Leyland in 1967, and the car never went into production.

Although production of aircraft engines and the 'S' family of armoured vehicles ceased in 1971, this was not the end of Alvis, as it had received a lucrative contract from the British government to build Scorpion and Scimitar light tanks. However, no more cars would be built.

◄ **1932 Alvis 12/50 Doctor's Drophead Coupé,** coachwork by Cross & Ellis, 1645cc, recently restored, engine rebuilt, new ash body framing, part original interior, finished in maroon over black, in need of new hood cover.
**£14,500–17,400 / €21,500–25,800
$25,500–30,000 ➚ H&H**
Launched in 1923, the 12/50 did much to establish Alvis as one of the leading manufacturers of the day. The 12/50TJ, introduced in 1930, employed a sturdy ladder chassis, leaf springs all-around, cable operated drum brakes and Marles steering box for much more accurate steering. With a high-revving, overhead-valve 1645cc four and crash box with right-hand change, most variants were good for 75–80mph.

ALVIS Model	ENGINE cc/cyl	DATES	CONDITION		
			1	2	3
12/50	1496/4	1923–32	£20,000	£13,000	£7,000
Silver Eagle	2148	1929–37	£16,000	£12,000	£8,000
Silver Eagle DHC	2148	1929–37	£20,000+	£13,000	£9,000
12/60	1645/4	1931–32	£15,000	£10,000	£7,000
Speed 20 (tourer)	2511/6	1932–36	£35,000+	£28,000	£18,000
Speed 20 (closed)	2511/6	1932–36	£25,000	£18,000+	£11,000
Crested Eagle	3571/6	1933–39	£10,000	£7,000	£4,000
Firefly (tourer)	1496/4	1932–34	£14,000+	£10,000	£6,000
Firefly (closed)	1496/6	1932–34	£7,000	£5,000	£4,000
Firebird (tourer)	1842/4	1934–39	£13,000	£10,000	£6,000
Firebird (closed)	1842/4	1934–39	£7,000	£5,000	£4,000
Speed 25 (tourer)	3571/6	1936–40	£38,500	£30,000	£20,000
Speed 25 (closed)	3571/6	1936–40	£23,000	£17,000	£12,000
3.5 Litre	3571/6	1935–36	£35,000	£25,000	£18,000
4.3 Litre	4387/6	1936–40	£44,000+	£30,000	£22,000
Silver Crest	2362/6	1936–40	£14,000	£10,000	£7,000
TA	3571/6	1936–39	£18,000	£12,000	£8,000
12/70	1842/4	1937–40	£10,000	£8,000	£6,000

◄ **1934 Alvis Speed 20 Tourer,** coachwork by Cross & Ellis, 2511cc, 6-cylinder engine, 90bhp at 4,000rpm, finished in dark blue with black wings and red wheels, dark blue interior.
£33,300–39,900 / €49,000–59,000
$58,000–70,000 ⚲ COYS
Aimed squarely at the upper end of the sports touring market, the Speed 20 model boasted a six-cylinder engine producing almost 90bhp at 4,000rpm, which, when clothed in the lightweight touring coachwork favoured by so many Alvis customers, resulted in cars capable of an impressive turn of speed.

► **1937 Alvis Speed 25,** coachwork by Charlesworth, 3571cc, rebuilt 6-cylinder engine, radiator renewed, original sliding sunroof, finished in dark blue over silver, blue leather interior.
£19,300–23,100 / €28,600–34,000
$34,000–40,000 ⚲ H&H
George Lanchester contributed to the design of the Speed 25, the first Alvis in which the accelerator was moved from the left to the right of the brake pedal.

1937 Alvis 4.3 Litre Tourer, coachwork by Charlesworth, 4387cc, 6-cylinder engine, finished in green, salmon leather interior, complete with original tool kit.
£28,700–34,000 / €42,000–50,000 / $50,000–60,000 ⚲ BB(S)
Development of the six-cylinder Alvis during the 1930s culminated in the announcement of the 4.3 Litre in August 1936. The new model was based on the 3.5 Litre introduced the previous year, and was powered by an enlarged version of Alvis's seven-bearing overhead-valve engine. The cruciform-braced chassis featured the independent front suspension and a four-speed all-synchromesh gearbox, together with driver controlled Luvax hydraulic dampers and servo-assisted brakes. Claimed to be the fastest non-supercharged saloon on the UK market, the Alvis 4.3 Litre was one of the few pre-war saloons capable of a genuine 100mph. Just 198 cars had been delivered when the outbreak of WWII stopped production.

◀ **1952 Alvis TA21 Drophead Coupé,** 2993cc, overhead-valve 6-cylinder engine, left-hand drive, restored in the USA, 760 miles recorded since, finished in white, beige interior, concours condition. **£11,300–13,500 / €16,700–20,000 $19,900–23,800** ✗ BB(S)
Looking much like its TA14 predecessor, but featuring independent front suspension and a new overhead-valve six-cylinder engine, the 3 litre Alvis TA21 was announced in 1950. Additions to the range were not long in coming, a sports two-seater and a Tickford-bodied two-door drophead coupé being announced for 1951.
The introduction of open-top models was calculated to boost sales in the United States, where Alvis was beginning to make an impact.

1963 Alvis TE21 Drophead Coupé, 2993cc, overhead-valve inline 6-cylinder engine, 3-speed automatic transmission, finished in black, tan leather interior.
£34,000–41,000 / €51,000–61,000 / $60,000–72,000 ✗ H&H
After WWII, Alvis specialized in sports saloons, the Grey Lady being capable of 100mph. In 1955, however, Graber styled an attractive two-door, pillarless coupé on a Grey Lady chassis, which could transport four at up to 110mph. Although the Swiss firm did body several Alvis chassis, its design was reproduced by celebrated English coachbuilder Park Ward which built both fixed-head and drophead versions. This particular example was owned by Group Captain Sir Douglas Bader. The WWII fighter ace had the TE21 with extended seat runners, bonnet louvres, rope door pulls, a larger ashtray to accommodate his pipe and a Hawker Hurricane mascot.

ALVIS Model	ENGINE cc/cyl	DATES	CONDITION 1	2	3
TA14	1892/4	1946–50	£9,500	£8,000	£4,500
TA14 DHC	1892/4	1946–50	£14,000	£11,000	£5,000
TB14 Roadster	1892/4	1949–50	£15,000	£10,000	£8,000
TB21 Roadster	2993/6	1951	£16,000	£10,000	£7,000
TA21/TC21	2993/6	1950–55	£10,000	£7,000	£5,000
TA21/TC21 DHC	2993/6	1950–55	£17,000	£13,000	£10,000
TC21/100 Grey Lady	2993/6	1953–56	£11,000	£7,000	£5,000
TC21/100 DHC	2993/6	1954–56	£19,000	£15,000	£9,000
TD21	2993/6	1956–62	£11,000	£8,000	£4,000
TD21 DHC	2993/6	1956–62	£20,000	£15,000	£10,000
TE21	2993/6	1963–67	£15,000	£10,000	£7,000
TE21 DHC	2993/6	1963–67	£22,000	£16,000	£8,000
TF21	2993/6	1966–67	£16,000	£12,000	£8,000
TF21 DHC	2993/6	1966–67	£28,000	£17,000	£13,000

Amphicar *(German 1961–68)*

◄ **1963 Amphicar,** 1147cc, restored 1996–2002.
£17,000–20,400 / €25,200–30,000
$30,000–36,000 ⌁ B(Mu)
Powered by a four-cylinder Triumph Herald engine mounted in the rear and driving the rear wheels, the Amphicar had a special transmission that turned its two propellers. The arrangement gave a maximum cruising speed of 6 knots (7mph) on water and a top speed on land of 70mph.

Armstrong-Siddeley *(British 1919–60)*

1934 Armstrong-Siddeley 12/6 Four-Seater,
1479cc, 6-cylinder engine, finished in blue, beige interior.
£5,900–7,000 / €8,700–10,300
$10,400–12,300 ⌁ H&H
In October 1928, Armstrong-Siddeley launched its 12hp six-cylinder model. Initially of 1236cc capacity, although bored out to 1431cc to boost performance from 1931, the new car had a 105in (266.5cm) wheelbase, separately mounted gearbox, cast-iron torque tube and banjo-type pressed-steel rear axle. From 1930, all Armstrong-Siddeleys were equipped with anti-dazzle headlamps, automatic spark advance and Triplex safety glass. The three-speed pre-selector gearbox, already used on larger models, became standard equipment on the 12hp from 1932.

1949 Armstrong-Siddeley Typhoon Coupé de Ville, 1991cc, overhead-valve 6-cylinder engine, 4-speed synchromesh gearbox, fully restored 1999.
£8,100–9,700 / €12,000–14,400 / $14,300–17,100 ⌁ B(Kn)
While most motor manufacturers entered the post-WWII era with cars little changed from those of 1939, Armstrong-Siddeley was able to launch its new Hurricane in May 1945. A stylish 4/5-seater, three-position drophead coupé, the Hurricane was soon joined by the mechanically similar Lancaster saloon, both cars using a developed version of the 1991cc, 16hp, overhead-valve six introduced in 1938.

ARMSTRONG–SIDDELEY Model	ENGINE cc/cyl	DATES	CONDITION 1	2	3
Hurricane	1991/6	1945–53	£10,000	£7,000	£4,000
Typhoon	1991/6	1946–50	£7,000	£3,000	£2,000
Lancaster/Whitley	1991/ 2306/6	1945–53	£8,000	£5,500	£2,500
Sapphire 234/236	2290/4 2309/6	1955–58	£7,500	£5,000	£3,000
Sapphire 346	3440/6	1953–58	£9,000	£5,000	£2,000
Star Sapphire	3990/6	1958–60	£10,000	£7,000	£4,000

Aston Martin *(British 1922–)*

ASTON MARTIN Model	ENGINE cc/cyl	DATES	CONDITION 1	2	3
Lionel Martin Cars	1486/4	1921–25	£26,000+	£18,000	£16,000
International	1486/4	1927–32	£50,000	£28,000	£16,000
Le Mans	1486/4	1932–33	£60,000	£40,000	£32,000
Mk II	1486/4	1934–36	£40,000	£30,000	£25,000
Ulster	1486/4	1934–36	£80,000+	£50,000	–
2 Litre	1950/4	1936–40	£40,000	£25,000	£18,000

Value is dependent upon racing history, originality and completeness.
Add 40% if a competition winner or works team car.

1934 Aston Martin 1½ Litre Mk II Saloon, 1486cc, 4-cylinder engine, completely restored, finished in dark blue, grey leather interior, 1 of 24 Mk II saloons built.
£35,000–42,000 / €52,000–62,000
$62,000–74,000 ➶ COYS
First-series 1½ Litre Astons used a separate engine and gearbox and worm-drive rear axle, while the second-series cars of 1932–33 had a gearbox mounted in unit with the dry-sump engine, which produced 60–70bhp, and a spiral-bevel rear axle. Suspension was by leaf springs with friction dampers, and the brakes were mechanically-operated front and rear, while an unusual feature was the steering box mounted high on the bulkhead. The final, third series of 1934 – the year after control of Aston Martin had passed from Augustus Bertelli to Gordon Sutherland – distinguishable by a flat scuttle and 73bhp engine, was known as the Mark II and, as before, a longer 120in (305cm) chassis was offered with tourer or saloon coachwork alongside short-chassis models plus the new Ulster. Production of the 1½ Litre ended in December 1935, by which time it had scooped many competition successes, including third overall at Le Mans the same year. This example was owned originally by Gordon Sutherland, who ran Aston Martin until its sale to David Brown in 1947.

1955 Aston Martin DB2/4 Drophead Coupé, 2922cc, 6-cylinder engine, 125bhp, 1 of 73 Drophead Coupés built, restored, concours condition.
£60,000–72,000 / €89,000–107,000
$106,000–127,000 ➶ B(Kn)
Widening the appeal of the DB2, the 2/4 had room for four, created by adding two occasional folding rear seats and raising the roof line, the resulting flat deck producing possibly the earliest form of hatchback. A one-piece windscreen replaced the earlier split screen, and a full set of bumpers was also provided. Standard specification included the 125bhp, 2.6 litre twin-overhead-camshaft engine, but from 1954 a bigger-bore 3 litre 140bhp engine was installed, providing 118mph top speed and 0–60mph in around 11 seconds.

► **1957 Aston Martin DB2/4 Mk II,** 2922cc, double-overhead-camshaft 6-cylinder engine, David Brown 4-speed manual gearbox, trailing-link suspension.
£15,500–18,600 / €22,900–27,500
$27,300–33,000 ➶ B(KN)
Just 199 Mk IIs were produced, making it the rarest of all DB Aston Martins.

1959 Aston Martin DB Mk III, 2922cc, double-overhead-camshaft 6-cylinder engine.
£30,000–36,000 / €44,000–53,000 / $53,000–63,000 ➶ H&H
What was, in effect, the Mk III version of the DB2/4, the DB Mk III had been restyled by Frank Feeley employing elements of the DB3S sports racer and was launched in August 1957. The biggest changes were to be found beneath its hand-crafted aluminium Tickford bodywork. Here was a DB that would actually stop when the brakes were hot, thanks to front disc brakes with hydro-booster, while to give it much longer legs than the earlier cars, an overdrive could be specified. The 3 litre twin-cam, six on SUs produced 178bhp, sufficient to propel the car to 140mph. From March 1957 until July 1959, when the DB4 replacement appeared, Aston Martin built 550 Mk IIs, 84 of them being soft-tops.

◄ **1962 Aston Martin DB4 Series IV,** 3670cc, double-overhead-camshaft 6-cylinder engine.
£51,000–61,000 / €75,000–90,000
$89,000–107,000 ➶ BB(S)
The DB4, introduced in 1954, was a complete departure from the models that had preceded it. The six-cylinder engine, designed by W. O. Bentley for the Lagonda, was replaced by a completely new, all-alloy, double-overhead-camshaft inline six of 3670cc. The platform chassis was fabricated from steel sheet, while the alloy body was designed using Touring's Superleggera construction technique.

1963 Aston Martin DB4 Series V, 3670cc, double-overhead-camshaft 6-cylinder engine, recent major mechanical and body overhaul, finished in dark green, red leather interior.
£33,000–40,000 / €49,000–59,000 / $58,000–70,000 ✗ COYS
The legendary 3.7 litre engine was conceived by Tadek Marek and first ran in 1956 and proven in competition in the DBR2 sports racer of 1957. There were five series of DB4. A number of features distinguish this final series: three SU carburettors, 9:1 compression-ratio pistons and larger valves, giving an output of 266bhp at 5,700rpm. Other improvements included a longer boot, adding space and enhancing the body shape, larger tyres and wheels, an oil cooler, a heavy-duty twin-plate clutch and a stronger wide-ratio gearbox.

1967 Aston Martin DB6, 3995cc, double-overhead-camshaft 6-cylinder engine, 282bhp, automatic transmission, 140mph, 0–60mph in 8.5 seconds.
£20,000–24,000 / €29,600–35,000 / $35,000–42,000 ✗ CGC
Launched in 1965, the DB6 was the first model to be engineered following the factory move from Feltham to Newport Pagnell. A total of 1,755 DB6s were built before production ceased in 1971.

1968 Aston Martin DB6, 3995cc, double-overhead-camshaft 6-cylinder engine, paintwork in need of attention.
£15,000–18,000 / €22,200–26,600
$26,400–31,000 ✗ CGC
The DB6 was visually distinguishable from the previous DB5 by its pronounced and aerodynamically effective Kamm tail, it also benefited from a 4in (10cm) increase in wheelbase. Combined with a marginally raised roof line and redesigned rear seats, courtesy of revised rear-suspension pick-up points, this gave a useful increase in rear passenger room, making the car a true four-seater.

ASTON MARTIN Model	ENGINE cc/cyl	DATES	CONDITION		
			1	2	3
DB1	1970/4	1948–50	£30,000+	£20,000	£16,000
DB2	2580/6	1950–53	£30,000+	£18,000	£14,000
DB2 Conv	2580/6	1951–53	£45,000+	£28,000+	£17,000
DB2/4 Mk I/II	2580/ 2922/6	1953–57	£30,000	£18,000	£14,000
DB2/4 Mk II Conv	2580/ 2922/6	1953–57	£45,000	£30,000	£15,000
DB Mk III Conv	2922/6	1957–59	£45,000	£28,000	£18,000
DB Mk III	2922/6	1957–59	£30,000	£20,000	£15,000
DB4	3670/6	1959–63	£40,000+	£25,000+	£16,000
DB4 Conv	3670/6	1961–63	£60,000+	£35,000+	–
DB4 GT	3670/6	1961–63	£150,000+	£100,000	–
DB5	3995/6	1964–65	£55,000	£35,000	£20,000
DB5 Conv	3995/6	1964–65	£65,000+	£40,000	–
DB6	3995/6	1965–69	£30,000	£20,000	£16,000
DB6 Mk I auto	3995/6	1965–69	£28,000	£18,000	£14,000
DB6 Mk I Volante	3995/6	1965–71	£60,000+	£40,000	£28,000
DB6 Mk II Volante	3995/6	1969–70	£70,000+	£40,000+	£30,000
DBS	3995/6	1967–72	£14,000+	£10,000	£8,000
AM Vantage	5340/8	1972–73	£15,000	£12,000	£9,000
V8 Vantage Oscar India	5340/8	1978–82	£30,000+	£20,000	£10,000
V8 Volante	5340/8	1978–82	£50,000+	£30,000	£20,000

Works/competition history is an important factor, as is Vantage and short-chassis specification.

◄ **1969 Aston Martin DB6,** 3995cc, double-overhead-camshaft 6-cylinder engine, automatic transmission, Webasto sun roof, finished in white, red leather interior.
£16,500–19,800 / €24,400–29,300 $29,000–35,000 ⚒ BRIT
The DB6 was available with a choice of ZF five-speed manual gearbox or automatic transmission.

The price paid for a car can vary according to the country in which it was sold. To discover where the car sold, cross reference the code at the end of each caption with the Key to Illustrations on page 251.

1970 Aston Martin DBS, 3995cc, 6-cylinder engine, automatic transmission, wire wheels, finished in white, tan leather interior.
£4,700–5,600 / €7,000–8,300 / $8,300–9,900 ⚒ BRIT
Introduced for 1967, the DBS ran concurrently with the DB6, both models sharing the 3995cc, double-overhead-camshaft six-cylinder engine developed from the W. O. Bentley-designed Lagonda unit. New was the wedge-shaped William Towns styling featuring quad headlamps and increased luggage space, while a new de Dion rear end improved handling. A total of 823 examples were built between 1967 and 1973.

1980 Aston Martin V8 Volante, 5340cc, V8 engine, 315bhp, 5-speed ZF manual gearbox, top speed 160mph, 0–100mph in under 14 seconds, export model, left-hand drive, European-spec chromed bumpers.
£40,000–48,000 / €60,000–72,000 $71,000–85,000 ⚒ B(Mu)
Introduced to meet a demand from the US market, the Volante convertible debuted in June 1978, boasting a lined, power-operated hood that endowed the interior with all the solidity and refinement associated with the saloon version.

Auburn (American 1903–36)

1931 Auburn Model 8-88 Boat-Tail Speedster, Lycoming 8-cylinder engine, restored, very good condition.
£44,000–53,800 / € 64,000–77,000
$76,000–91,000 ⚒ COYS
Erret Lobban Cord was hired as general manager of the Auburn Automobile Company in 1924, and became president of the company in 1926; within a few years, his empire included car makers Auburn, Cord and Duesenberg, and Lycoming, whose engines were used in all the cars. The first car to appear under his management was the eight-cylinder Model 8-88 of 1926.

1936 Auburn 852 Supercharged Roadster, 5000cc, Lycoming 8-cylinder engine, dickey seat.
£57,000–68,000 / € 84,000–101,000
$100,000–120,000 ⚒ COYS
In 1935, Auburn introduced the 851. The most revered model of the range was the Supercharged Roadster, with excellent performance and a sweeping, exaggerated body style. This example was built during the final year of production.

Audi (Germany 1910–39, 1965–)

◀ **1982 Audi 2.2 Quattro Coupé,** 2144cc, turbocharged 5-cylinder engine, 200bhp, 5-speed manual gearbox, 4-wheel drive, top speed 138mph.
£3,500–4,200 / € 5,200–6,200 / $6,200–7,400 ⚒ H&H

Austin (British 1906–80s)

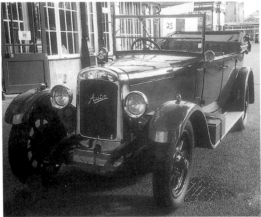

1926 Austin 20 Open Road Tourer, 3440cc, 4-cylinder engine.
£19,400–23,200 / € 28,700–34,000
$34,000–41,000 ⚒ H&H
Top of Austin's range in the 1920s was the alloy-bodied 20 Open Road Tourer. This featured three rows of seats and could accommodate up to seven adults. This car is believed to be the only example with alloy bodywork in existence.

AUSTIN Model	ENGINE cc/cyl	DATES	CONDITION 1	2	3
7 Swallow 2-Seater Sports	747/4	1927–32	£11,000	£8,500	£7,000
7 Swallow 4-Seater Saloon	747/7	1929–32	£10,000	£7,500	£6,000
Important coachbuilt versions.					

1927 Austin 7 Chummy Tourer, 747cc, 4-cylinder engine, restored, engine and chassis rebuilt, resprayed in dark green with black wings.
£5,100–6,100 / €7,500–9,000 / $9,000–10,700 ✗ CGC
The Austin 7 remained in production from 1922 until 1939.

1930 Austin 12/4 Burnham Saloon, 1535cc, side-valve 4-cylinder engine, cylinder head overhauled, new clutch, finished in blue and black, black interior.
£7,500–9,000 / €11,100–13,300 / $13,200–15,800 ✗ CGC

1933 Austin 7 Saloon, 747cc, side-valve 4-cylinder engine.
£1,500–1,800 / €2,200–2,650 / $2,650–3,150 ✗ COYS

1933 Austin 7 Two-Seater Tourer, 747cc, side-valve 4-cylinder engine, steering and brakes overhauled, finished in blue and black.
£4,400–5,200 / €6,500–7,700 / $7,700–9,200 ✗ BRIT
From 1932, the Austin 7 underwent a number of modifications, the chassis being given an 81in (205.5cm) wheelbase and wider track. For 1933, there was a rear-mounted fuel tank with mechanical pump and four-speed gearbox.

1933 Austin Light 12/6 Shooting Brake, coachwork by Angel Motor Bodies, 1496cc, side-valve 6-cylinder engine, fully restored, concours condition.
£9,100–10,900 / €13,400–16,100 / $16,000–19,200 ✗ BRIT
By 1930, it had become obvious that the gap between the diminutive Austin 7 and the 12/4 needed to be bridged. The vogue for small six-cylinder engines had been gathering momentum, and early in 1931 the new Light 12/6 went on sale, powered by a 1496cc, six-cylinder engine with an RAC rating of 13.9hp. This engine had good torque characteristics and excellent flexibility. In saloon form, the model was designated Harley, while open versions were the Open Road four-seat tourer and the Eton two-seater. This car began life as a standard Harley saloon, but it was rebodied as a shooting brake shortly after WWII.

1934 Austin 7 Nippy Sports, 858cc, side-valve 4-cylinder engine, 4-speed manual gearbox, completely restored, only 17 miles recorded since, engine rebuilt and rebored, body repaired and resprayed, rechromed, new upholstery.
£6,600–7,900 / €9,800–11,700 / $11,600–13,900 ✗ H&H

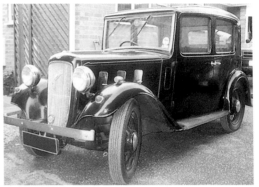

1935 Austin 10/4 Lichfield Saloon, 1125cc, side-valve 4-cylinder engine, 4-speed manual gearbox.
£1,750–2,100 / €2,600–3,100 / $3,100–3,700 ✗ BRIT
Introduced in April 1932, the Austin 10/4 filled the gap between the 7 and the 12/6 models. It was a popular car and was developed through many variants up to 1947.

Restored values

The cost of a professional restoration will have an influence on, but no direct relation to, a car's market value. A restored car can have a market value lower than the cost of its restoration.

1938 Austin 7 Pearl Cabriolet, 747cc, finished in dark blue with black wings, dark blue leather and Rexine upholstery.
£4,400–5,200 / €6,500–7,700 / $7,700–9,200 ✗ B(Kn)
The Austin 7 was nearing the end of its life by 1938. There had been countless modifications and improvements, but the original concept of an A-shaped frame with transverse-leaf front suspension and rear quarter-elliptic springing powered by a diminutive side-valve, 747cc engine remained. The top-of-the-range Pearl cabriolet was essentially a development of the Ruby, with a snug fitting roll-back hood, opening windscreen, and bumpers front and rear. The spare wheel was stored in the diminutive boot with a practical fold-out luggage carrier.

1935 Austin 7 Opal Tourer, 747cc, side-valve 4-cylinder engine, coil ignition, thermo-syphon cooling, 4-speed manual gearbox, concours condition.
£6,000–7,200 / €8,900–10,600 / $10,600–12,600 ✗ CGC
An extremely versatile design, the Austin 7's simple, but well-executed, A-frame, leaf-sprung chassis played host to a bewildering range of derivatives, from Brooklands single-seaters to two-speed tractors (all powered by the ubiquitous four-cylinder, side-valve 747cc engine). One of the most attractive was the Opal two-seater.

AUSTIN Model	ENGINE cc/cyl	DATES	CONDITION 1	2	3
25/30	4900/4	1906	£35,000	£25,000	£20,000
20/4	3600/4	1919–29	£20,000	£12,000	£6,000
12	1661/4	1922–26	£8,000	£5,000	£2,000
7/Chummy	747/4	1924–39	£7,000+	£5,000	£2,500
7 Coachbuilt/Nippy/Opal, etc	747/4	1924–39	£10,000	£9,000	£7,000
12/4	1861/4	1927–35	£6,500	£5,000	£2,000
16	2249/6	1928–36	£9,000	£7,000	£4,000
20/6	3400/6	1928–38	£12,500	£10,000	£8,000
12/6	1496/6	1932–37	£6,000	£4,000	£1,500
12/4	1535/4	1933–39	£5,000	£3,500	£1,500
10 and 10/4	1125/4	1932–47	£4,000	£3,000	£1,000
10 and 10/4 Conv	1125/4	1933–47	£5,000+	£3,500	£1,000
18	2510/6	1934–39	£8,000	£5,000	£3,000
14	1711/6	1937–39	£6,000	£4,000	£2,000
Big Seven	900/4	1938–39	£4,000	£2,500	£1,500
8	900/4	1939–47	£3,000	£2,000	£1,000
28	4016/6	1939	£6,000	£4,000	£2,000

Prices for early Austin models are dependent on body style: landaulette, tourer, taxi, Strachan, etc (eg. Austin Heavy 12/4 Tourer will command a higher price.

◀ **1939 Austin 8 Saloon,** 885cc, side-valve 4-cylinder engine, 4-speed manual gearbox, very good condition.
£2,500–3,000 / €3,700–4,400
$4,400–5,300 ⚲ H&H
The Austin 8 made its debut in 1939 and survived into the post-WWII era, production finally coming to an end in 1947.

1945 Austin 10 Saloon, 1125cc, side-valve 4-cylinder engine, 4-speed synchromesh gearbox.
£3,500–4,200 / €5,200–6,200 / $6,200–7,400 ⚲ CGC
The Austin 10 was built in various guises between 1932 and 1947.

c1952 Austin A30 Four-Door Saloon, 803cc, overhead-valve 4-cylinder engine, finished in black, red interior, original specification, unrestored.
£800–960 / €1,200–1,400
$1,400–1,650 ⚲ B(Kn)
The A30 was launched in 1951. A more cautious design than the Minor, nevertheless it was Austin's first unitary-construction car and the first to be powered by the famous A-series engine. The A30's selling price undercut the Minor's by £10 / €15 / $18, thanks in part to such cost cutting features as external door hinges, a solitary rear light, sliding windows and rear brakes operated by a single hydraulic cylinder via a mechanical linkage. A two-door model joined the original four-door in 1953; van and estate versions followed in 1954. The car was updated in 1956 with a wider rear window, remote-control gear-change and 948cc engine, becoming the A35. Saloon production ceased on the arrival of the Mini in 1959, although the A35 van would live on until 1968.

> ## Auction prices
> Miller's only includes cars declared sold.
> Our guide prices take into account the buyer's premium, VAT on the premium, and the extent of any published catalogue information relating to condition and provenance. Cars sold at auction are identified by the ⚲ icon; full details of the auction house can be found on page 251.

1953 Austin A90 Atlantic, 2660cc, overhead-valve 4-cylinder engine, 88bhp, 4-speed manual gearbox with column change, coil-sprung independent front suspension, hydro-mechanical brakes, restored, engine replaced, bare-metal respray, new electrics, finished in blue, grey leather interior.
£7,100–8,500 / €10,500–12,600 / $12,500–15,000 ⚲ B(Kn)
Aimed at the US market and styled accordingly, the A90 Atlantic met with a cool reception from American buyers, despite setting speed records at Indianapolis in 1949 by averaging over 70mph for seven days and nights. Based on A70 Hampshire running gear, the A90 was powered by a larger, 2660cc overhead-valve four producing 88bhp. Both convertible and saloon versions were built, the latter with a fabric covered roof and three-piece rear window with opening centre section.

Miller's Milestones

Austin A40 Farina and Countryman (1958–67)
Price range: £250–2,000 / €370–2,950 / $440–3,500
Built over almost a decade, the Pininfarina styled A40 never really achieved the sales levels its versatility and excellent handling deserved. Moreover, the Countryman version pointed the way ahead to the modern hatchback concept with its drop-down tailgate, lift-up rear window and fold-down rear seats.
Although the A40 boasted a modern style when launched in 1958, and some 340,000 were sold,

it was soon under fire from rivals such as the Triumph Herald and Ford Anglia. There was also in-house competition from BMC's advanced front-wheel-drive 1100 range and the Mini. Even so, the A40's good handling ensured its success in motor sport, in both circuit racing and rallying. A Mk II version arrived for 1961, featuring a slightly longer wheelbase. The Mk I had a 948cc four-cylinder engine, whereas for the second year of production, the Mk II received the more powerful 1098cc power unit, as fitted to the Morris Minor.

1956 Austin A50 Cambridge Four-Door Saloon, 1489cc, overhead-valve 4-cylinder engine, 4-speed manual gearbox, finished in red and white.
£1,550–1,850 / €2,300–2,750 / $2,750–3,250 ⚲ H&H
Austin and Morris merged in 1952 to become the British Motor Corporation. Among many other things, this led to an Austin engine powering the Morris Minor from late 1952. Austin's medium-sized saloon was the A40 Cambridge, which became the 1489cc A50 and, from 1957, the A55.

1975 Austin Allegro Vanden Plas Princess 1500, 1489cc, automatic transmission, 33,000 miles recorded, finished in white, brown leather interior.
£570–680 / €850–1,000 / $1,000–1,200 ⚲ B(Kn)
After the Austin 1100/1300 was phased out, the famous Vanden Plas name reappeared on the most luxurious version of its successor, the Allegro. Known as the Princess, the new car featured wood-veneer interior trim and leather upholstery.

AUSTIN Model	ENGINE cc/cyl	DATES	CONDITION 1	2	3
16	2199/4	1945–49	£3,000	£2,000	£1,000
A40 Devon	1200/4	1947–52	£2,000	£1,200	£750
A40 Sports	1200/4	1950–53	£6,000	£4,000	£2,000
A40 Somerset	1200/4	1952–54	£2,000	£1,500	£750
A40 Somerset DHC	1200/4	1954	£5,000	£4,000	£2,500
A40 Dorset 2-door	1200/4	1947–48	£2,000	£1,500	£1,000
A70 Hampshire	2199/4	1948–50	£3,000+	£1,500	£1,000
A70 Hereford	2199/4	1950–54	£3,000	£1,500	£1,000
A90 Atlantic DHC	2660/4	1949–52	£10,000	£6,000	£4,000
A90 Atlantic	2660/4	1949–52	£6,000	£4,000	£3,000
A40/A50 Cambridge	1200/4	1954–57	£1,200	£750	£500
A55 Mk I Cambridge	1489/4	1957–59	£1,000	£750	£500
A55 Mk II	1489/4	1959–61	£1,000	£750	£500
A60 Cambridge	1622/4	1961–69	£1,000	£750	£500
A90/95 Westminster	2639/6	1954–59	£2,000	£1,500	£750
A99 Westminster	2912/6	1959–61	£1,500	£1,000	£500
A105 Westminster	2639/6	1956–59	£3,000	£1,500	£750
A110 Mk I/II	2912/6	1961–68	£2,000	£1,500	£750
Nash Metropolitan	1489/4	1957–61	£3,500	£2,000	£750
Nash Metropolitan DHC	1489/4	1957–61	£6,000	£3,000	£1,500
A30	803/4	1952–56	£1,500	£800	–
A30 Countryman	803/4	1954–56	£1,500	£1,000	–
A35	948/4	1956–59	£1,000	£500	–
A35 Countryman	948/4	1956–62	£1,500	£1,000	–
A40 Farina Mk I	948/4	1958–62	£1,250	£750	£200
A40 Mk I Countryman	948/4	1959–62	£1,500	£1,000	£400
A40 Farina Mk II	1098/4	1962–67	£1,000	£750	–
A40 Mk II Countryman	1098/4	1962–67	£1,200	£750	£300
1100	1098/4	1963–73	£1,000	£750	–
1300 Mk I/II	1275/4	1967–74	£750	£500	–
1300GT	1275/4	1969–74	£1,800	£1,000	£750
1800/2200	1800/2200/4	1964–75	£1,500	£900	£600
3 Litre	2912/6	1968–71	£3,000	£1,500	£500

Austin-Healey *(British 1946–71)*

An accomplished designer and racing driver, Donald Healey had set up his own company to build sporting cars after WWII. Although they were successful in competition, production of the cars was never large.

Then came Healey's big moment. During 1952 he constructed a prototype car around the 2600cc Austin A90 engine. This was exhibited at the Earls Court Motor Show later that year as the Healey 100. The reception it received was massive, so much so that the design attracted the attention of Leonard Lord, managing director of the recently formed British Motor Corporation. Lord quickly reached an agreement with Healey that the new car would be produced at Austin's Longbridge works as the Austin-Healey 100, with a much more competitive price than could ever have been achieved by Healey alone.

Series production began in May 1953. Besides receiving a royalty for every car sold, Healey looked after the competition side and masterminded the 100S version, of which some 50 examples were constructed from 1954. A streamlined version with a supercharged engine topped 192mph at Bonneville Salt Flats, Utah, with Healey himself at the wheel.

In 1957, Donald Healey produced drawings which he sold to Austin for a new small sports car, powered by the A35 948cc engine. This entered production as the Austin-Healey Sprite in May 1958, becoming known affectionately as the 'frog-eye' because of the arrangement of its headlamps. Later it was restyled with conventional headlamps, and from May 1961 was also sold as the MG Midget with minor differences.

Next, in March 1959, came the larger-displacement 'big' Austin-Healey, uprated with an engine producing 124bhp to become the classic 3000 model. This was updated in 1961 as the Mk II, with triple SU carburettors and a 132bhp power output.

The 148bhp 3000 Mk II made its debut in early 1964, to be followed later in the year by the Phase II version, with revised rear suspension. Top speed now exceeded 120mph.

All the big Healeys enjoyed considerable success, especially in international rallying, but increasingly stringent safety and emissions regulations, particularly in North America, meant that the car's days were numbered, and in December 1967 – after over 16,000 Phase II models had been built (by far the most popular variant) – production was halted.

The Austin-Healey link ended in mid-1971 when the Sprite was phased out in favour of the MG Midget.

1953 Austin-Healey 100/4 BN1, 2660cc, overhead-valve 4-cylinder engine, 94bhp at 4,000rpm, 4-speed manual gearbox, left-hand drive, top speed 111mph, 0–60mph in 10.3 seconds, finished blue, dark blue interior.
£13,500–16,200 / €20,000–24,000
$23,800–28,500 ⚒ COYS

1954 Austin-Healey 100/4 BN1, 2660cc, overhead-valve 4-cylinder engine, completely restored, finished in white, newly refurbished red interior.
£15,500–18,600 / €22,900–27,500
$27,300–32,000 ⚒ H&H

1953 Austin-Healey 100/4 BN1, 2660cc, overhead-valve 4-cylinder engine, 4-speed synchromesh gearbox, uprated to 100M specification.
£16,200–19,400 / €24,000–28,700
$28,500–34,000 ⚒ H&H

1954 Austin-Healey 100/4 BN1, 2660cc, 4-cylinder engine, 3-speed manual gearbox, completely restored, finished in red, black interior.
£12,900–15,400 / €19,100–22,800
$22,700–27,100 ⚒ H&H
Although engines for the Austin-Healey 100 were built by BMC at Longbridge, the bodies (made from steel with aluminium bonnet and boot lid) were the work of Jensen at West Bromwich, where 100 cars a week were assembled from mid-1953 until 1957, when production was transferred to Abingdon. Early cars had a three-speed manual gearbox with overdrive as standard.

◀ **1955 Austin-Healey 100/4 BN1,** 2660cc, 110bhp, uprated to M specification, converted to right-hand drive.
£16,100–19,300 / €23,800–28,600
$28,300–34,000 ⚡ B(Kn)
After two mildly modified Austin-Healey 100s came 12th and 14th at Le Mans in 1953, a bolt-on 'Le Mans' tuning kit was offered through Austin-Healey dealers. The kit included modified carburettors and inlet manifold, a new distributor, new camshaft and valve springs, new pistons, an anti-roll bar and dampers. Just 1,159 factory M-specification cars were built, all offering a shade under 120mph.

▶ **1955 Austin-Healey 100/4 BN1,** 2660cc, overhead-valve 4-cylinder engine, 94bhp at 4,000rpm, 4-speed manual gearbox, top speed 111mph, 0–60mph in 10.3 seconds, 1 owner for last 35 years.
£17,600–21,100 / €26,000–31,000
$31,000–37,000 ⚡ COYS

◀ **1956 Austin-Healey 100M,** 2660cc, overhead-valve 4-cylinder engine, 110bhp, 4-speed manual gearbox with overdrive, top speed 120mph.
£17,600–21,100 / €26,000–31,200
$31,000–37,000 ⚡ BB(S)

▶ **1958 Austin-Healey 100/6,** 2639cc, 6-cylinder engine, converted to unleaded fuel, finished in red, black vinyl roof, 2 sets of side screens, tonneau cover.
£11,700–14,000 / €17,300–20,700
$20,600–24,600 ⚡ BRIT
The 100/6 was announced in 1956, subtly restyled and with a longer wheelbase to provide two occasional seats in the rear. As with its predecessor, the 100, a large proportion of 100/6 production was destined for export. The 100/6 remained in production until 1959, when it was superseded by the 3000, powered by a larger 2912cc engine.

AUSTIN-HEALEY Model	ENGINE cc/cyl	DATES	CONDITION 1	2	3
100 BN 1/2	2660/4	1953–56	£20,000	£14,000	£8,000
100/6, BN4/BN6	2639/6	1956–59	£18,000	£13,500	£8,000
3000 Mk I	2912/6	1959–61	£22,000	£13,000	£8,500
3000 Mk II	2912/6	1961–62	£23,000	£15,000	£9,000
3000 Mk IIA	2912/6	1962–64	£23,000	£15,000	£11,000
3000 Mk III	2912/6	1964–68	£25,000	£17,000	£11,000
Sprite Mk I	948/4	1958–61	£10,000	£6,000	£3,000
Sprite Mk II	948/4	1961–64	£5,000	£3,000	£2,000
Sprite Mk III	1098/4	1964–66	£4,500	£3,000	£1,500
Sprite Mk IV	1275/4	1966–71	£5,000	£3,000	£1,500

1958 Austin-Healey 100/6 BN6, 2639cc, 6-cylinder engine, 4-speed manual gearbox, wire wheels, finished in green and white, black leather interior, restored, concours condition.
£14,600–17,500 / €21,600–25,900 / $25,700–31,000 ⚒ H&H
A few pure two-seat versions of the 100/6 were built; this is one.

► **1958 Austin-Healey 100/6,** 2639cc, 6-cylinder engine, 102bhp, 4-speed manual gearbox with overdrive, top speed 103mph, completely restored at a cost of £38,000 / €56,000 / $67,000, finished in blue and white, hood, side screens and tonneau, dark blue leather interior.
£17,200–20,600 / €25,500–30,000 $30,000–36,000 ⚒ B(Kn)
The 100/6 employed BMC's 2.6 litre C-series engine. It was easily distinguishable from the previous model by its 'crinkle' radiator grille and bonnet-top air intake.

◄ **1959 Austin-Healey Sprite Mk I,** 948cc, overhead-valve 4-cylinder engine, 4-speed manual gearbox, finished in white, red interior.
£5,200–6,200 / €7,700–9,200 / $9,200–10,900 ⚒ H&H

1959 Austin-Healey Sprite Mk I, 948cc, liquid-cooled overhead-valve 4-cylinder engine, restored, hood, hardtop, spare windscreen, finished in white, red interior.
£6,300–7,500 / €9,300–11,100 / $11,100–13,200 ⚒ H&H
This Sprite is unusual in that it is a three-seater, believed to have been built at Donald Healey's factory. The extra seat required a cut-out in the bodywork, which has been trimmed with aluminium finishers.

◄ **1959 Austin-Healey 3000 Mk I BN7,** 2912cc, 6-cylinder engine, hardtop, restored 1997.
£19,200–23,000 / €28,400–34,000 $34,000–41,000 ⚒ H&H
This car was one of only 157 3000 Mk Is produced for the home market in right-hand-drive form.

1960 Austin-Healey 3000 Mk II, 2912cc, 6-cylinder engine, 4-speed manual gearbox with overdrive, converted to right-hand drive, fully restored.
£13,000–15,500 / € 19,200–23,100 $22,900–27,500 ✗ H&H

1960 Austin-Healey 3000 Mk I BN7, 2912cc, 6-cylinder engine, 4-speed manual gearbox, US export model, converted to right-hand drive, fully restored 1995, full-flow exhaust system, finished in red and black.
£17,000–20,400 / € 25,200–30,000 $29,900–36,000 ✗ BARO

1960 Austin-Healey 3000 Mk I, 2912cc, 6-cylinder engine, twin SU carburettors, 124bhp at 4,600rpm, 4-speed gearbox, independent coil-spring/wishbone front suspension, leaf-sprung rear axle located by Panhard bar, front disc brakes, top speed 110mph, 0–60mph in 11.4 seconds, left-hand drive, fully restored, 1,000 miles recorded since, finished in red and black, black weather equipment, red leather interior.
£20,500–24,600 / € 30,000–36,000 / $36,000–43,000 ✗ COYS

◀ **1963 Austin-Healey 3000 Mk IIA BST,** 2912cc, triple SU carburettors, 132bhp, fully restored at a cost of £25,000 / € 37,000 / $44,000.
£23,600–28,300 € 35,000–42,000 $42,000–50,000 ✗ H&H
The Mk IIA had wind-up windows, a curved windscreen and proper convertible hood.

▶ **1966 Austin-Healey 3000 Mk III BJ8,** 2912cc, 148bhp, top speed 120mph, 0–60mph in 9.5 seconds, finished in British racing green, black interior.
£23,400–28,000 / € 35,000–41,000 $41,000–49,000 ✗ COYS
The final 3000 model, the Mk III BJ8, appeared in February 1964 and incorporated myriad changes. Its engine was equipped with larger SU carburettors and a new camshaft, while the exhaust had been redesigned with four silencers. There was a new dashboard design trimmed in wood veneer, an electronic tachometer and a vacuum brake servo. The rear axle was located by twin radius arms rather than a Panhard bar.

Bentley *(British 1919–)*

Walter Owen Bentley was born in 1888. He was apprenticed to the Great Northern Railway works in Doncaster, but soon switched to the fledgling motor trade, selling French DFP cars in London's West End until the outbreak of WWI.

In 1919, Bentley went back to selling DFPs, but with F. T. Burgess (an ex-Humber draughtsman) also set about building a car to carry his name. Bentley Motors Ltd was formed in August 1919, and a prototype car with a 3 Litre overhead-camshaft four-cylinder engine was completed in December of that year. The first car was not sold until September 1921. An open four-seat tourer, it cost £1,350 / €2,000 / $2,400, making it one of the most expensive cars available in Great Britain at that time. Even so, 122 were sold in 1922, 204 in 1923 and 402 in 1924.

It was also in 1924 that Bentley gained its first Le Mans victory, but the Bentley enterprise was still seriously under capitalized. This led 'W. O.' to approach the millionaire sportsman Woolf Barnato for assistance in 1925. The result was the birth of an entirely new company with Barnato as chairman.

Between 1926 and 1931 Bentley enjoyed some of its greatest triumphs, including four successive Le Mans victories (1927–30).

Then came the depression caused by the Wall Street stock-market crash of 1929. By early 1931, Britain was feeling the full effects, and in June Bentley's debts had risen to such a level that it was unable to continue trading. Barnato was not prepared to bail out the company and shortly afterwards a receiver was appointed. At first it was

widely believed that Napier would acquire Bentley, but in the end it turned out to be Rolls-Royce.

'W. O.' continued to work for Rolls-Royce for the next four-and-a-half years, although he was never truly happy and left to join rival Lagonda, where he stayed for the next 11 years; he died in 1971.

The first fruit of the Rolls-Royce/Bentley merger was a 3.5 litre car nicknamed 'The Silent Sports Car'. This featured a modified Rolls-Royce 20/25 power unit mounted in a new chassis. Even though many Bentley buffs disapproved, the new car sold well, as did its successor, the 4¼ Litre, which utilized the Rolls-Royce 25/30 engine and was offered between 1936 and 1939.

The post-WWII cars, the Bentley Mk VI and Rolls-Royce Silver Wraith, were announced in 1946 and employed an inlet-over-exhaust version of the pre-war 4¼ Litre engine.

Following the disastrous RBII aero engine contract, which bankrupted Rolls-Royce and led to the formation of Rolls-Royce Motors to handle car production in 1971, the Bentley name was allowed to stagnate. Then, in August 1980, Rolls-Royce Motors became part of Vickers Ltd, and this spurred a Bentley revival, with cars such as the Mulsanne Turbo and Turbo R.

During the late 1990s there was a battle royal for the Rolls-Royce name, which ended with BMW buying Rolls-Royce and Volkswagen Bentley and, as the 21st century dawned, there was the exciting prospect of these famous marques competing directly against each other once more.

1924 Bentley 3 Litre Speed Model,
3500cc, fully restored regardless of cost.
**£85,000–100,000 / €125,000–148,000
$150,000–175,000** ➴ CGC
**The introduction of twin G5 SU
'sloper' carburettors to Bentley's TT
replica chassis in 1924 gave rise to
the Speed Model. About this time,
four-wheel brakes were also
introduced. With a top speed of
90mph, subject to coachwork, the
Red Label Speed Model was no slouch.**

1927 Bentley 4½ Litre Tourer, coachwork by Vanden Plas, 4398cc.
£126,000–151,000 / €186,000–223,000 / $223,000–266,000 🏁 B(Kn)
W. O. Bentley debuted his 3 Litre car in 1919. This was the model that was to become a legend in motor racing history and the archetypal vintage sports car. However, by the mid-1920s, the 3 Litre's competitiveness was on the wane and this, together with the fact that many customers fitted unsuitably heavy coachwork to the 3 Litre's excellent chassis rather than accept the expense and complexity of Bentley's 6½ Litre 'Silent Six' model, led to the introduction of the 4½ Litre. This effectively combined the chassis, transmission and brakes of the 3 Litre with an engine that was, in essence two-thirds of the six-cylinder 6½ Litre unit. It is believed that the first prototype engine went into the 3 Litre chassis of the 1927 Le Mans practice car. Subsequently, this same engine was fitted to the first production 4½ Litre chassis for that year's Grand Prix d'Endurance at the Sarthe circuit. The original 4½ Litre car, driven by Frank Clement and Leslie Callingham, promptly set the fastest race lap of 73.41mph before being eliminated in the infamous 'White House Crash' multiple pile-up. The 4½ Litre was produced for four years, all but nine of the 665 cars made being built on the 3 Litre's 'Long Standard' wheelbase.

1929 Bentley 4½ Litre Four-Seat Tourer, 4398cc, 100bhp, C-Type gearbox, originally fitted with close-coupled saloon coachwork by Maythorn, subsequently rebodied, finished in green, red leather interior.
£118,000–142,000 / €175,000–210,000
$208,000–250,000 🏁 H&H

1928 Bentley 3 Litre Sporting Tourer, coachwork by Freestone & Webb, 2996cc, 4-cylinder engine.
£58,000–70,000 / €86,000–103,000
$102,000–122,000 🏁 B(Kn)

BENTLEY Model	ENGINE cc/cyl	DATES	CONDITION 1	2	3
3 Litre	2996/4	1920–27	£100,000	£75,000	£40,000
Speed Six	6597/6	1926–32	£300,000	£250,000	£160,000
4½ Litre	4398/4	1927–31	£175,000	£125,000	£80,000
4½ Litre Supercharged	4398/4	1929–32	£600,000+	£300,000	£200,000
8 Litre	7983/6	1930–32	£300,000	£200,000	£100,000
3½ Litre Saloon & DHC	3699/6	1934–37	£70,000	£30,000	£15,000
4¼ Litre Saloon & DHC	4257/6	1937–39	£70,000+	£35,000	£20,000
Mk V	4257/6	1939–41	£45,000	£25,000	£20,000

Prices are dependent on engine type, chassis length, matching chassis and engine nos, body style and coachbuilder, and original extras like supercharger, gearbox ratio, racing history and originality. Many specials built upon the 'Derby' Bentley chassis and Mk VI.

1929 Bentley Speed Six 6½ Litre Tourer, 6597cc, Le Mans fuel tank, Lucas 'Bullseye' headlamps, finished in British Racing green.
£239,000–287,000 / €354,000–425,000
$421,000–505,000 ✗ B(Kn)

1934 Bentley 3½ Litre Tourer, 3675cc, coachwork believed to be by Vanden Plas fitted late 1990s.
£24,200–29,000 / €36,000–43,000
$43,000–51,000 ✗ H&H

1935 Bentley 3½ Litre Arthur Mulliner Sports Saloon, 3,699cc, finished in green with black wings, green leather interior.
£16,600–18,500 / €24,600–27,400
$29,200–33,000 ⊞ RCC

1935 Bentley 3½ Litre Coupé, 3699cc, 6-cylinder engine.
£21,800–26,200 / €32,000–38,000
$38,000–47,000 ✗ B(Kn)

1935 Bentley 3½ Litre Drophead Coupé, coachwork by Barker, 3½-litre 6-cylinder engine, 3-speed gearbox, finished in maroon and black, rear-mounted spare wheel with full cover, biscuit interior trim and hood.
£40,000–45,000 / €60,000–66,000
$70,000–79,000 ⊞ RCC

1936 Bentley 4¼ Litre 3-Position Drophead Coupé, 4257cc, overdrive, completely restored early 1990s, including new coachwork by Horsfield & Son.
£32,000–38,000 / €47,000–56,000
$56,000–67,000 ✗ H&H

◀ **1936 Bentley 4¼ Litre Drophead Coupé,** coachwork by Park Ward, 4257cc, 6-cylinder engine, very good condition.
£48,000–58,000 / €71,000–85,000
$85,000–102,000 ✗ COYS
This particular car was displayed at the 1936 London Motor Show. Subsequently, it was sold to Prince Bernhard of The Netherlands and then to Field Marshall Bernard Montgomery.

▶ **1938 Bentley 4¼ Litre Drophead Coupé,** coachwork by Vanden Plas, overdrive, servo brakes.
£84,000–100,000
€124,000–148,000
$148,000–176,000 ✗ COYS
This car was exhibited by Bentley at the Brussels and Geneva motor shows in 1939.

◀ **1939 Bentley 4¼ Litre High-Vision Saloon,** coachwork by H.J. Mulliner, 4257cc, overdrive, servo brakes, original specification, unrestored.
£27,600–33,000 / €41,000–49,000 $49,000–58,000 ⚹ B(Kn)

▶ **1939 Bentley Mk V Four-Door Sports Saloon,** 4257cc, matching engine and gearbox, full body-off restoration 1998.
£32,000–38,000 / €47,000–56,000 $56,000–67,000 ⚹ H&H
Only 16 of these models were handmade before WWII stopped play. The Mk V marked the transition between the MX Series of 1939 and the post-war Mk VI. The 124in (315cm) wheelbase was shorter than that of the 1939 model and 4in (11cm) longer than the 1946 cars; the wheel size was also smaller than previous Bentleys.

1947 Bentley Mk VI Saloon, 4257cc, 6-cylinder engine, 4-speed manual gearbox, finished in black, light brown interior.
£11,800–14,200 / €17,500–21,000 $20,800–25,000 ⚹ H&H

1947 Bentley Mk VI Saloon, 4257cc, 6-cylinder engine, finished in maroon and cream, beige leather interior.
£11,700–13,000 / €17,300–19,200 $20,600–22,900 ⊞ BLE

1949 Bentley Mk VI Saloon, 4257cc, finished in green, original, working radio, tan leather interior.
£12,400–14,900 / €18,400–22,000 $21,800–26,200 ⚹ B(Kn)

1949 Bentley Mk VI Saloon, 4257cc, 6-cylinder engine, 4-speed manual gearbox, finished in grey over silver-grey, grey leather interior.
£7,500–9,000 / €11,100–13,300 $13,200–15,800 ⚹ H&H

Restored values

The cost of a professional restoration will have an influence on, but no direct relation to, a car's market value. A restored car can have a market value lower than the cost of its restoration.

1949 Bentley Mk VI Two-Door Saloon, coachwork by James Young, 4257cc, restored 1985 at a cost of £36,000 / €53,000 / $63,000.
£13,500–15,000 / €20,000–22,200 / $23,800–26,400 ⚹ B(Kn)

1949 Bentley Mk VI Fixed Head Coupé, coachwork by Park Ward, 4257cc, 6-cylinder engine, recent full-engine rebuild, finished in dark blue and white, original blue leather interior.
£17,500–19,500 / €26,000–28,900 / $31,000–34,000 ⊞ RCC

1949 Bentley Mk VI Saloon, 4257cc, inlet-over-exhaust 6-cylinder engine, hydraulic front brakes, independent front suspension, extensive body-off restoration 1998.
£13,800–16,600 / €20,400–24,500 $24,300–29,200 ⚲ B(Kn)

▶ **1950 Bentley Mk IV Saloon,** 4257cc, 6-cylinder engine, twin SU carburettors, restored, finished in black over gold, tan leather interior, very good condition.
£16,700–20,000 / €24,700–29,600 $29,400–35,000 ⚲ B(Kn)

◀ **1950 Bentley Mk VI Drophead Coupé,** coachwork by Park Ward, 4257cc, finished in black and ivory, black leather interior, 1 owner for 40 years, good condition.
£29,700–33,000 / €44,000–49,000 $52,000–58,000 ⊞ RCC

1954 Bentley R-Type Saloon, 4566cc, 6-cylinder engine, 4-speed automatic transmission, finished in grey, black leather interior.
£12,800–15,400 / €19,000–22,800 $22,500–27,100 ⚲ H&H

1955 Bentley R-Type Saloon, 4566cc, inlet-over-exhaust 6-cylinder engine, 4-speed automatic transmission, hydraulic front brakes, independent front suspension, original leather interior.
£11,600–13,900 / €17,200–20,600 $20,400–24,500 ⚲ H&H

Miller's Milestones

Bentley R-Type Continental (1952–55)
Price range: £25,000–60,000 / €37,000–89,000 / $44,000–106,000
In the early 1950s, Bentley was at last able to break away from its Rolls-Royce parent and produce not only the fastest, genuine full-four-seat car in the world (it could top 120mph with ease), but also probably the most beautiful car of its era.
The Continental was a true classic, with an aerodynamically efficient, fastback profile.
Its stylish bodywork was manufactured in aluminium by H.J. Mulliner on a high-performance chassis.
At first, it was fitted with a 4566cc six-cylinder engine (later uprated to 4887cc), which featured a higher compression ratio than contemporary Bentleys and a big-bore exhaust system.
Another feature of the Continental was an excellent power-to-weight ratio. This was achieved not only by the alloy body, but also by attention to detail. For example, the bumpers were manufactured in aluminium rather than steel, while the armchair seats of the existing R-Type saloon had been dumped in favour of smaller sports buckets with aluminium frames.
Tall gearing provided the Continental with an ability to cruise serenely in excess of 100mph on the autoroutes of Europe, if not on the sub-standard British roads. The four-speed manual gearbox allowed the sporting driver to reach 80mph in second, 100mph in third and 124mph in top gear.
Only 208 Mulliner fastback Continentals were built, making it the most coveted of all post-war Bentley models.

1957 Bentley S1 Two-Door Saloon, coachwork by James Young, 4877cc, 6-cylinder engine, finished in blue, matching hide interior, original specification.
£26,000–31,000 / €38,000–45,000
$46,000–55,000 ↗ BARO
This car is one of only three two-door S1 saloons built by James Young between 1955 and 1959.

1958 Bentley S1 Saloon, 4887cc, 6-cylinder engine, 3-speed automatic transmission, extensively overhauled c2000.
£8,000–9,600 / €11,800–14,200
$14,100–16,900 ↗ H&H
This car has been fitted out as a Rolls-Royce Silver Cloud 1, with new grille, bumpers, wheel trims and speedometer. However, the engine still carries the Bentley badge and the car is still registered as a Bentley.

1960 Bentley S2 Continental, coachwork by H.J. Mulliner, 6230cc, aluminium V8 engine, automatic transmission, power steering, servo brakes.
£32,000–38,000 / €47,000–56,000 / $56,000–67,000 ↗ COYS

BENTLEY Model	ENGINE cc/cyl	DATES	CONDITION 1	2	3
Abbreviations: HJM = H.J. Mulliner; PW = Park Ward; M/PW = Mulliner/Park Ward					
Mk VI Standard Steel	4257/ 4566/6	1946–52	£16,000	£10,000	£5,000
Mk VI Coachbuilt	4257/ 4566/6	1946–52	£25,000	£20,000	£12,000
Mk VI Coachbuilt DHC	4566/6	1946–52	£45,000+	£30,000	£20,000
R-Type Standard Steel	4566/6	1952–55	£12,000	£10,000	£7,000
R-Type Coachbuilt	4566/6	1952–55	£25,000	£20,000	£15,000
R-Type Coachbuilt DHC	4566/ 4887/6	1952–55	£50,000+	£35,000	£25,000
R-Type Cont (HJM)	4887/6	1952–55	£90,000+	£40,000	£29,000
S1 Standard Steel	4887/6	1955–59	£15,000	£10,000	£7,000
S1 Cont 2-door (PW)	4877/6	1955–59	£30,000	£25,000	£20,000
S1 Cont Drophead	4877/6	1955–59	£80,000+	£75,000	£50,000
S1 Cont F'back (HJM)	4877/6	1955–58	£50,000+	£35,000	£25,000
S2 Standard Steel	6230/8	1959–62	£15,000	£9,000	£6,000
S2 Cont 2-door (HJM)	6230/8	1959–62	£60,000	£40,000	£30,000
S2 Flying Spur (HJM)	6230/8	1959–62	£45,000	£33,000	£22,000
S2 Conv (PW)	6230/8	1959–62	£60,000+	£50,000	£35,000
S3 Standard Steel	6230/8	1962–65	£16,000	£11,000	£9,000
S3 Cont/Flying Spur	6230/8	1962–65	£45,000	£30,000	£25,000
S3 2-door (M/PW)	6230/8	1962–65	£30,000	£25,000	£10,000
S3 Conv (modern conversion – only made one original)	6230/8	1962–65	£40,000	£28,000	£20,000
T1	6230/6 6750/8	1965–77	£10,000	£8,000	£4,000
T1 2-door (M/PW)	6230/6 6750/8	1965–70	£15,000+	£12,000	£9,000
T1 Drophead (M/PW)	6230/6 6750/8	1965–70	£30,000	£20,000	£12,000

◄ **1960 Bentley S2 Mulliner-Style Convertible,** 6230cc, rebuilt and fitted convertible coachwork 1990, finished in white, blue hood, magnolia hide interior piped in blue.
£40,000–45,000 / €60,000–66,000 $70,000–77,000 ⊞ RCC

1962 Bentley S2 Long-Wheelbase Saloon, coachwork by Park Ward, 6230cc, V8 engine, 4-speed automatic transmission, power steering, electric windows, glass division, finished in silver over green, beige leather interior.
£11,400–13,700 / €16,900–20,300 / $20,100–24,100 ⋌ CGC

► **1962 Bentley S3 Continental Flying Spur,** 6230cc, overhead-valve V8 engine, finished in grey, cream leather interior.
£29,600–35,000 / €44,000–52,000 $52,000–62,000 ⋌ H&H

1963 Bentley S3 Saloon, 6230cc, V8 engine, top speed 116mph, 0–60mph in 10.8 seconds, finished in silver over dark blue, grey leather interior.
£16,100–19,300 / €23,800–28,600 $28,400–34,000 ⋌ CGC

1964 Bentley S3 Saloon, 6230cc, V8 engine, original, good condition.
£17,100–19,000 / €25,300–28,100 $30,000–33,000 ⊞ BLE

1971 Bentley T1 Saloon, 6750cc, V8 engine, finished in 2-tone blue, matching leather interior.
£4,500–5,400 / €6,700–8,000 / $7,900–9,500 ⋌ CGC
Launched in 1965, the T-series was outsold by its Rolls-Royce Silver Shadow equivalent by 11 to one. Thus, today the Bentley is much rarer.

1975 Bentley T1 Saloon, 6750cc, V8 engine, automatic transmission, finished in green.
£5,600–6,700 / €8,300–9,900 / $9,800–11,800 ⋌ H&H

◀ **1983 Bentley Mulsanne Turbo Saloon**, 6750cc, V8 engine, 300bhp, 0–60mph in 6.9 seconds.
£15,000–18,000 / €22,200–26,600 $26,400–31,700 ✎ H&H
The Mulsanne Turbo was launched at the 1982 Geneva motor show. This particular car was owned originally by C. R. Giles, the cartoonist, whose witty artwork enlivened the pages of the *Daily Express* and *Sunday Express* newspapers for many years.

▶ **1984 Bentley Mulsanne Turbo Saloon**, 6750cc, V8 engine, finished in dark green, green leather interior with beige piping, burr-walnut facia.
£6,500–7,800 / €9,600–11,500 $11,400–13,700 ✎ H&H

1985 Bentley Mulsanne Turbo Saloon, 6750cc, V8 engine, automatic transmission, twin-headlamp conversion 1996, finished in dark blue, tan interior, 2 owners from new.
£11,300–13,600 / €16,700–20,100 $19,900–23,900 ✎ H&H

1985 Bentley Mulsanne Turbo Long-Wheelbase Saloon, 6750cc, V8 engine, automatic transmission, finished in royal blue, blue leather upholstery.
£8,000–9,600 / €11,800–14,200 $14,100–16,900 ✎ CGC

1986 Bentley Turbo R Long-Wheelbase Saloon, 6750cc, V8, finished in dark green, matching interior, 1 of 930 LWB examples built.
£10,600–12,700 / €15,700–18,800 $18,700–22,400 ✎ B(Kn)

1986 Bentley Turbo R Saloon, 6750cc, V8 engine, finished in green, magnolia interior, full service history carried out by Bentley main dealers and various handbooks, 89,000 miles.
£9,700–11,600 / €14,300–17,200 $17,100–20,400 ✎ H&H

◀ **1988 Bentley Eight Saloon**, 6750cc, V8 engine, magnolia leather interior.
£10,700–12,900 / €15,800–19,000 $18,800–22,600 ✎ H&H

1989 Bentley Eight Saloon, 6750cc, V8 engine,
automatic transmission.
£12,600–14,000 / €18,600–20,700
$22,200–24,600 ⊞ BLE

1991 Bentley Turbo R Saloon, 6750cc, V8 engine, active-
ride suspension, Continental alloy wheels, finished in black.
£14,800–17,800 / €21,900–26,300
$26,000–31,000 ⋏ H&H

1994 Bentley Brooklands, 6750cc, V8 engine, 4-speed automatic transmission, black interior with red piping, full service
history, 53,000 miles recorded.
£18,000–21,600 / €26,600–32,000 / $32,000–38,000 ⋏ H&H

► **1996 Bentley Turbo RL
Saloon,** 6750cc, V8 engine,
4-speed automatic
transmission, finished in
dark blue, dark blue interior.
£28,000–33,000
€41,000–49,000
$49,000–58,000 ⋏ H&H

BMA *(British 1954–56)*

◄ **1955 BMA Hazelcar,** 1.5hp electric motor,
steel chassis, aluminium bodywork, top speed
20mph, 50–60 miles per charge.
£1,500–1,800 / €2,200–2,650
$2,700–3,200 ⋏ B(Kn)
**Hazelcars were built during the mid-1950s,
but only seven examples were completed,
one of which had a Ford 8 petrol engine.**

BMW *(Germany 1929–)*

The early history of BMW (Bayerische Motoren Werke) was set firmly in the aero engine and motorcycle industries.

At the end of WWI, BMW was banned from manufacturing aircraft engines by the Treaty of Versailles. This led to the Munich company's entry into road transport, through motorcycles. By 1924, however, the firm had been able to restart aero engine production. Then, in 1928, BMW took a step that set it on the way to becoming the car giant it is today. It took over the plant of the Eisenach works together with a licence to build the Austin Seven. Sold in Germany as the Dixi, this vehicle marked BMW's arrival as a car builder, while Eisenach was to remain the centre of BMW car production until 1945.

In 1929, production of the Dixi boomed, and in 1930 one of the little cars won the 750cc class in the Monte Carlo Rally.

The first all-BMW designed car, the 3/20PS, appeared in 1932, followed in 1933 by the Type 303, a small six-cylinder model displacing 1200cc. That same year, Fritz Fiedler joined BMW from Horch and soon displayed his engineering talents by designing a cylinder head incorporating hemispherical combustion chambers with a single side-mounted camshaft. This was used in the famous 328 and 327/328 models.

Production of cars for civilian customers came to an end in September 1939, although BMW continued to manufacture small quantities of 321s, 326s and 335s until May 1941, after which only motorcycles were permitted by the German government. During the war years, BMW largely concentrated on aero engine manufacture.

At the end of WWII, BMW's Munich plant was in ruins, while Eisenach was in the Russian zone of the divided Germany. Eisenach returned to car production first, with pre-war BMW designs marketed under the EMW name. Motorcycle production resumed in Munich during 1948.

After experimenting with a small coupé powered by a flat-twin motorcycle engine, the company reverted to a 2 litre six-cylinder engine of pre-war design fitted into a saloon, which entered production as the Type 501 in December 1952. The 501 was built in various guises until 1958, being joined in 1954 by the 502, which featured a 2.6 litre V8 engine in the 501 body. There were also the low-volume 503 and 507.

However, during the 1950s, initially it was the motorcycles that kept BMW going, and later the Isetta (an Italian designed microcar). Towards the end of the decade, two-wheel sales began to slide, as did those of its big cars, and there were real fears that the company would fold.

In 1959, with a take-over by Daimler-Benz imminent, a small group of shareholders headed by Herbert Quandt saved the company, and as the 1960s dawned, BMW's fortunes began to look bright once more.

In 1961, BMW launched a new small car, the 700, powered by an engine based on the motorcycle unit, which proved a roaring success, while 1962 saw the 1500 saloon. This too became a top seller, and was followed by the 1600, 1800 and 1800 Ti models. In 1965, BMW produced 58,524 vehicles, and by 1969, production had climbed to 145,000 cars.

The 1980s saw the excellent E36 3-series, ranging from the 318 (90bhp) to the 323 (139bhp), together with larger 5- and 7-series saloons, and the 6-series coupé. Like its great rival, Mercedes-Benz, BMW favoured gradual development and improvement rather than dramatic innovation. It was also gaining a reputation for quality and performance.

During the last 20 years, BMW has continued to grow, and now produces over a million vehicles a year from plants in Germany and overseas.

1937 BMW 328, 1971cc, 6-cylinder engine, 3 Solex 305F carburettors, 80bhp, 4-speed manual gearbox.
£125,000–127,000 / €185,000–188,000 / $220,000–224,000 ⚲ COYS
The prototype 328 made its racing debut in 1936 during the annual Eifel race at the Nürburgring circuit. Driven by Ernst Henne – ironically under contract to rival Mercedes-Benz – it caused a sensation, winning first time out. In the following year, the 328 Roadster entered limited production. Lightweight engineering and a perfectly balanced rear-wheel drive made the car ideal for fast road use and motor sport.

BMW Model	ENGINE cc/cyl	DATES	CONDITION		
			1	2	3
Dixi	747/4	1927–32	£7,000	£3,000	£2,000
303	1175/6	1934–36	£11,000	£8,000	£5,000
309	843/4	1933–34	£6,000	£4,000	£2,000
315	1490/6	1935–36	£9,000	£7,000	£5,000
319	1911/6	1935–37	£10,000	£9,000	£6,000
326	1971/6	1936–37	£12,000	£10,000	£8,000
320 series	1971/6	1937–38	£12,000	£10,000	£8,000
327/328	1971/6	1937–40	£30,000+	£18,000	£10,000
328	1971/6	1937–40	£100,000+	–	–

◀ **1973 BMW 3.0 CS Coupé,** 2985cc, overhead-camshaft 6-cylinder engine.
£2,100–2,500 / €3,100–3,700 / $3,700–4,400 ⚒ B(Kn)
To create its new 3 litre, six-cylinder range in 1971, BMW refined the existing six-cylinder 2.8 cars while retaining many of their most successful features. The sporting two-door bodywork reflected strong Bertone influence, while Karmann reworked the chassis to incorporate much of the suspension design from the luxury 3 litre salons. The 2985cc, overhead-camshaft engine developed 180bhp at 6,000rpm, while power for the CS models was transmitted through a four-speed manual gearbox.

▶ **1974 BMW 3.0 CSi,** 2985cc, Bosch fuel injection, 4-wheel disc brakes, finished in red, beige velour interior trim.
£2,400–2,900 / €3,500–4,200 / $4,200–5,000 ⚒ BARO

1975 BMW 2002 Ti Lux, 1990cc, overhead-camshaft 4-cylinder engine, 4-speed manual gearbox.
£5,600–6,700 / €8,300–10,000 / $9,900–11,800 ⚒ H&H

Condition guide

1. A vehicle in top class condition but not 'concours d'elegance standard, either fully restored or in very good original condition.
2. A good, clean, roadworthy vehicle, both mechanically and bodily sound.
3. A runner, but in need of attention, probably both to bodywork and mechanics. Must have current MoT.

1980 BMW M535i, 3453cc, overhead-camshaft 6-cylinder engine, 5-speed manual gearbox, Mahle wheels, finished in silver, blue interior, 1 of 408 right-hand-drive models built.
£3,000–3,600 / €4,450–5,300 / $5,300–6,300 ⚒ H&H

1991 BMW Z1 Roadster, 2494cc, 6-cylinder engine, 5-speed manual gearbox, left-hand drive.
£12,400–14,900 / € 18,400–22,000 $21,800–26,200 ➚ CGC
Introduced at the 1987 Frankfurt show, the Z1 caused a furore. It was built around a galvanized steel spaceframe with fully detachable composite body panels, and boasted far greater torsional rigidity than its Z3 successor. This extra strength was partially derived from its zinc coating and bonded floor. The latter also doubled as an undertray, channelling airflow towards the specially shaped exhaust tail-box (inverted wing section), which provided meaningful downforce at speed. Always intended as a low-volume model (only 8,000 were built), the Z1 relied heavily on BMW's parts bins. It borrowed the front suspension design (albeit with a wider track), 2496cc straight-six engine and Getrag 260/5 gearbox from the 325i, but had a unique semi-trailing-arm Z-axle rear-suspension set-up. Lauded by the press for excellent handling and roadholding, it offered 170bhp and a top speed of 140mph. The car's electrically powered doors could be made to disappear inside the sills while on the move.

◀ **1985 BMW M635 Coupé,** 3453cc, 6-cylinder engine, 286bhp, 5-speed manual gearbox, finished in metallic grey, cream interior.
£3,350–4,000 / € 4,950–5,900 / $5,900–7,050 ➚ COYS

1986 BMW 635 CSi, 6-cylinder engine, 4-speed automatic transmission, ABS brakes, finished in red, black cloth interior.
£2,100–2,500 / € 3,100–3,700 / $3,700–4,400 ➚ CGC
Successor to the race-proven 3.0 CS/CSi high-performance sports coupés, the 6-series was introduced in August 1976. Altogether more forgiving and refined than its predecessors, it utilized a modified version of the 5-series saloon platform with independent coil-and-wishbone front suspension and trailing-arm rear suspension. Plenty of power was on tap from the various versions of BMW's mighty M30 overhead-camshaft straight-six engine fitted throughout the range. Second only to the BMW Motorsport tuned M6 version, the 635CSi's 3430cc unit developed some 218bhp, enough to propel it from rest to 60mph in 7.4 seconds and on to 142mph.

1992 BMW 320i Cabriolet, 1991cc, 6-cylinder engine, 150bhp, top speed 134mph, 4-speed automatic transmission, sports seats, power hood.
£4,800–5,800 / € 7,100–8,500 / $8,400–10,100 ➚ BARO

BMW Model	ENGINE cc/cyl	DATES	CONDITION 1	2	3
501	2077/6	1952–56	£9,000	£7,000	£3,500
501 V8/502	2580				
	3168/8	1955–63	£10,000+	£5,000	£3,000
503 FHC/DHC	3168/8	1956–59	£25,000+	£20,000	£15,000
507	3168/8	1956–59	£120,000+	£70,000	£50,000
Isetta (4 wheels)	247/1	1955–62	£7,000	£3,000	£1,200
Isetta (3 wheels)	298/1	1958–64	£8,000	£2,500	£1,500
Isetta 600	585/2	1958–59	£3,000+	£1,800	£500
1500/1800/2000	var/4	1962–68	£1,800	£800	£500
2000CS	1990/4	1966–69	£5,500	£4,000	£1,500
1500/1600/1602	1499/				
	1573/4	1966–75	£3,000+	£1,500	£800
1600 Cabriolet	1573/4	1967–71	£6,000	£4,500	£2,000
2800CS	2788/6	1968–71	£5,000	£4,000	£1,500
1602	1990/4	1968–74	£3,000	£1,500	£1,000
2002	1990/4	1968–74	£3,000	£2,000	£1,000
2002 Tii	1990/4	1971–75	£4,500	£2,500	£1,200
2002 Touring	1990/4	1971–74	£3,500	£2,000	£1,000
2002 Cabriolet	1990/4	1971–75	£5,000+	£3,000	£2,500
2002 Turbo	1990/4	1973–74	£10,000	£6,000	£4,000
3.0 CSa/CSi	2986/6	1972–75	£8,000	£6,000	£4,000
3.0 CSL	3003/				
	3153/6	1972–75	£16,000	£10,000	£7,500
MI	3500/6	1978–85	£50,000	£40,000	£30,000
633/635 CS/CSI	3210/3453/6	1976–85	£7,000	£3,000	£2,000
M535i	3453/6	1979–81	£4,500	£3,000	£2,500

Bristol *(British 1947–)*

◄ **1963 Bristol 407,** 5130cc, Chrysler V8 engine, automatic transmission, 4-wheel disc brakes, long-range lamps, original period radio.
£3,500–4,200 / €5,200–6,200
$6,200–7,400 ⤳ BRIT

1967 Bristol 409, 5211cc, V8 engine, restored over 2 years, concours winner.
£15,000–18,000 / €22,200–26,600
$26,400–31,700 ⤳ H&H

► **1972 Bristol 411,** 6277cc, Chrysler V8 engine, finished in blue, light blue leather interior.
£8,400–10,100 / €12,400–14,900
$14,800–17,800 ⤳ H&H

BRISTOL Model	ENGINE cc/cyl	DATES	CONDITION 1	2	3
400	1971/6	1947–50	£16,000	£14,000	£8,000
401 FHC/DHC	1971/6	1949–53	£28,000	£14,000	£8,000
402	1971/6	1949–50	£22,000	£19,000	£12,000
403	1971/6	1953–55	£20,000	£14,000	£10,000
404 Coupé	1971/6	1953–57	£22,000	£15,000	£12,000
405	1971/6	1954–58	£14,000	£11,000	£7,000
405 Drophead	1971/6	1954–56	£22,000	£19,000	£16,000
406	2216/6	1958–61	£12,000	£8,000	£6,000
407	5130/8	1962–63	£15,000	£8,000	£5,000
408	5130/8	1964–65	£14,000	£10,000	£8,000
409	5211/8	1966–67	£14,000	£11,000	£7,000
410	5211/8	1969	£14,000	£10,000	£6,000
411 Mk I–III	6277/8	1970–73	£16,000	£9,000	£6,000
411 Mk IV–V	6556/8	1974–76	£12,500	£9,500	£7,000
412	5900/ 6556/8	1975–82	£15,000	£9,000	£6,000
603	5211/ 5900/8	1976–82	£10,000	£7,000	£5,000

Brush *(American 1907–13)*

1911 Brush Model E Runabout, single-cylinder engine, brass acetylene headlamps and generator, kerosene cowl lamps, canvas top with glass windscreen, restored, finished in dark green.
£7,200–8,600 / € 10,700–12,700 / $12,700–15,100 ≯ BB(S)
Anson P. Brush designed the first car to bear his name in 1907, having already been involved in the design of the first Cadillac in 1902 and the earliest of the Oaklands. Brush sales were brisk, and the 6hp single-cylinder cars enjoyed a good reputation. The chassis and axles were of wood, while suspension was by coil spring. Top speed was approximately 35mph for this dual-chain-driven car. In 1908, a twin-cylinder model was offered, but it lasted for only a year. By the time this example was built in 1911, the little single was good for 10hp.

BSA *(British 1907–39)*

1934 BSA 10hp Four-Door Saloon, 1185cc, 4-cylinder engine, fluid flywheel transmission, 1 family ownership until 1997, fewer than 65,000 miles recorded.
£4,100–4,900 / € 6,100–7,200 / $7,200–8,600 ≯ COYS

1935 BSA 8.9hp Scout Sports, 1075cc, side-valve 4-cylinder engine, front-wheel drive, independent front suspension with quarter-elliptic springs, wire wheels.
£5,600–6,700 / € 8,200–9,800 / $9,900–11,800 ≯ B(Kn)

Bugatti *(France 1909–56, Italy 1994–98)*

◀ **1930 Bugatti Type 44 Tourer,** 2991cc, overhead-camshaft 8-cylinder engine, 3 valves per cylinder, 4-speed gate-change gearbox.
£72,000–86,000 / € 106,000–127,000 $126,000–151,000 ≯ BB(S)

BUGATTI Model	ENGINE cc/cyl	DATES	CONDITION 1	2	3
13/22/23	1496/4	1919–26	£40,000	£32,000	£25,000
30	1991/8	1922–36	£45,000	£35,000	£30,000
32	1992/8	1923	£45,000	£35,000	£30,000
35A	1991/8	1924–30	£110,000+	£90,000	£80,500
38 (30 update)	1991/8	1926–28	£44,500	£34,000	£28,000
39	1493/8	1926–29	£120,000	£90,000	£80,000
39A Supercharged	1496/8	1926–29	£140,000+	–	–
35T	2262/8	1926–30	£140,000+	–	–
37 GP Car	1496/4	1926–30	£110,000+	£90,000	£75,000
40	1496/4	1926–30	£50,000	£42,000	£35,000
38A	1991/8	1927–28	£48,000	£40,000	£35,000
35B Supercharged	2262/8	1927–30	£350,000+	£200,000	–
35C	1991/8	1927–30	£170,000+	–	–
37A	1496/4	1927–30	£125,000+	–	–
44	2991/8	1927–30	£60,000+	£40,000	£35,000
45	3801/16	1927–30	£150,000+	–	–
43/43A Tourer	2262/8	1927–31	£180,000+	–	–
35A	1991/8	1928–30	£140,000	£110,000	£90,000
46	5359/8	1929–36	£140,000	£110,000	£90,000
40A	1627/4	1930	£55,000	£45,000	£35,500
49	3257/8	1930–34	£60,000+	£45,000	£35,500
57 Closed	3257/8	1934–40	£60,000+	£35,000	£30,000
57 Open	3257/8	1936–38	£90,000++	£60,000	£55,000
57S	3257/8	1936–38	£250,000+	–	–
57SC Supercharged	3257/8	1936–39	£250,000+	–	–
57G	3257/8	1937–40	£250,000+	–	–
57C	3257/8	1939–40	£140,000+	–	–

Racing history is an important factor with the GP cars, also whether supercharged and low chassis.

Buick *(American 1903–)*

1936 Buick Century Sport Coupé, 5247cc, side-valve 8-cylinder engine, 3-speed manual gearbox, independent front suspension, hydraulic brakes, ground-up restoration 1994, finished in cream, tan wool broadcloth interior, concours winner.
£10,500–12,600 / € 15,500–18,600 / $18,500–22,200 ⚬ BB(S)

BUICK Model	ENGINE cc/cyl	DATES	CONDITION 1	2	3
Veteran	various	1903–09	£18,500	£12,000	£8,000
18/20	3881/6	1918–22	£12,000	£5,000	£2,000
Series 22	2587/4	1922–24	£9,000	£5,000	£3,000
Series 24/6	3393/6	1923–30	£9,000	£5,000	£3,000
Light 8	3616/8	1931	£18,000	£14,500	£11,000
Straight 8	4467/8	1931	£22,000	£18,000	£10,000
50 Series	3857/8	1931–39	£18,500	£15,000	£8,000
60 Series	5247/8	1936–39	£19,000	£15,000	£8,000
90 Series	5648/8	1934–35	£20,000	£15,500	£9,000
40 Series	4064/8	1936–39	£19,000	£14,000	£10,000
80/90	5247/8	1936–39	£25,000	£20,000	£15,000
McLaughlin	5247/8	1937–40	£22,000	£15,000	£10,000

Various chassis lengths and bodies will affect value. Buick chassis fitted with British bodies prior to 1916 were called Bedford-Buicks. Right-hand drive can have an added premium of 25%.

◄ **1951 Buick Roadmaster Series 70 Estate Wagon,** 5200cc, V8 engine, automatic transmission, factory sun visor and roof rack, 1 of only 679 Estate Wagons built in 1951, original.
£14,700–17,600 / €21,800–26,000
$25,900–31,000 ✗ B(Mon)
In 1951, the Buick Estate Wagon was the only car in General Motors' line-up that offered real wood body construction as opposed to simulated-wood trim. It was available on the mid-price Super and top-of-the-range Roadmaster chassis, the latter being powered by a 5.2 litre, 152bhp engine.

1955 Buick Century Convertible, 5247cc, V8 engine, automatic transmission, power steering, electric windows, radio, heater.
£15,600–18,700 / €23,100–27,700
$27,500–33,000 ✗ BJ

1968 Buick Skylark GS, 455cu.in, V8 engine, 480bhp, completely restored, chrome exhaust headers, 3in dual stainless steel exhaust, uprated Turbo 400 transmission, 12-bolt rear axle, new interior.
£9,100–10,900 / €13,500–16,100
$16,000–19,200 ✗ BJ

BUICK Model	ENGINE cu in/cyl	DATES	CONDITION 1	2	3
Special/Super 4-Door	248/364/8	1950–59	£6,000	£4,000	£2,000
Special/Super Riviera	263/332/8	1950–56	£8,000	£6,000	£3,000
Special/Super Convertible	263/332/8	1950–56	£8,500	£5,500	£3,000
Roadmaster 4-door	320/365/8	1950–58	£11,000	£8,000	£6,000
Roadmaster Riviera	320/364/8	1950–58	£9,000	£7,000	£5,000
Roadmaster Convertible	320/364/8	1950–58	£18,000	£11,000	£7,000
Special/Super Riviera	364/8	1957–59	£10,750	£7,500	£5,000
Special/Super Convertible	364/8	1957–58	£13,500	£11,000	£6,000

Cadillac (*American 1903–*)

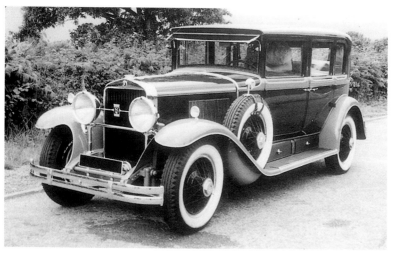

◄ **1929 Cadillac 353 Four-Door Saloon,** 5600cc, V8 engine, 4-wheel brakes, hydraulic shock absorbers, left-hand drive, older restoration.
£23,000–27,600
€34,000–40,000
$40,000–48,000 ✗ B(Kn)

CADILLAC (pre-war) Model	ENGINE cc/cyl	DATES	CONDITION 1	2	3
Type 57–61	5153/8	1915–23	£20,000+	£14,000	£6,000
Series 314	5153/8	1926–27	£22,000	£15,000	£6,000
Type V63	5153/8	1924–27	£20,000	£13,000	£5,000
Series 341	5578/8	1928–29	£22,000+	£15,000+	£6,000
Series 353–5	5289/8	1930–31	£50,000+	£30,000	£18,000
V16	7406/16	1931–32	£80,000+	£50,000+	£20,000
V12	6030/12	1932–37	£42,000+	£25,000	£15,000
V8	5790/8	1935–36	£30,000	£15,000	£6,000
V16	7034/16	1937–40	£50,000+	£30,000	£18,000

1959 Cadillac Eldorado Seville Custom, 6400cc, high-performance V8 engine, automatic ride-height control, wire wheels, lengthened sedanca de ville-style body, driver's compartment with fold-away roof, remote-control door catches, extended tail-fins, chrome continental spare-wheel kit, air conditioning, tinted glass, gold fittings, white leather interior, restored 1987.
£47,000–56,000 / €70,000–83,000
$83,000–99,000 ⚒ B(Mu)
The first owner of this particular car was ex-King Farouk of Egypt, who ordered all the changes. It cost £57,000 / €84,000 / $100,000 to build in 1959, when the standard Eldorado Seville cost £4,200 / €6,200 / $7,400.

▶ **1977 Cadillac Eldorado Biarritz,** 425cu.in, astro roof, air conditioning, 6-way power seats, power steering, brakes and windows, tilt/telescope steering column, 57,000 miles recorded.
£3,100–3,700 / €4,600–5,500 / $5,500–6,500 ⚒ BJ

CADILLAC Model	ENGINE cu in/cyl	DATES	CONDITION 1	2	3
4-door	331/8	1949	£8,000	£4,500	£3,000
2-door fastback	331/8	1949	£10,000	£8,000	£5,000
Convertible Coupe	331/8	1949	£22,000	£12,000	£10,000
Series 62 4-door	331/365/8	1950–55	£7,000	£5,500	£3,000
Sedan de Ville	365/8	1956–58	£8,000	£6,000	£4,000
Coupe de Ville	331/365/8	1950–58	£12,500	£9,500	£3,500
Convertible Coupe	331/365/8	1950–58	£25,000	£20,000	£10,000
Eldorado	331/8	1953–55	£35,000	£30,000	£18,000
Eldorado Seville	365/8	1956–58	£11,500	£9,000	£5,500
Eldorado Biarritz	365/8	1956–58	£30,000	£20,000	£15,000
Sedan de Ville	390/8	1959	£12,000	£9,500	£5,000
Coupe de Ville	390/8	1959	£15,000	£9,000	£5,500
Convertible Coupe	390/8	1959	£28,000	£20,000	£10,000
Eldorado Seville	390/8	1959	£13,000	£10,000	£6,000
Eldorado Biarritz	390/8	1959	£45,000+	£25,000	£15,000
Sedan de Ville	390/8	1960	£10,000	£8,000	£4,500
Convertible Coupe	390/8	1960	£27,000+	£14,000	£7,500
Eldorado Biarritz	390/8	1960	£25,000+	£17,000	£10,000
Sedan de Ville	390/429/8	1961–64	£7,000	£5,000	£3,000
Coupe de Ville	390/429/8	1961–64	£8,000	£6,000	£4,000
Convertible Coupe	390/429/8	1961–64	£20,000	£9,000	£7,000
Eldorado Biarritz	390/429/8	1961–64	£19,500	£14,000	£9,000

Caterham *(British 1973–)*

◄ **1998 Caterham 21,** 1796cc, Rover 1.8 4-cylinder engine, light grey interior, 1 of only 49 built.
£12,600–15,100 / €18,600–22,300
$22,200–26,600 ✗ BRIT

Chalmers *(American 1908–13)*

► **1912 Chalmers Model II Pony Tonneau,** 3700cc, 4-cylinder monobloc engine, exhaust pressure feed by Lunkenheimer valve, auxiliary air pump for starting, wooden-spoked wheels.
£16,100–19,300 / €23,800–28,600
$28,300–34,000 ✗ H&H
The Chalmers marque came about in 1907 when the former vice president of the National Cash Register Company, Hugh Chalmers, bought into the thriving Thomas-Detroit concern. The company was renamed Chalmers-Detroit in 1908 and became simply Chalmers in 1910. The first 30hp Chalmers model had a four-cylinder 3.7 litre monobloc engine in unit with a three-speed gearbox and multi-disc clutch.

Chevrolet *(American 1911–)*

CHEVROLET Model	ENGINE cc/cyl	DATES	CONDITION 1	2	3
H4/H490 K-Series	2801/4	1914–29	£9,000	£5,000	£2,000
FA5	2699/4	1918	£8,000	£5,000	£2,000
D5	5792/8	1918–19	£10,000	£6,000	£3,000
FB50	3660/4	1919–21	£7,000	£4,000	£2,000
AA	2801/4	1928–32	£5,000	£3,000	£1,000
AB/C	3180/6	1929–36	£6,000	£4,000	£2,000
Master	3358/6	1934–37	£9,000	£5,000	£2,000
Master De Luxe	3548/6	1938–41	£9,000	£6,000	£4,000

1951 Chevrolet Fleetline Four-Door Saloon, 3500cc, 6-cylinder engine, 3-speed manual gearbox, completely restored, 2,000 miles recorded since, concours condition.
£9,200–11,000 / €13,600–16,300
$16,200–19,400 ✗ H&H

1954 Chevrolet Corvette Roadster, 235cu.in, 6-cylinder engine, triple carburettors, 155bhp, automatic transmission, indicators, radio, concours winner.
£32,000–38,000 / €47,000–56,000
$56,000–67,000 ✗ BJ

1956 Chevrolet Belair Two-Door Hardtop,
completely rebuilt 1996, 454cu.in, V8 engine, supercharger,
750+bhp, B&M Turbo 400 automatic transmission, 9in Ford
rear axle, Wilwood disc brakes, braided brake and fuel
lines, Cragar alloy wheels, finished in
light green and white.
**£20,500–24,600 / €30,000–36,000
$36,000–43,000 ⋏ BJ**

1957 Chevrolet 210 Four-Door Saloon, 235cu.in,
6-cylinder engine, 140bhp, mechanics recently restored,
finished in metallic green and white, 2-tone green
upholstery, good condition.
£3,150–3,800 / €4,650–5,600 / $5,500–6,600 ⋏ CGC

1962 Chevrolet Corvette, 327cu.in, V8 engine, 4-speed manual gearbox.
£15,500–18,600 / €23,000–27,500 / $27,400–33,000 ⋏ B(Kn)

◄ **1963 Chevrolet Corvette Sting Ray Coupé,** 327cu.in,
V8 engine, 300bhp, automatic transmission, original knock-
off wheels, finished in red, red interior.
**£20,800–25,000 / €30,800–37,000
$37,000–44,000 ⋏ BJ**

1964 Chevrolet Malibu SS Convertible, 283cu.in,
numbers-matching V8 engine, complete 'nut-and-bolt'
rebuild, uprated GM camshaft, 10.5:1 Keith Black pistons,
Holley carburettor, aluminium valve covers, ceramic-coated
exhaust headers, c280bhp.
**£16,000–19,200 / €23,700–28,400
$28,200–33,800 ⋏ BJ**
**This car was found in a warehouse in Virginia,
having been in storage since 1979.**

1966 Chevrolet Corvette Sting Ray Roadster, 327cu.in,
V8 engine, Holley carburettor, 4-speed manual gearbox,
4-wheel disc brakes, top speed 120mph.
**£18,600–27,500 / €27,500–33,000
$32,800–39,000 ⋏ B(Kn)**

1967 Chevrolet Camaro RS Coupé, 327cu.in, V8 engine, 275bhp, factory 4-speed manual gearbox, de luxe interior.
£7,700–9,200 / €11,400–13,600 / $13,500–16,200 ✗ BJ

1972 Chevrolet Corvette Sting Ray Coupé, 454cu.in, V8 engine, M21 4-speed close-ratio manual gearbox, matching-numbers drivetrain, power steering, power brakes, T-top, completely restored, engine upgraded to 425bhp, electronic ignition, finished in white.
£17,400–21,000 / €25,800–31,000
$31,000–37,000 ✗ BJ

1972 Chevrolet Corvette Sting Ray Roadster, 350cu.in, V8 engine, automatic transmission, finished in yellow, black interior and hood, stored for last 14 years.
£8,600–10,300 / €12,700–15,200
$15,100–18,100 ✗ B(Kn)

Five years after the Sting Ray's arrival, a total restyle ushered in the 'Stingray' era, although the latter name was not officially applied to the model until 1969. Based on General Motors' 1965 Mako Shark II show car, the 1968 Corvette coupé became a 'notchback' with removable rear window and detachable two-piece 'T-top' (Targa) roof, while the roadster version could be ordered with an optional hardtop. The previous generation's pop-up headlights were retained, while the windscreen wipers were concealed beneath a vacuum operated panel. Beneath the skin, the chassis remained fundamentally unchanged.

1990 Chevrolet Corvette Coupé, 350cu.in, V8 engine, 4-speed automatic transmission, stainless steel exhaust.
£5,600–6,700 / €8,300–9,900 / $9,900–11,800 ✗ H&H

1979 Chevrolet Corvette Coupé, 350cu.in, V8 engine, 4-speed manual gearbox, 4-wheel independent suspension, 4-wheel disc brakes, alloy wheels, T-top, finished in dark green, 40,000 miles recorded, very good condition.
£7,000–8,400 / €10,300–12,400
$12,300–14,800 ✗ CGC

CHEVROLET Model	ENGINE cu in/cyl	DATES	CONDITION 1	2	3
Stylemaster	216/6	1942–48	£8,000	£4,000	£1,000
Fleetmaster	216/6	1942–48	£8,000	£4,000	£1,000
Fleetline	216/6	1942–51	£8,000	£5,000	£2,000
Styleline	216/6	1949–52	£8,000	£6,000	£2,000
Bel Air 4-door	235/6	1953–54	£6,000	£4,000	£3,000
Bel Air Sport Coupe	235/6	1953–54	£7,000	£4,500	£3,500
Bel Air convertible	235/6	1953–54	£12,500	£9,500	£6,000
Bel Air 4-door	283/8	1955–57	£8,000	£4,000	£3,000
Bel Air Sport Coupe	283/8	1955–56	£11,000	£7,000	£4,000
Bel Air convertible	283/8	1955–56	£16,000	£11,000	£7,000
Bel Air Sport Coupe	283/8	1957	£11,000	£7,500	£4,500
Bel Air convertible	283/8	1957	£22,000+	£15,000+	£8,000
Impala Sport Sedan	235/6, 348/8	1958	£12,500	£9,000	£5,500
Impala convertible	235/6, 348/8	1958	£14,500	£11,000	£7,500
Impala Sport Sedan	235/6, 348/8	1959	£8,000	£5,000	£4,000
Impala convertible	235/6, 348/8	1959	£14,000	£10,000	£5,000
Corvette	235/6	1953	£25,000+	£18,000	£10,000
Corvette	235/6, 283/8	1954–57	£20,000+	£13,000	£9,000
Corvette	283/327/8	1958–62	£24,000+	£16,000	£9,000
Corvette Sting Ray	327/427/8	1963–67	£19,000+	£15,000+	£10,000
Corvette Sting Ray Roadster	327/427/8	1963–66	£22,000+	£15,000	£8,000
Corvette Sting Ray Roadster	427/8	1967	£20,000+	£13,000	£10,000

Value will also be affected by build options, rare coachbuilding options and de luxe engine specifications, etc.

Chrysler *(American 1923–)*

1926 Chrysler E80 Imperial Rumble Seat Roadster, 4700cc, side-valve 6-cylinder engine, 3-speed manual gearbox.
£25,300–30,000 / €37,000–44,000 / $45,000–54,000 ✗ B(Kn)
Introduced in January 1924, Walter P. Chrysler's first automobile was an innovative, medium-priced six-cylinder car of better-than-average performance, as numerous motor sport successes would soon demonstrate. It featured hydraulic brakes, aluminium pistons, full-pressure lubrication and a tubular front axle, and was able to reach 70mph comfortably. Not surprisingly, it was a success, 32,000 being sold in the car's first year of production. The range soon expanded to encompass a four, a smaller six and the fabulous Imperial, the last being larger and more expensive than the original, and intended to compete with the likes of Cadillac, Lincoln and Packard. The Imperial boasted a powerful 4.7 litre side-valve six-cylinder engine coupled to a three-speed gearbox. Outwardly, it was distinguishable by its fluted radiator and bonnet, a feature legally challenged by Vauxhall and discontinued in 1929.

Cisitalia *(Italian 1946–65)*

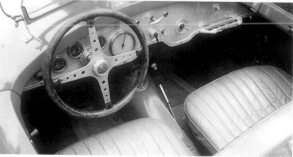

1952 Cisitalia Nuvolari Spyder, engine based on 5-main-bearing Simca 1100 block, tubular chassis, ventilated drum brakes
£47,000–56,000 / €70,000–83,000
$83,000–99,000 ✗ B(Mon)
Founded in 1939 by Piero Dusio to manufacture sports equipment, Consorzio Industriale Sportiva Italia (Cisitalia) amassed a fortune for its owner by making military uniforms during WWII. A motor racing enthusiast, Dusio used his wealth to become involved with the sport, building the first Cisitalia competition car in 1946. This was an advanced monoposto with spaceframe chassis – the first time this method of construction had been used for a series-built racing car – powered by a modified Fiat
1100 engine. The Cisitalia sold well and Dusio followed it with a two-seater sports car. Coupé and spyder versions were also made, a racing spyder almost winning the Mille Miglia in 1947 with Tazio Nuvolari at the wheel. In 1948, Cisitalia introduced the 202 Gran Sport coupé, styled by Pinin Farina. Its elegant lines and integrated, all-enveloping coachwork set the pattern for every Gran Turismo that followed. Ferdinand Porsche and Carlo Abarth helped Dusio develop a supercharged 12-cylinder Grand Prix car, which all but bankrupted Cisitalia, forcing Dusio to relocate his business to Argentina, where he founded Autoar. In 1952, Dusio began building Cisitalias again, beginning with this very car. Its aluminium bodywork was inspired by the 202SMM Nuvolari Spyder, with only minimal differences, while the tubular chassis was slightly shorter.

Citroën *(French 1919–)*

1925 Citroën 5CV, 856cc, side-valve 4-cylinder engine.
£3,150–3,800 / €4,650–5,600 / $5,500–6,600 ✈ BRIT
Built between 1922 and 1926, the 5CV was available as a two-seat or three-seat 'cloverleaf' tourer. It was also made under licence by Opel in Germany, where it was known as the 'Laubfrosch' ('Tree Frog').

1955 Citroën 11BD Normale Saloon, 1911cc, overhead-valve 4-cylinder engine, 60bhp, 3-speed manual gearbox with dash-mounted change, front-wheel drive, torsion-bar suspension, top speed 75mph.
£4,500–5,400 / €6,700–8,000 / $7,900–9,500 ✈ CGC

1925 Citroën B10 Tourer, 1452cc, fully restored, finished in green with black wings, green interior trim.
£4,800–5,700 / €7,000–8,400 / $8,400–10,000 ✈ BRIT
André Citroën's first car, a 10hp model with torpedo coachwork, was announced during 1919.
The company's products were the first European cars to be built using mass-production techniques and employing welded, all-steel bodies of the Budd principle. The new Citroën was not only the least expensive car available, but also frugal to run. It was followed by the B2 Series, subsequently known as the B10. These models were fitted with an enlarged engine, displacing 1452cc and developing 20bhp.

> The price paid for a car can vary according to the country in which it was sold. To discover where the car sold, cross reference the code at the end of each caption with the Key to Illustrations on page 251.

▶ **1968 Citroën DS21 Le Caddy Decapotable,** 2175cc, overhead-valve 4-cylinder engine, 4-speed semi-automatic transmission, finished in metallic maroon with black rear deck, aluminium side kick-plates, black vinyl hood, tan leather interior, Jaeger instruments.
£44,000–53,000 / €65,000–78,000 / $77,000–92,000 ✈ CGC
Built by famed coachbuilder Henri Chapron and launched in 1960, the Le Caddy Decapotable was built to special order, and only 34 cars were made over four series of the DS. Of those, only two were fifth-generation, faired-in headlamp models, and this car is one of them.

CITROËN Model	ENGINE cc/cyl	DATES	CONDITION 1	2	3
A	1300/4	1919	£4,000	£2,000	£1,000
5CV	856/4	1922–26	£7,000	£4,000	£2,000
11	1453/4	1922–28	£4,000	£2,000	£1,000
12/24	1538/4	1927–29	£5,000	£3,000	£1,000
2½ Litre	2442/6	1929–31	£5,000	£3,000	£1,500
13/30	1628/4	1929–31	£5,000	£3,000	£1,000
Big 12	1767/4	1932–35	£7,000	£5,000	£2,000
Twenty	2650/6	1932–35	£10,000	£5,000	£3,000
Ten CV	1452/4	1933–34	£5,000	£3,000	£1,000
Ten CV	1495/4	1935–36	£6,000	£3,000	£1,000
11B/Light 15/Big 15/7CV	1911/4	1934–57	£9,000	£5,000	£2,000
Twelve	1628/4	1936–39	£5,000	£3,000	£1,000
F	1766/4	1937–38	£4,000	£2,000	£1,000
15/6 and Big Six	2866/6	1938–56	£8,000	£4,000	£2,000

CITROËN Model	ENGINE cc/cyl	DATES	CONDITION 1	2	3
2CV	375/2	1948–54	£1,000	£500	£250
2CV/Dyane/Bijou	425/2	1954–82	£1,000	£800	£500
DS19/ID19	1911/4	1955–69	£5,000	£3,000	£800
Sahara	900/4	1958–67	£5,000	£4,000	£3,000
2CV6	602/2	1963 on	£1,200	£600	£250
DS Safari	1985/4	1968–75	£6,000	£3,000	£1,000
DS21	1985/4	1969–75	£6,000+	£3,000	£1,000
DS23	2347/4	1972–75	£6,000+	£4,000	£1,500
SM	2670/ 2974/6	1970–75	£9,000	£6,000	£4,500

1969 Citroën DS21 Saloon, 2175cc, 4-cylinder engine, top speed 110+mph.
£4,000–4,800 / €5,900–7,100 / $7,000–8,400 ✗ CGC

1972 Citroën SM Saloon, 2670cc, Maserati double-overhead-camshaft V6 engine, 170bhp, 5-speed manual gearbox, hydro-pneumatic independent suspension, power steering, disc brakes, top speed 140mph.
£7,200–8,600 / €10,700–12,700 $12,700–15,100 ✗ CGC

The acquisition of Maserati in 1968 gave Citroën's DS Sport project a great boost. Intended to follow in the tracks of such classics as the Facel Vega HK500, the SM's styling was all but finalized by 1967. One vital aspect was missing, however – a suitable powerplant. This was commissioned from Maserati. The resultant 90-degree V6 had a swept volume of 2670cc and four overhead camshafts. It developed a healthy 178bhp. The finished car, with two-door fastback bodywork, was unveiled at the 1970 Geneva Salon. In production for five years, only 12,920 were built.

1972 Citroën DS20 Pallas Saloon, 1985cc, 4-cylinder engine, semi-automatic transmission, air conditioning, leather interior.
£3,500–4,200 / €5,200–6,200 $6,200–7,400 ✗ BARO

▶ **1975 Citroën DS23 Safari,** 2347cc, 4-cylinder engine, 130bhp, 5-speed semi-automatic transmission.
£1,550–1,850 / €2,300–2,750 $2,750–3,250 ✗ H&H
This was the final year of production of the DS23 Safari.

1972 Citroën DS21 1E Decapotable, 2175cc, 4-cylinder engine, fuel injection, 4-speed semi-automatic transmission, top speed 115mph.
£53,000–64,000 / €80,000–95,000 / $93,000–112,000 ✗ CGC
Of the 1,456,115 Citroën DSs built during the model's 20-year production run, only 1,325 were Decapotables. Produced in collaboration with Chapron, the model was the flagship of the DS range.

Cord *(American 1929–37)*

1929 Cord L-29 Convertible, 4900cc, Lycoming 8-cylinder engine, 115bhp, front-wheel drive.
£13,500–16,200 / €20,000–24,000
$23,800–28,500 ⚒ COYS
The luxurious L-29 was dropped in 1932, after some 5,200 examples had been built.

Auction prices

Miller's only includes cars declared sold. Our guide prices take into account the buyer's premium, VAT on the premium, and the extent of any published catalogue information relating to condition and provenance. Cars sold at auction are identified by the ⚒ icon; full details of the auction house can be found on page 251.

1937 Cord 812 Phaeton, 4730cc, V8 engine, 170bhp, 4-speed manual gearbox, monocoque chassis, 1 of only 404 unsupercharged Phaetons built.
£49,000–59,000 / €73,000–87,000 / $86,000–103,000 ⚒ COYS

Crossley *(British 1904–39)*

◄ **1925 Crossley 15/30 Tourer,** 2100cc, 4-cylinder engine, 3-speed manual gearbox, completely restored.
£5,200–6,250 / €7,700–9,200 / $9,200–10,900 ⚒ H&H
The 15/30 was an export version of the Model 14, with a slightly different exhaust and wheels, and a more rugged cylinder block.

Colour Review

◄ **1983 Alfa Romeo 2000 Spider,** 1962cc, double-overhead camshaft 4-cylinder engine, fully restored, converted to right-hand drive, little use since.
£7,000–8,400 / €10,300–12,400 $12,300–14,800 ⚷ H&H
The Pininfarina styled Duetto roadster appeared in 1966, initially with a 1.6 litre engine and a few 1.3s. From 1967, the displacement was increased to 1750cc and, from 1970, there was a 2 litre option. This last version was offered with few changes until as late as 1994.

1930 Alvis 12/50 TJ Ducksback 3-seater, coachwork by Wilkinsons of Derby, 1645cc, 4-cylinder engine, opening windscreen, CAV headlamps, Toby torpedo side lamps, hood, side screens, tonneau cover.
£21,600–26,000 / €32,000–38,000 / $38,000–45,000 ⚷ B(Kn)

1936 Alvis Speed 20 SD Tourer, 2687cc, overhead-valve 6-cylinder engine, all-synchromesh gearbox.
£32,000–38,000 / €47,000–56,000 / $56,000–67,000 ⚷ H&H
London motor trader and entrepreneur Charles Follett funded a rescue investment for the ailing Alvis concern in 1930 and advised the firm as to which types of motor car the motoring public of the day would buy.
Thanks to Follett's money, the soundness of the basic designs, quality workmanship and motorsport success, Alvis prospered. The Silver Eagle was replaced in early 1932 by the Speed 20, which was powered by a similar 20hp engine, set in a massive, double-drop, beam-axled chassis, underslung at the rear.

1959 Alvis TD21 Drophead Coupé, 2993cc,
overhead-valve 6-cylinder engine, 3-speed automatic
transmission, beige leather interior.
£16,600–19,900 / €24,600–29,400
$29,200–35,000 ⋏ H&H

1979 Aston Martin V8 Volante, 5340cc,
concours condition.
£24,000–28,800 / €36,000–43,000
$42,000–50,000 ⋏ COYS

The DBS V8 was announced in September 1967,
and production began the following April. With four
overhead camshafts and Bosch electronic fuel
injection, the 5340cc V8 produced 320bhp at 5,000rpm
– good for 160+mph. After David Brown sold Aston
Martin in February 1972, the DBS V8 was replaced by
the Series 2 model, now simply called the Aston
Martin V8. Gone were the four headlamps and slatted
grille, in their place a black mesh grille flanked by
single headlamps; mechanical changes were limited
to electronic ignition and air conditioning as standard.
August 1973 saw the Series 3 arrive with quadruple
Weber carburettors, a larger bonnet bulge,
improved seats and central locking, with power
rising to 340bhp in June 1977.

◀ **1928 Austin 16/6 Doctor's Coupé,** 2249cc, side-valve
6-cylinder engine, Autovac fuel feed, 4-speed manual
gearbox, concours condition.
£7,800–9,400 / €11,500–13,800
$13,700–16,500 ⋏ CGC

1937 Austin Seven Ruby Saloon, 747cc, 4-cylinder
engine, 4-speed gearbox, completely restored 2000.
£3,900–4,700 / €5,800–7,000
$6,900–8,300 ⋏ B(Kn)

1954 Austin-Healey 100/4 BN1, 2660cc, overhead-valve
4-cylinder engine, wire wheels.
£12,500–15,000 / €18,500–22,200
$22,000–26,400 ⋏ H&H

1959 Austin-Healey 3000 Mk I Roadster, 2912cc, 6-cylinder engine, 124bhp, 4-speed gearbox, top speed 114mph,
0–60mph in 10 seconds.
£18,100–21,700 / €26,800–32,100 / $32,000–38,000 ⋏ H&H
The 3000 Mk1 arrived in 1959 and outwardly was the same shapely, low-slung two-seater, but now it featured
a 3 litre power plant. Also new were front disc brakes that improved stopping power.

1960 Austin-Healey 3000 Mk I BT7, 2912cc, 6-cylinder engine, 4-speed manual gearbox with overdrive, engine and gearbox rebuilt.
£14,200–17,000 / €21,000–25,200
$25,000–30,000 ✗ H&H
This car finished fourth overall in the 1990 Monte Carlo Rally Challenge.

1948 Bentley Mk VI Saloon, 4257cc, overhead-valve 6-cylinder engine, 4-speed manual gearbox, excellent condition.
£12,600–14,000 / €18,600–20,700
$22,200–24,600 ⊞ BLE

1950 Bentley Mk VI Drophead Coupé, coachwork by Park Ward, 4257cc, inlet-over-exhaust 6-cylinder engine, 1 owner for last 40 years.
£20,500–24,600 / €30,000–36,000
$36,000–43,000 ✗ COYS

1984 Bentley Mulsanne Turbo, 6750cc, V8 engine, automatic transmission, original specification, good condition.
£9,000–10,000 / €13,300–14,800
$15,800–17,600 ⊞ BLE

1988 BMW M635 CSi Coupé, 3453cc, 6-cylinder engine, manual gearbox, 1 of 524 right-hand-drive models built, concours condition.
£5,400–6,500 / €8,000–9,600 / $9,500–11,400 ✗ H&H
BMW's 6-series coupés changed little during the 1980s, being offered with three engine options: 2788cc (628CSi), 3430cc (635CS) and 3453cc (M635CSi). The last was a 24-valve, twin-overhead-camshaft motor that developed 255bhp and provided a top speed of 158mph.

◄ **1936 BSA Scout Sports Tourer,** 1203cc, 4-cylinder engine, 3-speed gearbox, completely rebuilt over 9 years.
£6,500–7,800 / €9,600–11,500
$11,400–13,700 ✗ BRIT
BSA described the Scout as 'the car for sporting people – a low-built, roomy, four-seat body with two adjustable front bucket seats designed for maximum comfort, and a full-width rear seat giving ample leg room.' Fitted with a four-cylinder, 9hp engine and three-speed manual gearbox, it was offered in two- and four-seat models. By mid-1936, the engine had been enlarged to 1203cc and was rated at 10hp. At this time, the range included a handsome two-seater fixed-head coupé. The Scout continued in production until 1940.

1956 Cadillac Coupe de Ville, 365cu in, overhead-valve V8 engine, Hydra-matic automatic transmission, servo-assisted brakes, power-assisted steering, automatic headlight dimmer, power windows, factory radio, seat belts, original, unrestored, concours winner.
£12,300–14,800 / €18,200–21,900
$21,600–26,000 ✣ BJ

1984 Cadillac Eldorado Biarritz, 425cu in, overhead-valve V8 engine, automatic transmission, power hood, defective rear window mechanism, full service history.
£5,600–6,700 / €8,300–9,900
$9,900–11,800 ✣ BJ

1952 Chrysler Crown Imperial, 5400cc, V8 engine, automatic transmission, servo-assisted disc brakes, power steering, beige Bedford cord interior, 1 of 338 built.
£8,000–9,600 / €11,800–14,200 / $14,100–16,900 ✣ B(Kn)
In the period immediately after WWII, the conservatively styled Chrysler Imperials looked little different from the marque's mainstream models. Based on the Chrysler New Yorker, the 1949 Imperial featured a canvas covered roof, and leather and broadcloth upholstery. The engine was a 5.3 litre side-valve straight-eight; Fluid Drive and Prestomatic (clutchless) transmission were standard equipment.
A Cadillac-style radiator grille was new for 1950, the last year of the straight-eight engine. The latter was replaced by Chrysler's classic 331cu in (5.4 litre) 'Hemi' V8. The Crown Imperial was Chrysler's top-of-the-range model and a direct competitor to Cadillac.

1952 Citroën Light 15, 1911cc, overhead-valve 4-cylinder engine, front-wheel drive, independent front suspension, hydraulic brakes, unitary construction.
£5,600–6,700 / €8,300–9,900 / $9,900–11,800 ✣ COYS

1937 Cord 812 Sportsmans Roadster, 4730cc, Lycoming side-valve V8 engine, 4-speed pre-selector gearbox, front-wheel drive, 4-wheel hydraulic drum brakes.
£54,000–65,000 / €80,000–96,000 / $95,000–114,000 ✗ COYS

Cord's first model was the luxurious and innovative, front-wheel-drive L-29 of 1929, but it was expensive and it did not survive the depression years, production ceasing in 1932. The marque staged a comeback in 1935 with the sophisticated and revolutionary 'coffin-nosed' 810, designed by Gordon Buehrig. This was propelled by a Lycoming V8 engine that produced 125bhp. The 812 followed in 1937, being basically the same car, but offered with an optional centrifugal supercharger (not fitted to this car). The chassis featured independent suspension by transverse springs and trailing arms, while the transmission was a four-speed pre-selector gearbox with column gear-change lever. The car boasted such features as a two-piece windscreen, concealed wind-up headlamps and an engine-turned dashboard with a comprehensive range of instruments.

1960 Daimler SP250, 2547cc, V8 engine, 4-speed manual gearbox, rack-and-pinion steering, stainless steel exhaust system, fibreglass body, fully restored.
£9,900–11,900 / €14,700–17,600 / $17,400–20,900 ✗ H&H

1967 Daimler 250 V8, 2547cc, automatic transmission.
£2,250–2,700 / €3,350–4,000 / $3,950–4,750 ⊞ BRIT

1968 Daimler 420 Sovereign, 4235cc, overhead-camshaft 6-cylinder engine, 3-speed automatic transmission, oatmeal leather interior.
£5,400–6,500 / €8,000–9,600 / $9,500–11,400 ✗ H&H

◀ **1975 Daimler 4.2 Vanden Plas,** 4235cc, overhead-camshaft 6-cylinder engine, automatic transmission, burr walnut fascia and door trims.
£2,300–2,750 / €3,400–4,050 / $4,050–4,850 ✗ B(Kn)

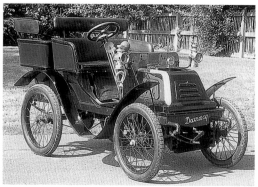

1901 Darracq 6½hp Rear-Entrance Tonneau, single-cylinder engine, shaft drive, tubular-steel chassis, regular Brighton Run competitor.
£49,000–59,000 / €73,000–87,000
$86,000–103,000 ⚲ B(Kn)

1972 Datsun 240Z Coupé, 2393cc, 6-cylinder engine, 5-speed manual gearbox, 150bhp at 6,000rpm, 0–60mph in 8.7 seconds, original, excellent condition.
£4,500–5,400 / €6,700–8,000 / $7,900–9,500 ⚲ H&H

a1924 Dodge Series 116 Tourer, 30hp, artillery wheels, left-hand drive, Auster screen for rear-seat passengers, folding hood.
£7,500–9,000 / €11,100–13,300
$13,200–15,800 ⚲ CGC

1963 Ferrari 250 GT Lusso Berlinetta, coachwork by Pininfarina, 2953cc, V12 engine, 1 of only 350 built, unrestored.
£105,000–126,000 / €155,000–186,000
$185,000–221,000 ⚲ B(Ge)

▶ **1965 Ferrari 275 GTS,** 3286cc, V12 engine, rear-mounted 5-speed transaxle, independent rear suspension, multi-tubular chassis, wire wheels, left-hand drive, 1 of only 200 built.
£89,000–107,000
€132,000–158,000
157,000–188,000 ⚲ BB(S)

1972 Ferrari 246 GT Dino, 2418cc, overhead-camshaft V6 engine, 5-speed transaxle, 1 owner from new.
£37,000–44,000 / €55,000–65,000 / $65,000–77,000 ⚲ B(Ge)

1974 Ferrari 365 GT4 Berlinetta Boxer, 4390cc, double-overhead-camshaft flat-12 engine, 360bhp, top speed 175mph.
£49,000–59,000 / €73,000–87,000 $87,000–104,000 ↗ B(Ge)
Only 367 365 GT4 BBs were built before the model was superseded by the 512 BB in 1976. It was the first road-going Ferrari not to have a V-configuration engine.

1976 Ferrari 308 GTB Berlinetta Vetroresina, 2926cc, double-overhead-camshaft V8 engine, 236bhp, top speed 155mph, 0–60mph in 6.7 seconds.
£20,300–24,400 / €30,000–36,000 / $36,000–43,000 ↗ B(Ge)

▶ **1980 Ferrari 308 GT4 2+2,** 2926cc, double-overhead-camshaft V8 engine, 5-speed manual gearbox, 4-wheel independent suspension, 4-wheel disc brakes.
£18,000–21,600 €26,600–32,000 $32,000–38,000 ↗ CGC

1987 Ferrari Testarossa Berlinetta, 4942cc, double-overhead-camshaft flat-12 engine, 4-valve cylinder heads, 390bhp, top speed 180mph, fitted luggage, fitted car cover, 1 owner from new, c14,000 miles recorded.
£32,000–38,000 / €47,000–56,000 / $56,000–67,000 ↗ B(Kn)

1966 Fiat 500F, 499.5cc, twin-cylinder engine, 4-speed manual gearbox.
£1,850–2,200 / €2,750–3,250 / $3,250–3,900 ✗ H&H

▶ **1931 Ford Model A Roadster,** 3285cc, side-valve 4-cylinder engine, splash lubrication, 3-speed manual gearbox, transverse-leaf suspension, left-hand drive, completely restored.
£7,800–9,300 / €11,500–13,800
$13,700–16,400 ✗ BB(S)
This was the final year of manufacture for the Model A.

1959 Ford Popular, 1172cc, side-valve 4-cylinder engine, 47,000 miles recorded, completely restored, concours condition.
£2,150–2,600 / €3,200–3,850 / $3,800–4,500 ✗ H&H

1968 Fiat Dino Spider, 1987cc, Ferrari double-overhead-camshaft aluminium V6 engine.
£13,500–16,200 / €20,000–24,000
$23,800–28,500 ✗ COYS

1955 Ford Thunderbird, 4785cc, overhead-valve V8 engine, 225bhp, top speed 110mph, concours condition.
£27,000–33,000 / €40,000–48,000
$48,000–57,000 ✗ BJ
This car was one of the first Thunderbirds built – the first example was assembled on 9th September, 1954; this one rolled off the assembly line on 24th September.

1966 Ford Mustang Convertible, 289cu in, overhead-valve V8 engine, concours condition.
£16,000–19,200 / €23,700–28,400 / $28,200–33,800 ✗ BB(S)

Daimler *(British 1896–)*

DAIMLER Model	ENGINE cc/cyl	DATES	CONDITION 1	2	3
Veteran (Coventry built)	var/4	1897–1904	£90,000+	£60,000	£30,000
Veteran	var/4	1905–19	£35,000	£25,000	£15,000
30hp	4962/6	1919–25	£40,000	£25,000	£18,000
45hp	7413/6	1919–25	£45,000+	£30,000	£20,000
Double Six 50	7136/12	1927–34	£40,000	£30,000	£20,000
20	2687/6	1934–35	£18,000	£14,000	£12,000
Straight 8	3421/8	1936–38	£20,000	£15,000	£12,000

Value is dependent on body style, coachbuilder and condition of the sleeve-valve engine.

1947 Daimler DB18 Three-position Drophead Coupé, coachwork by Barker, 2522cc, overhead-valve 6-cylinder engine, completely restored.
£12,700–15,200 / €18,800–22,500 / $22,400–26,800 ⚒ CGC

1950 Daimler DB18 Special Sports Drophead Coupé,
coachwork by Hooper, 2522cc, 85bhp, power-operated
hood, completely restored at a cost of c£80,000 /
€118,000 / $141,000.
£40,000–48,000 / €59,000–71,000
$70,000–84,000 ⚒ COYS
This car was the first of six DB18 drophead coupés
built on Super Sports chassis by Hooper, and was
ordered by King George VI for use by the Duke of
Edinburgh. Subsequently, it was owned by the singer
Max Bygraves.

1952 Daimler Empress Saloon, 2522cc, 6-cylinder
engine, finished in green and black, beige interior.
£9,200–11,000 / €13,600–16,200 / $16,300–19,400 ⚒ H&H

1952 Daimler DB18 Special Sports Drophead Coupé,
coachwork by Barker, 2522cc, 6-cylinder engine, 4-speed
pre-selector gearbox, finished in maroon and gold,
tan leather interior, complete mechanical overhaul 1999.
£12,900–15,500 / €19,100–22,900
$22,700–27,300 ⚒ H&H

1960 Daimler SP250, 2547cc, V8 engine, US export model.
£6,600–7,900 / €9,800–11,700 / $11,600–13,900 ⚒ BARO
The SP250, or Dart, was aimed at the American market. It was introduced in 1959, but its production run was cut short when Jaguar acquired Daimler in the early 1960s. Only 2,645 examples were built between 1959 and 1964, approximately 45 per cent being exported. The car was unusual for having a V8 engine and fibreglass bodywork.

1962 Daimler SP250, 2547cc, V8 engine, 4-speed manual gearbox.
£12,400–14,900 / €18,400–22,100 $21,800–26,200 ⚒ H&H

◄ **1964 Daimler 2.5 V8 Saloon,** 2547cc, V8 engine, 140bhp, finished in grey, red leather interior, stored last 19 years, paintwork faded in places, running.
£1,700–2,050 €2,500–3,000 $3,000–3,600 ⚒ B(Kn)
The 2.5 V8 ran from 1962 until 1967, then became the V8 250 with slimmer bumpers, which remained in production until 1969.

1966 Daimler 2.5 V8 Saloon, 2547cc, V8 engine, automatic transmission, 4-wheel disc brakes, in need of recommissioning.
£1,100–1,300 / €1,650–1,950 / $1,950–2,300 ⚒ CGC

1968 Daimler V8 250 Saloon, 2547cc, V8 engine, 4-speed manual gearbox with overdrive, wire wheels, completely restored.
£7,500–9,000 / €11,100–13,300 / $13,200–15,800 ⚒ CGC

1968 Daimler 420 Sovereign Saloon, 4235cc, 6-cylinder engine, 3-speed automatic transmission, wire wheels, older restoration.
£4,850–5,800 / €7,200–8,600 / $8,500–10,200 ⚒ H&H

1969 Daimler V8 250 Saloon, 2547cc, V8 engine, 3-speed automatic transmission, wire wheels, converted to unleaded fuel, steering and brakes overhauled, new exhaust, finished in black, beige interior, concours condition.
£4,000–4,800 / €5,900–7,100 / $7,000–8,400 ⚒ H&H
This car was built in the final year of production.

◀ **1969 Daimler V8 250,** 2547cc, V8 engine, 140bhp, top speed 115mph, matching body and mechanical components, completely restored.
£5,800–6,950 / €8,600–10,200 $10,200–12,100 ⚸ CGC

1972 Daimler DS420 Limousine, 4235cc, 6-cylinder engine, 245bhp, 3-speed automatic transmission, top speed 110mph, glass division.
£1,750–2,100 / €2,600–3,100 $3,100–3,700 ⚸ H&H
The DS420 arrived in 1968 and was based on the floorpan of Jaguar's 420G flagship, but with an extra 20in (510mm) of wheelbase.

1971 Daimler Sovereign Saloon, 4235cc, double-overhead-camshaft 6-cylinder engine, 180bhp, 4-wheel independent suspension, 4-wheel disc brakes, power steering, top speed 120mph.
£2,100–2,500 / €3,100–3,700 / $3,700–4,400 ⚸ CGC

1977 Daimler Double Six Saloon, 5343cc, double-overhead-camshaft V12 engine, 3-speed automatic transmission, finished in green, dark green interior, concours condition.
£4,500–5,400 / €6,700–8,000 / $7,900–9,500 ⚸ H&H

1977 Daimler 4.2 Vanden Plas, 4235cc, double-overhead-camshaft 6-cylinder engine, 180bhp, 3-speed automatic transmission, top speed 120mph, finished in silver-sand metallic, beige leather upholstery.
£530–640 / €800–950 / $960–1,150 ⚸ CGC

▶ **1985 Daimler Double Six Saloon,** 5343cc, double-overhead-camshaft V12 engine, 299bhp, 3-speed automatic transmission, 4-wheel independent suspension, 4-wheel disc brakes, power steering, 0–60mph in 7.5 seconds, top speed151mph, finished in metallic grey, grey leather upholstery.
£1,800–2,150 / €2,700–3,200 $3,200–3,800 ⚸ CGC

DAIMLER Model	ENGINE cc/cyl	DATES	CONDITION 1	2	3
DB18	2522/6	1946–49	£6,000	£3,000	£1,000
DB18 Conv S/S	2522/6	1948–53	£15,000+	£7,000	£2,000
Consort	2522/6	1949–53	£5,000	£3,000	£1,000
Conquest/Con Century	2433/6	1953–58	£4,000	£2,000	£1,000
Conquest Roadster	2433/6	1953–56	£12,000	£7,000	£4,000
Majestic 3.8	3794/6	1958–62	£5,000	£2,000	£1,000
SP250	2547/8	1959–64	£12,000	£9,000	£4,500
Majestic Major	4561/8	1961–64	£6,000	£4,000	£1,000
2.5 V8	2547/8	1962–67	£8,000	£5,250	£2,500
V8 250	2547/8	1968–69	£8,000+	£4,000	£2,000
Sovereign 420	4235/6	1966–69	£6,500	£3,500	£1,500
Double Six Coupé	5343/12	1975–77	£8,000	£3,000	£1,500

Darracq *(French 1896–1959)*

1911 Darracq GII Tourer, 2410cc, 4-cylinder engine, 3-speed manual gearbox, shaft final drive, finished in blue and black, matching leather interior.
£14,400–17,300 / € 21,300–25,600 / $25,300–30,000 ↗ B(Kn)

Datsun *(Japanese 1933–)*

| DATSUN | ENGINE | DATES | CONDITION | | |
Model	cc/cyl		1	2	3
240Z	2393/6	1970–71	£6,000	£4,000	£2,000
240Z	2393/6	1971–74	£5,000	£3,250	£1,500
260Z	2565/6	1974–79	£4,000	£2,800	£1,200
260Z 2+2	2565/6	1974–79	£4,000	£2,600	£1,000

De Dion Bouton *(French 1895–1932)*

◄ **1901 De Dion Bouton 4½hp Three-Seater Voiturette,** coachwork by H.J. Mulliner, Dietz oil side lamps, Phare Ducellier centre-mounted headlamp, finished in dark green with black and silver lining, deep-buttoned black leather upholstery.
£41,000–49,000
€ 61,000–73,000
$72,000–86,000 ↗ B(Kn)

Delage *(French 1905–53)*

1932 Delage D8S Sportsman's Coupé, coachwork by Lancefield, 4050cc, 8-cylinder engine, 145bhp, top speed 100mph.
£75,000–90,000 / €111,000–133,000 / $132,000–158,000 ✗ B(Kn)
Having spent some time in the experimental design department at Peugeot, Louis Delage set up his own company in 1905. Success was instant, with a second place in the Coupe de l'Auto in 1906 and a string of victories mainly in the voiturette classes. These were boosted in 1924 by René Thomas's World Speed Record of 143.24mph at Arpajon in a 10.5 litre V12 racing car. The D8 was launched in 1929 and offered three chassis lengths. The car's 4050cc straight-eight engine gave a cruising speed of 80+mph. The D8S of 1932 featured improvements to the chassis, which was significantly lower and lighter, while the engine output was increased from 120bhp to 145bhp.

DeLorean *(N Ireland/USA 1976–82)*

◀ **1982 DeLorean DMC-12,** 2849cc, Volvo V6 engine, 5-speed manual gearbox, stainless steel body, fewer than 3,500 miles recorded.
£8,300–10,000 / €12,300–14,800
$14,600–17,500 ✗ BJ
John DeLorean joined Chrysler in 1950, gaining a degree in auto engineering. Subsequently, he made a career with General Motors, rising steadily through the ranks until he left in 1973 to pursue his dream of building his own sports car. He set up the DeLorean Motor Company with a new factory in Northern Ireland, thanks to substantial grants from the British government. Production began in 1981, and although the car was built in some numbers, the operation was a financial disaster and liquidation followed in 1982.

DeSoto *(American 1928–60)*

▶ **1929 DeSoto Series K Espanol Rumble Seat Roadster,** 2900cc, side-valve 6-cylinder engine, 55bhp, hydraulic brakes, 1 of only 7 Series K Roadsters known to survive.
£17,200–20,600
€25,500–30,000
$30,000–36,000 ✗ B(Kn)
DeSoto took its name from the 16th-century Spanish explorer Hernando DeSoto, and the Espanol model continued the Spanish theme with a yellow and black livery.

De Tomaso *(Italian 1961–95)*

◀ **1968 De Tomaso Mangusta,** 4727cc, mid-mounted Ford V8 engine, 305bhp, ZF 5-speed transaxle, backbone chassis, top speed 155mph, left-hand drive, 1 of only 150 built for European market.
£20,900–25,100 / €31,000–37,000 $37,000–44,000 ⚡ B(Mu)
De Tomaso enjoyed close links with Ford during the late 1960s, and the American manufacturer helped put the Mangusta into larger-scale production than otherwise would have been possible. Around 400 examples were built between 1967 and 1972.

Detroit Electric *(American 1907–38)*

◀ **1918 Detroit Electric Brougham Coupé,** wire wheels, restored, very good condition.
£16,300–19,600 / €24,100–29,000 $28,700–34,000 ⚡ BB(S)
The first Detroit Electric cars appeared in 1907, and by the end of that year, 125 had been built. However, by the time this example was built, petrol-engined cars had improved substantially, while electric models had stagnated.

Dodge *(American 1914–)*

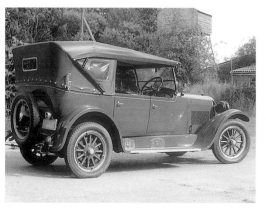

◀ **1926 Dodge De Luxe Tourer,** 3000cc, 4-cylinder engine.
£9,400–11,300 / €13,900–16,700 / $16,500–19,800 ⚡ CGC
Shareholders in, and engine suppliers to, the Ford Motor Company, brothers John and Horace Dodge became increasingly disgruntled with Henry Ford's staid design process and refusal to implement their ideas. Deciding they could do better, they set up their own car manufacturing company in 1914, the Dodge 4 appearing that November. Known for its speed and dependability, it was a largely convential design except for for its 12 volt electrics and back-to-front gear-change. The 4's abundant torque and good ground clearance proved their worth during General Pershing's punishing 1916 Mexico expedition. Subsequently established as an American Army favourite, the 4 was pressed into further use during WWI as a staff car and ambulance.

▶ **1964 Dodge Dart Convertible,** 3772cc, overhead-valve 6-cylinder engine, push-button 3-speed automatic transmission.
£4,800–5,800 €7,200–8,600 $8,500–10,200 ⚡ H&H
The Dart series was launched in 1959.

1969 Dodge Coronet 500 Convertible, 383cu.in, V8 engine, automatic transmission, power steering, alloy wheels, bucket seats, resprayed red, new hood with original zip-out glass window, new water pump, new power steering pump, new seat inserts.
£6,600–7,900 / €9,800–11,700 / $11,600–13,900 ⚒ BJ

1987 Dodge Diplomat Saloon, 5200cc, V8 engine, 3-speed automatic transmission, modified to resemble a US sheriff's car, police lights and siren.
£3,800–4,600 / €5,700–6,800 / $6,800–8,100 ⚒ H&H
Like most American cars, Dodges were downsized during the 1970s. By 1982, the largest Dodge in the catalogue was the 5.2 litre Diplomat, which was continued with little change until 1989.

Durant *(American 1921–32)*

◀ **1931 Durant Four-Door Saloon,** 3300cc, 6-cylinder engine, 3-speed manual gearbox, wire wheels, finished in red and black, red leather interior, completely restored, concours condition.
£8,500–10,200 / €12,600–15,100
$15,000–18,000 ⚒ BARO
The Durant Motor Company was part of William C. Durant's automotive empire, which encompassed Star, Eagle, Flint, Princeton, Rugby and Locomobile. The original four-cylinder model was introduced in 1921, while the first six appeared in 1922, using an Ansted engine. In 1927, Durant suspended production, but it began again in 1928 with a new range of fours and sixes. Another new model arrived in 1930, but only with the six-cylinder engine. Durant disappeared from the American market in 1932, but continued under the Frontenac name in Canada until 1933.

Essex *(American 1917–32)*

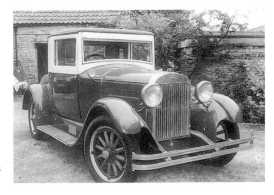

▶ **1928 Essex Super Six Doctor's Coupé,** 2.5 litre, 6-cylinder engine, 4-wheel brakes, artillery wheels.
£4,800–5,700 / €7,100–8,400 / $8,400–10,000 ⚒ CGC
Introduced by Hudson as its low-priced line in 1919, the Essex models became best-sellers thanks to their build quality and the value for money they offered. Sales of Essex cars helped push Hudson into America's top three by 1929.

Ferrari *(Italian 1940–)*

1956 Ferrari 250 GT Boano Coupé Prototype, coachwork by Pinin Farina/Boano, 2953cc, 12-cylinder engine, wire wheels, detachable bonnet, wood-rimmed steering wheel, restored early 1990s.
£100,000–120,000 / €148,000–178,000 / $176,000–211,000 ✗ B(Ge)
The introduction of the 250 Europa (Ferrari's first series-production road car) in 1953 heralded a significant change in the company's preferred coachbuilder. Whereas previously Vignale had been the most popular among Ferrari customers, from now on Pinin Farina (later Pininfarina) would be the number-one choice. Pinin Farina's experiments eventually crystalized in a new 250 GT road car, which appeared in 1956. At the time, however, the coachbuilder was not in a position to cope with the increased workload, resulting in production being entrusted to Boano after Pinin Farina had completed a handful of prototypes. Although this car's chassis number suggests it was the 21st of the 250 GT Boano sequence, it is believed that in fact it was built by Pinin Farina, since chalk marks were found on the inside of the body panels, and the rear wings feature a double curvature not found on production models. Features such as the front wing vents and outside filler cap are known to be later additions.

1958 Ferrari 250 GT Coupé, coachwork by Pininfarina, 2953cc, 12-cylinder engine, matching engine/chassis numbers, 4-wheel disc brakes, knock-off wire wheels, finished in white, tan leather interior, wood-rimmed steering wheel.
£40,000–48,000 / €59,000–67,000
$70,000–84,000 ✗ B(Mon)
A number of important developments occurred during 250 GT production. The original 3 litre 128C engine was superseded by the twin-distributor 128D. This, in turn, was supplanted in 1960 by the outside-plug 128F engine, which dispensed with siamesed inlets in favour of six separate ports. Four-wheel disc brakes arrived late in 1958, and a four-speed overdrive gearbox the following year.

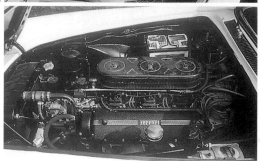

◄ **1964 Ferrari 500 Superfast Speciale,** 4390cc, V12 engine, finished in green, tan leather interior, bench front seat, power windows, 1 of 37 built, previously owned by Prince Bernhard of Holland.
£185,000–222,000 / €274,000–329,000
$326,000–391,000 ✗ B(Ge)
The 500 Superfast sprang from a series of styling exercises executed by Pininfarina between 1956 and 1962.

1966 Ferrari 275 GTB Aluminium Berlinetta, 3286cc, 60-degree V12 engine, 5-speed transaxle, 4-wheel independent suspension, wire wheels.
£152,000–182,000 / €225,000–269,000
$268,000–320,000 ♪ B(Mon)

1964 Ferrari 330 America Coupé, coachwork by Pininfarina, 3967cc, V12 engine, finished in metallic blue, black leather interior, Nardi wood-rimmed steering wheel, 1 of only 50 built.
£34,000–41,000 / €50,000–60,000
$60,000–72,000 ♪ B(Ge)
Towards the end of 250 GTE production in 1963, Ferrari began delivering a revised and improved version of the four-seater fitted with the new 330 engine. Ferrari road cars with large engines had traditionally formed part of the America/Superamerica series, and the new 4 litre model was duly christened 330 America. Based on the engine of the contemporary 400 Superamerica, the 330 America's 60-degree V12 engine incorporated many advances, including wider-spaced cylinder bores and revised combustion chambers to improve cooling and breathing. Although the 330 engine was superior to the 400 SA unit, it was nevertheless conservatively rated at 300bhp, 40bhp less than its progenitor. Chassis-wise, the 330 America was identical to the late-production 250 GTE Series III and outwardly indistinguishable, although some examples carried the legend 'America' on the boot.

1967 Ferrari 275 GTB/4, 3286cc, double-overhead-camshaft 60-degree V12 engine, 5-speed transaxle.
£222,000–266,000 / €329,000–394,000
$391,000–468,000 ♪ B(Ge)
The 1964 introduction of the 275 GTB signalled an important evolution for Ferrari – the adoption of full independent suspension, which had been developed in the marque's sports-racing cars. Bodied by Scaglietti to a Pinifarina design, the 275 GTB echoed the purposeful appearance of the 250 Tour de France and GTO, with its long bonnet, covered headlights, fastback roofline, Kamm tail, and vents in the front wings and roof sail panel. The engine was Ferrari's highly developed overhead-camshaft V12 displacing 3.3 litres. With three dual-choke Weber carburettors, the 275 GTB delivered 280bhp, 20bhp more than the 250 SWB Berlinetta. Two years later, Ferrari made a substantial change to the 275 GTB by giving it twin-cam cylinder heads. To take advantage of the heads' higher rpm capabilities, it breathed through six dual-choke Webers and had dry-sump lubrication for high-speed durability. Power increased only slightly to 300bhp. The big benefits were in increased torque and a wider range of usable power.

1969 Ferrari 365 GTB/4 Daytona, 4390cc, 60-degree V12 engine, top speed 175mph.
£66,000–79,000 / €98,000–117,000
$116,000–139,000 ♪ B(Ge)
The 'Daytona' name was unofficial, having been bestowed on the 365 GTB/4 by the press in honour of Ferrari's 1-2-3 victory at that circuit's 24-hour race in 1967. When introduced in 1968, it was the most expensive car Ferrari had ever made; it was also the fastest production car in the world. The Daytona was manufactured for only two years.

◄ **1971 Ferrari 365 GTB/4 Daytona**, 4390cc, 60-degree V12 engine, air conditioning, finished in metallic blue, beige leather interior, ex-1971 London Motor Show car, only 2,800 miles recorded.
£101,000–121,000
€149,000–178,000
$178,000–213,000
♪ B(Kn)

1972 Ferrari 365 GTB/4A Daytona, 4390cc, 60-degree V12 engine, 352bhp, 5-speed gearbox, finished in yellow, black leather interior, 1 owner from new, ex-1972 Geneva show car, unrestored.
£83,000–99,000 / € 123,000–147,000 / $146,000–174,000 ⚒ B(Ge)

◀ **1972 Ferrari 365 GTS/4 Daytona Spyder,** 4390cc, 60-degree V12 engine 5-speed manual gearbox, finished in red, black leather interior, black hood, air conditioning, 1 of 25 built to European specification, 52,000km recorded, 1 owner from new.
£245,000–294,000
€ 363,000–435,000
$431,000–517,000 ⚒ B(Mu)

▶ **1973 Ferrari 246 GT Dino,** coachwork by Pininfarina, 2418cc, double-overhead-camshaft V6 engine, 5-speed transaxle, 4-wheel independent suspension.
£40,000–48,000 / € 59,000–70,000
$71,000–84,000 ⚒ COYS

The Dino was named after Enzo Ferrari's son, Alfredino, who died in 1956, aged 24. Ferrari credited his son with the inspiration for a series of successful small- and medium-capacity V6 racing engines that bore his name. Subsequently, it was applied to a range of mid-engined production Ferrari V6 coupés, which were introduced in 1969 in 2 litre form. The definitive 246 Dino appeared in late 1969, and fewer than 4,000 were built before they were replaced by the slightly larger and completely restyled 308 Dino in 1973.

FERRARI Model	ENGINE cc/cyl	DATES	CONDITION 1	2	3
250 GTE	2953/12	1959–63	£32,000	£22,000	£20,000
250 GT SWB (steel)	2953/12	1959–62	£500,000+	£300,000	–
250 GT Lusso	2953/12	1962–64	£100,000	£60,000	£50,000
250 GT 2+2	2953/12	1961–64	£32,000	£24,000	£18,000
275 GTB	3286/12	1964–66	£150,000	£100,000	£70,000
275 GTS	3286/12	1965–67	£90,000+	£70,000	£50,000
275 GTB 4–cam	3286/12	1966–68	£190,000+	£150,000	£100,000
330 GT 2+2	3967/12	1964–67	£27,000+	£18,000	£11,000
330 GTC	3967/12	1966–68	£55,000+	£40,000+	£25,000
330 GTS	3967/12	1966–68	£90,000+	£70,000+	£60,000
365 GT 2+2	4390/12	1967–71	£30,000+	£20,000	£15,000
365 GTC	4390/12	1967–70	£40,000+	£35,000	£30,000
365 GTS	4390/12	1968–69	£190,000+	£130,000+	£80,000
365 GTB (Daytona)	4390/12	1968–74	£80,000	£60,000	£50,000
365 GTC4	4390/12	1971–74	£50,000+	£38,000+	£30,000
365 GT4 2+2/400GT	4390/ 4823/12	1972–79	£25,000	£20,000	£10,000
365 BB	4390/12	1974–76	£40,000	£32,000	£25,000
512 BB/BBi	4942/12	1976–81	£45,000	£35,000	£28,000
246 GT Dino	2418/6	1969–74	£40,000+	£30,000	£20,000
246 GTS Dino	2418/6	1972–74	£50,000+	£32,000	£20,000
308 GT4 2+2	2926/8	1973–80	£15,000	£10,000	£8,000
308 GTB (fibreglass)	2926/8	1975–76	£20,000	£15,000	£12,000
308 GTB	2926/8	1977–81	£22,000	£16,000	£10,000
308 GTS	2926/8	1978–81	£22,000	£18,000	£11,000
308 GTBi/GTSi	2926/8	1981–82	£24,000	£17,000	£10,000
308 GTB/GTS QV	2926/6	1983–85	£21,500	£16,500	£9,500
400i manual	4823/12	1981–85	£12,000	£10,000	£8,000
400i auto	4823/12	1981–85	£11,000	£9,000	£7,000

1974 Ferrari 365 GTB/4 Daytona, 4390cc, V12 engine, Chromodoro alloy wheels, finished in red, black leather interior, air conditioning.
£69,000–83,000 / €102,000–123,000
$121,000–146,000 ✍ B(Mon)

1973 Ferrari 365 GTC/4, coachwork by Pininfarina, 4390cc, 60-degree V12 engine, 320bhp, 5-speed manual gearbox.
£55,000–66,000 / €81,000–98,000
$97,000–116,000 ✍ B(Ge)
The GTC was built between 1971 and 1974.

1975 Ferrari 365 GT4/BB, coachwork by Pininfarina, 4823cc, mid-mounted flat-12 engine.
£75,000–90,000 / €111,000–133,000
$133,000–158,000 ✍ B(Ge)
The 365 GT4/BB was unveiled at the 1971 Turin show.

1976 Ferrari 308 GTB, 2962cc, double-overhead-camshaft V8 engine, fibreglass body, finished in red, brown leather interior, 7,000 miles recorded.
£28,000–33,000 / €41,000–49,000
$49,000–58,000 ✍ B(Kn)

1976 Ferrari 365 GT4/BB, 4390cc, double-overhead-camshaft flat-12 engine, 360bhp, 1 of only 367 built.
£34,000–41,000 / €50,000–60,000 / $60,000–72,000 ✍ B(Kn)
This was the last year of the production for the BB model.

> A known continuous history can add value to and enhance the enjoyment of a car.

◀ **1977 Ferrari 400,** 4823cc, V12 engine, automatic transmission, finished in red, beige interior, running, but in need of recommissioning.
£4,250–5,100 / €6,300–7,500 / $7,500–9,000 ✍ BRIT

▶ **1978 Ferrari 400 GT,**
4823cc, V12 engine,
5-speed manual gearbox,
finished in metallic blue,
tan leather interior.
£19,900–23,900
€29,500–35,400
$35,000–42,000 ✍ BB(S)

1978 Ferrari 400 GT, 4823cc, V12 engine, 5-speed manual gearbox, stainless steel exhaust, finished in metallic dark green, tan leather interior.
£7,500–9,000 / €11,100–13,300
$13,200–15,800 ✗ H&H
The 400 was an updated version of the 365 GT4 2+2 coupé. It was aimed at buyers seeking high performance with spacious accommodation, and Ferrari hoped that many sales would come from America, but increasingly stringent vehicle regulations prevented this. The 400 was launched in 1976 and was offered with a five-speed manual gearbox or, for the first time, a three-speed automatic transmission. A total of 502 400s were built before fuel injection was introduced in 1979 and the model became the 400i.

1980 Ferrari 400i, 4823cc, V12 engine, alloy wheels.
£6,100–7,300 / €9,000–10,800
$10,700–12,800 ✗ COYS

1982 Ferrari 400i, 4823cc, V12 engine, fuel injection, 240bhp, automatic transmission, 4-wheel independent suspension, 4-wheel disc brakes, new stainless steel exhaust, finished in gold, brown interior.
£10,700–12,800 / €15,800–18,900
$18,800–22,500 ✗ H&H

1986 Ferrari Mondial QV Convertible, 3200cc, air conditioning, new hood, finished in red, cream leather interior.
£19,000–22,700 / €28,000–33,000
$33,000–39,000 ✗ BARO
Penned by Pininfarina, the Mondial was based on the Bertone designed 308 GT4 and used the same 3 litre engine. Although deemed less sporty than the traditional 308 GTB, the Mondial could still top 150mph and accommodate four people. In 1982, the engine was enlarged to 3.2 litres, and in 1984 the convertible was launched.

1979 Ferrari 512 BB, 4.9 litre, flat-12 engine, fuel injection replaced by Weber carburettors, new clutch, flywheel and exhaust, concours condition.
£30,000–36,000 / €44,000–53,000
$53,000–63,000 ✗ COYS

1981 Ferrari 400i Spyder, 4823cc, V12 engine, fuel injection, automatic transmission, magnolia leather interior, minor damage to windscreen, 1 of only 12 converted to Spyder configuration by Autokraft for dealer H.R. Owen.
£4,500–5,400 / €6,700–8,000 / $7,900–9,500 ✗ H&H
This 400i was previously owned by rock musician Pete Townsend.

1983 Ferrari 400i, 4823cc, V12 engine, fuel injection, 3-speed automatic transmission, finished in light blue, tan interior.
£5,900–7,000 / €8,700–10,400
$10,400–12,300 ✗ H&H

1988 Ferrari 328 GTS Spyder, 3186cc, 270bhp, ABS, Targa top, top speed 160mph, 0–60mph in 5.5 seconds, 3,800km recorded, original, excellent condition.
£26,000–31,000 / €39,000–46,000
$46,000–55,000 ✗ B(Ge)

Fiat *(Italian 1899–)*

In 1899, three wealthy young men met in Turin to discuss the possibility of forming a company to manufacture cars. The trio were Giovanni Agnelli, Emanuele di Bricherasio and Count Roberto Biscaretti di Ruffia. And the new company's name? They chose Fabbrica Italiana Automobili Torino (Italian Motorcar Works Turin) – or more simply, FIAT.

In fact, they had selected the name before they had come up with a product to sell, but this was soon solved simply by buying Giovanni-Battista Ceirano's small factory and his prototype car. The latter was a 697cc, twin-cylinder rear-engined vehicle with belt drive. Agnelli replaced the drive belt with a chain, and the design became the Fiat Tipo A; eight were made in 1899–1900.

As well as the design, Fiat acquired the services of the car's creator, Aristide Faccioli, and some 50 workers, two of whom were destined to become famous Fiat racing drivers – Vincenzo Lancia (who later formed his own marque) and Felice Nazzaro.

Faccioli left in 1901, by which time Fiat was building 8 and 12hp cars in the style of contemporary Panhards.

Faccioli's position was taken by Giovanni Enrico, under whom Fiat's fortunes rose. By the time he retired in 1906, he had designed several four-cylinder engines, including one that displaced a massive 10.6 litres! Another, of 6.4 litres, was used in Fiat's first purpose-built commercial vehicles, including double-decker buses.

Enrico had also been responsible for creating Fiat's racing cars, which achieved numerous victories throughout Europe during 1904–08, helping to promote the company's name. Fiat also crossed the Atlantic to win the 1908 American Grand Prix. That year, the New York distributor, Hollander & Tangeman, sold 181 Fiats, which prompted an American Fiat operation, with a factory at Poughkeepsie, New York. It lasted from 1910 until 1918.

Agnelli, who was the driving force behind the marque, had already begun to diversify into other fields. For example, in 1905, he founded the RIV bearing company, then started ship building the following year. Fiat had begun manufacturing marine engines in 1903 and entered the aero engine market in 1908. It even made bicycles (1909–12), but never motorcycles.

Fiat's next chief designer was Guido Fornaco, who gave the company a new direction with the Tipo 1 of 1908. This was a smaller car than before and was the first Fiat to employ shaft final drive.

During WWI, Fiat factories built a range of military vehicles, including the Italian Army's first tank. It also produced 1,336 aircraft and 15,830 aero engines.

Profits made during the war enabled Fiat to extend its peacetime production considerably, a new factory being opened at Lingotto in 1922. This was Italy's first reinforced concrete structure, and it incorporated a test track on the roof. Production rocketed.

The 501 was Fiat's first mass-produced car, over 80,000 being built up to 1926. The first agricultural tractor arrived in 1919. In 1925, the Tipo 509 appeared, and over 92,000 were sold in under five years. The 509 was Fiat's best selling model until the famous 500 Topolino of 1936–48; even then, it took 12 years to sell 122,000.

By 1930, Fiat was co-operating with several foreign manufacturers, including NSU in Germany and Walter in Czechoslovakia; in Spain, the company opened its own factory, which led to the Seat marque in later years.

Fiat's best series of the period was the Balinna/1100 range, 237,000 examples of which were built, excluding French, Czech, German and Polish versions.

During WWII, Fiat made a major contribution to the Italian war effort. Post-war, production centred initially on trucks, but by mid-1946, cars were rolling off the lines again, specifically 500, 1100 and 1500 models.

The new 1100, produced between 1953 and 1962, was the first Fiat to top a million sales, but the figures were dwarfed by the new 500 and an improved 500D, which together had exceeded 3 million units by 1973.

Other notable post-war designs are the XI/9 sports car, 127, 130 Coupé, Uno, Panda and Punto. Another aspect of Fiat's post-war operations has been its acquisition of such famous Italian marques as Alfa Romeo, Lancia, Maserati and Ferrari.

However, at the beginning of the 21st century, Fiat has found the going tough, and doubts have even been expressed about its long-term survival.

◀ **1925 Fiat 505B Torpedo Tourer,** 2299cc, side-valve 4-cylinder engine, 4-speed manual gearbox, excellent condition.
£10,000–12,000 / € 14,800–17,800 $17,600–21,000 ⚲ CGC
Introduced in 1919, the 505 was based on a leaf-sprung ladder-frame chassis powered by a torquey four-cylinder, side-valve engine mated to a four-speed manual gearbox complete with multi-plate wet clutch. The later 505B benefited from four-wheel brakes and an electric starter. This example was one of the last 505s to be built.

FIAT Model	ENGINE cc/cyl	DATES	CONDITION 1	2	3
501	1460/4	1920–26	£6,000	£3,500	£1,500
519	4767/6	1923–29	£9,000	£7,000	£3,000
503	1473/4	1927–29	£10,000	£4,000	£2,000
507	2297/4	1927–28	£9,000	£5,500	£3,500
522/4	2516/6	1932–34	£10,000	£8,000	£3,500
508	994/4	1934–37	£5,000	£2,500	£1,500
527 Sports	2516/6	1935–36	£14,000	£8,000	£3,500
1.5 litre Balilla	1498/6	1936–39	£10,000	£7,000	£3,000
500	570/4	1937–55	£6,000	£2,500	£1,000
1100 Balilla	1089/4	1938–40	£4,500	£2,000	£1,000

1937 Fiat 500A Topolino, 569cc, side-valve 4-cylinder engine.
£1,800–2,100 / €2,650–3,100 / $3,150–3,700 ⚡ B(Kn)
The Topolino (Mouse) brought a degree of refinement to small cars when launched in 1936. Lockheed hydraulic brakes, independent front suspension and 12 volt electrics were all part of the specification, while the power unit was mounted ahead of the front axle line to maximize cabin space.

▶ **1958 Fiat 600 Multipla Marianella Beach Car,** coachwork by Fissore, 633cc, 4-cylinder engine, finished in blue and white, wicker upholstery, completely restored.
£20,300–23,600 / €30,000–35,000
$36,000–42,000 ⚡ B(Mon)

1959 Fiat 600 Jolly Beach Car, coachwork by Ghia, 633cc, finished in red, wicker upholstery.
£14,400–17,300 / €21,300–25,600
$25,300–30,000 ⚡ B(Mon)
Introduced in 1955 and produced for 15 years, Fiat's 600 and 600D were an outstanding success for the company, some 2.5 million being built. The compact, rear-engined saloon spawned numerous variants, from sporting and competition versions by Abarth to the Multipla people carrier. Many of Italy's coachbuilders offered alternatives to the original, perhaps the best known being Ghia's Jolly Beach Car, a novel concept that transformed the 600 from basic transport to conspicuous indicator of wealth. Lacking doors and equipped with wicker seats, the Jolly was only suitable as leisure transport, confirming its owner's status as someone who could afford a car 'just for fun'.

▶ **1968 Fiat Dino Coupé,** 1987cc, V6 engine, alloy wheels.
£1,550–1,850 / €2,300–2,750 / $2,750–3,250 ⚡ COYS

1955 Fiat Belvedore, sun roof, original.
£8,000–9,600 / €11,800–14,200
$14,100–16,900 ⚡ COYS
The Belvedore was a shooting-brake version of the Topolino and now is extremely rare.

1966 Fiat 500F, 499.5cc, twin-cylinder engine, 4-speed manual gearbox, finished in blue, black upholstery, fully restored, concours condition.
£3,650–4,400 / €5,400–6,500 / $6,400–7,700 ⚡ B(Kn)

1971 Fiat Dino Spyder, 2418cc, V6 engine, original Pininfarina hardtop, Campagnolo alloy wheels, finished in red, black leather seats, wood-rimmed steering wheel.
£14,900–17,900 / €22,100–26,500
$26,300–32,000 ⚘ BARO
Of the 424 Dino Spyders built, 242 were 2.4 litre models.

1972 Fiat Dino Spyder, 2418cc, double-overhead-camshaft V6 engine, 5-speed manual gearbox, 4-wheel independent suspension.
£16,100–19,300 / €23,800–28,600
$28,300–34,000 ⚘ B(Kn)
Production of the Fiat Dino ended in 1972.

1972 Fiat Abarth 695 Replica, 689cc, uprated suspension and brakes, alloy wheels, widened wheel arches, nudge bars, roll-back sunroof, finished in yellow, black interior, good condition.
£4,350–5,200 / €6,400–7,700 / $7,700–9,200 ⚘ B(Kn)

1978 Fiat 124 CS1 Spyder, 1756cc, new seats, new rear window, front suspension overhauled, unrestored.
£1,400–1,650 / €2,050–2,450 / $2,450–2,900 ⚘ COYS
Touring built the first convertible 124, known as the 124 Cabriolet C4. The body was made by Pininfarina, while finishing was done by Fiat. The 124 AS came with a 90bhp engine (1438cc) and had a flat bonnet. In 1969, the B model with 110bhp (1608cc) arrived. Its engine had twin carburettors and the bonnet received two blisters because of the taller engine. From August 1972, in Europe, it was named CS1 and received a stronger engine (118bhp/1756cc).

◄ **1982 Fiat X1/9,** 1498cc, mid-mounted 4-cylinder engine, 5-speed manual gearbox, cream interior.
£1,350–1,600 / €2,000–2,350 / $2,350–2,800 ⚘ H&H
Production of the X1/9 began in 1972. It was based on Fiat 128 components with styling by Bertone.

FIAT Model	ENGINE cc/cyl	DATES	CONDITION 1	2	3
500B Topolino	569/4	1945–55	£7,000	£3,000	£1,000
500C	569/4	1948–54	£4,000	£1,700	£1,000
500 Nuova	479,/499/2	1957–75	£3,000	£1,500	£750
600/600D	633/767/4	1955–70	£3,000	£2,000	£1,000
500F Giardiniera	479/499/2	1957–75	£3,000	£1,500	£1,000
2300S	2280/6	1961–68	£3,000	£1,700	£1,000
850	843/4	1964–71	£1,500	£1,000	–
850 Coupé	843/903/4	1965–73	£1,500	£1,000	–
850 Spyder	843/903/4	1965–73	£3,000	£2,000	£1,000
128 Sport Coupé 3P	1116/ 1290/4	1971–78	£2,500	£1,800	£1,000
130 Coupé	3235/6	1971–77	£5,500	£4,000	£2,000
131 Mirafiori Sport	1995/4	1974–84	£1,500	£1,000	£500
124 Sport Coupé	1438/ 1608/4	1966–72	£3,000	£2,000	£1,000
124 Sport Spyder	1438/ 1608/4	1966–72	£5,500	£2,500	£1,500
Dino Coupé	1987/ 2418/6	1967–73	£8,000	£5,500	£2,500
Dino Spyder	1987/ 2418/6	1967–73	£18,000+	£10,000	£5,000
X1/9	1290/ 1498/4	1972–89	£4,000	£2,000	£1,500

Ford *(British 1911–)*

◀ **1937 Ford 10 7W Four-Door Saloon,** 1172cc, side-valve 4-cylinder engine, finished in black with green leather upholstery, 1 of only 34 known to exist.
£1,400–1,650 / €2,050–2,450 / $2,450–2,900 ⚲ CGC
Introduced in 1932, the 8hp Model Y was intended to win back sales lost by Ford's larger-engined models in a British market subject to a horsepower tax. It faced fierce competition from rival Austin and Morris products, locking Ford into a price war. In 1937, revised 8hp 7Y and 10hp 7W models were released. Built on a transverse-leaf-sprung chassis fitted with an 1172cc, side-valve four-cylinder engine, the latter was the first Ford to be designed outside Detroit, Michigan.

▶ **1948 Ford Prefect Four-Door Saloon,** 1172cc, side-valve 4-cylinder engine, Girling mechanical brakes, top speed 60mph.
£2,650–3,150 / €3,900–4,650 / $4,650–5,500 ⚲ CGC
Launched in 1938, the Prefect offered practical, reliable transport with just a dash of transatlantic glamour. It was built on a ladder-frame chassis with a beam front axle and transverse semi-elliptic leaf springs front and rear.

1950 Ford V8 Pilot, 3622cc, side-valve V8 engine, 3-speed manual gearbox, finished in black, brown leather interior, concours condition.
£6,100–7,300 / €9,000–10,800 / $10,700–12,800 ⚲ BRIT
Introduced in 1947, the V8 Pilot was Ford's first new post-war model in the UK. Its design was based on the pre-war V8-62, the restyled front end featuring a high-fronted bonnet and imposing radiator grille. In prototype form, it was fitted with a 2.5 litre engine, but this made the car underpowered, so the tried-and-tested 3.6 litre V8 was utilized. Hydro-mechanical brakes were employed, and the specification included built-in hydraulic jacks. The engine ensured that the Pilot was a formidable performer, being capable of approximately 85mph. By the time production ceased in 1951, around 35,600 Pilots had been built. Some were used by police forces, including this car, which was supplied new to the Devonshire Constabulary; it has the police-specified 12 volt electrical system.

1954 Ford 103E Popular, 1172cc, side-valve 4-cylinder engine, completely restored 2001, engine rebuilt, stainless steel exhaust, finished in dark green, beige interior.
£1,950–2,350 / €2,900–3,450
$3,500–4,150 ⚲ BARO
The 103E was introduced in 1953. Capable of over 60mph and an economical 30+mpg, the Popular sold well.

FORD Model	ENGINE cc/cyl	DATES	CONDITION		
			1	2	3
Model T	2892/4	1908–27	£15,000+	£8,000	£4,000
Model A	3285/4	1928–32	£10,000+	£7,000	£4,000
Model Y & 7Y	933/4	1932–40	£5,000	£3,000	£1,500
Model C, CX & 7W	1172/4	1934–40	£4,000	£2,000	£1,000
Model AB	3285/4	1933–34	£10,000	£8,000	£4,500
Model ABF	2043/4	1933–34	£9,000	£6,000	£4,000
Model V8	3622/8	1932–40	£8,500	£6,000	£4,500
Model V8–60	2227/8	1936–40	£7,000	£5,000	£2,000
Model AF (UK only)	2033/4	1928–32	£9,000	£6,000	£3,500

A right-hand-drive vehicle will always command more interest than a left-hand-drive example in the UK. Coachbuilt vehicles, and in particular tourers, achieve a premium at auction. Veteran cars (ie. manufactured before 1919) will often achieve a 20% premium.

◄ **1961 Ford Zephyr Mk II,** 2553cc, 6-cylinder engine, 3-speed manual gearbox with column change, period windscreen visor, finished in green and white, red interior.
£1,350–1,600 / €2,00–2,350
$2,350–2,800 ♪ H&H
Ford's first European assembly plant was actually set up in the North West at Trafford Park, where Detroit-made Model Ts were shipped via the Manchester Ship Canal and assembled. Their main UK factory did not open until 1931 at Dagenham to build model AA 1.5-ton trucks and Model Y Saloons. Post-WWII, while production resumed in 1945 with Anglias and Prefects, the first all-new postwar models were the four-cylinder Consul and the six-cylinder Zephyr.

▶ **1962 Ford 100E Popular,** 1172cc, side-valve 4-cylinder engine, finished in sapphire blue, 2 owners from new, 31,000 miles recorded.
£1,200–1,400 / €1,750–2,050 / $2,100–2,450 ♪ CGC
The ultimate development of Ford's side-valve four-cylinder engine was fitted to the 100E range, introduced in 1953. McPherson-strut independent front suspension made its first appearance in a small car, giving ride and handling qualities far removed from the earlier 'upright' models. Escort and Squire estate versions followed, but in 1959 the introduction of the all-new 105E Anglia, with its overhead-valve engine and four-speed gearbox, brought an end to the 100E's development.

◄ **1964 Ford Zodiac Mk III,** 2553cc, overhead-valve 6-cylinder engine, automatic transmission, brakes and suspension overhauled, stainless steel exhaust system, finished in blue, blue pleated vinyl upholstery, imitation wood dashboard inserts.
£1,000–1,200 / €1,500–1,800 / $1,750–2,100 ♪ CGC

The price paid for a car can vary according to the country in which it was sold. To discover where the car sold, cross reference the code at the end of each caption with the Key to Illustrations on page 251.

1966 Ford Cortina Lotus Mk I, 1558cc, double-overhead-camshaft 4-cylinder engine, 105bhp, 4-speed manual gearbox, top speed 108mph, finished in white and green, near-concours condition.
£13,000–15,600 / €19,200–23,100
$22,900–27,500 ♪ H&H
A total of 4,012 Mk I Cortina Lotuses were built.

1966 Ford 105E Anglia, 997cc, overhead-valve 4-cylinder engine, restored.
£1,250–1,500 / €1,850–2,200 / $2,200–2,650 ⌁ **B(Kn)**
Ford belatedly switched to an overhead-valve engine for its small saloon with the introduction of the 105E Anglia in 1959. The running gear had been sourced from the previous 100E model, but the new four-speed gearbox represented a welcome advance. Distinctively styled with its 'grinning' radiator grille and reverse-slope rear window, the 105E Anglia was an outstanding success for Ford, selling more than a million before production ceased in 1967. This example was offered as first prize by the *Daily Mirror* in the newspaper's 'Win the Harry Potter Car' competition of 2002.

1970 Ford Capri Mk I 3000GT, 2792cc, overhead-valve V6 engine, 136bhp, 4-speed manual gearbox, top speed 115mph, 0–60mph in 10.3 seconds, engine rebuilt, 5,000 miles recorded since, finished in metallic red, black vinyl interior.
£2,150–2,550 / €3,200–3,750 / $3,800–4,500 ⌁ **CGC**
Intended as a European equivalent of the Mustang, the Capri was launched in 1969. A four-seater with good handling and respectable performance, it was an immediate sales hit. Although styling evolved through the three marks, the Capri's underpinnings remained largely unchanged. Front suspension was by McPherson struts, the rear axle was leaf-sprung, steering was by rack-and-pinion, and braking was handled by front discs and rear drums. Over the course of production, engine options ranged from a 1.3 litre four to the homologation special 3.1 litre V6.

◄ **1972 Ford Escort Mexico,** 1601cc, double-overhead-camshaft 4-cylinder engine, 40mm carburettors, new floorpan, suspension, brakes and wiring.
£5,700–6,800 / €8,400–10,100 / $10,000–12,000 ⌁ **B(Kn)**
An instant hit when it arrived in 1968, the Escort was destined to be Britain's best-selling car for many years. It was built in two- and four-door saloon, estate and van models, and came with either a 1098cc or 1298cc overhead-valve four-cylinder engine, with a choice of manual gearbox or automatic transmission.
Those with an appetite for high performance could choose between GT and 1.6 litre Twin Cam or – later on – RS1600 and Mexico models.

FORD (British built) Model	ENGINE cc/cyl	DATES	CONDITION 1	2	3
Anglia E494A	993/4	1948–53	£2,000	£850	£250
Prefect E93A	1172/4	1940–49	£3,500	£1,250	£900
Prefect E493A	1172/4	1948–53	£2,500	£1,000	£300
Popular 103E	1172/4	1953–59	£1,875	£825	£300
Anglia/Prefect 100E	1172/4	1953–59	£1,350	£625	£250
Prefect 107E	997/4	1959–62	£1,150	£600	£200
Escort/Squire 100E	1172/4	1955–61	£1,000	£850	£275
Popular 100E	1172/4	1959–62	£1,250	£600	£180
Anglia 105E	997/4	1959–67	£1,400	£500	£75
Anglia 123E	1198/4	1962–67	£1,550	£575	£150
V8 Pilot	3622/8	1947–51	£7,000	£4,000	£1,500
Consul Mk I	1508/4	1951–56	£2,250	£950	£400
Consul Mk I DHC	1508/4	1953–56	£6,000+	£3,500	£1,250
Zephyr Mk I	2262/6	1951–56	£3,000	£1,250	£600
Zephyr Mk I DHC	2262/6	1953–56	£7,000+	£4,000	£1,300
Zodiac Mk I	2262/6	1953–56	£3,300	£1,500	£700
Consul Mk II/Deluxe	1703/4	1956–62	£2,900	£1,500	£650
Consul Mk II DHC	1703/4	1956–62	£5,000	£3,300	£1,250
Zephyr Mk II	2553/6	1956–62	£3,800	£1,800	£750
Zephyr Mk II DHC	2553/6	1956–62	£8,000	£4,000	£1,500
Zodiac Mk II	2553/6	1956–62	£4,000	£2,250	£750
Zodiac Mk II DHC	2553/6	1956–62	£8,500	£4,250	£1,800
Zephyr 4 Mk III	1703/4	1962–66	£2,100	£1,200	£400
Zephyr 6 Mk III	2552/6	1962–66	£2,300	£1,300	£450
Zodiac Mk III	2553/6	1962–66	£2,500	£1,500	£500
Zephyr 4 Mk IV	1994/4	1966–72	£1,750	£600	£300
Zephyr 6 Mk IV	2553/6	1966–72	£1,800	£700	£300
Zodiac Mk IV	2994/6	1966–72	£2,000	£800	£300
Zodiac Mk IV Est.	2994/6	1966–72	£2,800	£1,200	£300
Zodiac Mk IV Exec.	2994/6	1966–72	£2,300+	£950	£300
Classic 315	1340/ 1498/4	1961–63	£1,400	£800	£500
Consul Capri	1340/ 1498/4	1961–64	£2,100	£1,350	£400
Consul Capri GT	1498/4	1961–64	£2,600+	£1,600	£800

1979 Ford Granada GL Limousine, 2800cc, V6 engine, 3-speed automatic transmission, coil-spring suspension, disc front brakes, power steering, finished in black, blue velour interior.
£300–360 / €440–530 / $530–630 ✗ CGC

1983 Ford Capri 1600 Mk III Cabaret, 1593cc, 4-cylinder engine, 4-speed manual gearbox, sunroof, boot spoiler, finished in metallic blue and silver, grey interior, 1 owner from new, 19,000 miles recorded.
£2,150–2,600 / €3,200–3,850 / $3,800–4,600 ✗ H&H

▶ **1989 Ford Escort Mk III RS Turbo,** 1600cc, turbocharged 4-cylinder engine, 130bhp, 5-speed manual gearbox, Recaro seats, top speed 130mph, finished in red, grey interior.
£2,800–3,350 / €4,150–4,950 / $4,950–5,900 ✗ H&H

1980 Ford Escort Mk II Harrier, 1599cc, overhead-valve 4-cylinder engine, 4-speed manual gearbox, fully restored, concours condition.
£3,300–3,950 / €4,900–5,800 / $5,800–6,900 ✗ BRIT
Introduced in 1980 as a limited edition of 1,500 cars, the Harrier was derived from the 1600 Sport and was fitted with Recaro seats, a rear spoiler and RS alloy wheels. It was the last sporting special edition of the Mk II to appear before the introduction of the front-wheel-drive Mk III Escort later in the year.

FORD (British built) Model	ENGINE cc/cyl	DATES	CONDITION 1	2	3
Cortina Mk I	1198/4	1963–66	£1,550	£600	£150
Cortina Crayford Mk I DHC	1198/4	1963–66	£3,500	£1,800	£950
Cortina GT	1498/4	1963–66	£1,800	£1,000	£650
Cortina Lotus Mk I	1558/4	1963–66	£10,000	£7,500	£4,500
Cortina Mk II	1599/4	1966–70	£1,000	£500	£100
Cortina GT Mk II	1599/4	1966–70	£1,200	£650	£150
Cortina Crayford Mk II DHC	1599/4	1966–70	£4,000	£2,000	£1,500
Cortina Lotus Mk II	1558/4	1966–70	£6,000+	£3,500	£1,800
Cortina 1600E	1599/4	1967–70	£4,000	£2,000	£900
Consul Corsair	1500/4	1963–65	£1,100	£500	£250
Consul Corsair GT	1500/4	1963–65	£1,200	£600	£250
Corsair V4	1664/4	1965–70	£1,150	£600	£250
Corsair V4 Est.	1664/4	1965–70	£1,400	£600	£250
Corsair V4GT	1994/4	1965–67	£1,300	£700	£250
Corsair V4GT Est.	1994/4	1965–67	£1,400	£700	£350
Corsair Convertible	1664/ 1994/4	1965–70	£4,300	£2,500	£1,000
Corsair 2000	1994/4	1967–70	£1,350	£500	£250
Corsair 2000E	1994/4	1967–70	£1,500	£800	£350
Escort 1300E	1298/4	1973–74	£1,900	£1,000	£250
Escort Twin Cam	1558/4	1968–71	£8,000	£5,000	£2,000
Escort GT	1298/4	1968–73	£3,000	£1,500	£350
Escort Sport	1298/4	1971–75	£1,750	£925	£250
Escort Mexico	1601/4	1970–74	£4,000	£2,000	£750
RS1600	1601/4	1970–74	£5,000	£2,500	£1,500
RS2000	1998/4	1973–74	£4,500	£2,200	£1,000
Escort RS Mexico	1593/4	1976–78	£3,500	£2,000	£850
Escort RS2000 Mk II	1993/4	1976–80	£6,000	£3,500	£2,000
Capri Mk I 1300/ 1600	1298/ 1599/4	1969–72	£1,500	£1,000	£550
Capri 2000/ 3000GT	1996/4 2994/6	1969–72	£2,000	£1,000	£500
Capri 3000E	2994/6	1970–72	£4,000	£2,000	£1,000
Capri RS3100	3093/6	1973–74	£6,500	£3,500	£2,000
Cortina 2000E	1993/4	1973–76	£2,500	£550	£225
Granada Ghia	1993/4 2994/6	1974–77	£3,000	£900	£350

Ford – USA (*American 1903–*)

1909 Ford Model T Touring Car, 2898cc, side-valve
4-cylinder engine, 2-speed planetary transmission,
transverse-leaf-spring suspension, acetylene headlamps
and generator, cowl-mounted kerosene lamps, bulb horn,
rear light, speedometer, canvas top.
£17,800–21,400 / €26,000–31,000
$31,000–37,000 ↗ BB(S)
This example dates from the first year of
Model T production.

1921 Ford Model T Centre-Door Saloon, 2898cc,
side-valve 4-cylinder engine, completely restored,
standard specification apart from Bayer tilt steering wheel,
concours condition.
£4,900–5,900 / €7,300–8,700 / $8,600–10,400 ↗ BB(S)

1930 Ford Model A Roadster, 3285cc, side-valve
4-cylinder engine, finished in dark green, dark tan leather
interior, excellent condition.
£9,100–10,900 / 13,500–16,100
16,000–19,200 ↗ BB(S)

1939 Ford Standard V8 Station Wagon, 3622cc,
side-valve V8 engine, Lockheed hydraulic drum brakes.
£32,000–38,000 / €47,000–56,000
56,000–67,000 ↗ BB(S)
The Station Wagon (nicknamed 'Woody') was one of
four body styles offered for the 1939 Standard V8
series; 3,277 of these vehicles were made,
the smallest run in the Ford line-up that year.

1931 Ford Model A Roadster, 3285cc, side-valve
4-cylinder engine, finished in blue, brown leather interior.
£7,800–9,400 / €11,500–13,900
$13,700–16,500 ↗ BB(S)

1947 Ford V8 Station Wagon, 3622cc, side-valve V8 engine, fully restored, engine uprated to 100bhp, new radiator.
£38,000–46,000 / €57,000–68,000 $67,000–81,000 ⚖ BB(S)

1953 Ford Customline Two-Door Saloon, 215cu.in, overhead-valve 6-cylinder engine, 3-speed manual gearbox with overdrive, 61,000 miles recorded, original.
£4,300–5,100 / €6,300–7,500 / $7,600–9,000 ⚖ BJ

◀ **1953 Ford Crestline Victoria Two-Door Hardtop,** 239cu.in, side-valve V8 engine, automatic transmission, radio, heater, full wheel covers, subject of body-off restoration, concours winner.
£14,400–17,300 €21,300–25,600 $25,300–30,000 ⚖ BJ
This was the last year of the famous flathead V8 engine.

▶ **1955 Ford Thunderbird,** 5113cc, overhead-valve V8 engine, 3-speed automatic transmission, power steering, hardtop, electric seats and windows, export model with engine dress-up kit and chrome driving lamps, finished in red, red and white interior.
£9,900–11,900 / €14,700–17,600 $17,400–20,900 ⚖ BARO
The Thunderbird was launched in 1955 and outsold the rival Chevrolet Corvette by 24 to one.

1957 Ford Thunderbird, 292cu.in, overhead-valve V8 engine, hardtop, restored, excellent condition.
£19,000–22,800 / €28,300–34,000 / $34,000–40,000 ⚖ BB(S)

1962 Ford Country Squire Station Wagon, 390cu.in, V8 engine, triple carburettors, automatic transmission, Kelsey Hayes wire wheels, power steering, electric seats.
£8,700–10,400 / €12,900–15,400 / $15,300–18,300 ⚖ BJ

1962 Ford Thunderbird Convertible, 390cu.in, V8 engine, Kelsey Hayes wire wheels, continental spare wheel kit, tonneau cover, air conditioning, finished in black, black leather interior.
£10,700–12,800 / €15,800–18,900 / $18,800–22,500 ➤ H&H

1965 Ford Mustang Fastback, 298cu.in, overhead-valve V8 engine, tuned to produce 330bhp, Holley carburettor, Offenhauser inlet manifold, Mallory ignition, large-capacity sump, Superlite cast-alloy wheels.
£23,500–28,200 / €35,000–42,000 $42,000–50,000 ➤ COYS

1965 Ford Mustang GT Coupé, 289cu.in, 4-speed automatic transmission, front disc brakes, Rally Pac, engine dress-up package, chromed steel wheels.
£7,800–9,350 / €11,500–13,800 / $13,700–14,600 ➤ BJ
This car was built for export to Germany; it is the only example known to exist.

▶ **1965 Ford Mustang Shelby GT350 Replica,** 302cu.in, V8 engine, tuned to produce 325bhp.
£12,200–14,600 €17,800–21,600 $21,500–25,700 ➤ BARO

Miller's Milestones

Ford Mustang (1964–69)
Price Range; £3,000–25,000 / €4,450–46,000 / $5,300–44,000
The Mustang rewrote America's sports car design rules and was a runaway sales success. It had crisp styling that showed European influence, being available in 'notchback', 'fastback' and convertible guises. Moreover, it was a salesman's dream and could be ordered with a vast array of options, which allowed buyers to tailor the car to suit their needs and pocket.
For power, the choice ranged from a straight-six displacing 2788cc right up to a mighty 4.7 litre, 335bhp V8, backed by a manual gearbox or automatic. There were sports handling packages and optional front disc brakes (to replace the standard drums), as well as countless trim options.

In the showroom, the Mustang was quite simply a record breaker, becoming one of the car industry's fastest-ever sellers – 418,000 Mustangs whizzed out of the door in the first year, and over a million had been sold by 1966.
The Mustang was also a hit with speed freaks, tuning wizard Carroll Shelby creating a range of high-performance models, including 1,000 for the Hertz car rental company. Before long, however, Hertz was forced to withdraw them, not because of mechanical problems, but because the black and gold road-burners were being used by weekend customers for drag racing.
After 1969, the Mustang slowly lost its way, effectively ruined by ever more stringent emissions regulations. Into the 1970s, it gradually became bigger and heavier until eventually it lost its magic completely.

1965 Ford Mustang Convertible, 289cu.in, V8 engine,
3-speed manual gearbox, unrestored,
in need of recommissioning.
£6,300–7,600 / €9,300–11,200 / $11,100–13,400 ⚒ CGC

1966 Ford Thunderbird Coupé, 3900cc, V8 engine,
3-speed automatic transmission, in need of new cylinder
head gasket, finished in yellow, black interior and hood.
£3,000–3,600 / €4,450–5,300 / $5,300–6,300 ⚒ H&H

1966 Ford Mustang Coupé, 289cu.in, V8 engine, 210bhp,
3-speed automatic transmission, completely restored, finished
in red, red interior, excellent condition, concours winner.
£8,000–9,600 / €11,800–14,200 / $14,100–16,900 ⚒ BJ

1969 Ford Mustang Mach 1 Fastback, 351cu.in, V8 engine,
4-speed manual gearbox, Traction-Loc rear axle, power steering,
front disc brakes, completely restored 2000, fewer than 1,500
miles since, Hurst shifter, Flowmaster dual exhaust, Magnum
500 wheels, finished in yellow and black, black interior.
£11,300–13,600 / €16,700–20,100 / $19,900–23,900 ⚒ BJ

◀ **1977 Ford Thunderbird,** 5700cc, V8 engine, 3-speed
automatic transmission, finished in white, green leather interior.
£3,900–4,700 / €5,800–7,000 / $6,900–8,300 ⚒ CGC

▶ **1990 Ford Mustang ASC McLaren Convertible,**
5000cc, V8 engine,
automatic transmission,
servo-assisted brakes, ASC
McLaren alloy wheels,
tinted glass, electric windows,
air conditioning, leather seats,
last of only 65 models built
1990, 11,000 miles recorded.
£8,300–10,000
€12,300–14,800
$14,600–17,600 ⚒ BJ

FORD (American built) Model	ENGINE cu in/cyl	DATES	CONDITION 1	2	3
Thunderbird	292/312/8	1955–57	£20,000	£14,000	£9,000
Edsel Citation	410/8	1958	£9,000	£4,500	£2,500
Edsel Ranger	223/6, 361/8	1959	£6,000	£3,500	£2,000
Edsel Citation convertible	410/8	1958	£12,000	£6,000	£4,000
Edsel Corsair convertible	332/361/8	1959	£10,500	£7,000	£4,500
Fairlane 2-door	223/6, 352/8	1957–59	£8,000	£4,500	£3,000
Fairlane 500 Sunliner	223/6, 352/8	1957–59	£12,000	£8,000	£6,500
Fairlane 500 Skyliner	223/6, 352/8	1957–59	£14,000	£10,000	£8,000
Mustang 4.7 V8 FHC/Conv.		1964–66	£9,000	£4,000	£2,000
Mustang GT 350		1966–67	£15,000	£10,000	£6,000
Mustang hardtop	260/6, 428/8	1967–68	£6,000	£4,000	£3,000
Mustang GT 500		1966–67	£20,000	£14,000	£6,000

Fuller *(American 1908–12)*

◄ **1910 Fuller Model K Touring Car,** flat-twin engine, leaf-spring suspension, brass headlamps, acetylene generator, windscreen frame and kerosene side lamps, finished in red with white chassis, red leather interior, restored.
£10,700–12,800 / € 15,800–18,900 $18,800–22,500 ↗ BB(S)

Not content with being a director of the modestly successful Jackson Automobile Company, George Matthews wanted to build his own vehicle, so he formed the Fuller Buggy Company. In 1908, the Fuller Model B was introduced. Powered by a flat-twin engine producing 15–18bhp, it had a Mott & Wesson planetary transmission and shaft drive to the rear wheels. Suspension was by semi-elliptic leaf springs all round, while the wheels were fitted with solid rubber tyres. The Model B was offered in four body styles: runabout, four-passenger touring car, open delivery wagon and closed delivery wagon. The Model K followed shortly after. Although it retained the twin-cylinder engine, it came with pneumatic tyres.

Gordon Keeble *(British 1964–67)*

GORDON KEEBLE Model	ENGINE cc/cyl	DATES	CONDITION 1	2	3
GKI/GKIT	5355/8	1964–67	£20,000	£15,000	£10,000

Hillman *(British 1907–78)*

1932 Hillman Minx Four-Door Saloon, 1124cc, side-valve 4-cylinder engine, Bendix brakes, finished in black, red interior.
£2,150–2,600 / € 3,200–3,850 / $3,800–4,550 ↗ H&H
The Minx, destined to be Hillman's best-known model, was launched at London's Olympia Motor Show in 1931.

1954 Hillman Minx Convertible, 1494cc, 4-cylinder engine, 4-speed manual gearbox, fully restored, concours condition.
£4,200–5,000 / € 6,200–18,900 / $7,400–8,800 ↗ COYS

◄ **1967 Hillman Husky,** 875cc, rear-mounted overhead-camshaft 4-cylinder engine, excellent condition.
£2,250–2,500 € 3,350–3,700 $3,950–4,400 🚗 IMP
The Husky was an estate version of the Imp; it is quite rare.

HILLMAN Model	ENGINE cc/cyl	DATES	CONDITION 1	2	3
Minx Mk I–II	1184/4	1946–48	£1,750	£800	£250
Minx Mk I–II DHC	1184/4	1946–48	£3,500	£1,500	£250
Minx Mk III–VIIIA	1184/4	1948–56	£1,750	£700	£350
Minx Mk III–VIIIA DHC	1184/4	1948–56	£3,750	£1,500	£350
Californian	1390/4	1953–56	£2,000	£750	£200
Minx SI/II	1390/4	1956–58	£1,250	£450	£200
Minx SI/II DHC	1390/4	1956–58	£3,500	£1,500	£500
Minx Ser III	1494/4	1958–59	£1,000	£500	£200
Minx Ser III DHC	1494/4	1958–59	£3,750	£1,500	£400
Minx Ser IIIA/B	1494/4	1959–61	£1,250	£500	£200
Minx Ser IIIA/B DHC	1494/4	1959–61	£3,750	£1,250	£500
Minx Ser IIIC	1592/4	1961–62	£900	£500	£200
Minx Ser IIIC DHC	1592/4	1961–62	£3,000	£1,500	£500
Minx Ser V	1592/4	1962–63	£1,250	£350	£150
Minx Ser VI	1725/4	1964–67	£1,500	£375	£100
Husky Mk I	1265/4	1954–57	£1,000	£600	£200
Husky SI/II/III	1390/4	1958–65	£1,000	£550	£150
Super Minx	1592/4	1961–66	£1,500	£500	£100
Super Minx DHC	1592/4	1962–64	£3,500	£1,250	£450
Imp	875/4	1963–73	£1,000	£500	£100
Husky	875/4	1966–71	£800	£450	£100
Avenger	var/4	1970–76	£550	£250	£60
Avenger GT	1500/4	1971–76	£950	£500	£100
Avenger Tiger	1600/4	1972–73	£2,000	£1,000	£500

1968 Hillman Imp Californian, 875cc, rear-mounted overhead-camshaft 4-cylinder engine, 42bhp.
£1,800–2,000 / €2,650–2,950 / $3,150–3,500 🚗 IMP
The Californian was the coupé version of the Imp.

1971 Hillman Imp, 875cc, rear-mounted overhead-camshaft engine, 42bhp, top speed 80mph.
£1,350–1,500 / €2,000–2,200 / $2,400–2,650 🚗 IMP
The Imp series was in production from 1963 to 1976.

Honda *(Japanese 1948–)*

HONDA Model	ENGINE cc/cyl	DATES	CONDITION 1	2	3
S800 Mk I Convertible	791/4	1966–69	£7,000	£4,000	£2,500
S800 Mk I Coupé	791/4	1966–69	£5,000	£3,500	£1,000
S800 Mk II Convertible	791/4	1968–69	£7,000	£5,000	£3,000
S800 Mk II Coupé	791/4	1968–69	£6,500	£4,000	£1,200

HRG *(British 1935–65)*

◀ **1939/46 HRG Aerodynamic 1500 Prototype,** 1496cc, Meadows 4-cylinder engine, Moss 4-speed manual gearbox, ENV live rear axle, aluminium bodywork.
£19,300–23,100 / €28,600–34,000 $34,000–40,600 🔨 H&H
HRG Engineering was formed in 1935 by E.A. Halford, Guy H. Robins and H.R. Godfrey – the marque name was derived from the first letter of each founder's surname. This prototype was built in 1939, but not registered until 1946. It is notable for being the first British sports car with all-enveloping, streamlined bodywork.

Hudson *(American 1909–57)*

◀ **1935 Hudson Big 6 Saloon,** 3500cc, 6-cylinder engine, 3-speed manual gearbox, right-hand drive.
£1,800–2,150 / €2,650–3,200 $3,150–3,800 ⚲ H&H
Howard Earl Coffin and Roy Dikeman Chapin helped form Thomas-Detroit (later Chalmers-Detroit) in 1906. Three years later, they set up a subsidiary line of cheaper cars named Hudson – after the Detroit tycoon who owned the largest department store in the world and gave financial backing to the company. This particular car was assembled in the UK.

Humber *(British 1901–76)*

1923 Humber 8/18, 985cc, inlet-over-exhaust 4-cylinder engine, 3-speed manual gearbox, finished in blue over black, black leather interior.
£7,200–8,000 / €10,700–11,800 / $12,700–14,100 🚗 HUMB
Like many early motor manufacturers, Humber started out making bicycles. Having built its first three-wheeler in 1896, the company became the very first manufacturer of series-production motor cars in Britain.
Humber also opened an aircraft engine manufacturing division in 1909 and made motorcycles until 1930.
The marque was eventually absorbed into the Rootes Group, which, in turn, was taken over by Chrysler before being off-loaded to Peugeot.

HUMBER Model	ENGINE cc/cyl	DATES	CONDITION 1	2	3
Veteran	various	1898			
		1918	£30,000+	£20,000+	£14,000
10	1592/4	1919	£7,000	£5,000	£3,000
14	2474/4	1919	£8,000	£6,000	£4,000
15.9–5/40	2815/4	1920–27	£9,500	£7,000	£4,000
8	985/4	1923–25	£7,000	£5,000	£2,500
9/20–9/28	1057/4	1926	£7,000	£5,000	£4,000
14/40	2050/4	1927–28	£10,000	£8,000	£5,000
Snipe	3498/6	1930–35	£8,000	£6,000	£4,000
Pullman	3498/6	1930–35	£8,000	£6,000	£4,000
16/50	2110/6	1930–32	£9,000	£7,000	£5,000
12	1669/4	1933–37	£7,000	£5,000	£3,000
Snipe/Pullman	4086/6	1936–40	£7,000	£5,000	£3,000
16	2576/6	1938–40	£7,000	£5,000	£3,000

Pre-1906 or Brighton Run eligible cars are very popular. Vintage tourers add more.

1926 Humber 12/25 Tourer, 1795cc, 4-cylinder engine, folding hood, 1 of 40 known to survive.
**£14,100–16,900 / € 20,900–25,000
$24,800–29,700** ⚲ BRIT
Powered by a 1.8 litre engine, the 12/25 was available as a two-seat tourer with dickey seat, four-seat tourer or saloon. Around 3,000 12/25s were produced, approximately half of this number having tourer coachwork.

1924 Humber 8/18, 985cc, inlet-over-exhaust 4-cylinder engine, magneto ignition, 3-speed gearbox, side screens, finished in beige and black, brown leather interior.
£7,000–8,400 / € 10,400–12,400 / $12,300–14,800 ⚲ H&H

▶ **1935 Humber 12 Saloon,** 1669cc, side-valve 4-cylinder engine, 4-speed synchromesh gearbox, Bendix servo brake system, hydraulic shock absorbers, finished in maroon, maroon interior.
£2,000–2,400 / € 2,950–3,550 / $2,950–4,200 ⚲ B(Kn)

1937 Humber Snipe Drophead Coupé, 4086cc, side-valve 6-cylinder engine, independent front suspension, vacuum servo brakes, finished in grey, black hood, maroon leather interior.
**£9,200–11,000 / € 13,600–16,300
$16,200–19,400** ⚲ B(Kn)

1949 Humber Super Snipe Drophead Coupé,
coachwork by Tickford, 4086cc, 6-cylinder engine, 4-speed manual gearbox, restored over 2 years.
**£16,500–19,800 / € 24,400–39,300
$29,000–34,800** ⚲ BARO
The Super Snipe was launched in 1948 and could be ordered in four-door saloon, estate and limousine form, or with special coachbuilt bodies. The Tickford drophead coupé was the rarest of all, and only a handful survive today.

1967 Humber Super Snipe Estate Series V, 2965cc, 6-cylinder engine, 4-speed manual gearbox with overdrive, finished in silver-grey, red interior, unrestored, good running order.
£2,700–3,250 / € 4,000–4,800 / $4,750–5,700 ⚲ H&H

HUMBER Model	ENGINE cc/cyl	DATES	CONDITION 1	2	3
Hawk Mk I–IV	1944/4	1945–52	£3,700	£1,500	£600
Hawk Mk V–VII	2267/4	1952–57	£3,000	£1,500	£400
Hawk Ser I–IVA	2267/4	1957–67	£3,000	£850	£325
Snipe	2731/6	1945–48	£5,000	£2,600	£850
Super Snipe Mk I–III	4086/6	1948–52	£4,700	£2,400	£600
Super Snipe Mk IV–IVA	4138/6	1952–56	£5,500	£3,000	£550
Super Snipe Ser I–II	2651/6	1958–60	£3,800	£1,800	£475
Super Snipe Ser III VA	2965/6	1961–67	£3,500	£1,800	£400
Super Snipe Ser III–VA Est.	2965/6	1961–67	£3,950	£1,850	£525
Pullman	4086/6	1946–51	£5,000	£3,000	£800
Pullman Mk IV	4086/6	1952–54	£6,000	£2,850	£1,200
Imperial	2965/6	1965–67	£3,900	£1,600	£450
Sceptre Mk I–II	1592/4	1963–67	£2,200+	£1,000+	£300
Sceptre Mk III	1725/4	1967–76	£2,000	£900	£200

Hupmobile
(American 1909–1940)

Auction prices

Miller's only includes cars declared sold. Our guide prices take into account the buyer's premium, VAT on the premium, and the extent of any published catalogue information relating to condition and provenance. Cars sold at auction are identified by the ⚒ icon; full details of the auction house can be found on page 251.

◀ **1910 Hupmobile Model 20 Runabout,** completely restored, engine, transmission, suspension, rear axle and brakes rebuilt.
£8,800–10,600 / € 13,000–15,600 $15,500–18,600 ⚒ BB(S)

ISO (Italian 1953–79)

▶ **1974 Iso Lele,** 5359cc, V8 engine, automatic transmission, finished in silver, tan interior, 1 of only 317 built.
£3,400–4,100 / € 5,000–6,100 $6,000–7,200 ⚒ COYS

ISO Model	ENGINE cc/cyl	DATES	CONDITION 1	2	3
Rivolta V8	5359/8	1962–70	£15,000	£10,000	£3,500
Grifo V8	5359/6899/8	1963–74	£28,000+	£16,000+	£12,000
Lele 2-door fastback coupé	5359/8	1967–74	£12,000	£8,000	£4,000
Fidia V8 4-door exec. saloon	5359/8	1967–74	£10,000	£7,000	£4,000

Jaguar *(British 1927–)*

◀ **1937 Jaguar SSII Saloon,** 1608cc, Standard 4-cylinder engine, finished in black, beige interior, original, excellent condition.
£9,100–10,900 / € 13,500–16,100 $16,000–19,200 ✈ **H&H**

▶ **1938 Jaguar SS Special Sports,** 2663cc, 6-cylinder engine, 4-speed manual gearbox, finished in black with red wheels, red interior.
£5,600–6,700 / € 8,300–9,900 / $9,900–11,800 ✈ **H&H**
This car was originally manufactured as a 2.5 litre saloon, but in 1991 was fitted with Vanden Plas-style coachwork with hood and side screen. At the same time, the chassis and propshaft were shortened, and a new radiator shell fabricated.

1948 Jaguar Mk IV 2½ Litre Drophead Coupé, 2663cc, 6-cylinder engine, fully restored 1988–89, finished in red, red leather interior, concours condition.
£26,100–31,000 / € 39,000–47,000 $48,000–57,000 ✈ **BB(S)**

▶ **1949 Jaguar Mk V 2½ Litre Saloon,** 2663cc, 6-cylinder engine, fully restored, concours condition.
£14,700–17,600 / € 21,800–26,000 $25,900–31,000 ✈ **H&H**

JAGUAR Model	ENGINE cc/cyl	DATES	CONDITION		
			1	2	3
SSI	2054/6	1932–33	£35,000	£18,000	£12,000
SSI	2252/6	1932–33	£22,000+	£17,000	£13,500
SSII	1052/4	1932–33	£18,000	£15,000	£11,000
SSI	2663/6	1934	£26,000	£22,000	£15,000
SSII	1608/4	1934	£18,000	£15,000	£12,000
SS90	2663/6	1935	£60,000+	–	–
SS100 (3.4)	3485/6	1938–39	£90,000+	–	–
SS100 (2.6)	2663/6	1936–39	£90,000+	–	–
Value dependent on body style, completeness and originality, particularly original chassis to body.					

1950 Jaguar XK120 Roadster Lightweight, 3442cc, double-overhead-camshaft 6-cylinder engine, aluminium bodywork.
£50,000–60,000 / €75,000–90,000/ $93,000–111,000 ✗ COYS
The first 57 right-hand-drive XK120s and first 183 left-hand-drive models were handbuilt with aluminium bodies, but demand for the car forced Jaguar to tool up for volume production in steel.

1951 Jaguar Mk V Drophead Coupé, 3485cc, 6-cylinder engine, 4-speed synchromesh gearbox, independent front suspension, hydraulic brakes, concours condition.
£32,000–38,000 / €48,000–57,000
$59,000–70,000 ✗ H&H
This was the last year of production of the Mk V Drophead Coupé.

1951 Jaguar XK120 Coupé, 3442cc, 6-cylinder engine, left-hand drive, replica C-Type cylinder head, seam-welded chassis, uprated suspension, servo-assisted front disc brakes, Borrani wire wheels, finished in metallic green, green leather interior, concours condition.
£55,000–66,000 / €83,000–99,000
$102,000–122,000 ✗ B(Kn)

1952 Jaguar XK120 Roadster, 3442cc, double-overhead-camshaft 6-cylinder engine, subject of 'no expense spared' restoration, converted to right-hand drive, finished in silver, red leather interior.
£31,000–37,000 / €47,000–56,000
$57,000–68,000 ✗ B(Mon)

1952 Jaguar XK120 Coupé, 3442cc, double-overhead-camshaft 6-cylinder engine.
£15,200–18,200 / €22,500–26,900
$26,800–32,000 ✗ COYS

 Miller's Milestones

Jaguar XK120/140/150 (1948–61)
Price Range: £6,000–65,000 / €8,900–96,000 / $10,6000–114,000
When Jaguar's XK120 arrived in 1948, it looked like an unbeatable package. The company's boss, William Lyons, was responsible for styling this superb roadster, which would have sold on its handsome lines alone. But the XK120 was not just about style, there was substance under the bonnet in the shape of a brand-new, twin-camshaft, straight-six engine displacing 3442cc. This classic power unit would survive well into the 1990s, powering everything from Le Mans winning cars to armoured vehicles and even fire engines. The first few hundred cars (built between 1948 and 1949) sported aluminium bodies, and today these are the most valuable of all the XK models. With a super-smooth 160bhp on tap, they were capable of 120mph, hence the '120' monicker. For a short time, the new Jaguar was the world's fastest series-production car.

Jaguar was totally overwhelmed by the massive demand for the car, which had been intended only as a limited-production model. As a result, the company tooled up for volume production with a steel body for 1950.
From then on, there was no looking back. A fixed-head coupé was launched in 1951, while a roomier drophead coupé arrived for 1953. A large percentage of production was exported to North America.
For 1954, Jaguar released the XK140, which had larger bumpers and, more usefully, rack-and-pinion steering. This was followed by the XK150 for 1957. Essentially, this was based on the original chassis, but it had all-new body panels. Concerns over lack of braking performance on previous models were addressed by fitting Dunlop discs to all four wheels, and with the arrival of the 3.8 litre 'S' version in 1959, power rose to an impressive 265bhp, giving a top speed of 135mph.

1952 Jaguar XK120 Coupé, 3422cc, double-overhead-camshaft 6-cylinder engine, restored, C-Type cylinder head, concours condition.
£48,000–58,000
€73,000–87,000
$89,000–107,000
➤ COYS

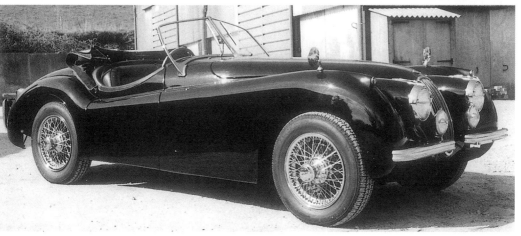

c1952 Jaguar XK120 Roadster, 3442cc, double-overhead-camshaft 6-cylinder engine, wire wheels, export model, converted to right-hand drive, finished in black, red leather interior.
£21,000–25,000 / €31,000–37,000 / $37,000–44,000 ➤ B(Kn)

JAGUAR Model	ENGINE cc/cyl	DATES	CONDITION 1	2	3
1½ Litre	1775/4	1945–49	£8,500	£5,500	£2,000
2½ Litre	2663/6	1946–49	£10,000	£7,500	£2,000
2½ Litre DHC	2663/6	1947–48	£17,000	£11,000	£8,000
3½ Litre	3485/6	1947–49	£12,000+	£6,000	£4,000
3½ Litre DHC	3485/6	1947–49	£19,000+	£13,500	£5,500
Mk V 2½ Litre	2663/6	1949–51	£14,000+	£8,000+	£1,500
Mk V 3½ Litre	3485/6	1949–51	£13,000	£8,000	£3,000
Mk V 3½ Litre DHC	3485/6	1949–51	£26,000+	£17,000+	£8,500
Mk VII	3442/6	1951–57	£10,000	£7,500	£2,500
Mk VIIM	3442/6	1951–57	£12,000	£8,500	£2,500
Mk VIII	3442/6	1956–59	£8,500	£5,500	£2,000
Mk IX	3781/6	1958–61	£9,000	£7,000	£2,500
Mk X 3.8/4.2	3781/6	1961–64	£7,500+	£3,500	£1,500
Mk X 420G	4235/6	1964–70	£6,000+	£3,000	£1,200
Mk I 2.4	2438/6	1955–59	£7,000+	£5,500	£2,000
Mk I 3.4	3442/6	1957–59	£12,000	£6,000	£2,500
Mk II 2.4	2483/6	1959–67	£10,000+	£6,000	£3,000
Mk II 3.4	3442/6	1959–67	£12,000+	£8,000	£4,000
Mk II 3.8	3781/6	1959–67	£20,000+	£11,000	£5,000
S-Type 3.4	3442/6	1963–68	£9,000+	£6,500+	£2,000
S-Type 3.8	3781/6	1963–68	£10,000	£6,500	£2,000
240	2438/6	1967–68	£9,000	£6,000	£2,500
340	3442/6	1967–68	£8,000	£7,000	£3,000
420	4235/6	1966–68	£6,000	£3,000	£2,000

Manual gearboxes with overdrive are at a premium.
Some concours examples make as much as 50% over Condition 1.

1953 Jaguar XK120 Roadster, 3442cc, double-overhead camshaft 6-cylinder engine, drum brakes, finished in grey, red leather interior.
£23,300–28,000 / € 35,000–42,000
$42,000–50,000 ✗ B(Kn)

1954 Jaguar XK120SE Drophead Coupé, 3422cc, finished in black, black hood, red leather interior, fully restored, concours condition.
£37,000–44,000 / € 56,000–66,000
$68,000–81,000 ✗ B(Kn)

1953 Jaguar Mk VIIM Saloon, 3442cc, double-overhead-camshaft 6-cylinder engine, sunroof.
£7,000–8,400 / € 10,400–12,400
$12,300–14,800 ✗ BRIT

▶ **1956 Jaguar XK140 Coupé,** 3442cc, double-overhead-camshaft 6-cylinder engine, completely restored.
£12,700–15,200 / € 18,800–22,500
$22,400–26,800 ✗ BARO
The XK120 became the XK140 in 1955, offering 130mph performance and useful upgrades, like rack-and-pinion steering and better weight distribution.

◀ **1956 Jaguar XK140 Drophead Coupé,** 3442cc, double-overhead-camshaft 6-cylinder engine, 4-speed manual gearbox with overdrive, fully restored, concours condition.
£46,000–55,000 / € 69,000–83,000
$85,000–102,000 ✗ COYS

1957 Jaguar XK150 Coupé, 3442cc, double-overhead-camshaft 6-cylinder engine, left-hand drive, completely restored at a cost of c£30,000 / € 44,000 / $53,000.
£22,600–27,100 / € 34,000–41,000 / $40,000–50,000 ✗ H&H

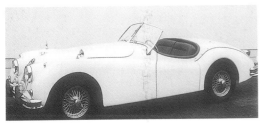

1958 Jaguar XK150 Coupé, 3442cc, double-overhead-camshaft 6-cylinder engine, automatic transmission, 4-wheel disc brakes, converted to unleaded fuel, front disc brake conversion.
£16,800–20,200 / €24,900–29,900
$29,900–36,000 ⚘ COYS
The XK150, introduced in 1957, was the last of the XK line. Although built on the same basic chassis, it had all-new body panels. Braking performance was improved by Dunlop discs on all four wheels. In 1959, the 3442cc engine was replaced by a 3781cc, triple-carburettor unit, the car becoming known as the XK150S.

1959 Jaguar XK150 Coupé, 3781cc, double-overhead-camshaft 6-cylinder engine, rebuilt wire wheels, stainless steel exhaust, Kenlowe fan.
£19,500–23,400 / €28,900–35,000
$34,000–41,000 ⚘ BRIT

◀ **1957 Jaguar XK140 Roadster**, 3442cc, 6-cylinder engine, chrome wire wheels, finished in white, black leather interior.
£37,000–44,000 / €56,000–66,000
$68,000–81,000 ⚘ COYS

1958 Jaguar Mk I Saloon, 2438cc, 6-cylinder engine, 4-speed manual gearbox, finished in dark green, brown interior.
£2,250–2,700 / €3,350–4,000 / $3,950–4,750 ⚘ H&H

1959 Jaguar Mk II 3.4 Saloon, 3442cc, double-overhead-camshaft 6-cylinder engine, 210bhp, 4-wheel disc brakes, finished in British Racing green, green leather interior, concours condition.
£7,200–10,400 / €10,700–15,400 / $12,700–18,300 ⚘ CGC

1959 Jaguar XK150 Coupé, 3781cc, double-overhead-camshaft 6-cylinder engine, 4-speed manual gearbox, finished in dark green, matching interior.
£18,000–21,600 / €26,600–32,000
$32,000–38,000 ⚘ H&H

JAGUAR Model	ENGINE cc/cyl	DATES	CONDITION 1	2	3
XK120 Roadster aluminium	3442/6	1948–49	£65,000	£30,000	£20,000
XK120 Roadster	3442/6	1949–54	£30,000+	£20,000+	£15,000
XK120 DHC	3442/6	1953–54	£25,000+	£17,000+	£12,000
XK120 Coupé	3442/6	1951–55	£20,000	£12,000+	£10,000
C-Type	3442/6	1951	£150,000+	–	–
D-Type	3442/6	1955–56	£500,000+	–	–
XKSS (original)	3442/6	1955–57	£400,000+	–	–
XK140 Roadster	3442/6	1955–58	£32,000+	£23,000	£16,000
XK140 DHC	3442/6	1955–58	£35,000	£22,000	£15,000
XK140 Coupé	3442/6	1955–58	£18,000	£12,000	£7,500
XK150 Roadster	3442/6	1958–60	£38,000	£22,000	£15,000
XK150 DHC	3442/6	1957–61	£28,000	£18,000	£10,000
XK150 Coupé	3442/6	1957–60	£20,000	£12,000	£6,000
XK150S Roadster	3442/ 3781/6	1958–60	£45,000+	£26,000+	£20,000
XK150S DHC	3442/ 3781/6	1958–60	£38,000	£22,000	£18,000
XK150S Coupé	3442/ 3781/6	1958–61	£24,000	£18,000	£10,000

D-Type with competition history considerably more.
Watch out for left- to right-hand-drive conversions in the XK series.

1960 Jaguar Mk II 3.4 Saloon, 3442cc, double-overhead-camshaft 6-cylinder engine.
£4,500–5,400 / €6,700–8,000 / $8,000–9,500 ➤ H&H

1960 Jaguar XK150 Coupé, 3781cc, 6-cylinder engine, stainless steel exhaust, Koni shock absorbers, bumpers missing, in need of mechanical attention.
£10,800–13,000 / 16,000–19,200 / $19,000–22,800 ➤ CGC

1960 Jaguar XK150S Coupé, 3781cc, 6-cylinder engine, 210bhp, finished in British Racing green, green interior, fully restored, concours condition.
£24,700–29,600 / €37,000–44,000
$46,000–55,000 ➤ H&H

1961 Jaguar E-Type, 3781cc, double-overhead-camshaft 6-cylinder engine, hardtop, finished in white, red interior.
£40,000–48,000 / €60,000–72,000
$74,000–89,000 ➤ COYS

1961 Jaguar XK150 Coupé, 3781cc, 6-cylinder engine, original fitted suitcases, in need of some restoration.
£14,900–17,900 / €22,100–26,500
$26,200–32,000 ➤ BRIT
This was the final year of production for the XK150.

1961 Jaguar Mk II 3.4 Saloon, 3442cc, 6-cylinder engine, 4-speed manual gearbox, Vicarage power steering conversion, finished in metallic grey, red interior, excellent condition.
£16,100–19,300 / €23,800–28,600
$28,300–34,000 ➤ H&H

Cross Reference
See Colour Review (page 145-152)

1961 Jaguar Mk II 2.4 Saloon, 2483cc, double-overhead-camshaft 6-cylinder engine, unrestored, interior in need of attention.
£4,000–4,800 / €5,900–7,100 / $7,000–8,400 ➤ H&H
A new generation of more compact Jaguar saloons had come on to the market in 1956, employing unitary construction rather than separate chassis and bodies as before. The Mk II arrived in 1959 and ran until 1967, by which time more than 80,000 examples had been sold.

1963 Jaguar Mk II 3.4 Saloon, 3442cc, 6-cylinder engine, 4-speed manual gearbox, finished in maroon, cream interior.
£8,100–9,700 / €12,000–14,400 / $14,300–17,100 ➤ H&H

◀ **1964 Jaguar S-Type 3.8,** 3781cc, double-overhead-camshaft 6-cylinder engine, 4-speed manual gearbox with overdrive, 4-wheel independent suspension, completely restored 1991, finished in white, red leather interior.
£6,300–7,600 / €9,300–11,200 / $11,100–13,400 ⚒ **BARO**

1964 Jaguar Mk II 3.8 Saloon, 3781cc, 6-cylinder engine, 4-speed manual gearbox with overdrive, finished in British Racing green, tan leather interior.
£12,900–15,500 / €19,100–22,900 $22,700–27,300 ⚒ **H&H**

1964 Jaguar E-Type Series 1 Roadster, 3781cc, double-overhead-camshaft 6-cylinder engine, finished in yellow, black interior, completely rebuilt for competition, 300bhp engine, Getrag 5-speed gearbox, race-spec suspension, Dunlop 15in knock-off wheels, grp bonnet, full roll cage.
£31,000–37,000 / €47,000–56,000 $57,000–68,000 ⚒ **H&H**

1965 Jaguar Mk II 2.4 Saloon, 2483cc, 6-cylinder engine, 4-speed manual gearbox, chrome wire wheels, finished in British Racing green, Motalita wood-rim steering wheel.
£3,750–4,500 / €5,600–6,700 / $6,600–7,900 ⚒ **H&H**

◀ **1965 Jaguar S-Type 3.4 Saloon,** 3442cc, double-overhead-camshaft 6-cylinder engine, 4-speed manual gearbox with overdrive, 4-wheel independent suspension, finished in grey, blue interior, 47,000 miles recorded, original, excellent condition.
£7,300–8,800 / €10,800–13,000 $12,800–15,500 ⚒ **H&H**

1965 Jaguar E-Type Series 1 Coupé, 4235cc, double-overhead-camshaft 6-cylinder engine, Webasto sun roof, finished in black, beige leather interior, completely restored.
£32,000–38,000 / €48,000–57,000 / $59,000–70,000 ⚒ **B(Kn)**

1965 Jaguar Mk II 3.8 Saloon, 3781cc, double-overhead-camshaft 6-cylinder engine, completely restored by Vicarage 1986, cut-down rear wheel spats, finished in white, dark blue leather interior, Daimler Vanden Plas front seats.
£15,000–18,000 / €22,200–26,600
$26,400–32,000 ➤ B(Kn)

1965 Jaguar E-Type Series 1 Coupé, 4235cc, 6-cylinder engine, restored, engine rebuilt, bare-metal respray.
£18,500–22,200 / €27,400–33,000
$27,400–39,000 ➤ H&H

1966 Jaguar E-Type 2+2 Coupé, 4235cc, 6-cylinder engine, stainless steel exhaust, finished in silver-grey, grey leather interior.
£12,800–15,400 / €18,900–22,700
$22,500–27,100 ➤ BRIT

1962 Jaguar 420 Saloon, 4235cc, double-overhead-camshaft 6-cylinder engine, 23,000 miles recorded.
£11,000–13,200 / €16,300–19,500
$19,400–23,200 ➤ CGC
The 420 saloon was built only between 1966 and 1968.

◀ **1967 Jaguar E-Type Series 1½ Coupé,** 4235cc, rebuilt double-overhead-camshaft 6-cylinder engine, triple SU carburettors, converted to unleaded fuel, Getrag 5-speed manual gearbox.
£16,400–19,700 / €24,300–29,200 / $29,500–35,000 ➤ CGC
Compared to the original Series 1 E-Type, the Series 1½ featured more luxurious upholstery and improved cabin space. Less noticeable improvements included the adoption of covers for the boot hinges to prevent them from squashing luggage. The model was known as the Series 1½ because it combined features of the Series 1 and later Series II, which had been designed to accommodate increasingly stringent US regulations.

JAGUAR Model	ENGINE cc/cyl	DATES	CONDITION 1	2	3
E-Type 3.8 flat-floor Roadster (RHD)	3781/6	1961	£40,000+	£30,000	£22,000
E-Type SI 3.8 Roadster	3781/6	1961–64	£35,000	£19,000	£15,000
E-Type 3.8 FHC	3781/6	1961–64	£20,000+	£13,000	£10,000
E-Type SI 4.2 Roadster	4235/6	1964–67	£30,000	£18,000	£14,000
E-Type 2+2 manual FHC	4235/6	1966–67	£16,000+	£11,000	£9,000
E-Type SI 2+2 auto FHC	4235/6	1966–68	£14,000	£10,000	£9,000
E-Type SII Roadster	4235/6	1968–70	£30,000	£21,000	£14,000
E-Type SII FHC	4235/6	1968–70	£18,000	£12,000	£10,000
E-Type SII 2+2 manual FHC	4235/6	1968–70	£15,000	£10,000	£8,000
E-Type SIII Roadster	5343/12	1971–75	£30,000+	£26,000	£17,000
E-Type SIII 2+2 manual FHC	5343/12	1971–75	£14,000	£10,000	£9,000
E-Type SIII 2+2 auto FHC	5343/12	1971–75	£13,000	£9,000	£7,000
XJ6 2.8 Ser I	2793/6	1968–73	£3,000	£1,500	£1,000
XJ6 4.2 Ser I	4235/6	1968–73	£3,500	£2,000	£1,000
XJ6 Coupé	4235/6	1974–78	£8,000	£5,000	£3,500
XJ6 Ser II	4235/6	1973–79	£3,500	£2,000	£750
XJ12 Ser I	5343/12	1972–73	£3,500+	£2,250	£1,500
XJ12 Coupé	5343/12	1973–77	£9,000	£5,000	£3,000
XJ12 Ser II	5343/12	1973–79	£3,000	£2,000	£1,000
XJS manual	5343/12	1975–78	£5,000	£4,000	£2,500
XJS auto	5343/12	1975–81	£4,000	£3,000	£2,000

E-Type Series III Commemorative Roadster fetches more than SIII Roadster – 50 limited editions only.

1967 Jaguar Mk II 2.4 Saloon, 2483cc, double-overhead-camshaft 6-cylinder engine, 4-speed manual gearbox, finished in dark blue, blue interior.
£6,500–7,800 / €9,600–11,500 / $11,400–13,700 ⚡ BARO

1967 Jaguar Mk X Saloon, 4235cc, double-overhead-camshaft 6-cylinder engine, 4-speed manual gearbox, finished in metallic grey, grey leather interior.
£1,950–2,350 / €3,000–3,500 / $3,450–4,150 ⚡ H&H
The Mk X debuted in 1961, and at the time of its launch was easily the most sophisticated Jaguar saloon built. It featured the triple-carburettor 3.8 XK engine from the E-Type, power steering as standard and fully independent suspension. The 4.2 litre version arrived in 1964 and not only had more torque for improved acceleration, but also better power steering.

◀ **1967 Jaguar 340 Saloon,** 3442cc, double-overhead-camshaft 6-cylinder engine, 210bhp.
£6,600–7,900 / €9,800–11,700 / $11,600–13,900 ⚡ COYS

1968 Jaguar 340 Saloon, 3442cc, double-overhead-camshaft 6-cylinder engine, finished in white, blue-grey vinyl interior.
£5,500–6,600 / €8,100–9,800 / $9,700–11,600 ⚡ CGC
The last evolution of the Mk II line, the 240 and 340 models were introduced for 1967. They had new slimline bumpers and a variety of hidden changes, including the E-Type's straight-port cylinder head design.

1968 Jaguar E-Type Series 1½ Coupé, 4235cc, 6-cylinder engine, Weber carburettors, 220bhp, 5-speed Getrag gearbox, totally restored, uprated brakes, widened rear suspension.
£18,100–21,700 / €26,800–32,000
$32,000–38,000 ⚡ H&H

1968 Jaguar E-Type Series 1½ Roadster, 4235cc, double-overhead-camshaft 6-cylinder engine, 264bhp, 4-speed gearbox, 28,000 miles recorded.
£25,400–30,000 / €38,000–45,000 / $47,000–56,000 ⚡ BJ

▶ **1969 Jaguar E-Type Series II Coupé,** 4235cc, double-overhead-camshaft 6-cylinder engine, 3-speed automatic transmission, finished in maroon, beige interior, 61,000 miles recorded.
£15,300–18,400 / €22,600–27,200
$26,900–32,000 ⚡ H&H

1969 Jaguar 420G Saloon, 4235cc, double-overhead-camshaft 6-cylinder engine, air conditioning, finished in black, beige leather interior.
£5,500–6,600 / €8,100–9,800 / $9,700–11,600 ⚹ COYS

1970 Jaguar E-Type Series II Coupé, 4235cc, double-overhead-camshaft 6-cylinder engine, 4-speed manual gearbox, chrome wire wheels, finished in black, black interior, 49,000 miles recorded.
£13,500–16,200 / €20,000–24,000
$23,800–28,500 ⚹ COYS

1972 Jaguar E-Type Series III Coupé, 5343cc, V12 engine, automatic transmission, wire wheels, finished in metallic dark red, black leather interior.
£8,900–10,700 / €13,200–15,800 / $15,700–18,800 ⚹ CGC
By 1971, the E-Type had been in production for a decade. Despite continual improvements, new emissions legislation in the all-important American market threatened to strangle the big cat's performance. Jaguar responded by giving its revered sports car new claws in the shape of a 5343cc V12, which had been developed from the doomed XJ13 Le Mans project car. With some 272bhp on tap, the Series III E-Type once again had 150mph in its sights. A revised wheelbase yielded better cabin space, while wider tracks front and rear, anti-dive front suspension geometry and wider tyres gave improved road-holding.

▶ **1973 Jaguar E-Type Series III Roadster,** 5343cc, V12 engine, power steering, servo-assisted 4-wheel disc brakes, finished in silver, black interior, 58,000 miles recorded.
£29,000–35,000 / €44,000–53,000
$54,000–65,000 ⚹ H&H

1969 Jaguar E-Type Series II Coupé, 4235cc, double-overhead-camshaft 6-cylinder engine, 4-speed manual gearbox, left-hand drive, engine reconditioned, little use since.
£10,000–12,000 / €14,800–17,800
$17,600–21,100 ⚹ COYS

1970 Jaguar E-Type Series II Coupé, 4235cc, double-overhead-camshaft 6-cylinder engine, suspension overhauled, new wire wheels, stainless steel exhaust, resprayed in red, original black interior.
£13,500–16,200 / €20,000–24,000
$23,800–28,500 ⚹ H&H

1973 Jaguar E-Type Series III Coupé, 5343cc, V12 engine, fully restored, finished in red, black interior.
£19,100–22,900 / €28,300–34,000
$34,000–41,000 ⚹ H&H

◀ **1973 Jaguar E-Type Series III Roadster,** 5343cc, V12 engine, 171bhp, automatic transmission, anti-dive front suspension, ventilated front disc brakes, 18-gallon fuel tank, top speed 145mph.
£21,500–25,800
€32,000–39,000
$38,000–48,000 ⚹ COYS

1975 Jaguar XJ6 Saloon, 4235cc, double-overhead-camshaft 6-cylinder engine, 3-speed automatic transmission, finished in grey, green interior, 24,000 miles recorded.
£3,100–3,700 / €4,600–5,500 / $5,500–6,500 🖎 H&H

1983 Jaguar XJ6 Saloon, 4235cc, double-overhead-camshaft 6-cylinder engine, 3-speed automatic transmission, finished in gold, beige interior.
£1,050–1,250 / €1,550–1,850 / $1,850–2,200 🖎 H&H

1984 Jaguar XJS Coupé, 5343cc, double-overhead-camshaft V12 engine, 244bhp, automatic transmission, top speed 142mph.
£3,050–3,650 / €4,500–5,400 / $5,400–6,400 🖎 BJ

1985 Jaguar XJS Cabriolet, 5343cc, double-overhead-camshaft V12 engine, electric windows, air conditioning, cruise control, central locking, rear seat, refurbished wheels, finished in red, magnolia leather interior.
£4,750–5,700 / €7,000–8,400 / $8,400–10,000 🖎 CGC

1985 Jaguar XJ12 Sovereign Saloon, 5343cc, double-overhead-camshaft V12 engine, sunroof, correct 'pepperpot' alloy wheels, finished in maroon, tan leather interior.
£9,200–11,100 / €13,600–16,300 $16,200–19,500 🖎 COYS

1986 Jaguar XJS 3.6 Coupé, 3590cc, double-overhead-camshaft 24-valve 6-cylinder engine, automatic transmission, finished in red, black leather interior, 59,000 miles recorded.
£4,150–5,000 / €6,200–7,400 / $7,400–8,800 🖎 CGC
Introduced in 1983, the XJS 3.6 was intended to be a sharper, more sporting foil to the established 5.3 litre model. It was fitted with a Getrag five-speed manual gearbox as standard. With some 225bhp on tap courtesy of its 3590cc, double-overhead-camshaft straight-six engine, it had a 140mph top speed and a 0–60mph time of 7.4 seconds. Yet it could return 30mpg. The brand-new engine also had the advantage of being considerably lighter than the V12. This allowed Jaguar to alter the suspension spring rates to give notably better turn-in and less body roll. A revised, more positive feel to the power steering improved the handling still further. Available as either a coupé or cabriolet, the 3.6 was a strong seller.

1987 Jaguar XJS Coupé, 5343cc, double-overhead-camshaft V12 engine, automatic transmission, finished in metallic dark red, cream leather interior.
£2,850–3,400 / €4,200–5,000 / $5,000–6,000 🖎 H&H

▶ **1988 Jaguar XJS TWR Coupé,** 6000cc, double-overhead-camshaft V12 engine, 4-speed automatic transmission, finished in metallic grey, cream interior.
£2,650–3,200 / €4,000–4,750 $4,650–5,600 🖎 H&H
This car has been modified by Tom Walkinshaw Racing.

1988 Jaguar Sovereign HE Saloon, 5300cc, V12 engine, air conditioning, electric sun roof, cruise control, finished in green, doeskin leather interior.
£1,250–1,500 / €1,850–2,200 / $2,200–2,650 ✒ BARO
The six-cylinder 4.2 litre Series III XJ6 went out of production in 1987, but the 5.3 litre V12 model remained on the Jaguar list until 1993, when it was finally replaced by the 6 litre V12 XJ40.

1989 Jaguar XJR 3.6 Saloon, 3590cc, double-overhead-camshaft 6-cylinder engine, 4-speed automatic transmission, uprated suspension, body kit, finished in metallic blue, cream leather interior.
£3,200–3,850 / €4,750–5,700 / $5,700–6,800 ✒ H&H

1990 Jaguar XJS 3.6 Coupé, 3590cc, V12 engine, alloy wheels, TWR body kit, finished in metallic red, magnolia leather interior.
£4,250–5,100 / €6,300–7,500 / $7,500–9,000 ✒ BARO
The XJS remained in production until the early 1990s. This car is one of the last of the 3.6 models.

▶ **1996 Jaguar XJ6 Chasseur 450 Tornado,** 450bhp, ZF manual gearbox, push-button gear-change, Race Logic traction control, lowered suspension, 5-spoke alloy wheels.
£20,600–24,700 / €30,000–36,000
$36,000–43,000 ✒ COYS
This car cost a staggering £95,000 / €143,000 $176,000 when new.

1988 Jaguar XJSC Cabriolet, 4522cc, V12 engine, automatic transmission, hardtop, left-hand drive, c50,000 miles recorded, excellent condition.
£4,450–5,300 / €6,600–7,800 / $7,800–9,300 ✒ BJ

1990 Jaguar XJS Cabriolet, 5343cc, double-overhead-camshaft V12 engine, 4-speed automatic transmission, finished in dark grey, black interior.
£4,300–5,100 / €6,400–7,500 / $7,600–9,000 ✒ H&H

1993 Jaguar XJS Coupé, 5993cc, V12 engine, automatic transmission, finished in red, magnolia leather interior.
£4,750–5,700 / €7,000–8,400 / $8,400–10,000 ✒ H&H

◀ **1998 Jaguar XJ220 Sports,** 3498cc, double-overhead-camshaft 24-valve V6 engine, twin turbochargers, 542bhp, 5-speed manual gearbox.
£88,000–105,000 / €132,000–155,000
$163,000–194,000 ✒ H&H
Jaguar pitched the XJ220 directly at the Ferrari F40 and Porsche 959, the prototype being unveiled in 1988. It was powered by a 530bhp, 48-valve V12 engine with four-wheel drive. Following the take-over of Jaguar by Ford, XJ220 production was entrusted to Tom Walkinshaw in 1992. TWR replaced the V12 with a twin-turbo V6, which had been developed in the Group C XJR-10 race programme and was just as powerful. At the same time, the prototype's four-wheel-drive system was replaced by rear-wheel drive.

Jensen *(British 1935–92)*

The Jensen marque was created by brothers Allen and Richard Jensen, who had made their names in the motor industry as stylists and coachbuilders during the late 1920s.

They had begun by rebodying a 1923 Austin Chummy as a more sporting two-seater, which they took to a Shelsley Walsh hill climb. There, it was seen by Arthur Wilde, chief engineer of the Standard Motor Company, who was sufficiently impressed to ask the Jensens to build a similar body on a Standard Nine chassis. Completed in 1928, this was so well received that Allen Jensen was recruited by specialist coachbuilder Avon Bodies, resulting in a production version, the Avon Standard.

Subsequently, the brothers worked for Edgbaston Garages, where their hard work and engineering talent saw them join the board of directors. Then they moved to W.J. Smith & Sons as joint managing directors. In 1934, they took over the company and renamed it Jensen Motors, building bodies for a wide range of cars.

Next they began work on the first car to carry the Jensen name. A luxuriously equipped, four-seat tourer powered by a 3.6 litre Ford V8 engine, it appeared in 1935. Clark Gable was one of the first to buy one, and the car was soon in demand.

Besides Ford engines, Jensen put Nash and Lincoln engines in its cars in the period leading up to the outbreak of WWII in 1939. During the war, it built ambulances, fire engines, amphibious tank conversions and even a high-speed bulk carrier.

Jensen's first post-war design, the PW saloon, was launched in 1946. It employed a Nash engine, although originally the company had intended building its own power unit. This car led to dealings with Austin, which supplied Jensen with a batch of 4 litre Sheerline engines. Another project was the 1950 Austin A40 Sports, for which Jensen built around 3,500 bodies.

Then, in 1953, Jensen launched the fibreglass-bodied 541, a GT saloon capable of 115 mph. In addition, the company was still undertaking outside work, including building bodies for Austin-Healey and Volvo.

In 1963, the 541 was replaced by the CV8, powered by a 5.9 litre Chrysler V8, with a choice of manual or automatic transmission and a top

speed of over 130mph. There was also the CV8FF, with four-wheel drive and anti-lock brakes.

By then, the Jensen brothers were approaching retirement. Allen resigned as an executive director in 1963, but stayed on the board, while Richard quit as chairman three years later, before leaving the board completely in 1967.

Kevin Beattie had taken over as chief designer in 1960 and was the man behind Jensen's most famous 'modern' car, the Interceptor. This was introduced in 1966 with a Vignale styled and built body, and a 6.2 litre Chrysler V8 engine. It was capable of 140mph; in FF guise, it remained in production until 1972.

However, just as the Interceptor arrived, so Jensen's financial problems began. At that time, by far the biggest chunk of the company's turnover came through building car bodies for other firms, notably the Rootes Group, and in 1967 Jensen made a loss in this area of the business. Subsequently, American car dealer Kjell Qvale bought a major shareholding, and appointed Donald Healey and his son, Geoffrey, to the Jensen board.

The Healeys set about producing a replacement for the Austin-Healey in an attempt to provide Jensen with a volume car to build alongside its exclusive and expensive Interceptor. Known as the Jensen-Healey, it debuted in 1972, by which time Jensen was back in profit. The prototype employed a 2.3 litre, overhead-camshaft, Vauxhall four-cylinder engine, but the production version came with a 16-valve Lotus four. This power unit proved unreliable, and customers didn't buy the car in sufficient numbers to make the project a commercial success.

But worse was to come. The onset of the oil crisis in 1974 and serious unrest among the workforce saw Jensen in the red again, and in late 1975, it went into receivership.

The following year, the receiver set up the Jensen Parts & Service organisation, later renamed International Motor Importers. This handled UK imports for companies such as Hyundai, Maserati and Subaru.

In 1983, besides continuing to service and restore Jensens, IMI announced that it could build to order a limited number of new Interceptors, exact replicas of the 1972 version.

1956 Jensen 541, 3993cc, 6-cylinder engine, 4-speed manual gearbox, grp bodywork, finished in red, cream interior.
£6,400–7,700 / € 9,500–11,400 / $11,300–13,600 ⚡ H&H

1964 Jensen CV8, 6276cc, Chrysler V8 engine, automatic transmission, extensively restored 1999, little use since, new engine, finished in dark metallic green, beige leather interior.
£9,200–11,000 / € 13,600–16,300
$16,200–19,400 ⚡ B(Kn)

1971 Jensen Interceptor Mk II, 6276cc, Chrysler V8 engine, 325bhp, automatic transmission, left-hand-drive, unrestored.
£5,100–6,100 / €7,500–9,000 / $9,000–10,700 ➚ B(Kn)

1971 Jensen Interceptor Mk II, 6276cc, Chrysler V8 engine, restored 1998–2002, resprayed in blue, beige leather interior.
£8,500–10,200 / €12,600–15,100
$15,000–18,000 ➚ BARO

1974 Jensen Interceptor Mk III Convertible, 7212cc, V8 engine, automatic transmission, finished in blue, tan interior.
£17,200–20,600 / €25,500–30,000
$30,000–36,000 ➚ H&H

1990 Jensen Interceptor Mk IV Convertible, 5910cc, Chrysler V8 engine, fuel injection replaced by carburettors, finished in blue, magnolia leather interior, 19,000 miles recorded, 1 of only 4 Mk IV convertibles built.
£31,000–37,000 / €47,000–56,000
$57,000–68,000 ➚ H&H

JENSEN Model	ENGINE cc/cyl	DATES	CONDITION 1	2	3
541/541R/541S	3993/6	1954–63	£13,000	£7,000	£4,500
CV8 Mk I–III	5916/				
	6276/8	1962–66	£14,000	£7,000	£6,000
Interceptor Ser I–III	6276/8	1967–76	£9,000	£5,500	£4,000
Interceptor DHC	6276/8	1973–76	£22,000	£15,000	£10,000
Interceptor SP	7212/8	1971–76	£12,000	£8,000	£5,000
FF	6766/8	1967–71	£15,000	£10,000	£7,000

CV8 and 541 are particularly sought after.

Jensen-Healey *(British 1972–76)*

1975 Jensen-Healey, 1973cc, Lotus double-overhead-camshaft 4-cylinder engine, Getrag 5-speed manual gearbox, finished in bronze, black interior.
£1,750–2,100 / €2,600–3,100 / $3,100–3,700 ➚ H&H

1976 Jensen-Healey GT, 1973cc, 4-cylinder engine, 5-speed manual gearbox, 4-wheel disc brakes, air conditioning, 2 owners from new, fewer than 43,000 miles recorded.
£1,600–1,900 / €2,350–2,800 / $2,800–3,350 ➚ BJ

JENSEN-HEALEY Model	ENGINE cc/cyl	DATES	CONDITION 1	2	3
Healey	1973/4	1972–76	£4,500	£3,000	£1,500
Healey GT	1973/4	1975–76	£5,000	£3,000	£2,000

Jowett (British 1906–53)

◀ **1952 Jowett Jupiter,** 1486cc, flat-4 engine, 4-speed manual gearbox with column gear-change, restored 1998, finished in red, leather interior.
£14,000–16,800 / €20,700–24,900 $24,600–29,600 ⨍ **H&H**

Lagonda (British 1908–)

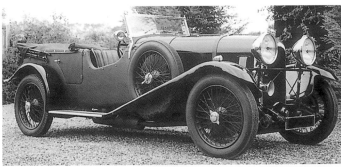

1932 Lagonda 2 Litre Supercharged Low Chassis Tourer, 1954cc, 4-cylinder engine, Zoller supercharger, SU carburettor, older restoration.
£35,000–42,000 / €53,000–63,000 / $65,000–78,000 ⨍ **B(Kn)**

> A known continuous history can add value to and enhance the enjoyment of a car.

1934 Lagonda M45 Rapide Close-Coupled Pillarless Saloon, coachwork by Gurney Nutting, 4429cc, 6-cylinder engine, 1 of only 6 fitted with Gurney Nutting coachwork, fully restored, concours condition.
£43,000–51,000 / €65,000–77,000 $80,000–94,000 ⨍ **B(Kn)**
This car was exhibited by Lagonda at Olympia in 1934. With pillarless saloon coachwork, it was offered at £1,250 / €1,850 / $2,200 and was the most expensive car on the stand by a considerable margin.

1936 Lagonda LG45 Tourer, 4429cc, 6-cylinder engine, wire wheels, finished in grey, red leather interior, fully restored, concours condition.
£43,000–52,000 / €65,000–78,000 $80,000–96,000 ⨍ **BRIT**

LAGONDA Model	ENGINE cc/cyl	DATES	CONDITION 1	2	3
12/24	1421/4	1923–26	£14,000	£10,000	£8,000
2 Litre	1954/4	1928–32	£28,000	£25,000	£19,000
3 Litre	2931/6	1928–34	£40,000+	£30,000	£22,000
Rapier	1104/4	1934–35	£15,000	£9,000	£5,000
M45	4429/6	1934–36	£50,000+	£30,000	£20,000
LG45	4429/6	1936–37	£45,000+	£32,000	£22,000
LG6	4453/6	1937–39	£40,000+	£28,000	£20,000
V12	4480/V12	1937–39	£75,000+	£50,000	£25,000

Prices are dependent upon body type, dhc or saloon, originality and competition history.

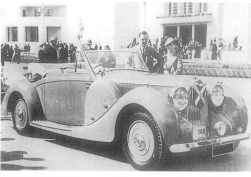

1938 Lagonda V12 Drophead Coupé, 4480cc, V12 engine, completely restored at a cost of c£300,000 / €444,000 / $555,000.
£70,000–84,000
€105,000–126,000
$130,000–155,000 ↗ COYS
This car was sold new to Lord Waleran. He drove it with success in a number of rallies. Subsequently, it appeared in Lagonda's advertising.

1938 Lagonda V12, 4480cc, V12 engine, 180bhp, finished in grey and royal blue, grey leather interior.
£20,600–24,700 / €30,000–37,000
$36,000–46,000 ↗ COYS
The prototype V12 made its debut in 1936.

1938 Lagonda LG6 Short Chassis Drophead Coupé, 4453cc, Meadows 6-cylinder engine, 4-speed manual gearbox, independent torsion-bar front suspension, Lockheed hydraulic drum brakes.
£61,000–74,000 / €93,000–111,000
$115,000–137,000 ↗ CGC

Restored values

The cost of a professional restoration will have an influence on, but no direct relation to, a car's market value.
A restored car can have a market value lower than the cost of its restoration.

▶ **1939 Lagonda V12 Saloon,** 4480cc, V12 engine, sun roof, fully restored late 1990s, converted to 4-carburettor set-up.
£25,300–30,000 / €38,000–45,000
$47,000–56,000 ↗ COYS

1962 Lagonda Rapide Four-Door Saloon, 3995cc, double-overhead-camshaft 6-cylinder engine, 3-speed automatic transmission, dual-circuit 4-wheel disc brakes, finished in blue, cream leather interior. 1 of only 55 built.
£22,000–26,500 / € 33,000–40,000 $39,000–49,000 ↗ H&H

1964 Lagonda Rapide Four-Door Saloon, 3995cc, double-overhead-camshaft 6-cylinder engine, twin SU carburettors, finished in metallic green, magnolia leather interior.
£12,900–15,500 / € 19,100–22,900 $22,700–27,300 ↗ H&H

LAGONDA (post-war) Model	ENGINE cc/cyl	DATES	CONDITION		
			1	2	3
3 Litre	2922/6	1953–58	£10,500	£7,000	£4,500
3 Litre DHC	2922/6	1953–56	£17,000	£12,000	£9,000
Rapide	3995/6	1961–64	£11,000+	£7,000	£4,500

Lamborghini *(Italian 1963–)*

1965 Lamborghini 350GT, 3500cc, double-overhead-camshaft V12 engine, 280bhp, 5-speed all-synchromesh gearbox, 4-wheel disc brakes, 4-wheel independent suspension, top speed 165mph.
£33,000–40,000 / € 49,000–59,000 $59,000–70,000 ↗ COYS

1967 Lamborghini 350GT, coachwork by Touring, 3500cc, double-overhead-camshaft V12 engine, 1 of 143 built.
£26,000–31,000 / € 38,000–45,000 $46,000–55,000 ↗ B(Kn)

1967 Lamborghini 400GT 2+2, 4000cc, double-overhead-camshaft V12 engine, 6 Weber 40DCOE carburettors, 320bhp, 5-speed manual gearbox, top speed 175mph, fully restored.
£38,000–46,000 / € 57,000–68,000 / $67,000–81,000 ↗ BB(S)

▶ **1970 Lamborghini Miura S,** 4000cc, double-overhead-camshaft V12 engine, 375bhp, top speed 180mph, finished in red, white leather interior.
£52,000–62,000 € 77,000–92,000 $91,000–109,000 ↗ COYS

1971 Lamborghini Miura P400S Jota Spyder, coachwork by Bertone/Lambomotor, 4000cc, double-overhead-camshaft V12 engine, resprayed in silver over grey, black and grey leather interior.
£59,000–71,000 / €88,000–105,000 / $104,000–125,000 ➤ B(Mon)
Lamborghini's challenge to Ferrari began in 1964 with the 350GT, but it was the arrival of the Miura that established Lamborghini as a major manufacturer of luxury sporting cars. Initial Miura development concentrated on chassis strengthening, the improvements being consolidated in the S version introduced in 1968. The Miura S featured a more powerful 375bhp engine. There was also a solitary competition version. Brainchild of Lamborghini development engineer Bob Wallace and known as the Jota, it featured light-alloy bodywork, plastic side windows, racing suspension, Campagnolo magnesium wheels and a 440bhp engine. Sadly, it was destroyed in a crash in 1972. Inspired by Bertone's one-off open-top Miura Roadster of 1968, this car features Jota-style bodywork and special suspension. It was built as a Jota Spyder by Swiss company Lambomotor.

LAMBORGHINI Model	ENGINE cc/cyl	DATES	CONDITION 1	2	3
350 GT FHC	3500/12	1964–67	£55,000+	£45,000	£25,000
400 GT	4000/12	1966–68	£50,000	£40,000	£25,000
Miura LP400	4000/12	1966–69	£70,000	£50,000	£30,000
Miura S	4000/12	1969–71	£75,000	£60,000+	£40,000
Miura SV	4000/12	1971–72	£90,000+	£75,000	£60,000
Espada	4000/12	1969–78	£12,000+	£10,000	£7,000
Jarama	4000/12	1970–78	£15,000+	£13,000	£11,000
Urraco	2500/8	1972–76	£12,000+	£10,000	£8,000
Countach	4000/12	1974–82	£60,000+	£40,000	£30,000

Countach limited editions are sought after as well as Miura SV.

1973 Lamborghini P250 Urraco, 2463cc, V8 engine, completely rebuilt, interior retrimmed in grey leather.
£10,100–12,100 / €14,900–17,900 $17,800–21,300 ➤ BRIT

1974 Lamborghini Urraco, 2463cc, transverse-mounted V8 engine, 5-speed gearbox, in need of some recommissioning.
£6,100–7,300 / €9,000–10,800 / $10,700–12,800 ➤ COYS
Lamborghini expected the Urraco to sell in relatively large numbers, but it entered production just as the 1970s oil crisis began to bite and only 520 examples were sold.

Lanchester *(British 1895–1956)*

◀ **1938 Lanchester 14/6 Coupé,** coachwork by Charlesworth, 1809cc, 6-cylinder engine, 4-speed pre-selector gearbox, finished in black and blue, 57,000 miles recorded.
£4,000–4,800 / €5,900–7,100 $7,000–8,400 ➤ H&H
Frederick Lanchester was one of the pioneers of the British car industry. He and his younger brother, George, were known for innovative and high-quality engineering. Their company became a victim of the depression of the early 1930s and was absorbed by the giant BSA group in 1931. From then on, there were many similarities between Lanchester models and those of Daimler, which was another member of the group.

LANCHESTER Model	ENGINE cc/cyl	DATES	CONDITION		
			1	2	3
LD10	1287/4	1946–49	£2,500	£1,500	£750
LD10 (Barker bodies)	1287/4	1950–51	£2,800	£1,500	£700

Lancia (Italian 1906–)

1935 Lancia Astura 3rd Series Limousine, 2604cc, V8 engine, sliding-pillar independent front suspension, finished in dark blue, original grey cloth interior.
£30,000–36,000 / €44,000–53,000 $53,000–63,000 ⚒ B(Mon)
The Astura series was built from 1931 until 1939.

1937 Lancia Aprilia Four-Door Saloon, 1352cc, V4 engine, independent front suspension, older restoration, in need of minor mechanical attention.
£4,900–5,900 / €7,300–8,700 / $8,600–10,400 ⚒ B(Kn)
The Aprilia went into production early in 1937. It was a compact model with seating for five, and combined speed with economy. The aerodynamic saloon was of unitary construction, and featured sliding-pillar front suspension, transverse-leaf trailing-arm rear suspension and a 1352cc V4 engine, which developed 47.8bhp.

1954 Lancia Aurelia B20 4th Series Coupé, coachwork by Pininfarina, 1754cc, V6 engine, finished in beige with matching interior.
£22,700–27,200 / €34,000–40,000 $40,000–48,000 ⚒ BB(S)
Launched in 1950, the Aurelia was the first car ever to employ a V6 engine. The 1754cc 60-degree V6 was of all-aluminium construction and had overhead valves operated by short pushrods instead of Lancia's traditional overhead camshafts. An advanced unitary-construction design, the Aurelia retained Lancia's sliding-pillar independent front suspension, but used a novel semi-trailing-arm layout at the rear. The transmission was also unusual, comprising a two-piece propshaft and combined gearbox/rear transaxle with inboard brakes were mounted.

1954 Lancia Aurelia B20 GT 4th Series Coupé, coachwork by Pininfarina, 2451cc, V6 engine, Nardi-type high-lift camshaft, Weber 40DCZ carburettor with modified chokes, Nardi floor-mounted gear-change, de Dion rear suspension, completely restored early 1990s.
€30,000–36,000 / €44,000–53,000 $53,000–63,000 ⚒ B(Kn)

LANCIA Model	ENGINE cc/cyl	DATES	CONDITION 1	2	3
Theta	4940/4	1913–19	£24,000	£16,500	£8,000
Kappa	4940/4	1919–22	£24,000	£16,000	£8,000
Dikappa	4940/4	1921–22	£24,000	£16,000	£8,000
Trikappa	4590/4	1922–26	£25,000	£18,000	£10,000
Lambda	2120/4	1923–28	£40,000	£20,000	£12,000
Dilambda	3960/8	1928–32	£35,000	£16,000	£10,000
Astura	2604/8	1931–39	£30,000	£20,000	£10,000
Artena	1925/4	1931–36	£9,000	£5,000	£2,000
Augusta	1196/4	1933–36	£9,000	£4,000	£2,000
Aprilia 238	1352/4	1937–39	£10,000	£5,000	£3,000

Coachbuilt bodywork is more desirable and can increase prices.

1974 Lancia Fulvia 1.3S Coupé, 1298cc, V4 engine, 5-speed manual gearbox, front-wheel drive, 4-wheel disc brakes, finished in black, beige interior, fully restored, blueprinted engine, 53,000 miles recorded.
£4,500–5,400 / €6,700–8,000 / $7,900–9,500 ✦ H&H

1990 Lancia Delta HF Integrale, 1995cc, double-overhead-camshaft 16-valve 4-cylinder engine, turbocharger, 4-wheel drive, finished in red, grey interior, engine rebuilt.
£4,100–4,900 / €6,100–7,300 / $7,200–8,600 ✦ BARO

LANCIA Model	ENGINE cc/cyl	DATES	CONDITION 1	2	3
Aprilia 438	1486/4	1939–50	£11,000	£6,000	£3,000
Ardea	903/4	1939–53	£10,000	£5,000	£3,000
Aurelia B10	1754/6	1950–53	£9,000	£6,000	£3,000
Aurelia B15–20–22	1991/6	1951–53	£15,000+	£10,000	£8,000
Aurelia B24–B24 Spyder	2451/6	1955–58	£40,000+	£17,000	£12,000
Aurelia GT	2451/6	1953–59	£18,000+	£11,000	£9,000
Appia C10–C105	1090/4	1953–62	£10,000	£5,000	£2,000
Aurelia Ser II/IV	2266/6	1954–59	£11,000	£6,000	£4,000
Flaminia Zagato	2458/6	1957–63	£20,000+	£12,000	£7,000
Flaminia	2458/6	1957–63	£18,000	£10,000	£5,000
Flavia 1500	1500/4	1960–75	£6,000	£4,000	£2,000
Fulvia	1091/4	1963–70	£3,000	£2,000	£1,000
Fulvia S	1216/4	1964–70	£5,000	£4,000	£1,500
Fulvia 1.3	1298/4	1967–75	£6,000	£4,000	£2,000
Stratos	2418/6	1969–71	£50,000+	£20,000+	£10,000
Flavia 2000	1991/4	1969–75	£3,000	£2,000	£1,000
Fulvia HF/1.6	1584/4	1969–75	£9,000	£5,000	£2,000
Beta HPE	1585/4	1976–82	£3,000	£1,500	£500
Beta Spyder	1995/4	1977–82	£4,000	£1,500	£800
Monte Carlo	1995/4	1976–81	£6,000	£3,000	£1,000
Gamma Coupé	2484/4	1977–84	£2,500	£1,500	£500
Gamma Berlina	2484/4	1977–84	£2,500	£1,200	£300

Competition history and convertible coachwork could cause prices to vary.
Zagato coachwork striking and sometimes pricey.

Land Rover *(British 1948–)*

LAND ROVER Model	ENGINE cc/cyl	DATES	CONDITION 1	2	3
Ser 1	1595/4	1948–51	£6,000	£3,000	£1,500
Ser 1	1995/4	1951–53	£4,500	£2,500	£1,000
Ser 1	1995/4	1953–58	£4,000	£2,000	£500
Ser 1	1995/4	1953–58	£3,000	£1,800	£800
Ser 2	1995/4	1958–59	£2,000	£950	£500
Ser 2	1995/4	1958–59	£2,800	£1,200	£500
Ser 2	2286/4	1959–71	£2,000	£950	£500
Ser 2	2286/4	1959–71	£2,500	£1,200	£500

Series 1 Land Rovers are very sought after.

1950 Land Rover Series 1 Station Wagon, 1595cc, 4-cylinder engine, 80in (203.2cm) wheelbase, older restoration, new steering box.
£11,200–13,400 / €16,600–19,800
$19,700–23,600 ⟶ B(Kn)
The seven-seat estate car/station wagon was manufactured between 1948 and 1951. Being classed as a passenger car, it was subject to punitive purchase tax.

1958 Land Rover Series 2, 2052cc, 4-cylinder diesel engine, 109in (276.9cm) wheelbase, factory heater, oil and water gauges, electrics updated with flashing indicators and alternator charging, finished in green, grey Rexine upholstery.
£2,200–2,600 / €3,250–3,850 / $3,850–4,600 ⟶ B(Kn)

▶ **c1974 Land Rover Air Portable 88 Series III,** 3528cc, V8 petrol engine, hardtop with side windows, one-piece windscreen, triple front wipers, rear wash-wipe, alloy wing extensions, civilian-type dash panel, Land Rover deluxe seats, carpets and door trims, finished in metallic blue.
£3,200–4,900 / €4,750–5,600 / $5,600–6,700 ⟶ B(Kn)

Lea-Francis
(British 1903–60, 1980–)

Despite building its first car in 1903, it was not until the 1922 announcement of a new 9hp chassis that Lea-Francis could truly be classified as a notable manufacturer. Once firmly established, however, the marque lost little time in embarking upon an impressive competition programme, which led to such fine sports cars as the 14/40, Ace of Spades and Hyper. Closing its doors temporarily in 1935, the company was invigorated by the arrival of Riley designer Hugo Rose in 1937; for 1938, fresh 12hp and 14hp models were announced. With styling that bore a close resemblance to contemporary SS Jaguars and powered by Rose designed, Riley-esque, twin-cam four-cylinder engines of 1496cc and

1629cc respectively, the new 12/14hp cars proved sufficiently advanced to form the basis of an immediate post-WWII range. Equipped with all-round leaf-sprung suspension (an independent torsion-bar set-up was soon made optional for the front), its ladder chassis had four-wheel drum brakes and was powered by an enlarged 1767cc version of the twin-cam engine. Connaught chose the same engine for its A-type racers.
Suitably modified, it produced 135bhp at 6,600rpm, but the Lea-Francis 14hp produced just 65bhp. Driving the rear wheels via a four-speed, all-syncromesh gearbox, this more modest figure still translated into a top speed of over 70mph.

Auction prices
Miller's only includes cars declared sold. Our guide prices take into account the buyer's premium, VAT on the premium, and the extent of any published catalogue information relating to condition and provenance. Cars sold at auction are identified by the ⟶ icon; full details of the auction house can be found on page 251.

◀ **1949 Lea-Francis 14hp Sports Saloon,** 1767cc, double-overhead-camshaft 4-cylinder engine, sun roof, completely restored.
£5,300–6,400 / €7,800–9,500
$9,300–11,300 ⟶ CGC

LEA-FRANCIS Model	ENGINE cc/cyl	DATES	CONDITION 1	2	3
12hp	1944/4	1923–24	£10,000	£5,000	£3,000
14hp	2297/4	1923–24	£10,000	£5,000	£3,000
9hp	1074/4	1923–24	£7,000	£4,000	£2,000
10hp	1247/4	1947–54	£10,000	£5,500	£3,000
12hp	1496/4	1926–34	£12,000	£6,000	£4,000
Various 6-cylinder models	1696/6	1927–29	£13,500	£9,500	£5,000
Various 6-cylinder models	1991/6	1928–36	£10,500	£8,750	£5,000
14hp	1767/4	1946–54	£10,000	£6,000	£4,000
1.5 Litre	1499/4	1949–51	£11,000	£6,000	£3,000
2.5 Litre	2496/4	1950–52	£14,000	£8,000	£4,000

Lincoln (American 1920–)

LINCOLN Model	ENGINE cu in/cyl	DATES	CONDITION 1	2	3
Premiere Coupé	368/8	1956–57	£6,000	£4,000	£2,000
Premiere Convertible	368/8	1956–57	£14,000	£8,000	£5,000
Continental Mk II	368/8	1956–57	£10,000	£6,000	£4,000
Continental 2-door	430/8	1958–60	£6,000	£4,000	£2,000
Continental Convertible	430/8	1958–60	£18,000+	£10,000+	£7,000+

◄ **1927 Lincoln Model L Roadster,** 357.8cu.in, side-valve V8 engine, 90bhp, 3-speed manual gearbox, transverse leaf-spring suspension, shaft drive, wood-spoked artillery wheels, unrestored, engine in need of attention.
£20,900–20,100 / €31,000–38,100
$37,000–46,000 ➤ BB(S)

1947 Lincoln Continental Convertible, 430cu.in, side-valve V12 engine, 3-speed manual gearbox with overdrive, 4-wheel hydraulic drum brakes.
£26,100–31,000 / €39,000–46,000
$46,000–55,000 ➤ BB(S)

◄ **1954 Lincoln Capri Hardtop,** 317.5cu.in, overhead-valve V8 engine, 205bhp, 4-barrel Holley carburettor, automatic transmission.
£4,550–5,500 / €6,700–8,100 / $8,000–9,600 ➤ BB(S)

Lotus (British 1948)

1958 Lotus Eleven Series 2 Le Mans, 1500cc, Coventry Climax FWB 4-cylinder engine, de Dion rear axle, inboard disc brakes.
£55,000–65,000 / €82,000–96,000
$97,000–114,000 🚗 HLR

1962 Lotus Elite S, 1216cc, Coventry Climax all-aluminium double-overhead-camshaft engine, finished in white, black interior, 1 owner for 33 years.
£17,800–21,800 / €26,300–32,000
$31,000–37,000 ➤ COYS

1966 Lotus Elan S2, 1558cc, double-overhead-camshaft 4-cylinder engine, 4-wheel disc brakes, 4-wheel independent suspension, rack-and-pinion steering, new alloy wheels, finished in blue over silver, black interior.
£5,600–6,700 / €8,300–9,900 / $9,900–11,800 ➤ B(Kn)

1967 Lotus Elan S3 SE, 1558cc, double-overhead-camshaft 4-cylinder engine, big-valve conversion, original Weber carburettors, finished in British Racing green, original black interior, concours condition.
£9,700–11,600 / €14,400–17,200 $17,200–20,600 ➤ BB(S)

1968 Lotus Elan +2, 1558cc, double-overhead-camshaft 4-cylinder engine, 4-speed manual gearbox, steel backbone chassis, grp bodywork, brakes and suspension overhauled, finished in yellow, black interior.
£3,850–4,600 / €5,700–6,800 / $6,800–8,100 ➤ H&H

1972 Lotus Europa John Player Special, 1558cc, double-overhead-camshaft 4-cylinder engine, completely restored over 4 years, concours condition.
£15,800–18,900 / €23,400–28,000 $27,800–33,000 ➤ COYS

1973 Lotus Elan Sprint, 1558cc, double-overhead-camshaft 4-cylinder engine, converted to unleaded fuel, gearbox rebuilt, finished in red, gold and white, black interior.
£14,900–17,800 / €22,100–26,300 $26,200–31,000 ➤ BRIT

1987 Lotus Excel SE, 2174cc, double-overhead-camshaft 4-cylinder engine, 5-speed manual gearbox, air conditioning, finished in metallic British Racing green, magnolia leather interior.
£2,750–3,300 / €4,100–4,900 / $4,850–5,800 ➤ BARO

 Miller's Milestones

Lotus Elan (1962–74)
Price range: £3,000–15,000 / €4,450–22,200 / $5,250–26,400
The forerunner of the Lotus Elan was the Elite, but although it was a good car, it proved too specialized to build at a profit – and it was plagued by a host of problems. Lotus needed something simpler, less ambitious, but still sporty – and the Elan delivered on all three counts. Like the Elite, the Elan employed a fibreglass body, but it was mounted on a backbone chassis sprung by ingenious Chapman-conceived struts, which combined ride comfort with superb agility. And there would be no more Coventry-Climax engines. Instead, Lotus built its own twin-cam, four-cylinder 1558cc unit, based on a Ford block, which produced 106bhp. In the lightweight Elan, this gave impressive performance.
There is absolutely no doubt that the Elan built Lotus's reputation during the late 1960s and early 1970s. That said, it was not perfect, build quality always being questionable, but most owners didn't mind, simply because no other car came close to the driving experience for the money. The S2 variant of 1964 featured centre-lock wheels instead of the previous discs, while the 1966 S3 had a higher final-drive ratio together with a close-ratio gearbox.
The SE (Special Equipment) Elan offered 115bhp, close-ratio gears and servo-assisted brakes. Next came the S3 SE (1968) with wider wheel arches – needed to accommodate low-profile rubber. For 1970, the power was upped to 126bhp in the big-valve Sprint model, some of which came with five-speed gearboxes. The Elan also spawned the Elan +2 and 2+2 versions, giving the car a wider appeal.
Production finally ended in 1973 to make way for the new Elite, but this move up market wasn't particularly successful.

LOTUS Model	ENGINE cc/cyl	DATES	CONDITION 1	2	3
Six		1953–56	£13,000+	£7,000+	£5,000+
Elite	1172/4	1957–63	£22,000+	£15,000+	£10,000
7 S1 Sports	1172/4	1957–64	£12,000+	£9,000+	£5,000+
7 S2 Sports	1498/4	1961–66	£10,000+	£8,000+	£5,000+
7 S3 Sports	1558/4	1961–66	£13,000+	£8,000+	£5,000+
7 S4	1598/4	1969–72	£8,000	£5,000	£3,000
Elan S1 Convertible	1558/4	1962–64	£12,000+	£8,000	£4,500
Elan S2 Convertible	1558/4	1964–66	£12,000+	£7,000	£4,000
Elan S3 Convertible	1558/4	1966–69	£12,000+	£8,000	£5,000
Elan S3 FHC	1558/4	1966–69	£13,000	£7,000	£5,000
Elan S4 Convertible	1558/4	1968–71	£14,000+	£9,500	£7,000
Elan S4 FHC	1558/4	1968–71	£10,000+	£7,500	£5,000
Elan Sprint Convertible	1558/4	1971–73	£15,000+	£8,500+	£7,000
Elan Sprint FHC	1558/4	1971–73	£10,000+	£7,000	£6,000
Europa S1 FHC	1470/4	1966–69	£4,000+	£3,500	£2,000
Europa S2 FHC	1470/4	1969–71	£5,500+	£3,000	£2,000
Europa Twin Cam	1558/4	1971–75	£8,000	£6,000	£4,000
Elan +2S 130	1558/4	1971–74	£8,000	£5,000	£4,000
Elite S1 FHC	1261/4	1974–80	£3,500	£2,500	£1,500
Eclat S1	1973/4	1975–82	£3,500	£3,000	£1,500
Esprit 1	1973/4	1977–81	£6,500	£5,000	£3,000
Esprit 2	1973/4	1976–81	£7,000	£4,000	£2,500
Esprit S2.2	2174/4	1980–81	£7,000	£5,500	£3,000
Esprit Turbo	2174/4	1980–88	£10,000	£7,000	£4,000
Excel	2174/4	1983–85	£5,000	£3,000	£2,500

Prices vary with some limited-edition Lotus models and with competition history.

Marcos *(British 1959–)*

Launched in January 1966, the Mini-Marcos had already made a spectacular circuit debut at Castle Coombe during September of the previous year, having been driven to a second-place finish by Geoff Mabbs. Further glory came at Le Mans in 1966, when a Mini-Marcos driven by Claude Ballot-Lena and Jean-Louis Marnat was the only British car to finish, coming home 15th overall. The Mini-Marcos was the product of a collaboration between Jem Marsh of Marcos and designer Malcolm Newell. The original cars lacked an opening rear hatch, although this was offered as an option in 1967 on the Mk III version This model was produced until 1971 in both fully built and

kit forms. Following financial troubles, the company was sold to Rob Walker's Corsley Garages and traded as Marcos Limited. A new Mk IV was introduced, having a substantially redesigned body with rear hatch as standard. Based on the longer-wheelbase floorpan of the Mini Traveller, the Mk IV was also taller than its predecessors, giving improved interior space and a better driving position. During 1975, production passed to D&H Fibreglass Techniques, which traded as Midas Cars from 1981. Following the aftermath of a fire at the Midas works, the rights and moulds reverted to Jem Marsh, who re-established Marcos in Westbury, Wiltshire.

1967 Marcos Mini-Marcos Mk IV, 998cc, overhead-valve 4-cylinder engine, 4-speed manual gearbox, finished in yellow, red interior.
£2,500–3,000 / €3,700–4,450 / $4,400–5,300 ⚘ BRIT

1968 Marcos 1600GT, 1600cc, 4-cylinder engine, 4-speed manual gearbox, grp body, finished in 2-tone blue, black interior, bonnet in need of attention, 1 owner for last 31 years.
£4,800–5,700 / €7,100–8,400 / $8,400–10,000 ⚘ H&H

MARCOS Model	ENGINE cc/cyl	DATES	CONDITION 1	2	3
1500/1600/1800	1500/1600/1800/4	1964–69	£8,000	£5,000	£2,500
Mini-Marcos	848/4	1965–74	£3,500	£2,500	£1,500
Marcos 3 Litre	3000/6	1969–71	£9,000	£6,000	£4,000
Mantis	2498	1970–71	£10,000	£4,500	£1,500

Maserati *(Italian 1926)*

Formed in 1914 by three brothers, Officine Alfieri Maserati SpA was a tuning establishment closely linked to Isotta-Fraschini. When Italy entered WWI, Maserati not only serviced Isotta aero engines, but also began manufacturing spark plugs. Much of the early post-war period was spent building and racing cars, the few road cars being essentially converted track cars.

A major blow came in early 1932 with the death of Alfieri Maserati, who had acted as the company's chief engineer. This led to a lack of competitive cars during the 1930s, which seriously affected the sales of Maserati's customer racing and sports cars. The resulting financial problems saw the company being taken over by industrialist Adolfo Orsi, although the Maserati brothers were retained on a ten-year contract.

After WWII, Maserati returned to the race-tracks, winning the first post-war Grand Prix at Nice in April 1946, while in early 1947, it unveiled a Farina bodied version of its A6-1500 sports racing model. At the time, the company's main money spinners were spark plugs and batteries.

The A6-1500 was the final project undertaken by the Maserati brothers before their contract expired in 1947, and they left to form OSCA (Officine Specializzata Costruzione Automobili).

Maserati continued making small numbers of sports racing cars, spark plugs, batteries and, from 1953, motorcycles. In the mid-1950s, light trucks, hydroplanes and machine tools were also offered. During the same era, Maserati went Grand Prix racing with some success, notably in 1957,

when Juan Fangio won the World Championship. Maserati almost won that year's sports car championship too. Unfortunately, all four factory cars were destroyed in serious accidents. This so crippled the organization that Maserati was forced to quit racing at the end of that year.

This led to an emphasis on road car production, and 1958 was the first year that Maserati had built in excess of 100 cars of all types in a single year. This was largely thanks to the arrival of the 3500GT model. In 1963, the four-door Quattroporte appeared, followed in 1966 by the Ghibli and Mexico.

In 1968, Maserati concluded a deal to build a new luxury car, the Citroën SM, and that same year Citroën acquired a majority shareholding in the company, taking over completely in 1971.

The SM proved a commercial failure, however, and Citroën was absorbed by Peugeot in 1975. The outlook was bleak for Maserati until Alejandro de Tomaso took it over.

Maserati production resumed in early 1976, and later that year the luxurious, Frua bodied Kyalami, a new Quattroporte and a 2 litre Merak made their debut.

In 1982, Maserati produced the Bi-Turbo saloon. With a twin-turbocharged, 2 litre V6 engine, this proved a major sales success, over 6,000 being sold in 1983.

Although Maserati contined to grow during the 1980s, ill health overtook de Tomaso and sales began to decline. Eventually, the company was acquired by Fiat, which meant better quality and new cars in the shape of the Coupé and Spyder.

1961 Maserati 3500GT Spyder, coachwork by Vignale, 3485cc, V12 engine, ZF 5-speed manual gearbox, disc brakes, finished in black, grey leather interior.
£89,000–106,000 / €132,000–158,000 / $156,000–186,000 ⋟ B(Mon)
Launched in 1957, the 2+2 3500GT drew on the marque's competition experience, employing a tubular frame and an engine derived from the 350S sports car unit. Suspension was independent at the front by wishbones and coil springs, while at the rear there was a conventional live axle with semi-elliptic leaf springs. The rarer Vignale-bodied Spyder, of which only 245 examples were made, arrived in 1959 and continued in production until 1964.

1962 Maserati 3500GT Coupé, 3485cc, V12 engine,
ZF 5-speed manual gearbox, front disc brakes, finished in
metallic grey, black leather upholstery.
**£14,000–16,800 / €20,700–24,800
$24,600–29,600** ✠ B(Mon)

1962 Maserati Sebring 3500GTI Coupé, 3485cc,
V12 engine, fuel injection, 5-speed manual gearbox,
finished in metallic maroon, beige interior.
£19,300–23,100 / €28,600–34,000 / $34,000–41,000 ✠ H&H

1965 Maserati Quattroporte I, 4136cc, V8 engine,
ZF 5-speed manual gearbox, gearbox in need of overhaul,
paintwork in need of attention.
£1,750–2,100 / €2,600–3,100 / $3,100–3,700 ✠ H&H

1967 Maserati Mistral Coupé, 4012cc, V12 engine,
fuel injection, aluminium body, left-hand drive, finished in
silver-green, black interior trim.
£15,000–18,000 / €22,200–26,600 / $26,400–32,000 ✠ H&H
**The Mistral was a derivative of the 3500GT,
but featured a shorter, stiffer and lighter Sebring
chassis with Frua styled bodywork incorporating a
lifting tailgate. A total of 948 Mistrals were built
between 1963 and 1970.**

1971 Maserati Indy Coupé, coachwork by Vignale,
4136cc, V8 engine, 260bhp, automatic transmission,
top speed 155mph, finished in red, tan leather upholstery,
fewer than 45,000 miles recorded.
**£9,000–10,800 / €13,300–16,000
$15,800–19,000** ✠ H&H

1978 Maserati Khamsin, 4930cc, V8 engine, finished in
red, fawn leather interior, 51,000 miles recorded.
**£13,000–15,600 / €19,200–23,100
$22,900–27,500** ✠ COYS

MASERATI Model	ENGINE cc/cyl	DATES	CONDITION 1	2	3
AG-1500	1488/6	1946–50	£40,000+	£30,000	£20,000
A6G	1954/6	1951–53	£50,000+	£35,000	£22,000
A6G-2000	1985/6	1954–57	£45,000+	£35,000	£20,000
3500GT FHC	3485/6	1957–64	£20,000+	£14,000	£10,000
3500GT Spyder	3485/6	1957–64	£40,000+	£22,000	£15,000
5000GT	4935/8	1960–65	£60,000+	£20,000	£15,000
Sebring	3694/6	1962–66	£20,000	£15,000	£10,000
Quattroporte	4136/8	1963–74	£11,000	£9,000	£7,000
Mistral	4014/6	1964–70	£18,000	£12,000	£9,000
Mistral Spyder	4014/6	1964–70	£30,000+	£18,000	£12,000
Mexico	4719/8	1965–68	£15,000	£12,000	£9,000
Ghibli	4719/8	1967–73	£20,000+	£15,000	£12,000
Ghibli Spyder/SS	4136/8	1969–74	£50,000+	£40,000	£25,000
Indy	4136/8	1969–74	£18,000	£13,000	£10,000
Bora	4719/8	1971–80	£25,000	£18,000	£11,000
Merak/SS	2965/6	1972–81	£16,000+	£14,000	£9,000
Khamsin	4930/8	1974–81	£16,000+	£11,000	£9,000

Early cars with competition/berlinetta coachwork, eg. Zagato, command a premium; A6, A6G and A6G-2000,
rare coupé and Gran Sport coachwork can see prices of £180,000–250,000.

1982 Maserati Quattroporte III, 4930cc, V8 engine, 290bhp, automatic transmission, finished in blue, beige interior.
£4,000–4,800 / €5,900–7,100 / $7,000–8,400 ➶ H&H

1994 Maserati Ghibli GT, 2790cc, V6 engine, twin turbochargers, adjustable suspension, stainless steel exhaust system, automatic climate control.
£7,000–8,400 / €10,400–12,400
$12,300–14,800 ➶ H&H

> A known continuous history can add value to and enhance the enjoyment of a car.

1988 Maserati Bi-Turbo Spyder, 2500cc, V6 engine, twin turbochargers, 5-speed manual gearbox, 4-wheel disc brakes, 4-wheel independent suspension, factory body kit, finished in red, cream leather interior, 23,000 miles recorded.
£8,300–10,000 / €12,300–14,800
$14,600–17,600 ➶ H&H

▶ **1994 Maserati Ghibli Gran Turismo Coupé,** 2790cc, V6 engine, 4-position suspension, finished in metallic blue, leather interior.
£7,000–8,400 / €10,400–12,400
$12,300–14,800 ➶ H&H

Mazda *(Japanese 1960–)*

◀ **1981 Mazda RX7 GSL SE Series 2,** 1146cc, twin-rotor rotary engine, 5-speed manual gearbox, 4-wheel disc brakes, alloy wheels, sun roof, electric windows, finished in red, brown interior.
£230–270 / €340–400
$400–480 ➶ CGC

Mercedes-Benz (German 1886–)

1953 Mercedes-Benz 300S Convertible, 2996cc, 6-cylinder engine, floor-mounted gear-change, restored 1990s, concours condition.
£84,000–101,000 / € 125,000–150,000 $148,000–178,000 ↗ COYS

1936 Mercedes-Benz 170V Cabriolet B, 1700cc, 4-cylinder engine, 4-speed manual gearbox, in need of restoration.
£9,000–10,800 / € 13,300–16,000 $15,800–19,000 ↗ CGC

▶ **1956 Mercedes-Benz 190SL,** 1897cc, 4-cylinder engine, twin carburettors, hood and hardtop, Blaupunkt radio, finished in white, red interior, fewer than 30,000 miles recorded, believed to be the first right-hand-drive example supplied to the UK.
£16,000–19,200 / € 23,700–28,400 $28,200–34,000 ↗ BRIT

1956 Mercedes-Benz 300SL Gullwing, 2996cc, overhead-camshaft 6-cylinder engine, dry-sump lubrication, Bosch direct fuel injection, 4-speed manual gearbox.
£100,000–120,000 / € 148,000–176,000 $176,000–211,000 ↗ H&H

 ## Miller's Milestones

Mercedes-Benz 300SL Gullwing (1954–57)
Price Range: £70,000–150,000 / € 104,000 / $123,000
The Mercedes-Benz 300SL Gullwing coupé was one of the truly great cars of the 1950s. In 1952, the German marque stormed back on to the racing scene with a space-framed car that didn't allow for conventional doors. Its engine was a development of the 3 litre unit of the 300-series saloons.

This aluminium-bodied coupé was called the 300SL ('SL' standing for Super Light) and it was a winner from the very beginning, making headlines by finishing second in its first ever event, the 1952 Mille Miglia. Then it went one better with outright victory in the Berne Grand Prix in Switzerland. Next came an impressive 1–2 at Le Mans, another victory at the Nürburgring, then a 1–2 in the gruelling Carrera Pan-Americana Mexican road race.

This success spurred Mercedes-Benz to turn its attention to Grand Prix events, while New York importer Max Hoffman persuaded the German marque to build the 300SL as a production car, guaranteeing to take 1,000 if Mercedes would build them.

Thus, in February 1954, the first of the production 300SLs arrived. The body – built in steel with alloy panels – was supported by a complex space-frame. Under the bonnet was an advanced, fuel injected, overhead-cam, 2996cc six-cylinder engine producing 240bhp. This was canted over to ensure a low frontal profile.

Although the 300SL was magnificent, it was not without its faults. Its swing-axle rear suspension needed an expert driver to tame it when the car was being driven hard, while the body was prone to water leaks and the space-frame was difficult to repair in the event of an accident.

So, in 1957, after 1,400 Gullwing coupés had been sold, the model was replaced by the more civilized 300SL roadster.

1957 Mercedes-Benz 190SL, 1897cc, 4-cylinder engine, twin Weber carburettors, free-flow exhaust system, 78,000 miles recorded.
£17,600–21,100 / €26,000–31,000 $31,000–37,000 ✗ COYS

1957 Mercedes-Benz 220S Cabriolet, coachwork by Sindelfinger, 2195cc, overhead-camshaft 6-cylinder engine, completely restored, many new body panels, resprayed by Mercedes-Benz in original colour scheme, original leather interior reproduced.
£39,000–46,000 / €57,000–68,000 / $68,000–81,000 ✗ B(Mon)

▶ **1958 Mercedes-Benz 220S Cabriolet,** 2195cc, overhead-camshaft 6-cylinder engine, servo-assisted brakes, left-hand drive, finished in dark blue, cream and grey interior.
£21,600–25,700 / €32,000–38,000 $38,000–45,000 ✗ COYS

1958 Mercedes-Benz 300SL Roadster, 2996cc, overhead-camshaft 6-cylinder engine, 4-speed manual gearbox, finished in silver, original red leather interior, concours condition.
£69,000–82,000 / €102,000–122,000 / $121,000–144,000 ✗ COYS

MERCEDES-BENZ Model	ENGINE cc/cyl	DATES	CONDITION 1	2	3
300A/B/C/D	2996/6	1951–62	£15,000	£10,000	£8,000
300D Cabriolet	2195/6	1951–62	£80,000	£50,000	£30,000
220A/S/SE Ponton	2195/6	1952–60	£10,000	£5,000	£3,000
220S/SEB Coupé	2915/6	1956–59	£11,000	£7,000	£5,000
220S/SEB Cabriolet	2195/6	1958–59	£28,000+	£18,000	£7,000
190SL	1897/4	1955–63	£20,000+	£15,000+	£10,000
300SL Gullwing	2996/6	1954–57	£120,000+	£100,000	£70,000
300SL Roadster	2996/6	1957–63	£110,000+	£90,000	£70,000
230/250SL	2306/ 2496/6	1963–68	£16,000	£12,000+	£7,000
280SL	2778/6	1961–71	£18,000	£13,000+	£9,000
220/250SE	2195/ 2496/6	1960–68	£10,000	£7,000	£4,000
300SE	2996/6	1961–65	£11,000	£8,000	£6,000
280SE Convertible	2778/6	1965–69	£25,000	£18,000	£12,000
280SE V8 Convertible	3499/8	1969–71	£40,000+	£20,000	£15,000
280SE Coupé	2496/6	1965–72	£12,000	£8,000	£5,000
300SEL 6.3	6330/8	1968–72	£12,000	£7,000	£3,500
600 & 600 Pullman	6332/8	1964–81	£40,000+	£15,000	£8,000

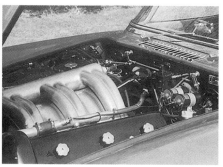

1959 Mercedes-Benz 300SL Roadster, 2996cc, overhead-camshaft 6-cylinder engine, fuel injection, 4-speed manual gearbox, 4-wheel independent suspension, 0–60mph in 7 seconds, top speed 130mph, hardtop, fully restored, concours condition.
£130,000–156,000 / €192,000–230,000 / $229,000–275,000 ✗ B(Mon)

1961 Mercedes-Benz 190SL, 1897cc, overhead-camshaft 4-cylinder engine, twin carburettors, dry-sump lubrication, fully restored 1990s, only 500 miles recorded since, bare-metal respray, mohair hood, blue leather interior, concours condition.
£19,200–23,000 / €28,400–34,000
$34,000–40,000 ✗ B(Kn)

1961 Mercedes-Benz 190SL, 1897cc, 4-cylinder engine, twin Solex carburettors, 120bhp, 4-speed manual gearbox, servo-assisted drum brakes, top speed 115mph, finished in red, magnolia leather interior.
£16,1000–19,300 / €23,800–28,600
$28,300–34,000 ✗ H&H

▶ **1962 Mercedes-Benz 300SE Cabriolet,** 2996cc, 6-cylinder engine, mohair hood, leather interior, in need of refurbishment.
£5,400–6,500 / €7,800–9,600
$9,300–11,400 ✗ BRIT

1964 Mercedes-Benz 300SE Coupé, 2996cc, 6-cylinder engine, fuel injection, 4-speed manual gearbox, self-levelling air suspension, finished in maroon, black interior.
£5,500–6,600 / €8,100–9,800 / $9,700–11,600 ✗ H&H

1965 Mercedes-Benz 230SL, 2306cc, overhead-camshaft 6-cylinder engine, automatic transmission, power steering, servo-assisted brakes, swing-axle rear suspension, hood and hardtop, fully restored.
£11,800–14,100 / €17,500–20,900
$9,300–24,800 ✗ H&H

◀ **1965 Mercedes-Benz 600 Short-Wheelbase Limousine,** 6300cc, V8 engine, fuel injection, hydraulic windows, sun roof, glass partition, air conditioning, finished in maroon, grey leather interior.
£15,400–18,500 / €22,800–27,400
$27,100–32,000 ✗ COYS

1967 Mercedes-Benz 250SL, 2496cc, 6-cylinder engine, 4-speed automatic transmission, finished in white, black interior.
£17,200–20,600 / €25,000–30,000
$30,000–36,000 ≯ H&H

1968 Mercedes-Benz 280SE Coupé, 2496cc, 6-cylinder engine, 4-speed automatic transmission, fuel injection system overhauled, finished in silver-blue, blue leather interior.
£5,900–7,100 / €8,700–10,500 / $10,400–12,500 ≯ BJ

1968 Mercedes-Benz 280SL, 2778cc, 6-cylinder engine, automatic transmission, 4-wheel disc brakes, 4-wheel independent suspension, new radiator, converted to unleaded fuel, catalytic converter, new hood, hardtop, fully restored, concours condition.
£11,500–13,800 / €17,000–20,400
$20,000–24,300 ≯ B(Kn)

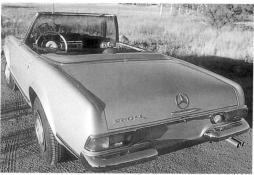

1969 Mercedes-Benz 280SL, 2778cc, 6-cylinder engine, finished in silver, burgundy leather interior, fitted luggage, fully restored, concours condition.
£31,000–37,000 / €46,000–55,000
$55,000–65,000 ≯ BB(S)

◄ **1970 Mercedes-Benz 280SE Coupé,** 3499cc, V8 engine, automatic transmission, finished in gold, black leather interior, additional chromework.
£9,800–11,800 / €14,500–17,500
$17,200–20,800 ≯ BJ

> A known continuous history can add value to and enhance the enjoyment of a car.

▶ **1970 Mercedes-Benz 280SE Cabriolet,** 3499cc, V8 engine, automatic transmission, finished in silver, black hood, black leather upholstery, 80,000 miles recorded, 1 of only 68 right-hand-drive Cabriolets built in 1970, previously owned by racing driver Roy Salvadori.
£36,000–43,000 / €53,000–64,000
$63,000–76,000 ≯ H&H

1972 Mercedes-Benz 350SLC, 3499cc, V8 engine, automatic transmission, left-hand drive, factory alloy wheels, steel sun roof, finished in white, blue velour interior.
£500–600 / €740–890 / $880–1,050 ≯ CGC

1972 Mercedes-Benz 350SL, 3499cc, V8 engine, manual gearbox, 4-wheel disc brakes, 4-wheel independent suspension, hardtop, finished in burgundy, brown leather interior.
£2,500–3,000 / €3,700–4,450 / $4,400–5,300 ≯ CGC

1975 Mercedes-Benz 350SE Saloon, 3499cc, V8 engine, 4-speed automatic transmission, 4-wheel disc brakes, 4-wheel independent suspension, power steering, 76,000 miles recorded.
£2,800–3,350 / €4,150–4,950 / $4,950–5,900 ⚖ COYS

1976 Mercedes-Benz 280E Saloon, 2746cc, 6-cylinder engine, automatic transmission, 4-wheel independent suspension, finished in brown.
£1,600–1,900 / €2,350–2,800 / $2,800–3,350 ⚖ CGC

1978 Mercedes-Benz 280SL, 2778cc, 6-cylinder engine, finished in yellow, beige leather interior.
£5,800–6,900 / €8,600–10,200
$10,200–12,100 ⚖ BARO

1978 Mercedes-Benz 450SLC, 4520cc, V8 engine, 225bhp, automatic transmission, 3 owners from new, unrestored.
£1,050–1,250 / €1,550–1,850 / $1,850–2,200 ⚖ COYS

◄ **1979 Mercedes-Benz 350SL,** 3499cc, finished in black, black and white interior.
£4,300–5,100 / €6,400–7,500
$7,600–9,000 ⚖ H&H
The SL (Sport Leucht) range was a major sales and publicity success for Mercedes-Benz.

▶ **1979 Mercedes-Benz 350SL,** 3499cc, V8 engine, 3-speed automatic transmission, finished in metallic green, black interior.
£6,100–7,300 / €9,000–10,800
$10,700–12,800 ⚖ H&H
A total of 15,304 350/450SL models were built.

1979 Mercedes-Benz 450SL, 4520cc, V8 engine, automatic transmission, cruise control, finished in dark blue, red leather interior, in need of some work.
£4,000–4,800 / €5,900–7,100 / $7,000–8,400 ⚖ BRIT

▶ **1980 Mercedes-Benz 280E Saloon,** 2746cc, 6-cylinder engine, automatic transmission, finished in white, black interior.
£1,350–1,600 / €2,000–2,350 / $2,400–2,800 ⚖ H&H

1980 Mercedes-Benz 380SL, 3818cc, overhead-camshaft V8 engine, cruise control, hood and hardtop, finished in bronze, cream leather interior.
£5,800–6,600 / €8,100–9,800 / $9,700–11,600 ✗ COYS

1980 Mercedes-Benz 450SL, 4520cc, V8 engine, finished in metallic green, green interior, 3 owners from new, excellent condition.
£3,150–3,800 / €4,650–5,600 / $5,500–6,600 ✗ BARO

1981 Mercedes-Benz 280SL, 2778cc, 6-cylinder engine, manual gearbox, factory alloy wheels, finished in bronze, beige interior.
£1,850–2,200 / €2,750–3,250 / $3,250–3,850 ✗ COYS

1981 Mercedes-Benz 380SLC, 3818cc, V8 engine, finished in gold, brown interior, fewer than 55,000 miles recorded.
£4,700–5,600 / €7,000–8,300 / $8,300–9,900 ✗ COYS

◄ **1981 Mercedes-Benz 380SL,** 3818cc, V8 engine, reconditioned 4-speed automatic transmission, new brake discs, new calipers, alloy wheels, new leather trim, hood and frame.
£5,500–6,600 / €8,100–9,800 $3,250–11,600 ✗ H&H

▶ **1981 Mercedes-Benz 500SL,** 4973cc, V8 engine, 4-speed automatic transmission, finished in white, blue hood, blue interior.
£4,950–5,900 / €7,300–8,700 $8,700–10,400 ✗ H&H

1982 Mercedes-Benz 380SE Saloon, 3839cc, V8 engine, 204bhp, 4-speed automatic transmission, 4-wheel disc brakes, 4-wheel independent suspension, power steering.
£2,350–2,800 / €3,500–4,150 / $4,150–4,950 ✗ CGC

1983 Mercedes-Benz 280CE Coupé, 2746cc, 6-cylinder engine, automatic transmission, finished in silver, dark blue interior.
£2,150–2,550 / €3,200–3,750 / $3,800–4,500 ✗ H&H

1985 Mercedes-Benz 280CE Coupé, 2746cc, 6-cylinder engine, automatic transmission, dark grey cloth interior, subject of £10,000 / €14,800 / $17,600 rebuild 1994.
£2,250–2,700 / €3,350–4,000 / $3,950–4,750 ⚒ H&H

1985 Mercedes-Benz 280SL, 2746cc, 6-cylinder engine, automatic transmission, hardtop, finished in blue, grey interior, c80,000 miles recorded.
£9,000–10,800 / €13,300–4,000 / $16,000–19,000 ⚒ H&H

1985 Mercedes-Benz 500SEC, 4973cc, V8 engine, automatic transmission, ABS, leather interior, electric seats, air conditioning, 2 owners from new.
£4,550–5,500 / €6,700–8,100 / $8,000–9,600 ⚒ COYS

1985 Mercedes-Benz 500SEL Saloon, 4973cc, V8 engine, automatic transmission, AMG performance suspension package, finished in black, black leather interior.
£5,200–6,200 / €7,700–9,200 / $9,200–10,900 ⚒ BJ

1985 Mercedes-Benz 500SL, 4973cc, V8 engine, automatic transmission, hood and hardtop, finished in red, cream leather interior.
£5,700–6,800 / €8,400–10,100 / $10,000–12,000 ⚒ JNic

► **1986 Mercedes-Benz 300SL,** 2977cc, 6-cylinder engine, 4-speed automatic transmission, power-steering, electric windows, central locking, cruise control.
**£10,200–12,200
€15,100–18,100
$18,000–21,500** ⚒ H&H

1988 Mercedes-Benz 500SEC Coupé, 4973cc, V8 engine, BBS alloy wheels, finished in dark green, blue leather upholstery.
£2,000–2,400 / €2,950–3,550 / $3,500–4,300 ⚹ CGC
Introduced in 1981, the W126 S-class four-seat coupé featured all-round independent suspension, disc brakes, power steering and a range of V8 engines mated to automatic transmission. Top of the range, the 500SEC was continuously updated, gaining Bosch KE-jetronic fuel injection in 1985. Developing 245bhp, the 4973cc overhead-camshaft V8 was capable of propelling the coupé to 60mph in 7.2 seconds and on to a top speed of 146mph.

1990 Mercedes-Benz 190 2.5–16, 2498cc, 16-valve 4-cylinder engine, aluminium body, leather upholstery, completely restored, 300 miles recorded since, 72,000 miles recorded.
£11,500–13,800 / €17,000–20,400 / $20,200–24,300 ⚹ CGC
The 2.3–16 was conceived in the late 1970s as a rally weapon. However, the Audi Quattro's arrival put paid to Mercedes-Benz's dreams of dominance on the forest stages, and the decision was taken to remould the project as a road car. Cosworth was commissioned to design a 16-valve cylinder head for the M102 2299cc, four-cylinder engine. Producing 185bhp, the resultant power plant exceeded expectations. Equipped with a five-speed Getrag manual gearbox, the 2.3–16 was capable of 145mph and 0–60mph in eight seconds. To harness such performance, the car featured an electronically controlled limited-slip differential and powerful ABS anti-lock brakes. The body kit reduced the model's coefficient of drag to just 0.32. For 1988, Mercedes created the 2.5–16. Engineered in-house, its 2498cc unit produced 204bhp. The new model was notably quicker (150mph, 0–60mph in 7.1 seconds) and achieved success in the German touring car championship. Campaigned by AMG, the distinctive silver and black machines won 50 races over the next five years, as well as a variety of championship titles.

The price paid for a car can vary according to the country in which it was sold. To discover where the car sold, cross reference the code at the end of each caption with the Key to Illustrations on page 251.

◀ **1986 Mercedes-Benz 560SL,** 5600cc, V8 engine, 227bhp, automatic transmission, finished in white, grey leather interior, 1 owner from new, good condition.
£11,500–13,800 / €17,000–20,400 $20,200–24,300 ⚹ BJ

1987 Mercedes-Benz 560SEC, 5547cc, V8 engine, automatic transmission, new radiator, finished in silver, grey leather interior, heated electric seats.
£2,950–3,500 / €4,350–5,200 / $5,200–6,200 ⚹ BARO

1989 Mercedes-Benz 300SE Saloon, 2962cc, 6-cylinder engine, automatic transmission, finished in metallic dark red, beige leather interior.
£1,750–2,100 / €2,600–3,100 / $3,100–3,700 ⚹ H&H

1992 Mercedes-Benz 300SL, 2993cc, 6-cylinder engine, 4-speed manual gearbox, finished in metallic black, grey leather interior, fewer than 50,000 miles recorded.
£13,400–16,000 / €19,800–23,700 $23,600–28,200 ⚹ H&H

1992 Mercedes-Benz 500SEC Coupé, 4973cc, V8 engine, 4-speed automatic transmission, finished in white, silver-grey leather interior.
£5,800–6,900 / €8,600–10,200 $10,200–12,100 ⚹ H&H

Mercury (American 1938–)

1953 Mercury Custom Four-Door Saloon, 255cu.in, side-valve V8 engine, 3-speed manual gearbox with overdrive, completely restored, fitted Jamco front and rear anti-roll bars, servo-assisted brakes, finished in yellow and black.
£8,500–10,200 / €12,600–15,100 / $15,000–18,000 ⚒ BJ

1954 Mercury Monterey Two-Door Hardtop, 265cu.in, overhead-valve V8 engine, 3-speed manual gearbox with overdrive, completely restored, finished in red and black, red and black interior, concours winner.
£19,000–22,800 / €21,800–33,000 / $33,000–39,000 ⚒ BJ

MG (British 1924–80, 1985–)

The origins of MG can be traced to the arrival of Cecil Kimber at Morris Garages in Oxford in 1921. The following year, he took charge of the business when the general manager committed suicide. Almost immediately, he began designing special bodywork for the Morris Oxford and Cowley. Then, in 1923, Kimber commissioned Raworth of Oxford to construct six open two-seaters on Cowley chassis; these cars are now recognized as the first MGs.

In November 1927, an MG secured the marque's first race victory in Buenos Aires. Then came the Morris Minor derived Midget, with 847cc overhead-cam engine, and the 18/80, with a 2.5 litre, overhead-cam six. Largely due to these two cars, MG production trebled to 900 in 1929.

During the early and mid-1930s, MG's racing activities really began to show success, notably in 1933 when the great Nuvolari won the Ulster Grand Prix and the factory took the team prize in the Italian Mille Miglia. In 1935, however, Lord Nuffield (as William Morris had become) sold MG to Morris Motors. Thus, Kimber came under the direction of Leonard Lord, later to become head of Austin. Lord wanted to cut costs, which resulted in MG's racing department being closed and the overhead-cam engines being axed in favour of normal overhead-valve assemblies.

Production of MGs reached a pre-war peak of 2,850 cars in 1937. During WWII, MG worked on military contracts.

After the war, MG resumed production earlier than most, announcing the TC Midget in October 1945. Exports to the USA began in 1947, the TC Midget becoming very much an icon of its era. The TC's successor, the TD, was built in considerably larger numbers, many being exported.

The arrival of the Austin-Healey 100 badly affected MG sales, and Leonard Lord vetoed a proposal to launch a new Midget in 1953. He reasoned that the newly created British Motor Corporation did not require two competing sports car designs. Over the years, there were many examples of such snubs, MG becoming very much the 'poor relation' at BMC and subsequently British Leyland.

However, there were bright spots, one being the MGA, which from 1955 to 1962 amassed sales of 101,181 – the largest production figure for any MG up to that time.

The MGA was replaced by the MGB, which was even more popular, selling over 460,000 and remaining in production until MG's demise in 1980. The same bodyshell was also used for some 9,000 MGCs, which had Austin-Healey 3000 six-cylinder engines, and almost 2,600 cars equipped with the Rover 3.5 litre V8.

In 1958, a new small BMC sports car, the Austin-Healey Sprite, arrived. The Mk II version appeared in 1961 and had an MG equivalent, which revived the Midget name.

◀ **1932 MG F1 Magna Tourer,** 1271cc, 6-cylinder engine, chrome wire wheels, fog and spot lights.
£16,300–19,600 / €24,100–29,000 $28,700–34,000 ⚒ BB(S)
The F1 Magna used a development of the underslung chassis first seen on the racing C-Type Midget, but with a longer wheelbase.

Cross Reference
See Colour Review (page 145–152)

◄ **1933 MG L1 Magna Four-Seater Tourer,** 1087cc, 6-cylinder engine, wire wheels, finished in red and black, red leather interior.
£24,100–29,000 / €36,000–43,000
$42,000–51,000 ➤ BRIT

1934 MG L1 Magna, 1087cc, 6-cylinder engine, wire wheels, engine rebuilt.
£17,400–20,900 / €25,800–31,000
$31,000–37,000 ➤ BRIT

1934 MG PA Midget, 847cc, 4-cylinder engine, wire wheels, restored, engine rebuilt, new hood, finished in black, red leather interior.
£10,200–12,200 / €15,100–18,100
$18,000–21,300 ➤ H&H
The 75mph PA Midget was launched in 1934. Compared to earlier models, its leaf-sprung chassis was stronger and had a longer wheelbase, while the 12in (30.5cm) diameter drum brakes were larger and more powerful.

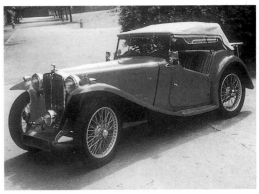

c1936 MG Midget Special, 1292cc, overhead-valve 4-cylinder engine, supercharger, wire wheels, restored, finished in red, beige interior.
£15,300–18,400 / €22,600–27,200
$26,900–32,000 ➤ COYS

▶ **1938 MG TA Midget,** 1292cc, overhead-valve 4-cylinder engine, 4-speed manual gearbox, hydraulic drum brakes.
£9,800–11,800 / €14,500–17,500
$17,200–20,800 ➤ H&H

MG Model	ENGINE cc/cyl	DATES	CONDITION 1	2	3
14/28	1802/4	1924–27	£26,000	£18,000	£10,000
14/40	1802/4	1927–29	£25,000	£18,000	£10,000
18/80 Mk I–III	2468/6	1927–33	£40,000	£28,000	£20,000
M-Type Midget	847/4	1928–32	£11,000	£9,000	£7,000
J-Type Midget	847/4	1932–34	£15,000	£12,000	£10,000
J3 Midget	847/4	1932–33	£18,000	£14,000	£12,000
PA Midget	847/4	1934–36	£13,000+	£10,000	£8,000
PB Midget	936/4	1935–36	£15,000+	£10,000	£8,000
F-Type Magna	1271/6	1931–33	£22,000	£18,000	£12,000
L-Type Magna	1087/6	1933–34	£26,000	£18,000	£12,000
K1/K2 Magnette	1087/6	1932–33	£35,000	£30,000	£20,000
N-Series Magnette	1271/6	1934–36	£30,000	£28,000	£20,000
TA Midget	1292/4	1936–39	£13,000+	£12,000	£9,000
SA 2 Litre	2288/6	1936–39	£22,000+	£18,000	£15,000
VA	1548/4	1936–39	£12,000	£8,000	£5,000
TB Midget	1250/4	1939–40	£15,000	£11,000	£9,000

Value will depend on body style, history, completeness, racing history, the addition of a supercharger and originality.

1946 MG TC Midget, 1250cc, overhead-valve 4-cylinder engine, restored at a cost of over £44,000 / €65,000 / $77,000.
£16,600–19,900 / €24,600–29,500 / $29,200–35,000 ⚐ COYS
The Midget originated with the 847cc M-Type in 1928 and progressed to the 939cc PB in 1936, always with an overhead-camshaft engine. The TA appeared in July 1936. It kept the slab tank, folding windscreen and cutaway doors of the J2 and its successors, but there were several major changes, which included a 1292cc overhead-valve engine, a longer wheelbase and hydraulic 9in (22.9cm) drum brakes instead of cable-operated 12in (30.5cm) drums. The cars were more comfortable and practical than their predecessors, as well as being faster and handling better; tuned versions were soon lapping Brooklands at more than 90mph. The 1250cc TB appeared in 1939 and was almost identical to the TA, but only a few hundred were made before the outbreak of WWII. After the war came the hugely successful TC. While fundamentally the same as the TA, it incorporated myriad detail changes, not least a substantially more flexible and powerful engine.

◀ **1947 MG TC Midget,** 1250cc, 4-cylinder engine, restored 1992, engine and chassis overhauled, resprayed in black, new hood, new red leather upholstery.
£10,800–13,000 / €16,000–19,200
$19,000–22,900 ⚐ CGC

1948 MG TC Midget, 1250cc, overhead-valve 4-cylinder engine, wire wheels, luggage rack, finished in black, red interior.
£10,500–12,600 / €15,500–18,600
$18,500–22,200 ⚐ COYS

◀ **1948 MG TC Midget,** 1250cc, overhead-valve 4-cylinder engine, 54bhp, top speed 80mph, restored.
£12,400–14,900 / €18,400–22,100
$21,800–26,200 ⚐ BB(S)

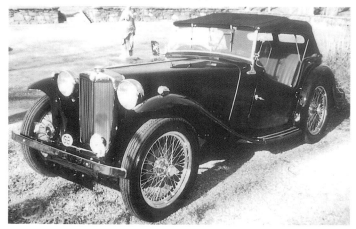

▶ **1948 MG TC Midget,** 1250cc, overhead-valve 4-cylinder engine, recently restored, mechanics rebuilt, chrome wire wheels, black top and side screens, Brooklands steering wheel, Alfin brake drums, light-alloy front wings, finished in black, red leather interior.
£17,300–20,800 / €25,600–31,000
$30,000–37,000 ⚐ BB(S)

1949 MG TC Midget,
1250cc, 4-cylinder engine,
wire wheels, restored,
finished in British Racing
green, cream interior,
concours winner.
£18,300–21,900
€27,100–32,000
$32,000–39,000 ⚒ B(Kn)

1949 MG YT Tourer, 1250cc, restored early 1990s,
wire wheels, finished in green, tan leather interior.
£10,600–12,700 / €15,700–18,800
$18,700–22,400 ⚒ BB(S)

Based on the Morris Eight, MG's first post-war saloon,
the Y-Type, employed such advanced features as coil-
spring independent front suspension and rack-and-
pinion steering, both of which would appear later on
the TD Midget. Underslung at the rear, the separate
chassis was unique to the Y-Type, which shared the
contemporary TC Midget's 1250cc four-cylinder engine,
albeit in single-carburettor, 46bhp form. An open,
four-seat tourer version – the YT – was launched in
1948. Altogether more sporting than the saloon,
the YT boasted twin carburettors, a TC camshaft and
a maximum power output of 54.5bhp for a top
speed of 76mph. The body had been redesigned as
a two-door, without compromising interior space,
and featured leather upholstery and a fold-flat
windscreen. The YT was destined for a relatively short
life, ceasing production in 1950 after only 877 had
been made, most of which were exported.

◄ **1949 MG YT Tourer,** 1250cc, 4-cylinder engine,
independent front suspension, restored.
£12,100–14,500 / €17,900–21,500
$21,300–25,500 ⚒ B(Kn)

MG Model	ENGINE cc/cyl	DATES	CONDITION 1	2	3
TC Midget	1250/4	1946–49	£15,000+	£11,000	£7,000
TD Midget	1250/4	1950–52	£14,000	£10,000	£5,000
TF Midget	1250/4	1953–55	£15,000	£13,000	£8,000
TF 1500	1466/4	1954–55	£16,000	£14,000	£9,000
YA/YB	1250/4	1947–53	£5,500+	£2,750	£1,500
Magnette ZA/ZB	1489/4	1953–58	£3,500	£2,000	£500
Magnette Mk III/IV	1489/4	1958–68	£3,500	£1,200	£350
MGA 1500 Roadster	1489/4	1955–59	£11,000+	£7,000	£4,000
MGA 1500 FHC	1489/4	1956–59	£8,000	£6,000	£3,000
MGA 1600 Roadster	1588/4	1959–61	£13,000	£9,000	£4,500
MGA 1600 FHC	1588/4	1959–61	£7,000	£5,000	£3,000
MGA Twin Cam Roadster	1588/4	1958–60	£16,000	£12,000	£9,000
MGA Twin Cam FHC	1588/4	1958–60	£13,000	£9,000	£7,000
MGA 1600 Mk II Roadster	1622/4	1961–62	£13,000+	£10,000	£4,000
MGA 1600 Mk II FHC	1622/4	1961–62	£9,000	£7,000	£3,000
MGB Mk I	1798/4	1962–67	£7,000	£4,000	£1,200
MGB GT Mk I	1798/4	1965–67	£5,000	£3,500	£1,000
MGB Mk II	1798/4	1967–69	£7,500	£4,000	£1,500
MGB GT Mk II	1798/4	1969	£4,500	£2,500	£850
MGB Mk III	1798/4	1969–74	£6,500	£4,000	£1,100
MGB GT Mk III	1798/4	1969–74	£4,500	£2,500	£1,000
MGB Roadster (rubber bumper)	1798/4	1975–80	£6,000	£4,500	£1,200
MGB GT	1798/4	1975–80	£5,000	£3,000	£1,000
MGB Jubilee	1798/4	1975	£5,000	£3,000	£1,200
MGB LE	1798/4	1980	£8,500	£4,750	£2,250
MGB GT LE	1798/4	1980	£6,000	£3,750	£2,000
MGC Roadster	2912/6	1967–69	£10,000	£6,500	£4,000
MGC GT	2912/6	1967–69	£7,000	£5,000	£2,000
MGB GT V8	3528/8	1973–76	£9,000	£6,000	£3,000
Midget Mk I	948/4	1961–62	£4,000	£2,000	£850
Midget Mk II	1098/4	1962–66	£3,000	£2,000	£850
Midget Mk III	1275/4	1966–74	£3,200	£2,000	£850
Midget 1500	1491/4	1975–79	£3,000	£2,000	£850

All prices are for British right-hand-drive cars. For left-hand-drive varieties, deduct 10–15% for UK values,
even if converted to right-hand drive.

1953 MG TD Midget Four-Seater, 1250cc, 4-cylinder engine, disc wheels, 1 of 10 four-seaters built.
£9,500–11,400 / €14,100–16,900
$16,700–20,100 ✗ BB(S)
The four-seat Midget was the brainchild of New York MG importer J.S. Inskip. The chassis was lengthened to accommodate the extra seats, the body panels and running gear being modified accordingly. A special folding hood and side screens were also made.

1953 MG TD Midget, 1250cc, overhead-valve 4-cylinder engine, 55bhp, independent front suspension, 4-wheel hydraulic drum brakes, restored 1990s.
£14,800–17,800 / €21,900–26,300
$26,000–31,000 ✗ H&H

1955 MG TF 1500 Midget, 1466cc, 4-cylinder engine, 63bhp, top speed 90mph, left-hand drive, fully restored, concours condition.
£12,100–14,500 / €17,900–21,500 / $21,300–25,500 ✗ BB(S)
A stop-gap model produced pending the arrival of the MGA, the TF was essentially a TD with a restyled front end. The TD's 1250cc engine was retained initially, but in November 1954, the TF 1500 arrived with a 1466cc engine. Ultimately, this model accounted for more than half of total TF production.

1955 MG ZA Magnette, 1489cc, 4-cylinder engine, red leather interior, fewer than 6,000 miles recorded.
£6,400–7,700 / €9,500–11,400
$11,300–13,600 ✗ BRIT

1956 MGA 1500 Roadster, 1489cc, overhead-valve 4-cylinder engine, 72bhp, top speed 95mph, left-hand drive, new wire wheels, fewer than 42,000 miles recorded, good condition.
£6,300–7,600 / €9,300–11,200
$11,100–13,400 ✗ BARO
When the MGA arrived in 1955, it caused a sensation, its sleek bodywork being far removed from that of the ageing TF Midget.

c1959 MGA 1600 De Luxe Roadster, 1622cc, 4-cylinder engine, disc brakes, extensively restored, concours condition.
£12,800–15,400 / €18,900–22,800
$22,500–27,100 ✗ BRIT

Condition guide

1. A vehicle in top class condition but not 'concours d'elegance standard, either fully restored or in very good original condition.
2. A good, clean, roadworthy vehicle, both mechanically and bodily sound.
3. A runner, but in need of attention, probably both to bodywork and mechanics. Must have current MoT.

1960 MGA 1600 Coupé, 1588cc, 4-cylinder engine, finished in pale blue, black interior.
£4,500–5,400 / €6,700–8,000 / $7,900–9,500 ✈ H&H
Only 2,800 MGA 1600 Mk I Coupés were built.

1960 MGA Twin Cam Roadster, 1588cc, double-overhead-camshaft 4-cylinder engine, 4-wheel disc brakes.
£14,700–17,600/ €21,800–26,000
$25,900–31,000 ✈ BRIT
Only 2,111 Twin Cam models were built.

1963 MG Midget Mk II, 1098cc, overhead-valve 4-cylinder engine, 4-speed manual gearbox, engine and gearbox rebuilt, new Minilite alloy wheels, bodywork restored, new black interior.
£4,100–5,600 / €6,100–8,300 / $7,200–9,900 ✈ H&H

1960 MG EX182 Le Mans Replica, 1588cc, 4-cylinder engine, Judson supercharger, close-ratio 4-speed gearbox, wire wheels, finished in red, single seat, wood-rimmed steering wheel.
£20,000–24,000 / €29,600–36,000
$35,000–42,000 ✈ COYS
This car was built as a cosmetic representation of one of MG's 1955 Le Mans team cars.

1961 MGA 1600 Mk II Roadster, 1588cc, 4-cylinder engine, wire wheels, rear luggage rack, completely restored late 1980s, original specification.
£11,900–14,200 / €17,600–21,000
$20,900–25,000 ✈ CGC
The restoration of this car was televised by Channel 4.

1965 MGB Mk I Roadster, 1798cc, overhead-valve 4-cylinder engine, 4-speed manual gearbox, fully restored, concours condition.
£15,100–18,100 / €22,300–26,800
$26,600–32,000 ✈ COYS

◄ **1967 MGB GT Mk I,** 1798cc, 4-cylinder engine, 4-speed manual gearbox, wire wheels, restored early 1990s, front suspension rebuilt, electric cooling fan, Webasto sun roof, finished in dark blue, black interior, good condition.
£2,950–3,550 / €4,350–5,300 / $5,200–6,200 ✈ BARO

1967 MGB Mk I Roadster, 1798cc, blue mohair hood, fully restored 2002 at a cost of £25,000 / €37,000 / $44,000, blue mohair hood, finished in light blue, grey leather interior.
£10,100–12,100 / €14,900–17,900 / $17,800–21,300 ✈ CGC

1968 MGB GT, 1798cc, 4-cylinder engine, wire wheels, restored, finished in red, new red interior.
£2,700–3,200 / €4,000–4,750 / $4,750–5,600 ⚒ H&H

1968 MGB Mk II Roadster, 1798cc, 4-cylinder engine, 4-speed manual gearbox with overdrive, finished in red, black interior.
£4,100–4,900 / €6,100–7,300 / $7,200–8,600 ⚒ H&H

1968 MGC Roadster, 2912cc, 6-cylinder engine, torsion-bar independent front suspension, converted to unleaded fuel, wire wheels, luggage rack.
£9,300–11,200 / €13,800–16,600 / $16,400–19,700 ⚒ H&H

1969 MGC GT, 2912cc, 6-cylinder engine, 4-speed manual gearbox with auto-shift, 2 owners from new, 58,000 miles recorded.
£5,500–6,600 / €8,100–9,800 / $9,700–11,600 ⚒ COYS

1970 MGC GT, 2916cc, 6-cylinder engine, 4-speed manual gearbox, wire wheels, finished in beige, brown leather interior.
£3,200–3,850 / €4,750–5,700 / $5,600–6,800 ⚒ H&H

1971 MGB GT Mk III, 1798cc, 4-cylinder engine, 1 owner from new.
£1,650–2,000 / €2,450–2,950 / $2,900–3,500 ⚒ CGC
The MGB GT Mk III was offered between late 1969 and 1974.

◀ **1972 MGB GT Mk III,** 1798cc, 4-cylinder engine, manual gearbox, sun roof, finished in British Racing green, in need of some attention.
£880–1,050 / €1,300–1,550 / $1,550–1,850 ⚒ COYS

1972 MGB Mk III Roadster, 1798cc, 4-cylinder engine, totally restored over 3 years, new floor and sills, new radiator, oil cooler, converted to unleaded fuel, finished in blue, matching blue interior.
£5,400–6,500 / €8,000–9,600 / $9,500–11,400 ⚒ H&H

◀ **1972 MG Midget Mk III,** 1275cc, 4-cylinder engine, completely restored 1997, new hood, finished in red, black vinyl interior.
£2,550–3,050 / €3,750–4,500 / $4,500–5,400 ⚒ BRIT

1973 MGB Mk III Roadster, completely restored 1994 and modified for road/competition use, original engine rebuilt, tuned and capacity increased to 1950cc, new brakes, fuel system, wheel bearings and steering, Moss coil-over suspension kit, lowering springs, Spax competition shock absorbers, anti-roll bar, new body panels, including Sebring-style valances and aluminium bonnet, works hardtop, plastic headlamp fairings, leather bonnet strap, resprayed in red, refurbished interior, full harnesses.
£9,600–11,500 / €14,200–17,000 $16,900–20,200 ➤ H&H

▶ **1973 MGB GT Mk III,** 1798cc, 4-cylinder engine, manual gearbox, finished in blue, black interior, original, unrestored.
£1,700–2,050 / €2,500–3,050 $3,000–3,600 ➤ H&H

1975 MGB GT Mk III, 1798cc, overhead-valve 4-cylinder engine, 4-speed manual gearbox with overdrive, stainless steel exhaust system, fewer than 68,000 miles recorded.
£1,950–2,350 / €2,900–3,500 / $3,450–4,150 ➤ H&H

1975 MGB GT V8, 3528cc, V8 engine, bare-metal respray in yellow, black interior.
£3,750–4,500 / €5,600–6,700 / $6,600–7,900 ➤ BRIT
Introduced in 1973, the MGB GT V8 was powered by the low-compression version of the 3.5 litre Rover engine, developing 137bhp, which equated to a top speed in excess of 125mph and 0–60mph in just over eight seconds. This car was the last factory-built, chrome-bumpered GT V8.

1977 MGB V8 Roadster, restored at a cost of £12,000 / €17,700 / $21,100, fitted modified 3500cc Rover SD1 V8 engine, automatic transmission, original 'rubber' bumpers replaced by chrome units, front spoiler.
£5,400–6,500 / €8,000–9,600 / $9,500–11,400 ➤ COYS

1978 MGB GT, 1798cc, 4-cylinder engine, 4-speed manual gearbox, fewer than 18,000 miles recorded, original, very good condition.
£2,700–3,250 / €4,000–4,800 / $4,750–5,700 ➤ BRIT

◀ **1978 MGB Roadster,** 1798cc, 4-cylinder engine, 4-speed manual gearbox, wire wheels, original 'rubber' bumpers removed, fitted earlier chrome grille, reduced ride height, finished in black, black interior, good condition.
£2,150–2,600 / €3,200–3,850 $3,800–4,600 ✗ BARO

1978 MG Midget, 1491cc, 4-cylinder engine, restored, finished in yellow, black interior.
£2,500–3,000 / €3,700–4,450 / $4,400–5,300 ✗ BARO

1977 MG Midget 1500, 1491cc, tuned 4-cylinder engine, modified exhaust, Minilite-style alloy wheels, finished in red, black interior.
£3,100–3,700 / €4,600–5,500 / $5,500–6,500 ✗ H&H

1975 MGB GT V8, 3528cc, V8 engine, finished in red, black interior.
£5,200–6,300 / €7,700–9,300 / $9,200–11,100 ✗ CGC
Despite the first prototype MGB GT V8 being registered in 1970, it took British Leyland a further three years to bring the car to market. By August 1973, the car had had its thunder stolen somewhat by Ken Costello's limited run of MGB V8s. However, the factory version was judged to be more thoroughly engineered. By modifying the bulkhead and using a low-rise exhaust manifold, MG was able to retain the standard front suspension and bonnet. Since the Rover V8 weighed less than the B-series four-cylinder engine that it replaced, if anything, handling was improved. Performance certainly benefited, with some 137bhp available. Fitted with a manual four-speed overdrive gearbox, the MGB GT V8 could achieve a top speed of 125mph and sprint to 60mph in 8.5 seconds. The rack-and-pinion steering of the standard GT was employed as were front disc/rear drum brakes.

◀ **1978 MGB GT,** 1798cc, 4-cylinder engine, manual gearbox, full-length sun roof, upgraded Lucas H4 headlamps, finished in black, striped grey cloth interior.
£1,000–1,200 / €1,500–1,800 / $1,750–2,100 ✗ CGC

1979 MGB GT, 1798cc, 4-cylinder engine, stainless steel exhaust, 1 owner for last 20 years, very good condition.
£1,200–1,450 / €1,800–2,150 / $2,100–2,550 ✗ CGC

◀ **1979 MGB Roadster,** 1798cc, 4-cylinder engine, 4-speed manual gearbox with overdrive, Rostyle wheels, finished in red, black leather interior.
£2,400–2,850 / €3,550–4,200 / $4,200–5,000 ✗ CGC

Colour Review

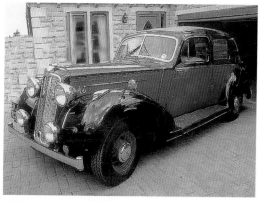

1902 Haynes-Apperson 12hp 4/6-Seater Surrey,
3900cc, twin-cylinder engine, 3-speed epicyclic gearbox.
£29,300–35,000 / €43,000–52,000
$51,000–61,000 ⌁ H&H
America's first commercially-built, petrol-driven car
was the Haynes-Apperson, built at Kokomo, Indiana.
The marque was founded by Elwood Haynes, who was
also the first man to recognise the properties of and
manufacture stainless steel; he also invented Stellite
alloy. Having hired Elmer and Edgar Apperson,
Haynes made the first trial run in his new automobile
on 4th July, 1894, when, in the interests of safety to
the onlookers and to prevent scaring the city's horses,
he pulled the car behind a horse and buggy to beyond
the city limits before firing it up. After being driven
about six miles around the countryside that day at up
to 7mph, the first Haynes-Apperson was considered
a huge success; production of replicas began in 1898.
During 1902, however, the founding partners split
up and started their own automobile companies.
Haynes never sold his prototype, donating it instead
to the Smithsonian Institute, Washington, in 1910.
Before his death at 67 in 1925, Haynes car production
had risen to an impressive 40 vehicles per day.

1937 Humber Snipe Limousine, 2731cc, side-valve
6-cylinder engine, 4-speed manual gearbox, beige
leather interior.
£6,000–7,000 / €8,900–10,600
$10,600–12,700 ⌁ H&H
Humber bought its Coventry rival Hillman in 1928,
and four years later was taken over itself by the
Rootes Group. With the Hillman Minx catering for
budget buyers, Rootes moved its newly acquired
brand up market. The smallest Humber became the
1933–37 1669cc Twelve, while the larger Snipe,
Super Snipe and Pullman dominated the range.
The Snipe, which first appeared in 1930, combined
chassis and body styles of the 16/50 with a six-
cylinder engine. A long-wheelbase Snipe with
limousine body coachbuilt by Thrupp and Maberly
was called the Pullman. From 1933, Humber
abandoned inlet-over-exhaust valves in favour of
sidevalves for their engines. From 1934, gearboxes
had synchromesh, cars had built-in jacks and radiators
sloped. And from 1936, Snipe coachwork became
more curvaceous, while transverse-leaf independent
front suspension was employed.

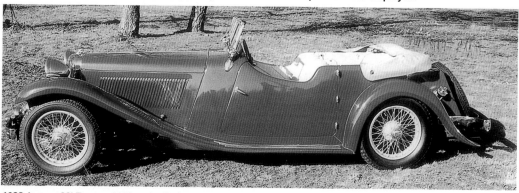

1933 Jaguar SSI Tourer, 2052cc, 6-cylinder engine.
£52,500–62,000 / €77,000–93,000 / $92,000–110,000 ⌁ COYS
Only 115 examples of the SSI Tourer were built.

▶ **1951 Jaguar XK120 Roadster,**
3442cc, double-overhead-camshaft
6-cylinder engine, twin SU carburettors,
160bhp, top speed 126mph, left-hand
drive, red leather interior, fully restored.
£29,400–35,000 / €43,000–52,000
$51,000–62,000 ⌁ COYS
It was at the 1948 London Motor
Show that Jaguar virtually threw
the sports car world into turmoil
with its stunning XK120. Here was
a car with incredible style and
looks, a powerful six-cylinder
engine installed in an outstanding
chassis and a remarkably low price
– a quarter that of a V12 Ferrari
with similar performance.

◀ **1957 Jaguar XK140 Roadster,** 3442cc, double-overhead-camshaft 6-cylinder engine, C-type cylinder head, matching numbers, left-hand drive, original, 1 owner from new, stored since late 1960s, recently recommissioned.
£34,100–40,900 / €50,000–60,000 $60,000–72,000 ⚒ COYS

1958 Jaguar XK150 Roadster, 3442cc, double-overhead-camshaft 6-cylinder engine, green leather interior, Nardi wood-rimmed steering wheel.
£32,200–38,600 / €47,600–57,100 $56,600–67,900 ⚒ B(Kn)

A progressive development of the XK120 and XK140, the XK150 retained its predecessors' basic chassis, engine and transmission, but benefited from an entirely new body that provided increased interior space and improved visibility courtesy of a one-piece windscreen. The new model's main talking point, though, was its Dunlop disc brakes, which at last provided stopping power to match the XK's prodigious straight-line speed. At 190bhp, the 3.4 litre engine's maximum power output was identical to that of the XK140, so the already high level of performance was maintained.

1960 Jaguar XK150S Roadster, 3442cc, double-overhead-camshaft 6-cylinder engine, 4-speed manual gearbox, fully restored, engine rebuilt, 600 miles recorded since, front disc brake conversion kit, Harvey Bailey handling kit with 4 adjustable Koni shock absorbers, improved anti-roll bar, rear-suspension anti-tramp bar kit, stainless steel exhaust, additional electric radiator cooling fan, black leather interior, Moto-Lita steering wheel.
£28,200–34,000 / €42,000–50,000 $60,000–70,000 ⚒ COYS

▶ **1965 Jaguar 3.4 S-Type Saloon,** 3442cc, double-overhead-camshaft 6-cylinder engine, 3-speed automatic transmission, restored.
£5,800–6,900 / €8,600–10,200 $10,200–12,100 ⚒ H&H

1967 Jaguar E-Type Series 1½ Roadster, 4235cc, double-overhead-camshaft 6-cylinder engine, matching numbers, completely restored mid-1990s at a cost of c£30,000, little use since, engine rebuilt, new wire wheels and hood, black leather interior.
£27,600–33,000 / €41,000–49,000 / $48,000–58,000 ⚒ COYS

Officially, there was no such thing as a Series 1½ E-Type; the term was applied retrospectively to some late Series 1 cars that featured the Series 2 mechanical upgrades and interior, prior to the launch of that model in 1968. They are easily recognised by the unusual bonnet, which combines the Series 1 assembly with the exposed headlamps of the Series 2. Most of these cars were destined for the USA, where new legislation had outlawed the stylish, but ineffective, glass-covered headlamps of the original E-Type.

◄ **1970 Jaguar E-type Series 2 Roadster,** 4235cc, double-overhead-camshaft 6-cylinder engine, blue interior, restored 1989, concours condition.
£29,000–35,000 / €43,000–51,000
$51,000–61,000 ⚒ H&H
This E-Type was owned originally by Bill Heynes, chief engineer of Jaguar Cars and co-designer of the famous XK engine.

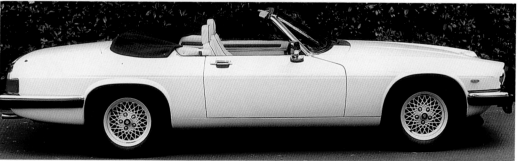

1991 Jaguar XJS Convertible, 5343cc, V12 engine, 3-speed automatic transmission, 51,000 miles recorded, magnolia leather interior.
£7,200–8,600 / €10,600–12,700 / $12,600–15,100 ⚒ H&H

1969 Jensen FF Mk I, 6276cc, V8 engine, 3-speed automatic transmission, rebuilt radiator, new Bosch cooling fan, black leather interior.
£9,700–11,600 / €14,300–17,100
$17,000–20,000 ⚒ H&H

1973 Lancia Fulvia 1.3S Coupé, 1298cc, V4 engine, 5-speed manual gearbox, lead-free conversion, tan interior, fewer than 20,000 miles recorded.
£3,300–3,900 / €4,800–5,700 / $5,800–6,900 ⚒ H&H

1965 Maserati Sebring 3500 GTI Coupé, 3485cc, V12 engine, Lucas fuel injection, ZF 5-speed gearbox, disc brakes, 32,000 miles recorded.
£17,200–20,600 / €25,500–30,000
$30,000–36,000 ⚒ H&H
In all, 444 Sebring models were produced, many with automatic transmissions; most were sold in the USA.

1988 Lamborghini Countach 5000QV, 4754cc, double-overhead-camshaft V12 engine, black leather interior, 1 owner from new, 25,000km recorded.
£35,000–42,000 / €52,000–63,000
$62,000–75,000 ⚒ COYS
Sensation of the 1971 Geneva Motor Show, the Countach was styled by Bertone and retained the quad-cam V12 of its predecessor, albeit mounted longitudinally. To achieve optimum weight distribution, the five-speed gearbox was positioned ahead of the engine, between the seats, while the differential at the rear was driven by a shaft that passed through the sump. The engine size was increased from 4000 to 4754cc in 1982.

1972 Lotus Elan Sprint, 1558cc, double-overhead-camshaft 4-cylinder engine, 4-speed manual gearbox, dynamo replaced by alternator, 68,000 miles recorded.
£8,600–10,300 / €12,700–15,200 / $15,000–18,000 ⚒ H&H
With its revolutionary backbone chassis, the Elan was a milestone design from Colin Chapman's Lotus marque. Each end of the chassis was fork-shaped, the front cradling the engine, and the rear the final drive. The suspension was similar to that of the Elite. The first Elans were open cars, although fixed-head versions were quickly offered as well. Lotus manufactured its own twin-cam motor, using a Ford cylinder block, and initially this produced 105bhp, latterly 130bhp. The same engine was employed in Ford's Cortina Lotus. A stretched and widened 2+2 Elan was available from 1967.

1960 Mercedes-Benz 300SL Roadster, 2996cc, overhead-camshaft 6-cylinder engine, fuel injection.
£108,000–129,500 / €160,000–192,000 / $190,000–228,000 ⚒ COYS
The 300SL Roadster was developed from the famous Gullwing 300SL Coupé of 1954. It was built between 1957 and 1963.

1967 Mercedes-Benz 250SL, 2495cc, 6-cylinder engine, 4-speed automatic transmission, concours condition.
£13,700–16,400 / €20,200–24,200
$24,100–28,900 ⚒ H&H
The 250SL appeared in 1966 as a replacement for the 230SL, which some had said was neither powerful nor fast enough. The new roadster was fitted with a 2.5 litre six-cylinder engine, and from 1967, it sold alongside the similar looking 2.8 litre 280SL. Transmission options were a five-speed manual and a four-speed automatic. The soft-top roadster was offered with an optional hardtop. A total of 5,196 250SLs were built between 1966 and 1968.

1983 Mercedes-Benz 280SL Roadster, 2746cc, factory hardtop, fog lights, grey leather interior.
£9,500–11,400 / €14,000–16,800
$16,700–20,000 ⚒ H&H

1989 Mercedes-Benz 500SEL Saloon, 4973cc, V8 engine, 4-speed automatic transmission, fully optioned.
£3,000–3,600 / €4,400–5,200 / $5,300–6,300 ⚒ H&H

1947 MG TC Midget, 1250cc, overhead-valve 4-cylinder engine, fully restored, fewer than 1,500 miles since, concours condition.
£13,500–16,200 / €20,000–24,000 / $23,700–28,400 ⚒ H&H
Announced in October 1945, the TC Midget was based on the TB, a short-lived pre-war model powered by the same 1250cc XPAG motor. With open two-seater bodywork widened by 4in and improved suspension incorporating Luvax-Girling hydraulic shock absorbers, the TC had a 78mph top speed. Production ceased at the end of 1949.

1958 MG ZB Magnette Varitone, 1489cc, overhead-valve 4-cylinder engine.
£3,500–4,200 / €5,200–6,200 / $6,100–7,300 ⚒ H&H

1960 MG MGA 1600 Coupé, 1588cc, 4-cylinder engine, 80bhp, Lockheed disc front brakes, 0–60mph in 14.2 seconds, top speed 100mph, completely restored, concours condition.
£9,500–11,400 / €14,000–16,500 / $16,700–20,000 ↗ COYS

1972 MG MGB Roadster, 1798cc, overhead-valve 4-cylinder engine, oil cooler, wire wheels, engine overhauled 2003, resprayed, new hood.
£5,500–6,600 / €8,100–9,700 / $9,700–11,600 ↗ H&H

1971 Mini 1275GT, 1275cc, 4-cylinder engine, 4-speed manual gearbox, fully restored 1998, 61,000 miles recorded.
£5,400–6,400 / €8,000–9,600 / $9,500–11,400 ↗ H&H
During a 41-year production run, the original pre-BMW Mini was available in numerous permutations, originally being offered by British Motor Corporation with either Austin or Morris badging and grilles.
By late 1969, however, all Minis were simply badged 'Mini', a practice that was continued by British Leyland and Austin Morris.

1991 Mini Cooper, 1275cc, 78bhp, adjustable shock absorbers, left-hand drive, fully restored, concours condition.
£5,200–6,200 / €7,700–9,200 / $9,200–11,000 ↗ B(Kn)

1995 Morgan 4/4 Four-Seater, 1800cc, Ford Zetec engine, wire wheels, boot-mounted luggage rack, cream leather interior.
£17,000–19,000 / €25,100–27,600 $30,000–33,000 ⊞ FHD

◀ **1926 Morris Cowley 11.9hp Two-Seater with Dickey,** 1550cc, restored, engine rebuilt, radiator recored, brakes overhauled, new wheel bearings, new tyres and tubes, new paintwork, reupholstered.
£11,700–14,000 / €17,300–20,700 $20,600–24,700 ↗ CGC

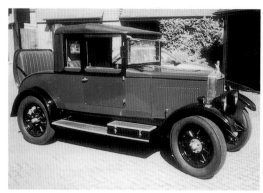

1928 Morris Oxford Drophead Coupé, 1803cc, 4-cylinder engine, 3-speed manual gearbox, dickey, blue interior trim, excellent condition.
£7,300–8,700 / €10,800–12,900
$12,800–15,300   ⊁ H&H

1953 Morris Minor Series II Two-Door Saloon, 803cc, overhead-valve 4-cylinder engine, new stainless steel exhaust, red interior trim.
£850–1,000 / €1,250–1,500 / $1,500–1,800   ⊁ BRIT

▶ **1934 Packard 11th Series Club Sedan,**
5275cc, 8-cylinder engine, 4-speed manual gearbox, electrics converted to 12 volts, brown interior.
£17,400–20,800 / €25,700–30,800
$30,000–36,000   ⊁ H&H
In 1898, James Ward Packard bought a Winton, but took it back to Alexander Winton with some suggested improvements. 'If you are so smart, you had better build a car yourself,' said Winton, so Packard did just that. His first Model A was completed in 1899. In 1923, the company introduced its first Straight 8, which was the first Packard to have four-wheel brakes. The 1924 models were known as the First Series, and this numbering system continued every year right up to the 26th Series, which was introduced for 1953.

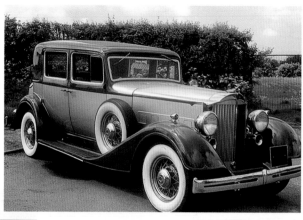

◀ **1964 Porsche 356C Coupé,** 1582cc, air-cooled flat-4 engine, 4-wheel torsion-bar independent suspension.
£13,500–16,200 / €20,000–24,000
$23,700–28,400   ⊁ COYS

1983 Porsche 911 3.2 Carrera, 3125cc, overhead-camshaft flat-6 engine, 5-speed manual gearbox, burgundy interior.
£6,500–7,800 / €9,600–11,500
$11,400–13,600   ⊁ H&H

1954 Riley RME 1½ Litre Saloon, 1496cc, 4-cylinder engine, flashing indicators, red interior.
£5,100–6,100 / €7,500–9,000 / $9,000–10,800   ⊁ CGC
Introduced in 1946, the Riley RMA was one of the first British cars launched after WWII to feature a new chassis design. With independent torsion-bar front suspension, rack-and-pinion steering and 80mph performance from its twin-cam, 1496cc four-cylinder engine, the RMA was praised by the contemporary motoring press for its excellent ride and handling qualities. Its successor, the RME, arrived in 1951 and featured a host of mechanical revisions. An open propshaft linked the four-speed manual gearbox to a new hypoid-bevel rear axle, while stopping power had been improved courtesy of Girling hydraulic brakes; an enlarged rear window gave welcome extra visibility.

◀ **1927 Rolls-Royce Phantom 1 Tourer,** 7668cc, 6-cylinder engine, restored early 1990s and fitted with new open tourer coachwork.
£26,900–32,000 / €39,000–47,000
$47,000–56,000   ⊁ H&H

1932 Rolls-Royce 20/25 Saloon, 3669cc, overhead-valve 6-cylinder engine, 4-speed manual gearbox, concours condition.
**£34,500–38,000 / €51,000–57,000
$60,000–66,000 ⊞ BLE**

1980 Rolls-Royce Corniche Convertible, 6750cc, V8 engine, 4-speed automatic transmission, excellent condition.
**£34,500–38,000 / €51,000–57,000
$60,000–66,000 ⊞ BLE**

◄ **1909 Rover 6hp Two-Seater,** vertically-mounted single-cylinder engine, leaf-spring suspension, cape cart-style hood, 2-piece folding windscreen, formerly owned by British Leyland Heritage Collection and National Motor Museum.
**£12,000–14,400 / €17,750–21,300
$21,000–25,000 ⚒ B(Kn)**
Like so many pioneers in the motor industry, Rover graduated from cycle and motorcycle manufacture to car production, its first four-wheeler appearing in 1904. Strangely, this model, with its 8hp engine, was considered too powerful for the novice motorist, and a 6hp option was soon added to the range. The car's simplicity, with its ash and steel flitch-plate chassis, undoubtedly contributed to its early popularity, and Rover's robust little single-cylinder models were to continue in production until 1912, by which time most other manufacturers had switched to multi-cylinder units.

1930 Sunbeam Twenty 2.9 Litre Saloon, 2916cc, overhead-valve 6-cylinder engine, vacuum servo brakes, reconditioned dynamo, original specification apart from electric fuel pump in place of Autovac, 1 owner since 1960.
**£7,600–9,100 / €11,200–13,400
$13,400–16,000 ⚒ B(Kn)**

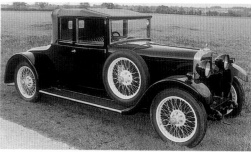

1929 Talbot 14/45 Doctor's Coupé, 1666cc, overhead-valve 6-cylinder engine, 45bhp, 4-speed manual gearbox, top speed 60mph, fully restored.
**£14,700–17,600 / €21,800–26,000
$26,000–31,000 ⚒ CGC**

1972 Triumph GT6 Mk III, 1998cc, overhead-valve 6-cylinder engine, 4-speed manual gearbox, bodywork restored and repainted 1999, new carpets.
£2,650–3,200 / €4,000–4,800 / $4,750–5,700 ⚒ H&H
To counter the Austin-Healey Sprite from rival BMC, Triumph rushed out the Spitfire, an open two-seater version of the Herald saloon, employing the same 1147cc engine, chassis and swing-axle rear suspension. Styled by Michelotti, the Spitfire was built between 1962 and 1980. Pitched against the MGB GT, a 1998cc, six-cylinder Vitesse-engined Spitfire with fixed-head fastback coupé body, the GT6, was offered between 1966 and 1973.

◄ **1976 Triumph Stag,** 2997cc, overhead-camshaft V8 engine, engine rebuilt with new crankshaft, Holley carburettor and air filter conversion, new manifold and exhaust system.
£4,200–5,000 / €6,200–7,400 $7,400–8,800 ⚞ H&H

1972 TVR 1600M, 1599cc, Ford 4-cylinder engine, tubular-steel backbone chassis, 4-wheel independent coil-sprung suspension, disc front brakes, rack-and-pinion steering.
£6,500–7,800 / €9,600–11,500 / $11,400–13,700 ⚞ CGC
Introduced in 1972 as the entry model in TVR's new M-series (named after company owner Martin Lilley), the 1600M was intended as a replacement for the firm's ageing Vixen S4.

1923 Vauxhall 14/40 Princeton Tourer, 2300cc, side-valve engine, detachable cylinder head, 3-speed manual gearbox, single-plate clutch, aluminium five-seat tourer coachwork, originally exported to Australia, imported to UK 1999, excellent condition.
£19,000–22,800 / €28,100–33,000 $33,000–39,000 ⚞ H&H

1972 Volkswagen 1300 Beetle, 1285cc, air-cooled overhead-valve 4-cylinder engine, 4-speed manual gearbox, fully restored.
£2,650–3,200 / €4,000–4,800 / $4,750–5,700 ⚞ H&H

◄ **1931 Wolseley Hornet,** coachwork by Swallow Cars, 1271cc, 6-cylinder engine, 4-speed manual gearbox, wire wheels, restored, concours condition.
£18,900–21,000 / €28,000–32,000 $33,000–37,000 ⊞ WHS
Specialist tuners such as Vic Derrington and Michael McEvoy were quick to see the potential of the Hornet's lively 1271cc engine. They developed four-speed remote-control gearboxes, improved camshafts, twin-carburettor conversions and even superchargers to extract more power. In April 1932, Wolseley bowed to pressure and marketed the Hornet Special in chassis form only. It featured 12in brakes, twin carburettors, three-branch exhausts and an oil cooler.

Mini *(British 1959–)*

1959 Morris Mini 850 DeLuxe, 850cc, 4-cylinder engine, finished in red, red/grey fleck vinyl upholstery, restoration bills for c£10,000 / €14,800 / $17,600, 1 family ownership for last 30 years, 30,000 miles recorded.
£3,750–4,500 / €5,600–6,700 / $6,600–7,900 ⚡ CGC
Following the Suez Crisis of 1957, Leonard Lord lost little time in ordering Alec Issigonis to drop everything in favour of a new small car project. Apart from the constraint of using existing BMC mechanical assemblies and a brief to house four adults and their luggage in as small a space as possible, Issigonis was given free rein. His response was the Mini. Featuring all-round independent 'rubber cone' suspension, a transverse, four-cylinder 850cc engine mounted in unit with its four-speed gearbox, and compact rack-and-pinion steering, it was a packaging masterpiece. Launched in August 1959, it proved an immediate success, fulfilling all Lord's criteria, but with the added bonus of exceptional handling and roadholding.

1964 Morris Mini Cooper, 998cc, overhead-valve 4-cylinder engine, 4-speed manual gearbox, converted to unleaded fuel, sump guard, adjustable suspension, brake servo, rev-counter, rally trip meter, roll cage, finished in green and white, matching interior.
£4,600–5,500 / €6,800–8,100 / $8,100–9,700 ⚡ B(Kn)
The Mini Cooper was launched in 1961, the brainchild of racing car manufacturer John Cooper. Enlarged to 997cc and suitably tweaked, the revised A-series engine easily met its target 55bhp, the extra power endowing it with an 85+mph top speed. To cope with the increased performance, Lockheed developed special 7in (17.8cm) diameter disc brakes for the front wheels. The new car soon established its credentials as a rally and race winner, and the stage was set for even faster versions.

1969 Mini Moke, 1000cc, new floor and chassis panels, period Weller wheels, full hood, seat belts to all 4 seats, heater.
£4,200–5,000 / €6,200–7,400 / $7,400–8,800 ⚡ COYS
Developed in the early 1960s, the Moke was intended for military use and was designed to be stacked on board aircraft prior to being dropped by parachute, then being capable of carrying four adults over rough terrain. Although it could easily be manhandled by its occupants if it got stuck, it was rejected for lack of ground clearance.

1967 Mini De Luxe, 848cc, overhead-valve 4-cylinder engine, 4-speed manual gearbox, original, good condition.
£6,000–7,000 / €8,900–10,400/ $10,600–12,300 🚘 MINI

▶ **1971 Mini Cooper S Mk II,** 1275cc, overhead-valve 4-cylinder engine, alloy wheels, wheel-arch extensions, 1 of last original Cooper S models built, concours condition.
£10,800–12,000
€16,000–17,800
$19,000–21,100 🚘 MINI

1979 Austin Mini 1000, 998cc, 4-cylinder engine, finished in beige, cream interior, 20,000 miles recorded.
£1,800–2,150 / €2,650–3,200 / $3,150–3,800 ➤ H&H

1979 Innocenti Mini Cooper, 1275cc, right-hand drive, Minilite alloy wheels, front quarterlights, improved interior, finished in red and black.
£2,600–3,100 / €3,850–4,600 / $4,600–5,500 ➤ COYS
While the Italian Innocenti-built cars remained close to their British counterparts in terms of specification, the trim and fittings were of a much higher standard, with additional instruments housed in moulded dashboards among their distinctive features (a rev-counter was one Innocenti luxury not available to UK buyers). Such was the demand that Innocenti Minis were also assembled in a factory in Britain.

1991 ERA Mini Turbo, 1275cc, Garrett T3 turbocharger, 5-speed manual gearbox, alloy wheels, sun roof, special dashboard, spotlamps, half leather grey interior, 25,000 miles recorded, last example built.
£7,000–8,400 / €10,400–12,400 / $12,300–14,800 ⊞ CARS
The ERA Mini Turbo was designed to replace the top-of-the-range Mini Cooper and S series of the late 1980s, but because of high development costs and an eventual price of £12,000 / €17,800 / $21,100, this model could not compete with the new VW Golf GTi.

1979 Mini 1275 GT, engine bored to 1380cc, modified cylinder head, 'fast road' camshaft, Maniflow exhaust, finished in red, grey striped upholstery.
£2,000–2,400 / €2,950–3,550 / $3,500–4,200 ➤ COYS

1990 ERA Mini Turbo, 1275cc, 4-cylinder engine, Garrett T3 turbocharger, lowered suspension, alloy wheels, ventilated brakes, twin spotlamps, bonnet power bulge, body kit, leather interior, fewer than 10,000 miles recorded, concours condition.
£7,000–8,400 / €10,400–12,400 / $12,300–14,800 ➤ COYS

1991 Rover Mini Cooper, 1275cc, 4-cylinder engine, finished in green and white, red and black interior.
£1,450–1,750 / €2,150–2,600 / $2,500–3,100 ➤ B(Kn)
John Cooper sold his own modified Minis under the 'Mini Cooper' name from the mid-1980s, before Rover's acquisition of the rights to the new name made it possible to officially relaunch the model in 1990. The new Mini Cooper was based on the Mini 30, the most luxuriously equipped limited-edition Mini to date, but fitted with the new 1275cc engine rather than the 30's 998cc unit. Power was not back to the old 1275 S level, but at 61bhp the new Cooper's maximum output was the highest since its predecessor's demise in 1971.

| MINI | ENGINE | DATES | CONDITION | | |
Model	cc/cyl		1	2	3
Mini	848/4	1959–67	£3,500	£1,200	–
Mini Countryman	848/4	1961–67	£2,500	£1,200	–
Cooper Mk I	997/4	1961–67	£8,000	£5,000	£2,500
Cooper Mk II	998/4	1967–69	£6,000	£4,000	£1,500
Cooper S Mk I	var/4	1963–67	£7,000	£5,000	£2,000
Cooper S Mk II	1275/4	1967–71	£6,000	£5,000	£2,000
Innocenti Mini Cooper	998/4	1966–75	£4,500	£2,000	£1,000

◄ **1994 Rover Mini 35 Limited Edition Radford,** 1275cc, automatic transmission, catalytic converter, Minilite-style alloy wheels, modified by Radford at a cost of £20,000 / €29,600 / 35,000, electric windows and sun roof, walnut dashboard and door cappings, central locking, 46,000 miles recorded, finished in green, matching interior.
£5,600–6,700 / €8,300–9,900 $9,900–11,800 ✗ B(Kn)

Morgan *(British 1910–)*

After serving an apprenticeship with the Great Western Railway, H.F.S. Morgan quit to open a garage in Malvern Link in 1906. Initially, the business sold Wolseleys and Darracqs; it also briefly operated a Wolseley bus between Malvern and nearby Worcester. This was followed by a car hire service, but already Morgan was beginning to experiment with vehicles of his own design.

The first of these arrived in 1908, in the shape of a motorcycle powered by a Peugeot V-twin engine, but this was soon forsaken in favour of a three-wheel car, also Peugeot V-twin powered. The engine was mounted at the front and drove a single rear wheel by means of a propshaft. This ran through a large tube that was the main chassis component. There was a two-speed gearbox, and the front wheels were provided with independent suspension by means of sliding, coil-sprung pillars at each end of a beam axle.

Even though the prototype had no body and only a single seat, it encouraged 'HFS' to consider a production version. That dream was realised in 1910, when, with a loan from his father, he was able to set up the Morgan Motor Company.

At the end of that year, the fledgling company displayed the first two 961cc, JAP-engined production cars at the Olympia Cycle & Motorcycle Show. This led to a two-seat version in 1911 and the appointment of the first Morgan agency – at Harrod's in central London.

By the outbreak of WWI, production was approaching 1,000 cars annually, and much publicity had been gained from sporting successes in the UK and Europe.

The first four-seater, known as the Family model, arrived in 1919. Engines used during the interwar years included JAP, Anzani, Precision, Blackburne and the Matchless V-twin.

Following an accident in 1924, three-wheelers were banned from racing, but in 1927 the Morgan Club was reorganised as the Cyclecar Club and thereby was able to re-establish the three-wheeler in racing. As a result, Morgans collected a string of victories and speed records.

From late 1933, a three-wheeler was listed with a four-cylinder Ford engine. Then, in 1935, Morgan axed the JAP power unit, thereafter fitting the Matchless as standard. Later, in December 1935, the company announced its first production four-wheeler. Coded 4/4, this employed a 1122cc Coventry-Climax engine. It arrived just as sales of Morgan's traditional three-wheelers were plummeting.

During WWII, Morgan made aircraft components. Post-war, it continued building three-wheelers until as late as February 1952, but the bulk of sales were of the new Plus 4, which had superseded the 4/4 in 1950. The later car employed a 2088cc Standard Vanguard engine.

In 1955, a new 4/4, with a Ford 10 engine, was offered as a budget-priced alternative to the Plus 4, which now used a Triumph TR2 power unit. Later, the 4/4 gained a Ford 1600GT engine, and the Plus 4 a Triumph TR3, then TR4 engine.

The 1960s were generally a lean time for Morgan, not helped by a fall in demand in the USA; from 1966, the company was unable to sell any cars in the States due to new vehicle legislation. However, this led to the Plus 8 in 1968. Powered by the 3.5 litre Rover V8, it allowed Morgan to re-enter the US market.

During the 1980s, Morgan offered a choice of four-cylinder Ford and Fiat engines for the 4/4 and Plus 4, while the Plus 8 continued with fuel injection and the Vitesse engine. By 1985, Morgan had a reported five- or six-year waiting list.

In the late 1990s, Morgan fans could look forward to the eagerly awaited Aero 8, and when Charles Morgan wrote the Foreword for the 2001 edition of *Miller's Collectors Cars Yearbook & Price Guide*, he was able to say, 'We are poised to enter one of the most exciting phases in the company's history...'

MORGAN Model	ENGINE cc/cyl	DATES	CONDITION 1	2	3
4/4 Series I	1098/4	1936–50	£10,000+	£6,000	£5,000
Plus 4	2088/4	1950–53	£15,000	£10,000	£7,000
Plus 4	1991/4	1954–68	£14,000	£11,000	£7,000
4/4 Series II–IV	997/4	1954–68	£10,000+	£7,000	£5,000
4/4 1600	1599/4	1960 on	£14,000+	£9,000	£6,000
Plus 8	3528/8	1969 on	£17,000+	£13,500	£10,000

1929 Morgan Aero Roadster, 1078cc, Anzani M3 overhead-valve 57-degree V-twin engine.
£15,100–18,100 / €22,300–26,800
$26,600–32,000 ⚒ B(Kn)

The appearance of Morgan's first three-wheeler in 1910 coincided with an upsurge of interest in cyclecars. Of simple construction with front-mounted motorcycle engine and two-speed chain transmission, the Morgan was light, fast and economical to run. V-twin engines from a wide variety of manufacturers were employed, including Blackburne, MAG and British Anzani, although those from J. A. Prestwich predominated. Competition from small sports cars forced the adoption of a three-speed-and reverse gearbox in 1931, the last two-speed model leaving the factory the following year. A more refined version – the F4, with 8hp Ford four-cylinder power unit – appeared soon after, later forming the basis of the first four-wheeled Morgan. Built from 1929 to 1932, the second-generation Aero Model could be ordered with either of two JAP engines – side- or overhead-valve – or an overhead-valve Anzani; 70+mph was attainable with either of the overhead-valve versions. From the mid-1930s onwards, Morgan three-wheelers were fitted with Matchless V-twin engines in preference to JAP units.

1934 Morgan Three-Wheeler, 998cc, JAP air-cooled overhead-valve V-twin engine, magneto ignition, high-level exhausts, drum brakes, wire wheels.
£16,200–18,000 / €24,000–26,600
$28,500–32,000 ⊞ PM

1978 Morgan 4/4, 1598cc, Ford 4-cylinder engine, wire wheels, roll bar, partially rebuilt, grey leather interior, 53,000 miles recorded.
£9,400–10,500 / €13,900–15,500
$16,500–18,500 ⊞ FHD

1980 Morgan 4/4, 1598cc, Ford 4-cylinder engine, finished in black, stone leather interior.
£11,200–12,500 / €16,600–18,500
$19,700–22,000 ⊞ FHD

1982 Morgan Plus 8, 3528cc, Rover V8 engine, 5-speed gearbox, alloy wheels, top speed 125mph, finished in metallic green, cream leather interior.
£11,200–12,500 / €16,600–18,500
$19,700–22,000 ⊞ FHD

Morris *(British 1912–83)*

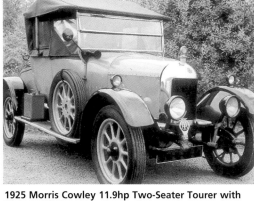

1924 Morris Cowley 11.9hp Two-Seater Tourer, 1550cc, side-valve 4-cylinder engine, rear brakes, reconditioned dynamotor, new exhaust, beaded-edge tyres.
£7,100–8,500 / €10,500–12,600 / $12,500–15,000 ➶ CGC

1925 Morris Cowley 11.9hp Two-Seater Tourer with Dickey, 1550cc, side-valve 4-cylinder engine, new clutch, radiator, hood and side screens, finished in grey, green leather upholstery.
£7,100–8,500 / €10,500–12,600 / $12,500–15,000 ➶ B(Kn)

1925 Morris Oxford Drophead Coupé with Dickey, 1550cc, side-valve 4-cylinder engine, 3-speed centre-change gearbox, finished in yellow and black, Bedford cord interior.
£8,200–9,800 / €12,100–14,500 / $14,400–17,200 ➶ B(Kn)

1926 Morris Cowley 11.9hp Two-Seater Tourer, 1550cc, side-valve 4-cylinder engine, leaf-spring suspension, finished in beige with black wings, wooden dashboard, Smiths instruments, grey interior.
£7,400–8,800 / €11,000–13,000 / $12,500–15,500 ➶ CGC

1929 Morris Cowley Four-Door Saloon, 1550cc, side-valve 4-cylinder engine, 4-wheel brakes, leaf-spring suspension, finished in maroon and black, grey interior.
£4,200–5,000 / €6,200–7,400 / $7,400–8,800 ➶ BRIT
September 1926 saw the appearance of the entirely redesigned Morris Cowley. Gone was the famous 'bull-nose' radiator, to be replaced by a more conventional flat radiator, while the coachwork, particularly on the two-seat tourer, displayed a certain amount of American influence.

MORRIS Model	ENGINE cc/cyl	DATES	CONDITION		
			1	2	3
Prices given are for saloons					
Cowley (Bullnose)	1550/4	1913–26	£12,000	£8,000	£6,000
Cowley	1550/4	1927–39	£10,000	£6,000	£4,000
Oxford (Bullnose)	1803/4	1924–27	£14,000	£10,000	£6,000
Oxford	1803/4	1927–33	£10,000	£8,000	£6,000
16/40	2513/4	1928–33	£8,000	£7,000	£6,000
18	2468/6	1928–35	£9,000	£7,000	£5,000
8 Minor	847/4	1929–34	£5,500	£4,000	£2,000
10/4	1292/4	1933–35	£5,000	£3,000	£1,500
25	3485/6	1933–39	£10,000	£8,000	£5,000
Eight	918/4	1935–39	£4,000	£3,000	£1,500
10hp	1140/4	1939–47	£4,500	£3,000	£1,500
16hp	2062/6	1936–38	£5,000	£3,500	£2,000
18hp	2288/6	1935–37	£5,000	£3,500	£2,500
21hp	2916/6	1935–36	£6,000	£4,000	£2,500

A tourer version of the above is worth approximately 30% more. Value is dependent on body type and is greater if coachbuilt.

◄ **1930 Morris Minor 8hp Two-Door Saloon,** 846cc, overhead-camshaft 4-cylinder engine, 20bhp, ladder chassis, leaf-spring suspension, drum brakes, top speed 50mph, rebuilt radiator, new exhaust system.
£2,750–3,300 / €4,050–4,900 / $4,800–5,800 ✗ CGC

1930 Morris Oxford Four-Door Saloon, 1803cc, 4-cylinder engine, wire wheels, restored, finished in red and black, brown interior.
£4,800–5,700 / €7,100–8,400 / $8,4000–10,000 ✗ H&H

1936 Morris Eight Two-Door Saloon, 918cc, 4-cylinder engine, converted to unleaded fuel.
£2,150–2,550 / €3,200–3,750 / $3,800–4,500 ✗ H&H

▶ **1936 Morris Eight Two-Door Deluxe Saloon,** 918cc, 4-cylinder engine, hydraulic drum brakes, non-standard Lucas lamp conversion.
£3,350–4,000 / €4,950–5,900 / $5,900–7,000 ✗ BRIT
Available as a two- or four-seat saloon in standard and deluxe forms, the Eight was capable of almost 60mph and able to return 45mpg.

1936 Morris Eight Tourer, 918cc, new engine, new clutch, finished in red and black, red upholstery, good condition.
£5,500–6,600 / €8,100–9,800 / $9,700–11,600 ✗ B(Kn)

▶ **1937 Morris 14/6 Four-Door Saloon,** 2062cc, 6-cylinder engine, 4-speed manual gearbox, unrestored, excellent condition.
£1,850–2,200 / €2,750–3,250 / $3,250–3,850 ✗ COYS

◄ **1953 Morris Minor Series II,** 803cc, overhead-valve 4-cylinder engine, 4-speed manual gearbox, rack-and-pinion steering.
£1,250–1,500 / €1,850–2,200 $2,200–2,650 ✗ B(Kn)
The Alec Issigonis designed Morris Minor was launched in 1948. Initially powered by the company's 918cc side-valve engine, it received the more efficient 803 overhead-valve unit in 1953.

1955 Morris Minor Series II Four-Door Saloon, 803cc, overhead-valve 4-cylinder engine, fully restored, finished in original green, de luxe specification interior.
£2,200–2,600 / €3,250–3,850 / $3,850–4,600 ✗ BARO
In all, 1,620,000 Minors were sold over a 23-year production life.

1957 Morris Minor 1000 Four-Door Saloon, 948cc, overhead-valve 4-cylinder engine, 4-speed manual gearbox, finished in grey, burgundy interior.
£1,600–1,900 / €2,350–2,800 / $2,800–3,350 ✗ CGC

1964 Morris Oxford Four-Door Saloon, 1622cc, overhead-valve 4-cylinder engine, 4-speed manual gearbox, front and rear anti-roll bars, fewer than 8,000 miles recorded.
£7,500–9,000 / €11,100–13,300 / $13,200–15,800 ✗ CGC
This car was the last private car purchased by Sir Winston Churchill.

1968 Morris Minor 1000 Series V Two-Door Saloon, 1098cc, 4-cylinder engine, 45bhp, 4-speed manual gearbox, top speed 77mph, 3 owners from new, finished in pale grey, blue vinyl upholstery.
£1,000–1,200 / €1,5000–1,800 / $1,750–2,100 ✗ CGC
The Series V Minor arrived in 1962, with engine size increased from 948 to 1098cc, giving a useful increase in performance.

MORRIS Model	ENGINE cc/cyl	DATES	CONDITION 1	2	3
Minor Series MM	918/4	1948–52	£3,000	£1,600	£800
Minor Series MM Conv	918/4	1948–52	£4,500	£2,200	£1,200
Minor Series II	803/4	1953–56	£2,000	£1,000	£500
Minor Series II Conv	803/4	1953–56	£5,500	£3,500	£1,500
Minor Series II Est	803/4	1953–56	£3,000	£1,250	£800
Minor 1000	948/4	1956–63	£1,750	£925	£250
Minor 1000 Conv	948/4	1956–63	£4,000+	£2,000	£750
Minor 1000 Est	948/4	1956–63	£4,000	£2,200	£1,200
Minor 1000	1098/4	1963–71	£2,000	£950	£250
Minor 1000 Conv	1098/4	1963–71	£4,500	£3,000	£1,500
Minor 1000 Est	1098/4	1963–71	£4,000	£3,000	£1,500
Cowley 1200	1200/4	1954–56	£1,675	£1,000	£300
Cowley 1500	1489/4	1956–59	£1,750	£950	£350
Oxford MO	1476/4	1948–54	£2,000	£850	£250
Oxford MO Est	1476/4	1952–54	£3,000	£1,500	£350
Oxford Series II–III	1489/4	1954–59	£2,000	£1,200	£300
Oxford Series II–IV Est	1489/4	1954–60	£2,250	£1,350	£250
Oxford Series V Farina	1489/4	1959–61	£1,800	£800	£250
Oxford Series VI Farina	1622/4	1961–71	£1,750	£750	£200
Six Series MS	2215/6	1948–54	£2,500	£1,500	£500
Isis Series I–II	2639/6	1955–58	£2,500	£1,300	£450
Isis Series I–II Est	2639/6	1956–57	£2,600	£1,350	£500

Nash *(American 1917–62)*

◄ **1959 Nash Metropolitan,** 1500cc, overhead-valve 4-cylinder engine, automatic transmission, fully restored.
£3,250–3,900 / €4,800–5,800 / $5,700–6,900 ⚒ BARO
The Metropolitan was built for Nash by Austin in the UK, production beginning in 1953. It was powered initially by the 1200cc A40 engine. The 1956 model year saw a new 1500cc engine fitted, resulting in a 24 per cent increase in power and a 10mph increase in top speed to a heady 80mph. Sales of the Metropolitan peaked in 1959, when 22,300 were sold, but by 1961 they had plummeted, and production came to an end in 1962.

NB *(British/Italian 1905–27)*

1913 NB 12hp Five-Seater Tourer, 2155cc, 4-cylinder engine, leaf-spring suspension, older restoration, original, good condition.
£27,000–32,400 / €40,000–47,000 / $48,000–56,000 ⚒ B(Kn)
John Newton of the Manchester company Newton & Bennett owned the Valt factory in Turin, which built the Newton Bennett car, commonly known as the NB. The 12hp model was powered by a four-cylinder engine displacing 2155cc. About 1,000 were manufactured.

Nissan *(Japanese 1937)*

◄ **1991 Nissan Figaro Targa Coupé,** 1000cc, 4-cylinder engine, turbocharger, automatic transmission, sliding soft top, finished in pale green and white, electric windows, air conditioning, cream leather upholstery.
£10,000–12,000 / €14,800–17,800
$17,600–21,100 ⚒ B(Kn)
Prompted by the burgeoning interest in European classics among Japanese car collectors in the 1980s, Nissan produced four retro-styled cars emulating 1960s European styling, but incorporating up-to-the-minute Japanese technology. Launched in 1991, the Figaro was the fourth of these. It was soon in such demand that a lottery was organized to determine the lucky owners of the limited run of 20,000.

Oldsmobile (American 1896–)

◀ **1972 Oldsmobile Cutlass Convertible,** 455cu.in, V8 engine, 400bhp, automatic transmission, completely restored, finished in yellow and white, white hood, concours winner.
£12,600–15,100 / € 18,600–22,300 $22,200–26,600 ✒ BJ

OLDSMOBILE Model	ENGINE cc/cyl	DATES	CONDITION 1	2	3
Curved Dash	1600/1	1901–04	£18,000+	£15,000	£12,000
30	2771/6	1925–26	£9,000	£7,000	£4,000
Straight Eight	4213/8	1937–38	£14,000	£9,000	£5,000

OM (Italian 1905–34)

▶ **1925 OM Tipo 469 11.9hp Roadster,** 1496cc, 4-cylinder engine, 4-speed manual gearbox, Brooklands-type windscreens, Bosch-style headlamps, Jaeger speedometer.
£10,000–12,000 / € 14,800–17,800 $17,600–21,100 ✒ B(Kn)
The first cars built by Officine Meccaniche (OM) were branded Züst, after the company it had taken over at the end of WWI. The OM Tipo 465 was introduced in 1920, a 1325cc, side-valve-engined car, but by 1923 this had become the Tipo 469 with a four-cylinder, 1496cc engine.

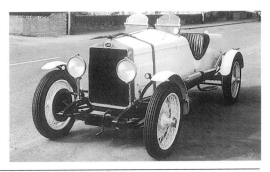

Orient (American 1898–1922)

◀ **1903 Orient Buckboard,** 6000cc, single-cylinder engine, trembler coil ignition, single-speed transmission, restored.
£10,800–12,900 / € 16,000–19,100 $19,000–22,700 ✒ H&H
The rear-engined Orient Buckboard was built by the Walham Manufacturing Company, and 1,800 examples were sold during 1903–04. Early models had a single speed transmission and no rear suspension; a two-speed version was introduced in 1904.

OSCA (Italian 1947–67)

▶ **1959 OSCA 1500 Coupé,** 1452cc, double-overhead-camshaft 4-cylinder engine, 5-speed manual gearbox, 4-wheel disc brakes, wire wheels, fully restored, concours condition.
£20,500–24,400 / € 30,000–36,000 $36,000–43,000 ✒ H&H
In 1938, the Maserati brothers sold their interest in the firm bearing their name to the industrialist Adolfo Orsi. In December 1947, the three surviving brothers set up Officina Specializzata Costruzione Automobili Fratelli Maserati (OSCA). Over the next two decades, this company built small quantities of racing and sports cars.

OSI *(Italian late 1960s)*

1967 OSI MTS Coupé, Ford V6 engine, 4-speed manual gearbox, original 2.3 litre engine replaced by 2.8 litre unit, 1 of 2,000 built.
£7,900–9,400 / €11,700–13,900 / $13,900–16,500 ↗ CGC
Italian styling house Ghia was keen to expand in the 1960s and took on ever more ambitious projects with a view to securing greater manufacturing capacity. Contracts for a new vehicle were won from Innocenti and Fiat, but it was soon discovered that full-scale production of this new vehicle would require additional financial backing. Manufacturing giant Olivetti was approached for assistance, leading to the formation of Olivetti Stamping Industries (OSI).

Owen *(American 1915–22)*

▶ **1918 Owen Magnetic Tourer,** 6-cylinder engine.
£23,500–28,000 / €35,000–41,000 / $35,000–49,000 ↗ BB(S)
The Owen Magnetic was a high-quality car that featured an electric transmission developed by Justin B. Entz, whose design had been incorporated in some Columbia cars and also the battleship *New Mexico*. The engine drove a generator to produce electric power, which was transmitted over an air gap to turn the propshaft. Brothers Raymond and Ralph Owen launched the first version of the Owen Magnetic in 1915. The car was advertised as having a thousand speeds; perhaps not entirely true, but it did dispense with clutch and gears, and also with a starter motor, magneto and battery. All of these functions were performed by parts of the transmission.

Packard *(American 1899–1958)*

1930 Packard 745 Phaeton, 384.8cu.in, side-valve 8-cylinder engine, 106bhp, 3-speed manual gearbox, wire spoke wheels.
£57,000–68,000 / €84,000–101,000 / $100,000–120,000 ↗ BB(S)

◀ **1937 Packard 120C Four-Door Saloon,** 4621cc, 8-cylinder engine, single Stromberg carburettor, 6 volt electrics, finished in back, maroon interior trim.
£11,800–14,100 / € 17,500–20,900 $20,800–24,800 ⚒ H&H

▶ **1955 Packard Caribbean Convertible,** 352cu.in, V8 engine, twin 4-barrel carburettors, 275bhp, 3-speed manual gearbox with overdrive, power steering and brakes, restored, finished in ivory and green, leather interior, working Wonder-Bar radio, 1 of only 500 examples built, concours condition.
£40,000–48,000 / € 59,000–71,000 $70,000–84,000 ⚒ BJ

PACKARD Model	ENGINE cc/cyl	DATES	CONDITION 1	2	3
Twin Six	6946/12	1916–23	£30,000	£20,000	£15,000
6	3973/6	1921–24	£20,000	£15,000	£12,000
6, 7, 8 Series	5231/8	1929–39	£45,000+	£25,000+	£14,000+
12	7300/12	1936–39	£50,000+	£30,000+	£18,000+

Panhard-Levassor
(French 1891–1967)

◀ **1899 Panhard-Levassor Type M2F 6hp Wagonette ,** Daimler Phoenix vertical twin-cylinder engine, 3 forward gears, chain drive to rear wheels, finished in green, red interior.
£107,000–117,000 / € 158,000–173,000 $188,000–205,000 ⚒ H&H
After acquiring the French rights to the Daimler engine, Panhard et Levassor built its first motor vehicles in 1890–91. Initially, all were rear- or mid-engined, but in 1891, to improve weight distribution, the company relocated the engine to the front. A bonnet also provided the motor with better protection from the elements. Emile Levassor's famous victory in the 1895 Paris-Bordeaux-Paris road race really caught the public imagination and ensured that a Panhard was the choice of the aspiring motorist. As a result, production climbed steadily.

▶ **1902 Panhard-Levassor Type A 7hp Four-Seater,** Daimler Phoenix vertical twin-cylinder engine, 1 family ownership from new, in need of some restoration.
£87,000–104,000 € 129,000–154,000 $153,000–183,000 ⚒ B(Kn)

Peugeot *(French 1889–)*

◀ **1953 Peugeot 203A Four-Door Saloon,** 1920cc, 4-cylinder engine, 4-speed manual gearbox, finished in black, pale grey interior.
£1,000–1,200 / €1,500–1,800
$1,750–2,100 🔧 CGC
Peugeot's first post-WWII model was the 203, introduced in 1947. A new, over-square 1290cc engine with hemispherical combustion chambers, all-round coil suspension and rack-and-pinion steering made it a winner from the outset. Renowned for its durability, it remained in production until 1960.

PEUGEOT Model	ENGINE cc/cyl	DATES	CONDITION 1	2	3
Bébé	856/4	1912–14	£25,000	£15,000	£8,000
153	2951/4	1913–26	£9,000	£5,000	£3,000
163	1490/4	1920–24	£5,000	£4,000	£2,000
Bébé	676/4	1920–25	£7,000	£6,000	£3,000
156	5700/6	1922–24	£7,000	£5,000	£3,000
174	3828/4	1922–28	£7,500	£5,000	£2,000
172	714/4	1926–28	£4,000	£3,000	£1,500
183	1990/6	1929–30	£5,000	£3,000	£1,500
201	996/4	1930–36	£6,000	£3,000	£1,500
402	2140/4	1938–40	£4,500	£3,000	£1,000
Good solid cars.					

Pick *(British 1898–1925)*

▶ **1912 Pick 20hp Coupé,** 3600cc, 4-cylinder engine, artillery wheels, brass acetylene headlamps, oil side lamps, bulb horn, 1 owner for last 41 years, 1 of 2 Picks known to survive.
£20,100–24,000 / €29,700–36,000
$35,000–42,000 🔧 B(Kn)

Pontiac *(American 1907–)*

◀ **1960 Pontiac Bonneville Convertible,** 389cu.in, V8 engine, Tri-Power 3-carburettor induction, 318bhp, power steering and brakes, finished in blue, 3-tone leather interior.
£26,000–28,500 / €38,000–42,000
$46,000–50,000 🔧 BJ
Edward M. Murphy incorporated the Pontiac Buggy Company in 1891 in Pontiac, Michigan, hence the name.

PONTIAC Model	ENGINE cc/cyl	DATES	CONDITION 1	2	3
Six–27	3048/6	1926–29	£9,000	£7,000	£4,000
Silver Streak	3654/8	1935–37	£12,000	£9,000	£5,500
6	3638/6	1937–49	£7,000	£4,000	£3,500
8	4078/8	1937–49	£7,000	£4,000	£3,500

Porsche *(German 1948–)*

In 1905, after working for Jacob Lohner, developing electric and petrol cars, Ferdinand Porsche became technical director of Austro-Daimler in Vienna Neustadt. From 1910, he designed a series of aero engines, including an air-cooled flat-four, which is widely seen as the ancestor to the Volkswagen and Porsche car engines.

In 1929, Porsche moved to Steyr, then Austria's largest car manufacturer, as chief designer, but later that year, following the failure of Steyr's bank, the company was absorbed by Austro-Daimler. This prompted Porsche to leave and set up his own design bureau in 1930. His right-hand man in the new venture was Karl Rabe, a young engineer whom he had met at Austro-Daimler. Rabe was a key figure in the rise of the Porsche marque and would serve as its chief designer until 1966. Ferdinand's son, Ferry, had also joined the company.

After doing work for Zündapp and NSU, in 1934 Porsche accepted a commission to build a 'people's car', which eventually became the Volkswagen Beetle. The first three prototypes were delivered in 1936.

But production cars were only one facet of the Porsche design bureau's work. It also developed the Auto Union V16 Grand Prix car and its record breaking derivatives, and the formidable Tiger tank.

Although Ferdinand Porsche had attempted to remain out of politics during the German Nazi era, he was arrested in 1945 by the Americans and handed over to the French, being imprisoned for two years. When released in 1947, he returned to Germany, where he began work on a Porsche sports car, based on his pre-war ideas for a sports version of the VW Beetle. Given the project number 356, it was a lightweight two-seat roadster with a tuned, 1131cc, air-cooled VW engine and VW suspension. A streamlined coupé model was displayed in Geneva in 1949.

The first 50 cars were built at Porsche's pre-war offices in Gmünd, but more capacity was needed, and Ferdinand managed to negotiate the return of his Stuttgart factory in 1950. Almost 300 cars were built that year. In 1951, Porsche made its first visit to the Le Mans 24-hour race, finishing 20th.

Ferdinand Porsche died in 1952, but by then, Ferry had been running the company for several years.

The basic 356 design continued to be developed until it was replaced by the 911 series in 1964. The most radical of the 356 series had been the Speedster, introduced in the USA during 1954. In fact, the American market took a large percentage of Porsche production. The 10,000th Porsche left the works in 1965, and by the end of that decade, production had reached around 8,000 cars annually.

Initially, the 911 featured a 1991cc, flat-six engine producing 130bhp, but it gradually grew in displacement and power. Fuel injection arrived in 1970, coinciding with an increase in engine size to 2195cc; in 1972, it rose to 2343cc; and, in late 1973, went up to 2687cc, after which fuel injection became standard. That year, Porsche built 15,415 cars, of which 75 per cent were exported. In 1975, a turbocharged version of the 911 was offered, but only 9,424 cars were sold.

From the late 1970s, there was a dramatic increase in sales, thanks in no small part to the debut of the low-priced 924 in 1975 and the top-of-the-range 928 in 1977, alongside improved versions of the ever popular 911.

The 924 was a radical move; it featured a liquid-cooled, 1984cc, front-mounted, four-cylinder engine and rear-wheel drive. By 1981, over 100,000 had been sold.

Throughout the 1980s, Porsche continued to expand, and in 1986 production reached almost 54,000 cars. Other significant models of this era included the Carrera Turbo, 928S and 944. Again, the USA was the top export market.

In the 1990s, the Boxster arrived, offering potential buyers the chance to own a Porsche for almost half the price of the latest 911.

1957 Porsche 356 Speedster, 1086cc, flat-4 engine, chrome wheels, finished in red, black interior.
£34,000–40,000 / €50,000–60,000 / $60,000–72,000 ⋌ COYS

1961 Porsche 356B Coupé, 1582cc, flat-4 engine,
torsion-bar front suspension, rear swing axles,
engine rebuilt, body restored.
**£11,800–14,100 / €17,500–20,900
$20,800–24,100** ✗ H&H
The first production Porsche was the rear-engined 356.
Early cars were powered by the air-cooled, 1131cc,
Beetle flat-four engine, albeit tuned to produce
40bhp, the brakes being cable-operated until 1951.

1961 Porsche 356B Roadster, 1582cc, flat-4 engine,
boot rack, Carerra VDM steering wheel, US export model,
concours condition.
**£29,500–35,000 / €44,000–52,000
$52,000–62,000** ✗ COYS

1964 Porsche 356SC Coupé, 1582cc, flat-4 engine,
finished in silver, black interior, fully restored,
concours condition.
**£14,000–16,800 / €20,700–24,900
$24,600–29,500** ✗ COYS

1964 Porsche 356C Coupé, 1582cc, flat-4 engine, 90bhp,
top speed 110+mph.
**£8,500–10,200 / €12,600–15,000
$15,000–18,000** ✗ BARO

▶ **1968 Porsche 911T,** 1991cc, flat-6 engine,
160bhp, 5-speed manual gearbox, finished in
grey, cream leather interior.
**£12,900–15,400 / €19,100–22,800
$22,700–27,100** ✗ H&H

PORSCHE Model	ENGINE cc/cyl	DATES	CONDITION		
			1	2	3
356	var/4	1949–53	£15,000+	£8,000+	£5,000
356 Cabriolet	var/4	1951–53	£20,000+	£14,000	£10,000
356A	1582/4	1955–59	£13,000	£9,000	£5,000
356A Cabriolet	1582/4	1956–59	£16,000	£10,000	£7,000
356A Speedster	1582/4	1955–58	£40,000	£22,000	£14,000
356B Carrera	1582/ 1966/4	1960–65	£50,000+	£30,000+	£18,000
356C	1582/4	1963–65	£17,000+	£11,000+	£5,000
356C Cabriolet	1582/4	1963–64	£25,000+	£16,000	£10,000
911/911L/T/E	1991/6	1964–68	£12,000	£7,000	£5,000
912	1582/4	1965–68	£6,500	£5,000	£2,000
911S	1991/6	1966–69	£12,000	£8,000	£5,500
911S	2195/6	1969–71	£13,000	£9,000	£6,000
911T	2341/6	1971–73	£13,000	£8,000	£6,000
911E	2341/6	1971–73	£12,000+	£8,000	£6,000
914/4	1679/4	1969–75	£4,000	£3,000	£1,000
914/6	1991/6	1969–71	£6,000	£3,500	£1,500
911S	2341/6	1971–73	£16,000	£10,000	£8,500
Carrera RS Lightweight	2687/6	1973	£40,000+	£28,000+	£16,000
Carrera RS Touring	2687/6	1973	£30,000+	£26,000+	£17,000
Carrera 3	2994/6	1976–77	£14,000	£9,000	£7,000
924 Turbo	1984/4	1978–83	£5,000	£4,000	£2,000
928/928S	4474/4664–V8	1977–86	£10,000	£7,000	£4,000
911SC	2993/6	1977–83	£13,000	£8,000	£6,000

Sportomatic cars are less desirable.

Miller's Milestones

Porsche 911S (1966–73)
Price range: £5,000–14,000 / €7,400–20,700 / $8,800–24,600
To many, the Porsche 911S is the purest of all the company's products – and one of the best. In its day, it was hot stuff, the air-cooled, 1991cc flat-six engine featuring a higher compression ratio, larger valves, forged pistons and twin triple-choke Weber carburettors. Power output was a potent 160bhp, which grew to 170bhp with fuel injection. Other features of the 911S were its five-speed gearbox (rare in those days), monocoque chassis, all-round disc brakes and independent suspension. The S came with 'starfish' alloy wheels, the only external indicator that it was actually an S rather than the standard version. The development potential of the 911 engine has been incredible. Power has leapt from the original 130bhp of the 1963 2 litre model to the Turbo's 360bhp, and the 450bhp of the 911-based 959, a technological tour de force that was created to take on the likes of Ferrari's 288 GTO and F40.

◄ **1970 Porsche 911E 2.2 Targa,** 2341cc, overhead-camshaft flat-6 engine, 4-speed semi-automatic gearbox, removable roof panel, finished in red, black half-leather interior, unrestored.
£3,300–3,900 / €4,800–5,800 / $5,800–6,900 ⚡ CGC

1970 Porsche 911E Targa, 2341cc, overhead-camshaft flat-6 engine, 165bhp, 5-speed manual gearbox.
£4,500–5,400 / €6,700–8,000 / $7,900–9,500 ⚡ COYS

◄ **1971 Porsche 911T,** 2195cc, overhead-camshaft flat-6 engine, triple Weber carburettors, 5-speed manual gearbox, left-hand drive, finished in red, grey interior trim, fewer than 55,000 miles recorded.
£6,200–7,400 / €9,200–11,000 / $10,900–13,000 ⚡ H&H

1973 Porsche 911 2.7 RS Carrera Touring, 2687cc, overhead-camshaft flat-6 engine, 210bhp, limited-slip differential, converted to right-hand drive, finished in orange, black interior, sports seats.
£24,700–29,600 / €37,000–44,000 $43,000–52,000 ⚡ B(Kn)

► **1973 Porsche 911 2.7 RS Carrera Touring,** 2687cc, overhead-camshaft flat-6 engine, left-hand drive, sun roof, finished in white, black interior.
£35,000–42,000 / €52,000–62,000 $62,000–74,000 ⚡ H&H

1975 Porsche 911S 2.7, 2687cc, overhead-camshaft flat-6 engine, electric sun roof, finished in green, black leather interior.
£6,600–7,900 / €9,800–11,700 / $11,600–13,900 ⚡ COYS

1976 Porsche 911 3.0 Carrera, 2994cc, overhead-camshaft flat-6 engine, 230bhp, left-hand drive, finished in silver, blue interior.
£5,200–6,200 / €7,700–9,200 / $9,200–10,900 ⚡ B(Kn)

◀ **1977 Porsche 911 3.0 Carrera,** 2994cc, flat-6 engine, 204bhp, 5-speed manual gearbox, 4-wheel disc brakes, rack-and-pinion steering, torsion-bar suspension, galvanized bodyshell, top speed 150mph.
£7,300–8,700 / €10,800–12,900
$12,800–15,300 ⚡ CGC

▶ **1980 Porsche 924 Turbo,** 1984cc, overhead-camshaft 4-cylinder engine, fuel injection, turbocharger, 170bhp, 5-speed manual gearbox, top speed 141mph, finished in silver, black interior.
£2,300–2,750 / €3,400–4,000 / $4,000–4,800 ⚡ H&H
The 924 was the first front-engined Porsche, and the first with a liquid-cooled engine.

1982 Porsche Ruf BTR-1, 3400cc, overhead-camshaft flat-6 engine, turbocharger, 369bhp, roll bar, sun roof, 17in alloy wheels, finished in metallic navy blue, leather interior.
£17,800–21,300 / €26,300–32,000
$31,000–37,000 ⚡ B(Kn)
Alois Ruf graduated from tuning and modifying Porsches to full-blown automobile manufacture in 1981. The first group of Ruf designated cars – numbered BTR-1, -2 and -3 – appeared in 1982. The Porsche 911 was the starting point for the trio, and the engine was based on that of the 3.3 litre Turbo, but enlarged to 3.4 litres. It was fed by an oversize KKK turbocharger with intercooler. The resulting 369bhp was transmitted to the road by a Ruf five-speed gearbox, while the suspension and brakes were also of Ruf design.

1983 Porsche 911SC 3.0 Cabriolet, 2994cc, overhead-camshaft flat-6 engine, Turbo spoiler, electric windows and mirrors.
£9,200–11,000 / €13,600–16,300
$16,200–19,400 ⚡ BARO
The 911SC was offered between 1977 and 1983.

Cross Reference
See Colour Review (pages 145–152)

◀ **1984 Porsche 928 S2,** 4664cc, V8 engine, fuel injection, 240bhp, 5-speed manual gearbox, top speed 143mph.
£3,500–4,200 / €5,200–6,200
$6,200–7,400 ⚲ **COYS**
The 928 differed in many ways from anything Porsche had offered before. These included the all-new V8 engine, the styling and the so-called 'Weissach axle' – named after the company's development centre – which incorporated flexible rubber bushes that provided the rear suspension with a degree of self-steering, improving cornering and stability under braking.

1986 Porsche 911 Carrera Supersport Cabriolet, 3125cc, air-cooled overhead-camshaft flat-6 engine, 5-speed manual gearbox, 17in (43.2cm) alloy wheels, finished in black, black leather interior.
£17,200–20,600 / €25,500–30,000 / $30,000–36,000 ⚲ **B(Kn)**

1986 Porsche 928 S2, 4664cc, overhead-camshaft V8 engine, 4-speed automatic transmission, 4-wheel disc brakes with ABS, finished in dark metallic green, tan leather interior, 88,000 miles recorded.
£2,000–2,400 / €2,950–3,550 / $3,500–4,200 ⚲ **CGC**
Introduced in 1977, the 928 was a luxurious GT intended to replace the ageing 911. Ultimately, however, it failed to usurp its tail-heavy sibling, despite strong critical acclaim. The 928 was built around a galvanized steel monocoque, but made extensive use of aluminium in its construction. This not only saved weight, but also contributed to near-perfect weight distribution. Blessed with excellent handling and roadholding, the 928 made the most of the 240bhp from its all-alloy, 4.5 litre, overhead-cam V8 engine. Available with a manual gearbox or automatic transmission in its passive rear-steer Weissach transaxle, the 928 was subject to a programme of continual upgrades. Thus, the 928S of 1979 gave way to the S2 some three years later. Inheriting the former's 4664cc engine, the S2 added electronic ignition and Bosch L H Jetronic fuel injection to boost output to 310bhp. It was capable of 160mph and 0–60mph in just over six seconds.

1986 Porsche 944 Turbo, 2500cc, 4-cylinder engine, turbocharger, 5-speed manual gearbox, finished in white, brown leather interior, excellent condition.
£5,600–6,700 / €8,300–9,900 / $9,900–11,800 ⚲ **H&H**
The engine of the 944 was essentially half the 928's V8 unit.

1988 Porsche 911 Carrera Targa, 3164cc, air-cooled overhead-camshaft flat-6 engine, 5-speed manual gearbox.
£12,500–15,000 / €18,500–22,200
$22,000–26,400 ⚲ **BRIT**

1988 Porsche 944S, 2500cc, 4-cylinder engine, 5-speed manual gearbox, finished in silver, black leather interior.
£3,300–3,950 / €4,850–5,800 / $5,800–6,900 ⚮ COYS

1997 Porsche 911 TechArt CT3, 3.8 litre, air-cooled overhead-camshaft flat-6 engine, supercharger, 462bhp, finished in black, grey leather interior.
£30,000–36,000 / €44,000–53,000
$53,000–63,000 ⚮ B(Mu)
TechArt is one of the few tuning specialists recognized by Porsche.

1998 Porsche 911 GT1, 2994cc, flat-6 engine, 4 valves per cylinder, forced induction, 6-speed gearbox, ABS brakes, power steering, carbon-fibre body tub, 1 owner from new, fewer than 5,000km recorded.
£64,000–76,000 / €95,000–112,000 / $112,000–134,000 ⚮ B(Mon)
This car is a road version of Porsche's Le Mans winning GT1 endurance racer. It is electronically limited to a top speed of 192mph.

Rambler
(American 1902–17, 1954–87)

1964 Rambler Classic Station Wagon, 2996cc, 6-cylinder engine finished in gold and white, beige interior, 43,000 miles recorded.
£2,200–2,600 / €3,250–3,850 / $3,850–4,550 ⚮ H&H
American Motors Corporation (AMC) was formed in 1954 through a merger of Hudson and Nash, the latter being the owner of the Rambler brand name. By 1958, all AMC cars were badged as Ramblers, apart from the sub-compact Metropolitan.

Range Rover *(British 1970–)*

◄ **1978 Range Rover Two-Door Estate,** 3528cc, V8 engine, 4-wheel drive.
£2,800–3,350 / €4,150–4,950 / $4,950–8,700 ⚒ H&H
The Range Rover arrived in 1970. With excellent cross-country performance, it was powered by the 3.5 litre V8 engine that had also been used in versions of the P5 and P6 Rover cars.

Reliant *(British 1934–)*

► **1977 Reliant Scimitar GTE SE6A,** 2994cc, Ford V6 engine, 4-speed manual gearbox, alloy wheels.
£850–1,850 / €1,250–2,750 / $1,500–3,250 ⚒ CGC
Launched in 1968, the Scimitar GTE was the original sports estate. Stablemate to the GT Coupé, it was the first car to offer split folding rear seats. It utilized a stiff, separate chassis to underpin its lightweight, rust-free fibreglass bodywork. With independent coil-and-wishbone front suspension, a rear axle located by Watts linkage, rack-and-pinion steering and front disc/rear drum brakes, handling and braking were strong points. Powered by a Ford 3 litre V6 engine developing 138bhp, the GTE was tested at over 120mph and could sprint to 60mph in 8.9 seconds.

RELIANT Model	ENGINE cc/cyl	DATES	CONDITION 1	2	3
Sabre 4 Coupé & Drophead	1703/4	1961–63	£5,500	£2,750	£1,000
Sabre 6 Coupé & Drophead	2553/6	1962–64	£6,000	£3,500	£1,500
Scimitar GT Coupé SE4	2553/6, 2994/6	1964–70	£4,500	£2,500	£1,000
Scimitar GTE Sports Estate SE5/5A	2994/6	1968–75	£5,000	£3,000	£750
Scimitar GTE Sports Estate SE6/6A	2994/6	1976–80	£5,000	£3,500+	£1,250
Scimitar GTE Sports Estate SE6B	2792/6	1980–86	£6,500	£5,000	£2,000
Scimitar GTC Convertible SE8B	2792/6	1980–86	£8,000	£7,000	£5,500

Reliable Dayton *(American 1906–15)*

◄ **1909 Reliable Dayton Type F Surrey,** 15hp, 4-stroke flat-twin engine, leaf-spring suspension, solid tyres, fully restored.
£8,100–9,700 / €12,000–14,400
$14,300–17,100 ⚒ BB(S)
Reliable Dayton was founded by William O. Dayton in Chicago. The company's first cars employed a twin-cylinder, two-stroke engine with chain drive to the rear wheels via a planetary transmission. Later the engine was changed to a four-stroke.

Renault (French 1899–)

Louis Renault was born in Paris during 1877, and although expected to enter the family button making business, he had other ideas. First came an apprenticeship with a boiler manufacturer, then military service and finally a small workshop in the grounds of the family home at Billancourt. There he built a small four-wheel car powered by a 270cc, single-cylinder, de Dion motorcycle engine. An outstanding feature of the design was the use of a propeller shaft and bevel gears for the drive, rather than a chain or belt, which were commonly used at the time. Another advanced feature was a direct-drive top gear in the three-speed 'box.

Renault completed the car on Christmas Eve, 1898. He had built it for his own amusement, but soon received orders from friends for replicas, and in March 1899, the Renault company was born. It exhibited at the Paris Salon later that year, taking orders for some 60 cars.

The first Renault 'factory' was actually a disused boathouse, which was reassembled in the Renault family garden. By the end of the year, 60 workers had constructed 71 cars. During 1900, 179 were manufactured. By then, the 270cc engine had been replaced by a 450cc unit. The classic Renault 'coal-scuttle' bonnet with dashboard radiator arrived on the 1904 models.

Renault had built its first engine in 1902, single-, twin- and four-cylinder versions soon appearing. By 1905, annual production had topped 2,000. That year, the 1060cc, twin-cylinder AG and AX cars appeared, going on to become Renault's top sellers prior to WWI. By 1913, Renault had become the biggest motor vehicle manufacturer in France, with an output of over 10,000, including heavy commercial vehicles like buses and lorries.

During WWI, the company underwent a huge expansion, producing large numbers of trucks, tanks and aero engines. In 1919, it acquired its own steel works in Alsace, which came by way of war reparations from Germany to France.

The early 1920's saw a massive rise in Renault car manufacture, growing to 46,000 in 1925; reaching a pre-WWII peak of 61,146 in 1936.

The final pre-war model was the 1 litre 8CV Javaquatre saloon. Over 27,000 had been built by the end of 1939, with many more after the war.

After the fall of France in 1940, Renault was forced to build trucks for the Germany Army. The factory was seriously damaged by air raids between 1942 and 1944, and on 23 July, 1944, closed indefinitely. A month later, Paris was liberated and soon afterwards Louis Renault was arrested and charged with helping the Germans. Although this was not strictly true, his dislike of the unions put him at the mercy of communist ex-resistance men, and he was put in prison. He died there in October 1944.

In early 1945, Renault was nationalized, and in 1946 the 4CV appeared, employing a 760cc, 4-cylinder engine and rear-wheel drive. By the time production ceased in 1961, a total of 1,150,000 had been made.

In 1956, the 2CV and 4CV were joined by a larger rear-engined car, the 845cc Dauphine; in only four years, over 1 million left the production lines. There was also a high-performance version tuned by Gordini, which appeared in 1959, and the Florida coupé.

During the 1960s, more expansion took place, with more factories and more cars, including the replacement for the 4CV, the R4. Other models included the 8, 10 and 16 saloons, and from 1969, the front-wheel-drive 12. The last rear-engined Renault was built in 1972. That same year saw the arrival of the 5 hatchback, one of the world's first 'super minis'. By 1984, nearly 5.5 million had been sold.

Notable Renault cars of the 1980s included the 9, 11 and 25, while the long running 2CV was still available and had become something of a style icon.

RENAULT Model	ENGINE cc/cyl	DATES	CONDITION 1	2	3
40hp	7540/6	1919–21	£30,000	£20,000	£10,000
SR	4537/4	1919–22	£10,000	£7,000	£5,000
EU-15.8HP	2815/4	1919–23	£8,000+	£5,000	£2,000
GS-IG	2121/4	1920–23	£5,000	£3,000	£2,000
JP	9123/6	1922–29	£25,000	£20,000	£15,000
KJ	951/4	1923–29	£6,000	£4,000	£2,000
Mona Six	1474/6	1928–31	£7,000	£5,000	£3,000
Reinastella	7128/8	1929–32	£25,000	£20,000	£15,000
Viva Six	3181/6	1929–34	£10,000	£7,000	£3,000
14/45	2120/4	1929–35	£7,000	£5,000	£2,000
Nervahuit	4240/8	1931	£12,000	£10,000	£7,000
UY	1300/4	1932–34	£7,000	£5,000	£2,000
ZC/ZD2	4825/8	1934–35	£12,000	£10,000	£7,000
YN2	1463/4	1934–39	£7,000	£5,000	£2,000
Airline Super and Big 6	3620/6	1935	£10,000	£8,000	£5,000
18	2383/4	1936–39	£9,000	£5,000	£3,000
26	4085/6	1936–39	£12,000	£8,000	£5,000

Veteran pre-war models like the twin-cylinder AX, AG and BB are very popular, with values ranging between £6,000 and £15,000. The larger four-cylinder cars, like the AM, AZ, XB and VB, are very reliable, and coachbuilt examples command £30,000+, with six-cylinder coachbuilt cars commanding a premium.

1914 Renault DM 13.9hp Tourer, 2120cc,
monobloc 4-cylinder engine, 3-speed manual gearbox.
**£11,500–13,800 / €17,000–20,400
$20,200–24,300** 🔨 BRIT

1958 Renault Dauphine R1090, 845cc, 4-cylinder engine,
Solex carburettor, 31bhp, 3-speed manual gearbox,
6 volt electrics.
£800–960 / €1,200–1,400 / $1,400–1,650 🔨 CGC
Launched in 1956, the Dauphine became the first
French car to top two million sales. There was also a
more highly tuned Gordini version, which had an
extra gear ratio.

◄ **2001 Renault Clio V6 Sport,** 2946cc, mid-mounted V6
engine, 6-speed manual gearbox, finished in silver, 2-tone
blue seats.
**£15,500–18,600/ €22,900–27,500
$27,300–33,000** 🔨 COYS
Only 1,600 examples of this model were built.
The main aim was to homologate the car for the new
Clio Cup race series.

RENAULT Model	ENGINE cc/cyl	DATES	CONDITION 1	2	3
4CV	747/ 760/4	1947–61	£3,500	£2,000	£850
Frégate	1997/4	1952–60	£3,000	£2,000	£1,000
Dauphine	845/4	1956–66	£1,500	£1,000	£350
Dauphine Gordini	845/4	1961–66	£2,000	£1,000	£450
Floride	845/4	1959–62	£3,000	£2,000	£600
Caravelle	956/ 1108/4	1962–68	£4,500	£2,800	£750
R4	747/ 845/4	1961–86	£2,000	£1,500	£350
R8/R10	1108/4	1962–71	£1,800	£750	£200
R8 Gordini	1108/4	1965–66	£8,000	£5,000	£2,000
R8 Gordini	1255/4	1966–70	£8,000	£5,500	£2,500
R8S	1108/4	1968–71	£2,000	£1,200	£400

Riley *(British 1898–1969)*

1924 Riley 11/40 10.8hp Tourer, 1498cc, 4-cylinder
engine, completely rebuilt 1991, new 4-seater aluminium
tourer body, excellent condition.
**£9,700–11,600 / €14,400–17,200
$17,00–20,400** 🔨 B(Kn)
The first sporting Riley is considered to be the 1498cc
11/40 introduced in 1922. Later known as the Redwing,
it came with a guarantee of 70mph. This car was
exported new to Australia, where it was discovered in
1980, having been converted to a pick-up.

1925 Riley 11/40 11.9hp Tourer, 1645cc, side-valve
4-cylinder engine, 42bhp, polished aluminium coachwork.
**£10,000–12,000 / €14,500–17,500
$17,500–21,000** 🔨 B(Kn)
In 1925, Riley's highly successful 11/40 model was
uprated to 11.9hp with an enlarged engine. A longer
chassis and front wheel brakes were also introduced.

1927 Riley 9 Mk I Sports Four, 1087cc, 4-cylinder engine, twin high-set camshafts, Riley PR cylinder head, early-type exhaust manifold without 'hot spot' connections, right-hand gear-change and handbrake, Perrot braking system, fabric coachwork.
£10,700–12,800 / €15,800–18,900
$18,800–22,500 ➤ BRIT
The Riley 9 was one of the greatest pre-WWII success stories and the choice of discerning motorists. Offered alongside the early touring models was the Special Tourer or Sports Four. Fitted with a twin-carburettor engine and carrying light fabric bodywork, this model was capable of achieving a maxium speed of 76mph.

1935 Riley Lynx Tourer, 1087cc, 4-cylinder engine, 4-speed manual gearbox, wire wheels, 4-wheel brakes, finished in black, red leather interior, excellent condition.
£21,500–25,800 / €32,000–38,000
$38,000–45,000 ➤ H&H

◄ **1936 Riley Kestrel Four-Door Saloon,** 1496cc, 4-cylinder engine, twin Zenith carburettors, pre-selector gearbox, alloy body.
£4,100–4,900 / €6,100–7,300 / $7,200–8,600 ➤ CGC
Introduced in 1934, the Kestrel was available with a choice of four- or six-cylinder engines.

1949 Riley RMC Roadster, 2443cc, 4-cylinder engine, fully restored, finished in red, magnolia leather interior.
£18,900–22,600 / €28,000–33,000
$33,000–40,000 ➤ B(Kn)
Most popular of the immediate post-WWII Rileys was the 1.5 litre RMA sports saloon, which came with torsion-bar independent front suspension, rack-and-pinion steering, Girling hydro-mechanical brakes, four-speed synchromesh gearbox and Riley's classic twin-camshaft, overhead-valve engine in four-cylinder guise. Farther up the range was the 2.5 litre RMB, which used the pre-war Big Four's 90bhp engine in a lengthened RMA chassis. Introduced in 1946, the RMB was blessed with 100bhp from 1948 and gained a brace of roadster companions – the two/three seater RMC and the four-seat RMD – that same year. Production of the open-top RMs lasted until 1951, by which time 507 RMCs and 502 RMDs had been completed.

1936 Riley Lynx-style Tourer, based on Merlin saloon chassis, 1056cc, twin-high-camshaft 4-cylinder engine, twin SU carburettors 4-speed pre-selector gearbox, finished in red and black, black interior.
£8,600–10,300 / €12,700–15,200
$15,100–18,100 ➤ H&H

1952 Riley RMB Saloon, 2443cc, 4-cylinder engine, twin-high-mounted camshafts, finished in green, beige leather interior.
£5,500–6,600 / €8,100–9,800 / $9,700–11,600 ➤ B(Kn)

RILEY Model	ENGINE cc/cyl	DATES	CONDITION		
			1	2	3
9hp	1034/2	1906–07	£9,000	£6,000	£3,000
Speed 10	1390/2	1909–10	£10,000	£6,000	£3,000
11	1498/4	1922–27	£7,000	£4,000	£2,000
9	1075/4	1927–32	£10,000	£7,000	£4,000
9 Gamecock	1098/4	1932–33	£14,000	£10,000	£6,000
Lincock 12hp	1458/6	1933–36	£9,000	£7,000	£5,000
Imp 9hp	1089/4	1934–35	£35,000	£28,000	£20,000
Kestrel 12hp	1496/4	1936–38	£10,000	£7,000	£2,000
Sprite 12hp	1496/4	1936–38	£40,000	£35,000	£20,000

Many Riley 9hp Specials available; ideal for VSCC and club events.

◀ **1955 Riley RME Saloon,** 1496cc, twin-camshaft
4-cylinder engine, 4-speed manual gearbox,
Girling hydraulic brakes, extensively restored,
resprayed in black and ivory, new roof covering.
£4,300–5,100 / €6,400–7,500 / $7,500–9,000 ⚲ CGC

1955 Riley RME Saloon 1496cc, twin-camshaft 4-cylinder engine, fully restored, finished in blue and white, blue interior,
concours condition.
£9,900–11,900 / €14,700–17,600 / $17,400–20,900 ⚒ H&H

1955 Riley Pathfinder Saloon, 2443cc, twin-camshaft
6-cylinder engine, 110bhp, 4-speed manual gearbox,
torsion-bar independent front suspension, coil-sprung rear
axle, top speed 98mph, completely restored, finished in
black, red leather interior.
£4,350–5,200 / €6,400–7,700 / $7,700–9,200 ⚲ B(Kn)
A sister car to the Wolseley 6/90, the Pathfinder
combined a separate box-section chassis and steel
bodyshell with Riley's classic twin-cam Big Four engine.

1960 Riley 1.5 Saloon 1489cc, overhead-valve
4-cylinder engine, twin SU carburettors, 68bhp, 12 volt
electrics, torsion-bar independent front suspension,
rack-and-pinion steering, leather upholstery, wood veneer
trim, top speed 85mph.
£1,400–1,650 / €2,050–2,450 / $2,450–2,900 ⚲ B(Kn)

RILEY Model	ENGINE cc/cyl	DATES	CONDITION 1	2	3
1½ Litre RMA	1496/4	1945–52	£6,000	£3,500	£1,200
1½ Litre RME	1496/4	1952–55	£6,000+	£3,500	£1,500
2½ Litre RMB/F	2443/4	1946–53	£8,000	£5,000	£3,000
2½ Litre Roadster	2443/4	1948–50	£18,000	£11,000	£9,000
2½ Litre Drophead	2443/4	1948–51	£15,000	£10,000	£7,000
Pathfinder	2443/4	1953–57	£3,500	£2,000	£750
2.6	2639/6	1957–59	£3,000	£1,800	£750
1.5	1489/4	1957–65	£3,000	£2,000	£850
4/68	1489/4	1959–61	£1,500	£700	£300
4/72	1622/4	1961–69	£1,600	£800	£300
Elf I–III	848/4	1961–66	£1,500	£850	£400
Kestrel I–II	1098/4	1965–67	£1,500	£850	£400

Rolls-Royce *(British 1904–)*

1909 Rolls-Royce 40/50 Silver Ghost, 7035cc, 6-cylinder engine, finished in silver and polished aluminium, dark green leather interior, 1 of 16 known to survive, fully restored, concours condition.
£363,000–435,000 / €537,000–644,000
$639,000–765,000 ⚒ B(Kn)

1922 Rolls-Royce 40/50 Silver Ghost, 7428cc, 6-cylinder engine, wire wheels, polished aluminium body with white wings, red leather interior.
£72,000–80,000 / €107,000–118,000
$127,000–141,000 ⊞ BLE

1925 Rolls-Royce 40/50 Silver Ghost, coachwork by Barker, 7438cc, side-valve 6-cylinder engine, exposed valve gear, 60bhp, leaf spring suspension.
£52,000–62,000 / €77,000–92,000
$92,000–109,000 ⚒ BB(S)

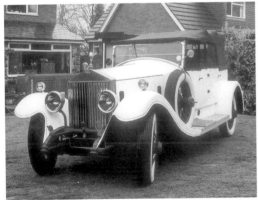

◀ **1926 Rolls-Royce Phantom I Tourer,** 7668cc, 6-cylinder engine, original cabriolet bodywork replaced by 4-seater tourer coachwork.
£21,500–25,800 / €32,000–38,000
$38,000–45,000 ⚒ H&H
The Phantom appeared in 1925. The chassis was based on that of the Ghost, while the long-stroke engine featured two blocks of three cylinders each and pushrod operated valves. It resembled the engine of the 20hp model, but had twice the swept volume.

ROLLS-ROYCE Model	ENGINE cc/cyl	DATES	CONDITION 1	2	3
Silver Ghost 40/50	7035/6	pre-WWI	£350,000+	£120,000	£80,000
Silver Ghost 40/50	7428/6	post-WWI	£110,000+	£70,000	£40,000
20hp (3-speed)	3127/6	1922–25	£29,000+	£23,000	£15,000
20hp	3127/6	1925–29	£30,000+	£24,000	£15,000
Phantom I	7668/6	1925–29	£50,000+	£28,000	£22,000
20/25	3669/6	1925–26	£30,000+	£18,000	£13,000
Phantom II	7668/6	1929–35	£40,000+	£30,000	£20,000
Phantom II Continental	7668/6	1930–35	£60,000+	£40,000	£28,000
25/30	4257/6	1936–38	£30,000+	£18,000	£12,000
Phantom III	7340/12	1936–39	£45,000+	£28,000	£14,000
Wraith	4257/6	1938–39	£38,000	£32,000	£25,000

Prices will vary considerably depending on heritage, originality, coachbuilder, completeness and body style. A poor reproduction body can often mean the value is dependent only upon a rolling chassis and engine.

1928 Rolls-Royce 20hp Limousine, coachwork by Windover, 3127cc, 6-cylinder engine, 4-speed gearbox, right-hand gear-change, 4-wheel servo-assisted brakes, restored over 8 years, updated with full-flow oil filter and flashing indicators.
£32,000–38,000 / €47,000–56,000
$56,000–67,000 ➢ B(Kn)

1929 Rolls-Royce 20hp Tourer, 3127cc, overhead-valve 6-cylinder engine, 4-speed gearbox, wire wheels, finished in white, dark green interior.
£22,700–27,200 / €34,000–40,000
$40,000–48,000 ➢ H&H

1930 Rolls-Royce 20/25 Torpedo Tourer, 3669cc, overhead-valve 6-cylinder engine, 4-speed gearbox, excellent condition.
£27,000–32,000 / €40,000–48,000 / $47,000–56,000 ➢ COYS

1932 Rolls-Royce 20/25 Sports Saloon, 3669cc, 6-cylinder engine, 4-speed manual gearbox, finished in light green and black, black leather interior.
£26,500–31,000 / €39,000–46,000
$47,000–55,000 ➢ BLE

1933 Rolls-Royce 20/25 Three-Position Drophead Coupé, 3669cc, 6-cylinder engine, 4-speed manual gearbox, wheel discs, 2 spare wheels, finished in beige and green, cream leather interior.
£32,000–38,000 / €47,000–56,000
$56,000–67,000 ➢ H&H

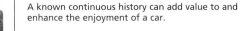

A known continuous history can add value to and enhance the enjoyment of a car.

◄ **1933 Rolls-Royce 20/25 Limousine,** coachwork by Hooper, 3669cc, 6-cylinder engine, 4-speed manual gearbox, D-back limousine body, sliding division, finished in white, black and red leather interior.
£9,600–11,500 / €14,200–17,000
$16,900–20,200 ➢ B(Kn)
In all, 3,827 examples of the 20/25 chassis were produced.

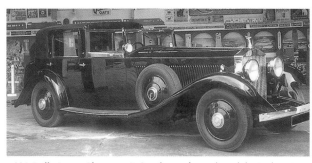
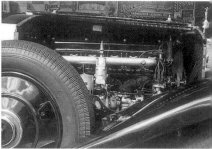

1933 Rolls-Royce Phantom II Continental, coachwork by Barker, 7668cc, 6-cylinder engine, 4-speed manual gearbox, fully restored, finished in dark blue, red leather and cloth interior, concours condition.
£61,000–73,000 / €92,000–108,000 / $109,000–128,000 ➤ B(Kn)
Reportedly the last model that Henry Royce designed himself, the Phantom II was introduced in 1929 as a successor to the Phantom I. The new model employed an entirely new chassis in two wheelbase lengths – 144 and 150in (365.8 and 381cm). This low-slung frame, with its radiator set well back, enabled coachbuilders to create sleeker designs than the upright styles of the past. The engine also had come in for extensive revision. The Phantom I's cylinder dimensions and basic layout – two blocks of three cylinders with a common aluminium cylinder head – were retained, but the combustion chambers had been redesigned, and the head was of the crossflow type. The magneto/coil dual ignition system remained the same. The result of these changes was improved performance and the ability to accommodate heavier coachwork. Built on the short-wheelbase chassis and introduced in 1930, the Continental had been conceived as an enthusiastic driver's car, and featured revised rear suspension, a higher axle ratio and a lowered steering column. By the end of production, the Phantom II Continental was good for 95mph.

1934 Rolls-Royce 20/25 Sports Saloon, coachwork by Rippon Brothers, 3669cc, overhead-valve 6-cylinder engine, 4-speed manual gearbox, completely overhauled.
£13,400–16,000 / €19,800–23,700
$23,600–28,200 ➤ H&H

1934 Rolls-Royce 20/25 Saloon, coachwork by Connaught, 3669cc, 6-cylinder engine, synchromesh gearbox, central chassis lubrication, finished in grey, maroon leather interior, 1 owner since 1958, in need of restoration.
£14,300–17,100 / €21,100–25,300
$25,100–30,000 ➤ B(Kn)

1934 Rolls-Royce 20/25 Wingham Cabriolet, coachwork by Martin Walker, 3669cc, 6-cylinder engine, finished in cream and black, 1 family ownership from new.
£31,000–37,000 / €46,000–55,000
$55,000–65,000 ➤ CGC

1934 Rolls-Royce Phantom II Sedanca de Ville, 7668cc, 6-cylinder engine, louvred bonnet and scuttle, rear-mounted trunk, polished alloy wheel discs, P100 headlamps, finished in grey, black interior.
£58,000–65,000 / €86,000–96,000
$102,000–114,000 ⊞ RCC

1935 Rolls-Royce 20/25 Saloon, coachwork by Park Ward, 3669cc, 6-cylinder engine, 4-speed manual gearbox, older restoration, excellent condition.
£20,700–24,800 / €31,000–37,000
$36,000–44,000 ➤ B(Kn)

1935 Rolls-Royce 20/25 Mayfair Limousine, 3669cc, overhead-valve 6-cylinder engine, 4-speed manual gearbox, finished in burgundy and cream, engine and chassis in excellent condition.
£17,500–19,500 / €25,200–28,900
$29,900–34,000 ⊞ RCC

◀ **1936 Rolls-Royce 25/30 Coupé,** 4257cc, 6-cylinder engine, completely restored, concours winner.
£21,700–26,000 / €32,000–38,000 $38,000–46,000 ✦ COYS

1936 Rolls-Royce 25/30 Four-Door Saloon, coachwork by Mayfair Carriage Company, 4257cc, 6-cylinder engine, 4-speed manual gearbox, hypoid rear axle, restored.
£13,700–16,400 / €20,300–24,300 $24,100–28,900 ✦ BB(S)
In all, 1,201 examples of the 25/30 were built.

1937 Rolls-Royce 25/30 Sedanca de Ville, coachwork by Mulliner, 4257cc, 6-cylinder engine, sliding roof, finished in 2-tone grey, grey leather interior, engine rebuilt, 5,000 miles recorded since, 1 owner for 34 years, in need of cosmetic restoration.
£26,500–29,500 / €39,000–44,000 / $47,000–52,000 ⊞ RCC

1937 Rolls-Royce Phantom III Saloon, coachwork by Barker, 7340cc, V12 engine, 4-speed manual gearbox, finished in black, beige interior.
£25,000–30,000 / €37,700–44,000 / $44,000–53,000 ✦ H&H
Launched in 1925, the Rolls-Royce 40/50 was sufficiently different from the Silver Ghost to warrant a new name, the New Phantom, subsequently becoming known as the Phantom I. After 2,212 six-cylinder Phantom 1s were built, the replacement Phantom II appeared in 1929. By the 1930s, however, 12-cylinder competition from rivals Daimler, Hispano-Suiza, Packard and Lincoln, not forgetting a V16 from Cadillac, had forced Rolls-Royce into the 12-cylinder sector. In 1935, the company launched the Phantom III with a V12 engine; 710 had been made by 1939.

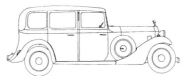

1939 Rolls-Royce 25/30 Saloon, coachwork by Barker, 4257cc, overhead-valve 6-cylinder engine, 4-speed manual gearbox, good condition.
£9,600–11,500 / €14,500–17,000
$16,900–20,000 ✗ H&H

1956 Rolls-Royce Silver Cloud I, 4887cc, 6-cylinder engine, stainless steel exhaust system, factory picnic tables, original push-button radio, finished in gold and brown, beige interior, partially refurbished.
£5,900–7,100 / €8,700–10,500 / $10,400–12,500 ✗ H&H

1952 Rolls-Royce Silver Wraith LWB, coachwork by H.J. Mulliner, 4566cc, 6-cylinder engine, 4-speed manual gearbox, finished in 2-tone green, grey interior.
£12,900–15,500 / €19,100–22,900
$22,7900–27,300 ✗ H&H
A new Silver Wraith started post-war production at the Rolls-Royce Crewe factory in 1946 and continued in production until 1959, becoming one of the longest running RR models. It had a significantly shorter wheelbase than its predecessor and an all-new, inlet-over-exhaust 4257cc engine. From 1951, capacity was increased to 4566cc and a long-wheelbase chassis option, like this car, was offered.

1957 Rolls-Royce Silver Cloud I Empress Limousine, coachwork by Hooper, 4887cc, 6-cylinder engine, automatic transmission, division, picnic tables, 1 of 12 examples built, good condition.
£20,100–24,100 / €29,700–36,000
$35,000–42,000 ✗ BARO
The Silver Cloud was introduced in 1955 as a direct replacement for the Silver Dawn.

◄ **1960 Rolls-Royce Phantom V Limousine,** 6230cc, V8 engine, 4-speed automatic transmission, finished in silver and black, grey leather interior, fewer than 73,000 miles recorded, engine and steering box in need of minor attention, otherwise good condition.
£21,000–24,700 / €31,000–37,000
$37,000–43,000 ✗ B(Mu)

Miller's
Milestones

Rolls-Royce Silver Cloud (1955–65)
Price range: £8,000–80,000 / €11,800–118,000 / $14,100–141,000
The Rolls-Royce Silver Cloud and near-identical Bentley S-Type were the Crewe factory's second 'standard steel' cars following the Rolls-Royce Silver Dawn and Bentley R-Type. This meant they rode on a box-section chassis and featured independent front suspension, while at the rear, the shock absorbers could be altered from the driver's seat for additional comfort and greater control. The power unit in the Cloud Series I was the 4887cc, six-cylinder engine carried over from the Silver Dawn/R-Type. This featured overhead inlet valves and side exhaust valves, twin SU carburettors and a four-speed automatic transmission. It could propel the Cloud to 106mph,

but was replaced in late 1958 by a new all-alloy, 6230cc V8 engine. In this guise, the car became the Silver Cloud II, and with it came much better performance (0–60mph in 11 seconds and a top speed of 116mph). The Series II arrived in 1962, still powered by the 6.3 litre V8. These cars can be identified by a lower bonnet line and four headlamps. Besides the saloons, which could be ordered with Mulliner or Hooper coachwork, there were a coupé (Series I only) and a convertible. All the Silver Cloud models had beautiful proportions, and were superbly built and well refined. In fact, everything a Rolls-Royce should be. Inside, there were luxurious leather seats and burr-walnut dashboard; power steering and air conditioning were just two of the options; automatic transmission was fitted as standard.

1960 Rolls-Royce Silver Cloud II, 6230cc, V8 engine, automatic transmission, finished in 2-tone grey, grey leather interior.
£18,000–20,000 / €26,600–29,600
$31,000–35,000 ⊞ BLE
The Silver Cloud II arrived in 1959, with a 6230cc V8 instead of the previous 4887cc straight-six.

1961 Rolls-Royce Silver Cloud II, 6230cc, V8 engine, 4-speed automatic transmission, finished in green, green leather interior, restored 1997, good condition throughout.
£18,400–22,100 / €27,200–33,000
$32,000–39,000 ⋏ B(Kn)

1963 Rolls-Royce Silver Cloud III, 6230cc, V8 engine, 4-speed automatic transmission, finished in metallic dark blue, new white leather upholstery.
£20,700–24,800 / €31,000–37,000
$37,000–44,000 ⋏ B(Kn)
Introduced in 1962, the Silver Cloud III was the last mainstream Rolls-Royce to employ a separate chassis, being superseded by the Silver Shadow in late 1965.

1963 Rolls-Royce Silver Cloud III, 6230cc, V8 engine, 4-speed automatic transmission, finished in black, brown leather interior, excellent condition.
£23,400–26,000 / €35,000–38,000
$41,000–46,000 ⊞ RCC

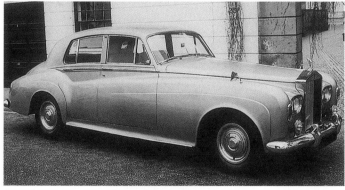

◀ **1964 Rolls-Royce Silver Cloud III,** 6230cc, V8 engine, automatic transmission, factory air conditioning, finished in grey, grey leather interior.
£19,400–23,200 / €28,700–34,000
$34,000–41,000 ⋏ COYS
The Silver Cloud III can be distinguished from its predecessors by twin headlamps and a lower radiator grille.

1965 Rolls-Royce Silver Cloud III Convertible, 6230cc, V8 engine, SU carburettors, power steering, restored 2002, 1,000 miles recorded since.
£40,000–48,000 / €59,000–71,000
$70,000–84,000 ⋏ BB(S)

1966 Rolls-Royce Silver Shadow I, 6230cc, V8 engine, 4-speed automatic transmission, servo-assisted brakes.
£11,100–13,300 / €16,400–19,700
$19,500–23,400 ⋏ BB(S)
The Silver Shadow appeared in 1965 and used the 6230cc V8 engine from the Silver Cloud. In 1970, the need to maintain power while conforming to American exhaust-emissions regulations saw the displacement rise to 6750cc.

◀ **1968 Rolls-Royce Phantom VI Limousine,** coachwork by Mulliner Park Ward, 6750cc, V8 engine, 4-speed automatic transmission, air conditioning, cocktail cabinet, finished in black and metallic grey, matching upholstery.
£29,700–35,000 / €44,000–52,000
$52,000–62,000 ⚒ B(Mu)

1969 Rolls-Royce Silver Shadow I, 6230cc, V8 engine, 4-speed automatic transmission, self-levelling suspension, disc brakes, left-hand drive, finished in white, blue leather interior, 1 family ownership for last 30 years.
£7,600–9,100 / €11,200–13,500
$13,400–16,000 ⚒ COYS

1975 Rolls-Royce Camargue, 6750cc, V8 engine, stainless steel exhaust, Harvey Bailey suspension, chromed alloy wheels, electric mirrors from later model, 1 owner for 20 years.
£13,400–16,100 / €19,800–23,800
$23,600–28,300 ⚒ H&H
Styled by Pininfarina, the two-door, coupé-style Camargue ran from 1975 to 1985, a total of 531 being built.

1975 Rolls-Royce Silver Shadow I, 6750cc, V8 engine, 4-speed automatic transmission, finished in metallic green, beige leather interior, fewer than 43,000 miles recorded.
£7,200–8,600 / €10,700–12,700
$12,700–15,100 ⚒ H&H

1975 Rolls-Royce Silver Shadow I, 6750cc, V8 engine, automatic transmission, 4-wheel independent self-levelling suspension, disc brakes, finished in 2-tone metallic blue, cream leather interior.
£6,900–8,300 / €10,200–12,300
$12,100–14,600 ⚒ H&H

▶ **1976 Rolls-Royce Silver Shadow I,** 6750cc, V8 engine, automatic transmission, finished in metallic blue black leather interior.
£9,000–10,000 / €13,300–14,800 / $15,800–17,600 ⊞ BLE
This was the final year of production for the Shadow I.

1977 Rolls-Royce Corniche Convertible, coachwork by Mulliner Park Ward, 6750cc, V8 engine, 4-speed automatic transmission, finished in dark green, light green leather interior.
£21,500–25,800 / €32,700–38,000 / $38,700–45,000 ⚒ H&H

1977 Rolls-Royce Silver Shadow II, 6750cc, V8 engine, automatic transmission, finished in metallic red, red leather interior, 3 owners from new.
£4,750–5,700 / €7,000–8,400 / $8,400–10,000 ⚒ CGC

1978 Rolls-Royce Corniche II Convertible, 6750cc, V8 engine, 4-speed automatic transmission, finished in gold, dark brown leather interior, excellent condition throughout.
£20,900–25,100 / €31,000–37,000 $37,000–44,000 ⚒ H&H

◄ **1978 Rolls-Royce Silver Shadow II,** 6750cc, V8 engine, 4-speed automatic transmission, finished in metallic blue, blue leather interior.
£9,000–10,000 / €13,300–14,800 / $15,800–17,600 ⊞ BLE
The Silver Shadow II was introduced in 1977. It featured a revised and more ergonomic fascia, improved front suspension geometry and power-assisted rack-and-pinion steering. There was also a new split-level air conditioning system.

1978 Rolls-Royce Silver Shadow II, 6750cc, V8 engine, radiator and brakes overhauled, new starter motor and brake pumps, finished in 2-tone metallic brown, beige leather upholstery, 35,000 miles recorded.
£7,500–9,000 / €11,100–13,300 / $13,200–15,800 ⚒ CGC

1979 Rolls-Royce Silver Shadow II Red Label, 6750cc, V8 engine, 4-speed automatic transmission, finished in 2-tone brown, brown leather interior.
£5,400–6,300 / €9,300–9,300 / $7,800–1,100 ⚒ H&H

ROLLS-ROYCE Model	ENGINE cc/cyl	DATES	CONDITION		
Abbreviations: HJM = H.J. Mulliner; MPW = Mulliner/Park Ward			1	2	3
Silver Wraith LWB	4566/ 4887/6	1951–59	£25,000	£15,000	£10,000
Silver Wraith SWB	4257/ 4566/6	1947–59	£20,000	£13,000	£10,000
Silver Wraith Drophead	4257/ 4566/6	1947–59	£50,000	£35,000	£25,000
Silver Dawn St'd Steel	4257/ 4566/6	1949–52	£25,000	£15,000	£10,000
Silver Dawn St'd Steel	4257/ 4566/6	1952–55	£30,000	£20,000	£15,000
Silver Dawn Coachbuilt	4257/ 4566/6	1949–55	£35,000+	£25,000	£18,000
Silver Dawn Drophead	4257/ 4566/6	1949–55	£60,000	£50,000	£30,000
Silver Cloud I	4887/6	1955–59	£18,000	£10,000	£8,000
SCI Coupé Coachbuilt	4887/6	1955–59	£30,000	£20,000	£15,000
SCI Conv (HJM)	4887/6	1955–59	£80,000+	£60,000+	£40,000
Silver Cloud II	6230/8	1959–62	£19,000	£10,000	£8,000
SCII Conv (HJM)	6230/8	1959–62	£80,000	£75,000	£40,000
SCII Conv (MPW)	6230/8	1959–62	£60,000	£40,000	£32,000
Silver Cloud III	6230/8	1962–65	£25,000	£12,000	£10,000
SCIII Conv (MPW)	6230/8	1962–65	£70,000	£45,000	£35,000
Silver Shadow	6230/ 6750/8	1965–76	£14,000	£9,000	£7,000
S Shadow I Coupé (MPW)	6230/ 6750/8	1965–70	£15,000	£10,000	£8,000
SSI Drophead (MPW)	6230/ 6750/8	1965–70	£33,000	£25,000	£18,000
Corniche FHC	6750/8	1971–77	£15,000	£11,000	£8,000
Corniche Convertible	6750/8	1971–77	£30,000+	£22,000	£18,000
Camargue	6750/8	1975–85	£28,000	£22,000	£17,000

1979 Rolls-Royce Silver Shadow II, 6750cc, V8 engine, 4-speed automatic transmission, finished in gold, dark brown leather interior, good condition.
£7,700–9,200 / €11,400–13,600 / $13,600–16,200 ⚡ H&H

1979 Rolls-Royce Silver Shadow II Red Label, 6750cc, V8 engine, finished in black and beige, fewer than 63,000 miles recorded.
£9,000–10,800 / €13,300–16,000
$15,800–19,000 ⚡ BRIT
The Silver Shadow II was produced until 1980. This car is a limited-edition Red Label model.

1980 Rolls-Royce Silver Shadow II, 6750cc, finished in silver, blue leather interior, 1 family ownership from new, 55,000 miles recorded, excellent condition throughout.
£11,200–13,400 / €16,600–19,800
$19,700–23,600 ⚡ BRIT

1980 Rolls-Royce Silver Shadow II Estate, coachwork by FLM (Panelcraft), 6750cc, V8 engine, automatic transmission, sun roof, finished in dark green, matching leather interior.
£23,500–28,000 / €35,000–41,600
$41,000–49,000 ⚡ B(Kn)

1984 Rolls-Royce Silver Spirit, 6750cc, V8 engine, 4-speed automatic transmission, finished in metallic grey, light brown leather interior.
£9,900–11,000 / €14,700–16,300
$17,400–19,400 ⊞ BLE

▶ **1990 Rolls-Royce Silver Spirit II,** 6750cc, V8 engine, fuel injection, self-levelling rear suspension.
£14,300–17,100
€21,200–25,300
$25,200–30,000 ⚡ B(Kn)

Rover *(British 1904–)*

In 1896, John Kemp Starley, already experienced in the manufacture of bicycles, formed the Rover Cycle Company in Coventry. At the time, there was a boom in bicycle sales, and the new company's first-year production reached around 11,000 machines. When Starley died in 1901, work was already well advanced on Rover's first motorcycle, which appeared in late 1902. Two years later, an 8hp light car was introduced.

The first Rover car had a 1327cc, four-cylinder engine, a chassis with integral three-speed gearbox and a rigidly mounted rear axle. It was followed by a cheaper, 780cc model with a more conventional chassis and sprung axle. From this second car came a whole range of models.

After becoming the Rover Motor Company in 1906, the marque went racing for a short period, gaining victory in the 1907 Tourist Trophy. However, it was soon decided that racing was too expensive to justify.

The next significant Rover design was the Twelve, which ran from 1912 until 1924. This featured a side-valve, monobloc, four-cylinder engine.

Two-wheelers were separated from the cars in 1912, bicycles continuing until 1923, and motorcycles until 1925. Rover built 426,530 of the former and 10,401 of the latter.

Next came the 998cc model Eight, some 17,000 of which were sold between 1920 and 1925. Rover suffered serious losses during 1925–26, which led to a series of management changes; in 1929, Spencer Wilks took over the reins of the company. During this period, a number of new cars appeared, having six-cylinder engines of various capacities. These ran until 1938.

Spencer Wilks' brother, Maurice, was in charge of engineering from 1931 until 1957, and with Robert Boyle created the excellent 10, 12, 14, 16 and 20hp cars of the 1930s – a time when Rover built a reputation for quality. During the mid- to late 1930s, production more than doubled, while profits went through the roof.

During WWII, Rover played a major part in the war effort by making aero engine components. The company was even involved in the development of Frank Whittle's revolutionary jet engine.

From 1945 onwards, car production was concentrated in Solihull, the first cars coming off the lines in December that year. These were the pre-war P2 saloons, in 10, 12, 14 and 16 hp guises. They were replaced in 1948 by the P3 series.

The P3s were available in 1595cc (four-cylinder) and 2103cc (six-cylinder) versions, being designated 60 and 75 respectively. This started a Rover tradition of numbering models by their approximate horsepower, which lasted until the 1960s.

The same inlet-over-exhaust engines that had been introduced on the P3 series were carried over to the newly styled P4 range in 1949. In the car's heyday during the 1950s, the car enjoyed a professional customer base – doctors, businessmen and the like. By the time production ceased in 1964, over 130,000 P4s had been built.

Another model to prove popular after the war was the four-wheel-drive Land Rover, which was launched in 1948. The concept came from Maurice Wilks and had been inspired by the wartime Jeep.

In 1959, the P4 was joined by the larger P5 with a 3 litre engine, while in 1963 a new 2 litre model, the P6 2000, arrived. Later, in 1968, a version appeared with the Buick designed 3.5 litre V8 engine, which was known as the P6 3500. This continued until 1976. Total production of all P6 variants was an impressive 327,208.

Then came a series of events that destabilized the successful and profitable organization. Spencer Wilks, who had been chairman since 1957, retired in 1962 in favour of his younger brother, Maurice, but he died suddenly in 1963 and was succeeded by George Farmer. Spencer Wilks died in 1971. Engineering was under Maurice's nephew, Peter Wilks from 1964 until 1971, when he was replaced by Spencer King.

In 1965, Rover purchased Alvis for its military vehicles, but in 1967 was acquired itself by Leyland. Less than a year later, Leyland was swallowed up by the British Motor Corporation, which became British Leyland.

In 1970, the four-wheel-drive Range Rover appeared, followed in 1976 by the SD1 saloon. At the same time, the decision was taken to axe all the remaining P-series cars, so Rover became dependant upon the SD1 and the Land Rover/Range Rover range.

In 1981, car production left Solihull for the Morris plant in Cowley, but the site was later occupied by the Land Rover operation, which had been a separate company since 1975.

Subsequently, there was the nationalization of BL, then the sale to British Aerospace (which included a tie-up with Honda), a take-over by BMW, and finally a management buy-out for £1 in 1999.

◀ **1939 Rover P2 12hp Four-Door Saloon,** 1496cc, 4-cylinder engine, 4-speed manual gearbox, Girling rod-operated drum brakes, completely restored.
£5,100–6,100 / €7,500–9,000
$9,000–10,700 ⚑ CGC
The P2 was restyled in 1937 with lower, more sweeping lines. By 1939, the specification boasted synchromesh gears, hydraulic shock absorbers and a Luxax-Bijur chassis lubrication system.

1947 Rover 12hp Tourer, 1500cc, 4-cylinder engine, 4-speed manual gearbox, Girling mechanical brakes, hydraulic shock absorbers, excellent condition.
£15,300–18,300 / € 22,600–27,100
$26,900–32,000 ➢ CGC

1948 Rover P3 75 Four-Door Saloon, 2103cc, 6-cylinder engine, 4-speed manual gearbox, independent coil-sprung front suspension, hydro-mechanical drum brakes, stainless steel exhaust, top speed 80mph, excellent condition.
£6,200–7,400 / € 9,200–11,000 / $10,200–13,000 ➢ CCG
The Rover P3 was built only during 1948–49, a total of 9,111 examples being completed.

1965 Rover P5 Saloon, 2995cc, overhead-valve 6-cylinder engine, automatic transmission, stainless steel exhaust, finished in green and grey, tan leather upholstery, excellent condition.
£6,300–7,000 / € 9,300–10,400
$11,100–12,300 ⊞ UMC

▶ **1970 Rover P5B Coupé,** 3528cc, V8 engine, automatic transmission, air conditioning, finished in white, tan leather interior, concours condition.
£9,600–11,500 / € 12,700–17,000
$15,100–20,000 ➢ B(Kn)

1947 Rover 16 Four-Door Saloon, 2147cc, 6-cylinder engine, finished in green, green leather interior.
£2,650–3,150 / € 3,900–4,650 / $4,650–5,500 ➢ BRIT
The Rover 16's long-stroke six-cylinder engine endowed it with excellent performance, allowing it to cruise effortlessly between 60 and 70mph.

1964 Rover P4 110 Four-Door Saloon, 2625cc, 6-cylinder engine, 4-speed manual gearbox, finished in grey and maroon, maroon leather interior, fewer than 44,000 miles recorded.
£2,750–3,300 / € 4,050–4,900 / $4,850–5,800 ➢ BARO

1968 Rover 2000TC, 1978cc, 4-cylinder engine, converted to unleaded fuel, new exhaust system, 35,000 miles recorded.
£1,150–1,350 / € 1,700–2,000 / $2,000–2,400 ➢ BRIT

ROVER Model	ENGINE cc/cyl	DATES	CONDITION 1	2	3
10hp	998/2	1920–25	£5,000	£3,000	£1,500
9/20	1074/4	1925–27	£6,000	£4,000	£2,000
10/25	1185/4	1928–33	£7,000	£4,000	£2,500
14hp	1577/6	1933–39	£6,000	£4,250	£2,000
12	1496/4	1934–37	£7,000	£4,000	£1,500
20 Sports	2512/6	1937–39	£7,000	£4,500	£2,500

ROVER Model	ENGINE cc/cyl	DATES	CONDITION		
			1	2	3
P2 10	1389/4	1946–47	£3,200	£2,500	£1,000
P2 12	1496/4	1946–47	£3,500	£2,800	£1,200
P2 12 Tour	1496/4	1947	£6,000	£3,500	£1,500
P2 14/16	1901/6	1946–47	£4,200	£3,000	£1,000
P2 14/16 Sal	1901/6	1946–47	£3,000	£2,000	£700
P3 60	1595/4	1948–49	£5,000	£2,500	£1,000
P3 75	2103/6	1948–49	£4,000	£3,000	£800
P4 75	2103/6	1950–51	£4,000	£2,000	£1,200
P4 75	2103/6	1952–64	£3,500	£1,800	£1,200
P4 60	1997/4	1954–59	£3,200	£1,200	£1,200
P4 90	2638/6	1954–59	£4,000	£1,800	£1,200
P4 75	2230/6	1955–59	£3,800	£1,200	£1,000
P4 105R	2638/6	1957–58	£4,000	£2,000	£1,000
P4 105S	2638/6	1957–59	£4,000	£2,000	£1,000
P4 80	2286/4	1960–62	£3,000	£1,200	£800
P4 95	2625/6	1963–64	£3,000	£1,600	£500
P4 100	2625/6	1960–62	£3,800	£2,000	£1,000
P4 110	2625/6	1963–64	£3,800	£2,000	£1,000
P5 3 Litre	2995/6	1959–67	£4,000	£2,500	£1,000
P5 3 Litre Coupé	2995/6	1959–67	£5,500	£3,800	£1,000
P5B (V8)	3528/8	1967–74	£6,250	£4,500	£1,500
P5B (V8) Coupé	3528/8	1967–73	£6,250	£4,500	£1,500
P6 2000 SC Series 1	1980/4	1963–65	£2,200	£800	–
P6 2000 SC Series 1	1980/4	1966–70	£2,000	£800	–
P6 2000 SC Series 1 Auto	1980/4	1966–70	£1,500	£600	–
P6 2000 TC Series 1	1980/4	1966–70	£2,000	£900	–
P6 2000 SC Series 2	1980/4	1970–73	£2,000	£900	–
P6 2000 SC Series 2 Auto	1980/4	1970–73	£1,500	£800	–
P6 2000 TC Series 2	1980/4	1970–73	£2,000	£900	–
P6 3500 Series 1	3500/8	1968–70	£2,500	£1,400	–
P6 2200 SC	2200/4	1974–77	£1,750	£850	–
P6 2200 SC Auto	2200/4	1974–77	£2,500	£1,000	–
P6 2200 TC	2200/4	1974–77	£2,000	£1,000	–
P6 3500 Series 2	3500/8	1971–77	£3,000	£1,700	–
P6 3500 S Series 2	3500/8	1971–77	£2,000	£1,500	–

1972 Rover P6 2000TC Series 2, 1978cc, 4-cylinder engine, 4-speed manual gearbox, finished in white, beige leather interior.
£910–1,100 / €1,400–1,650 / $1,650–1,950 ↗ CGC
The designation 'TC' stood for 'twin carburettor'.

1973 Rover P5B Saloon, 3528cc, V8 engine, finished in burgundy, beige leather interior, 1 family ownership from new, 41,000 miles recorded.
£5,300–6,300 / €7,800–9,300 / $9,300–11,100 ↗ BARO
The V8-engined P5B range was manufactured from 1967 to 1974.

Saab (*Swedish 1950–*)

SAAB Model	ENGINE cc/cyl	DATES	CONDITION		
			1	2	3
92	764/2	1950–53	£3,000	£1,500	£1,000
92B	764/2	1953–55	£3,500	£1,500	£1,000
93–93B	748/3	1956–60	£3,000	£1,500	£1,000
95	841/3	1960–68	£3,000	£1,500	£1,000
96	841/3	1960–68	£4,000	£1,800	£1,000
96 Sport	841/3	1962–66	£3,500	£1,500	£1,000
Sonnett II	1698/4	1967–74	£4,000	£2,000	£1,000
95/96	1498/4	1966–80	£3,000	£1,000	£800
99	1709/4	1968–71	£2,000	£1,200	–
99	1854/4	1970–74	£2,000	£1,000	–
99	1985/4	1972–83	£2,000	£1,000	£500
99 Turbo	1985/4	1978–83	£3,000	£1,000	£500

Salmson *(French 1921–57)*

◀ **1948 Salmson S4E Four-Door Saloon,** 2300cc, double-overhead-camshaft 4-cylinder engine, electrically-operated gearbox, finished in yellow and dark red, red cloth interior.
£2,950–3,550 / €4,350–5,300 / $5,200–6,200 ⚒ CGC
Famed for its aero engines, Salmson began constructing GN cars under licence in 1919, but by 1921 had begun building models of its own design. By the 1930s, however, demand for light sporting cars had diminished. Salmson's reaction was to produce small luxury machines, the most successful of which was the S4. By the late 1930s, the S4 had developed into the S4E, with a 2.3 litre, twin-cam engine and hydraulic brakes. After WWII, this model was reintroduced in 1946, but by 1950 its sales were in decline. Despite the introduction of a new Randonée model with a light alloy engine in 1951, the company ceased production in 1957.

Singer *(British 1905–70)*

SINGER Model	ENGINE cc/cyl	DATES	CONDITION 1	2	3
10	1097/4	1918–24	£5,000	£2,000	£1,000
15	1991/6	1922–25	£6,000	£3,000	£1,500
14/34	1776/6	1926–27	£7,000	£4,000	£2,000
Junior	848/4	1927–32	£6,000	£3,000	£1,500
Senior	1571/4	1928–29	£7,000	£4,000	£2,000
Super 6	1776/6	1928–31	£7,000	£4,000	£2,000
9 Le Mans	972/4	1932–37	£13,000+	£8,000	£5,000
Twelve	1476/6	1932–34	£10,000	£7,000	£6,000
1.5 Litre	1493/6	1934–36	£3,000	£2,000	£1,000
2 Litre	1991/6	1934–37	£4,000	£2,750	£1,000
11	1459/4	1935–36	£3,000	£2,000	£1,000
12	1525/4	1937–39	£3,000	£2,000	£1,000

▶ **1934 Singer Nine Le Mans,** 972cc, 4-cylinder engine, recently restored, 1,000 miles recorded since.
£12,700–15,200 / €18,800–22,500 / $22,400–26,800 ⚒ B(Kn)
The Singer Nine's predecessor was the 8hp Junior, a successful, high-quality light car powered by an 848cc, four-cylinder, overhead-camshaft engine. Built from 1932 to 1939, the Nine employed a 972cc, 26.5bhp version of this motor in an entirely new chassis. A four-speed freewheel gearbox was standard, while the Nine Sports, and more powerful and faster Nine Le Mans came with hydraulic brakes.

Standard *(British 1903–63)*

STANDARD Model	ENGINE cc/cyl	DATES	CONDITION 1	2	3
SLS	1328/4	1919–20	£5,000	£4,000	£1,000
VI	1307/4	1922	£5,000	£4,000	£1,000
SLO/V4	1944/4	1922–28	£5,000	£4,000	£1,000
6V	2230/6	1928	£10,000	£8,000	£5,000
V3	1307/4	1923–26	£4,000	£3,000	£1,000
Little 9	1006/4	1932–33	£4,000	£2,000	£1,000
9	1155/4	1928–29	£5,500	£3,000	£1,000
Big 9	1287/4	1932–33	£4,500	£3,250	£2,000
15	1930/6	1929–30	£6,000	£4,000	£2,000
12	1337/6	1933–34	£4,000	£3,000	£1,500
10hp	1343/4	1933–37	£4,000	£2,500	£1,000
9	1052/4	1934–36	£4,200	£2,500	£1,000
Flying 9	1131/4	1937–39	£3,200	£1,800	£750
Flying 10	1267/4	1937–39	£3,500	£2,200	£1,000
Flying 14	1176/4	1937–48	£4,500	£2,200	£1,000
Flying 8	1021/4	1939–48	£4,500	£2,400	£1,000

STANDARD Model	ENGINE cc/cyl	DATES	CONDITION 1	2	3
12	1609/4	1945–48	£2,000	£950	£250
12 DHC	1509/4	1945–48	£3,200	£2,000	£500
14	1776/4	1945–48	£3,000	£950	£250
Vanguard I–II	2088/4	1948–55	£2,200	£1,000	£250
Vanguard III	2088/4	1955–61	£1,800	£900	£200
Vanguard III Est	2088/4	1955–61	£2,000	£1,000	£250
Vanguard III Sportsman	2088/4	1955–58	£2,500	£1,200	£400
Vanguard Six	1998/6	1961–63	£2,000	£1,000	£500
Eight	803/4	1952–59	£1,250	£500	–
Ten	948/4	1955–59	£1,400	£800	–
Ensign I–II	1670/4	1957–63	£1,000	£800	–
Ensign I–II Est	1670/4	1962–63	£2,000	£1,100	–
Pennant Companion	948/4	1955–61	£1,800	£850	£300
Pennant	948/4	1955–59	£1,650	£825	£250

Stanley *(American 1897–1927)*

1909 Stanley Steamer 12hp Model R, Stanley designed their own wire-wound boiler and used it with a very light engine manufactured by J. W. Penny & Son, Maine.
£76,000–91,000 / €112,000–134,000 / $134,000–160,000 ⚘ BB(S)
One of the few cars to succeed without relying on an internal-combustion engine, the Stanley Steamer was also by far the most successful. The first prototype was completed in 1897, with production beginning the following year.

Star *(British 1898–1932)*

1926 Star 12/25 Scorpio Roadster, 1945cc, 4-cylinder engine, finished in red and black, beige leather interior, older restoration.
£13,500–15,000 / €20,000–22,200 $23,800–26,400 🚗 SBR

1932 Star Comet 18/50 Four-Door Saloon, overhead-valve 6-cylinder engine, thermostatically-controlled radiator shutters, central lubrication and self-jacking systems, older restoration.
£6,800–8,100 / €10,100–12,000 / $12,000–14,300 ⚘ CGC

Stevens-Duryea (American 1902–27)

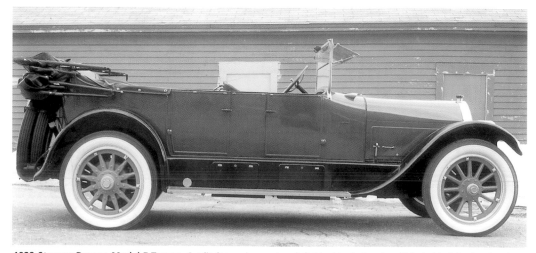

1922 Stevens-Duryea Model E Tourer, 6-cylinder engine, restored, finished in dark red and black, black leather interior. £17,000–19,900 / €25,100–29,400 / $29,900–35,000 ✗ BB(S)

In 1895, Charles and J. Frank Duryea established the Duryea Motor Wagon Company in Springfield, Massachusetts, the company being the first to actually manufacture automobiles in the USA. Two belt-driven vehicles were shipped to England to participate in the 1896 Emancipation Run celebrating the repeal of draconian laws restricting the use of motor cars. Frank Duryea's entry was the first to reach Brighton. The enterprise soon moved to Peoria, but shortly afterwards the brothers parted company. Returning to Massachusetts, Frank struck a deal with J. Stevens Arms & Tool Company – the result was the Stevens-Duryea Company. By the early 1920s, Duryea himself had long since left the company, which had changed hands several times. By then, it was building the Model E, which was powered by an 80bhp, six-cylinder engine. For 1922 and 1923, ten different bodies were offered on the Model E chassis.

Studebaker (American 1902–66)

1955 Studebaker President Speedster Coupé, 259cu.in, V8 engine, leather upholstery, restored to original condition. £29,700–35,000 / €44,000–52,000 $52,000–62,000 ✗ BJ

Studebaker's roots go back to 1852 and the establishment of a wagon works at South Bend, Indiana, by brothers Henry and Clem Studebaker. Later, they were joined by their dynamic younger brother, John Mohler Studebaker, who had already made a fortune making wheelbarrows for gold miners in California.

1956 Studebaker Golden Hawk Coupé, 352cu.in, V8 engine, automatic transmission, finished in white and black, cream interior, 4 owners from new. £14,800–17,700 / €21,900–26,200 $26,000–31,000 ✗ BJ

Subaru (Japanese 1958–)

◀ **1996 Subaru SVX Turbo Coupé,** 3300cc, double-overhead-camshaft 24-valve 6-cylinder engine, turbocharger, 4-speed automatic transmission, 4-wheel drive, alloy wheels, finished in red and black. £3,500–4,200 / €5,200–6,200 / $6,200–7,400 ✗ H&H

Sunbeam (British 1901–68)

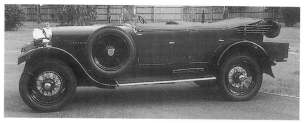

1929 Sunbeam 20.9hp Tourer, 2916cc, 6-cylinder engine, 4-speed gearbox, original paintwork, leather interior, engine rebuilt, 64,000 miles recorded.
£17,200–20,600 / €25,500–30,000 / $30,000–36,000 ➶ H&H

1927 Sunbeam 25hp Tourer, 3.6 litre, 6-cylinder engine, 4-speed manual gearbox, finished in maroon and black, maroon leather interior, excellent condition.
£22,500–27,000 / €33,000–40,000 $40,000–48,000 ➶ H&H
Sunbeam was formed in 1905 by John Marston. It soon became a force to be reckoned with in motor sport, achieving Grand Prix and record breaking success in the 1920s. To beat the 200mph Land Speed record, Sunbeam built a car for Sir Henry Segrave, which he used to achieve a new record of 203.79mph at Daytona Beach, Florida, in 1927.

1930 Sunbeam 16.9hp Drophead Coupé, 2116cc, 6-cylinder engine, finished in grey and black, dark blue leather interior.
£11,200–13,400 / €16,600–19,800 / $19,700–23,600 ➶ H&H

◄ **1951 Sunbeam-Talbot 90 Mk II,** 2267cc, 4-cylinder engine, 4-speed manual gearbox, fewer than 52,000 miles recorded.
£2,750–3,300 / €4,050–4,900 / $4,850–5,800 ➶ H&H
Sunbeams were known as Sunbeam-Talbots from 1935 to 1963.

1955 Sunbeam-Talbot 90 Mk III Drophead Coupé, 2267cc, 4-cylinder engine, 4-speed manual gearbox with overdrive, top speed 93+mph, finished red, white top, black interior, 1 of only 17 known to exist.
£7,100–8,500 / €10,500–12,600 / $12,500–15,000 ➶ H&H

◄ **1966 Sunbeam Tiger Mk I,** bored V8 engine with high-lift camshaft, high-compression pistons and high-output oil pump, 300bhp, hardtop, alloy wheels.
£10,100–12,100 / €14,900–17,900 / $17,800–21,300 ➶ H&H

SUNBEAM Model	ENGINE cc/cyl	DATES	CONDITION 1	2	3
12/16	2412/4	1910–14	£30,000	£18,000	£12,000
16/20	4070/4	1910–15	£32,000	£22,000	£15,000
24	4524/6	1919–22	£30,000	£19,000	£11,000
3 Litre	2916/6	1925–30	£48,000	£30,000	£20,000
14/40	2200/4	1925–30	£18,000	£10,000	£8,000
16	2040/6	1927–30	£16,000	£12,500	£10,000
20	2916/6	1927–30	£22,000	£15,000	£10,500
Speed 20	2916/6	1932–35	£15,000+	£10,000	£8,000
Dawn	1627/4	1934–35	£8,000	£5,000	£3,500
25	3317/6	1934	£12,000+	£8,000	£4,000

Prices can vary depending on replica bodies, provenance, coachbuilder, drophead, twin cam, etc.

1971 Sunbeam Stiletto, 875cc, overhead-camshaft engine, twin carburettors, 55bhp, alloy wheels, vinyl-covered roof, reclining seats.
£3,150–3,500 / €4,650–5,200 / $5,500–6,200 🚗 IMP
The Stiletto was an up-market, badge engineered Hillman Imp with running gear and engine from the Imp Sport.

1972 Sunbeam Imp Sport, 875cc, rear-mounted overhead-camshaft 4-cylinder engine, twin carburettors, uprated running gear, oil cooler, brake servo, fully restored, concours condition.
£2,700–3,000 / €4,000–4,450
$4,750–5,300 🚗 IMP

SUNBEAM-TALBOT/ SUNBEAM Model	ENGINE cc/cyl	DATES	CONDITION 1	2	3
Talbot 80	1185/4	1948–50	£3,500	£2,250	£1,000
Talbot 80 DHC	1185/4	1948–50	£6,000	£4,500	£2,000
Talbot 90 Mk I	1944/4	1949–50	£4,000	£2,100	£750
Talbot 90 Mk I DHC	1944/4	1949–50	£7,000	£4,750	£2,000
Talbot 90 II–III	2267/4	1950–56	£5,000	£3,000	£1,500
Talbot 90 II–III DHC	2267/4	1950–56	£7,000	£5,000	£2,250
Talbot Alpine I–III	2267/4	1953–55	£11,000	£7,500	£3,750
Talbot Ten	1197/4	1946–48	£3,500	£2,000	£750
Talbot Ten Tourer	1197/4	1946–48	£7,000	£4,000	£2,000
Talbot Ten DHC	1197/4	1946–48	£6,500	£4,000	£2,000
Talbot 2 Litre	1997/4	1946–48	£4,000	£2,500	£1,000
Talbot 2 Litre Tourer	1997/4	1946–48	£7,500	£4,000	£2,250
Rapier I	1392/4	1955–57	£1,200	£700	£300
Rapier II	1494/4	1957–59	£1,800	£900	£300
Rapier II Conv	1494/4	1957–59	£3,000	£1,500	£450
Rapier III	1494/4	1959–61	£2,000	£1,200	£400
Rapier III Conv	1494/4	1959–61	£3,500	£1,600	£600
Rapier IIIA	1592/4	1961–63	£2,000	£1,200	£400
Rapier IIIA Conv	1592/4	1961–63	£3,600	£1,700	£650
Rapier IV–V	1592/ 1725/4	1963–67	£2,000	£700	£250
Alpine I–II	1494/4	1959–62	£6,000	£3,500	£1,800
Alpine III	1592/4	1963	£6,500	£4,000	£1,250
Alpine IV	1592/4	1964	£5,500	£3,500	£1,250
Alpine V	1725/4	1965–68	£6,000	£4,000	£1,250
Harrington Alpine	1592/4	1961	£8,000	£4,750	£1,250
Harrington Le Mans	1592/4	1962–63	£10,000	£6,500	£3,000
Tiger Mk 1	4261/8	1964–67	£12,000+	£10,000	£6,000
Tiger Mk 2	4700/8	1967	£13,000+	£8,000	£6,000
Rapier Fastback	1725/4	1967–76	£1,100+	£700	£250
Rapier H120	1725/4	1968–76	£1,500+	£800	£300

Swift *(British 1898–1931)*

1926 Swift Model QA Two-Seater with Dickey, 1097cc, side-valve 4-cylinder engine, 3-speed manual gearbox, magneto ignition, partially restored.
£3,350–4,000 / €4,950–5,900 / $5,900–6,900 🔨 CGC

1929 Swift P-Type Tourer, 1190cc, side-valve 4-cylinder engine, 4-speed manual gearbox, engine rebuilt 2001, finished in maroon and black, red interior, good condition.
£5,800–6,900 / €8,600–10,200 / $10,200–12,100 🔨 H&H

Talbot *(British 1902–54)*

1935 Talbot BA75 Sports Saloon, stored for 33 years, recently recommissioned, new water pump, brakes overhauled, rewired, rear section of roof modified to allow sun roof to extend back to the waistline, 1 of only 6 known to exist.
£7,000–8,400 / €10,400–12,400 / $12,300–14,800 ✗ CGC

1936 Talbot BG110 Tourer, coachwork by Vanden Plas, 3377cc, 6-cylinder engine, 120bhp, top speed 110mph, engine and gearbox overhauled 1997–98, 1 of only 12 VDP Tourers built, concours condition.
£55,000–66,000 / €81,000–98,000
$97,000–116,000 ✗ CGC

1936 Talbot BG110 Speed Saloon, 3378cc, overhead-valve 6-cylinder engine, 4-speed manual gearbox, semi-cantilever rear suspension, hydraulic shock absorbers, adjustable steering column, finished in beige and black, 1 of only 2 Speed Saloons known to exist.
£35,000–42,000 / €52,000–62,000 / $62,000–74,000 ✗ B(Kn)

▶ **1936 Talbot Roesch Model 75 Four-Seater Sports,** 2366cc, engine overhauled, finished in white, green interior.
£21,500–25,800 / €32,000–38,000
$38,000–45,000 ✗ H&H
This car began life as a Model 75 saloon, but in 1998 it was fitted with a four-seater sports body.

TALBOT Model	ENGINE cc/cyl	DATES	CONDITION		
			1	2	3
25hp & 25/50	4155/4	1907–16	£35,000	£25,000	£15,000
12hp	2409/4	1909–15	£22,000	£15,000	£9,000
8/18	960/4	1922–25	£8,000	£5,000	£2,000
14/45	1666/6	1926–35	£16,000	£10,000	£5,000
75	2276/6	1930–37	£22,000	£12,000	£7,000
105	2969/6	1935–37	£30,000+	£20,000+	£15,000

Higher value for tourers and coachbuilt cars.

◀ **1938 Talbot Ten Sports Tourer,** 1185cc, side-valve 4-cylinder engine, 4-speed all-synchromesh gearbox, new wheel discs, finished in ivory, navy blue upholstery, full mechanical restoration 1991, excellent condition throughout.
£5,700–6,800
€ 8,400–10,100
$10,000–12,000   ✈ B(Kn)

▶ **1980 Talbot Sunbeam Lotus,** 2174cc, 4-cylinder engine, ZF 5-speed close-ratio gearbox, limited-slip differential, ventilated disc brakes with 4-piston calipers, Mk II interior with Recaro front seats, concours condition.
£6,900–8,200 / € 10,200–12,100
$12,100–14,400   ✈ H&H

Toyota *(Japanese 1936–)*

TOYOTA Model	ENGINE cc/cyl	DATES	CONDITION 1	2	3
Celica TA22 & TA23 Coupé	1588/4	1971–78	£2,500	£1,800	£500
RA28 Liftback	1968/4	1971–78	£3,500	£1,500	£400
Plus a premium of £200–500 for a Twin-Cam GT.					

◀ **1978 Toyota Celica TA23 1600,** 1588cc, overhead-camshaft 4-cylinder engine, 5-speed manual gearbox, finished in yellow, brown cloth interior, 1 owner from new, 29,000 miles recorded.
£1,800–2,150 / € 2,650–3,200
$3,150–3,800   ✈ CGC

TOYOTA Model	ENGINE cc/cyl	DATES	CONDITION 1	2	3
Crown MS65, MS63, MS75, Saloon, Estate, Coupé	2563/6	1972–75	£2,000	£1,000	£500
Plus a premium of £200–400 for the Coupé.					

Triumph *(British 1923–84)*

In 1890, German-born Siegfried Bettman and Mauritz Schulte began building bicycles under the Triumph name in Coventry. However, it was motorcycles that really set the Triumph brand on its way. Production of these began in 1902, using imported engines. By 1905, however, Triumph was manufacturing its own power units. With the outbreak of WWI in 1914, Triumph became a major supplier of motorcycles to the British and allied forces.

The first Triumph car, the 10/20hp model, appeared in 1923, being followed in 1924 by the larger 13/35 with an 1873cc engine. It was notable for being the first British car to feature Lockheed hydraulic brakes on all four wheels. In 1926, the engine's capacity rose to 2169cc; production continued until 1930.

However, it was not until 1927 that Triumph built a car that sold in any real numbers. It was the Super Seven, which came with an 832cc engine and worm drive. A total of 17,000 were built, compared to only 2,000 of all the previous Triumph cars.

By 1931, Triumph was suffering from the effects of the world-wide depression. Its motorcycle sales (the mainstay of the company) were down some 30 per cent, and to help balance the books, the bicycle business was sold off.

Triumph moved from building small cars to larger vehicles, and the mid- to late 1930s saw a family of very attractive models with four- and six-cylinder engines. These included the Gloria, Dolomite and Vitesse.

Although Triumph appeared to be doing well, in fact the opposite was true, with losses growing steadily. The situation came to a head in 1936, resulting in the sale of the motorcycle division.

In 1944, Sir John Black purchased the remains of Triumph, which became a subsidiary of his Standard Motor Company. Among the new post-war Triumphs were the Renown (1946) and the Mayflower (1950), but the big breakthrough occurred in 1953, when Triumph launched the TR2 sports car. This employed a Standard Vanguard engine tuned to give 90bhp. The TR2 and its descendants, the TR3 and TR3A, sold over 83,000 units up to 1962.

The next major post-war Triumph model was the Herald, which arrived in mid-1959. The Herald was powered originally by the 948cc Standard Ten engine, later replaced by a 1147cc unit. It was the first small British family car to sport all-round independent suspension. The two-door body was styled by Michelotti.

In 1961, Standard-Triumph was purchased by Leyland, and in 1962 a six-cylinder Herald, the Vitesse, was introduced. Next came the 2000, the various forms of which were manufactured until 1977. The Herald/Vitesse range was supplemented and eventually replaced by the 1300 (1965) and Toledo (1970). Other models included the Dolomite and more sporting 16-valve Dolomite Sprint. Triumph sports cars continued to be popular and included the TR4, TR5, TR6 and wedge-shaped TR7, plus the Spitfire.

In 1968, Triumph had become part of British Leyland. Rationalization was inevitable: the Triumph saloons lost out to Rover; production of the Spitfire ceased in 1980; and the TR7 and TR8 had been dropped by the end of 1981.

But the Triumph name lived on for another three years, thanks to the Acclaim saloon, which was a badge engineered Honda Ballade. In June 1984, its replacement, the Honda Civic, was given the name Rover 200, and so for marketing reasons, the Triumph marque finally disappeared.

1948 Triumph 1800 Roadster, 1776cc, overhead-valve 4-cylinder engine, 4-speed manual gearbox, unrestored, good condition. **£11,100–13,300 / €16,400–19,700 / $19,500–23,400 ⚹ COYS**
Introduced in 1946, the Triumph Roadster was one of the new designs from Triumph following its acquisition by the Standard Motor Company. For the first two years of production, it was powered by a 1776cc engine, effectively an overhead-valve version of the pre-war Standard 14 unit. The aluminium body was constructed on an ash framework, and the design was largely influenced by the pre-war Dolomite roadster. A dickey seat was incorporated, and as a bench front seat was fitted, the car could hold five at a pinch. By the time production came to an end, 4,501 had been built.

TRIUMPH Model	ENGINE cc/cyl	DATES	CONDITION		
			1	2	3
TLC	1393/4	1923–25	£6,000	£4,000	£1,500
TPC	2169/4	1926–30	£6,000	£4,000	£2,000
K	832/4	1928–34	£4,000	£2,000	£1,000
S	1203/6	1931–33	£5,000	£3,000	£1,500
G12 Gloria	1232/4	1935–37	£6,000	£4,000	£2,000
G16 Gloria 6	1991/6	1935–39	£7,000	£4,500	£2,000
Vitesse/Dolomite	1767/4	1937–39	£14,000	£10,000	£6,000
Dolomite	1496/4	1938–39	£7,000	£4,000	£2,000

1948 Triumph 1800 Roadster, 1776cc, 4-cylinder engine, completely restored, finished in metallic grey, red interior.
£13,800–16,500 / €20,400–24,7400
$24,300–29,000 ➤ BRIT

◀ **1953 Triumph Mayflower Saloon,** 1247cc, 4-cylinder engine, 1 of last Mayflowers built, unrestored, in need of attention.
£800–960 / €1,200–1,400
$1,400–1,700 ➤ B(Kn)

▶ **1957 Triumph TR3,** 1991cc, overhead-valve 4-cylinder engine, 4-speed manual gearbox, finished in beige, red interior.
£7,800–9,300 / €11,500–13,700
$13,700–16,400 ➤ H&H
The TR2 was responsible for Standard-Triumph taking motor sport seriously, the model's first big win being the 1954 RAC Rally victory of privateers Wallwork and Cooper. It was superseded in 1955 by the TR3 with a slightly more powerful (95bhp) engine and front disc brakes.

1958 Triumph TR3A, 1991cc, 100bhp, 4-speed manual gearbox with overdrive, left-hand drive, finished in black, red interior, excellent condition.
£13,400–16,100 / €19,900–23,900
$23,600–28,300 ➤ COYS
The Michelotti styled TR2/3/3A sports cars had rugged and reliable mechanics, which ensured buoyant sales in the UK and USA.

1966 Triumph Vitesse 1600 Convertible, 1569cc, overhead-valve 6-cylinder engine, wire wheels, luggage rack, finished in blue, black leather interior.
£2,100–2,500 / €3,100–3,700
$3,700–4,400 ➤ CGC

1967 Triumph Vitesse 2 Litre Mk I Convertible, 1998cc, overhead-valve 6-cylinder engine, 4-speed manual gearbox with overdrive, tonneau cover, finished in green, red interior. £2,900–3,450 / €4,300–5,100 / $5,100–6,100 ✗ H&H

1968 Triumph TR5, 2498cc, overhead-valve 6-cylinder engine, fuel injection, 150bhp, 4-speed manual gearbox, top speed 120mph, finished in blue, dark blue interior, near concours condition.
£9,100–10,900 / €13,400–16,100 $16,000–19,200 ✗ COYS

TRIUMPH Model	ENGINE cc/cyl	DATES	CONDITION 1	2	3
1800/2000 Roadster	1776/ 2088/4	1946–49	£14,000	£8,000	£5,000
1800	1776/4	1946–49	£4,000	£2,000	£1,000
2000 Renown	2088/4	1949–54	£4,000	£2,000	£1,000
Mayflower	1247/4	1949–53	£2,000	£1,000	£500
TR2 long door	1247/4	1953	£10,000	£8,000	£5,000
TR2	1247/4	1953–55	£10,000+	£7,500	£5,000
TR3	1991/4	1955–57	£10,000+	£9,000	£4,000
TR3A	1991/4	1958–62	£11,000	£9,000	£3,500
TR4	2138/4	1961–65	£10,000	£7,000	£3,000
TR4A	2138/4	1965–67	£10,000	£6,500	£3,000
TR5	2498/6	1967–68	£12,000	£7,500	£4,000
TR6 (PI)	2498/6	1969–74	£9,000	£8,000	£3,500
Herald	948/4	1959–61	£1,000+	£400+	£150
Herald FHC	948/4	1959–61	£1,500+	£550+	£300
Herald DHC	948/4	1960–61	£2,500+	£1,000+	£350
Herald S	948/4	1961–64	£800+	£400	£150
Herald 1200	1147/4	1961–70	£1,100	£500	£200
Herald 1200 FHC	1147/4	1961–64	£1,400	£800	£300
Herald 1200 DHC	1147/4	1961–67	£2,500	£1,000	£350
Herald 1200 Est	1147/4	1961–67	£1,300	£700	£300
Herald 12/50	1147/4	1963–67	£1,800	£1,000	£250
Herald 13/60	1296/4	1967–71	£1,300	£600	£200
Herald 13/60 DHC	1296/4	1967–71	£3,500	£1,500	£500
Herald 13/60 Est	1296/4	1967–71	£1,500	£650	£300
Vitesse 1600	1596/6	1962–66	£2,000	£1,250	£550
Vitesse 1600 Conv	1596/6	1962–66	£3,500	£1,800	£600
Vitesse 2 litre Mk I	1998/6	1966–68	£1,800	£800	£300
Vitesse 2 litre Mk I Conv	1998/6	1966–68	£4,500	£2,200	£1,000
Vitesse 2 litre Mk II	1998/6	1968–71	£2,000	£1,500	£300
Vitesse 2 litre Mk II Conv	1998/6	1968–71	£5,000	£2,500	£600
Spitfire Mk I	1147/4	1962–64	£2,000	£1,750	£300
Spitfire Mk II	1147/4	1965–67	£2,500	£2,000	£350
Spitfire Mk III	1296/4	1967–70	£3,500	£2,500	£450
Spitfire Mk IV	1296/4	1970–74	£5,000	£2,500	£350
Spitfire 1500	1493/4	1975–78	£3,500	£2,500	£750
Spitfire 1500	1493/4	1979–81	£5,000	£3,500	£1,200
GT6 Mk I	1998/6	1966–68	£5,000	£4,000	£1,200
GT6 Mk II	1998/6	1968–70	£6,000	£4,500	£1,400
GT6 Mk III	1998/6	1970–73	£7,000	£5,000	£1,500
2000 Mk I	1998/6	1963–69	£2,000	£1,200	£400
2000 Mk III	1998/6	1969–77	£2,000	£1,200	£500
2.5 PI	2498/6	1968–75	£2,000	£1,500	£900
2500 TC/S	2498/6	1974–77	£1,750	£700	£150
2500S	2498/6	1975–77	£2,500	£1,000	£150
1300 (FWD)	1296/4	1965–70	£800	£400	£150
1300TC (FWD)	1296/4	1967–70	£900	£450	£150
1500 (FWD)	1493/4	1970–73	£700	£450	£125
1500TC (RWD)	1296/4	1973–76	£850	£500	£100
Toledo	1296/4	1970–76	£850	£450	£100
Dolomite 1500	1493/4	1976–80	£1,350	£750	£125
Dolomite 1850	1854/4	1972–80	£1,450	£850	£150
Dolomite Sprint	1998/6	1976–81	£5,000	£4,000	£1,000
Stag	2997/8	1970–77	£9,000	£5,000	£2,000
TR7	1998/4	1975–82	£4,000	£1,200	£500
TR7 DHC	1998/4	1980–82	£4,000	£3,000	£1,500

◄ **1968 Triumph TR250,** 2498cc, overhead-valve 6-cylinder engine, 4-speed manual gearbox, servo-assisted front disc/rear drum brakes, top speed 120mph.
£10,500–12,600 / €15,500–18,600 $18,500–22,200 ≯ BRIT
The TR5 was the first of the six-cylinder TRs. It had Lucas fuel injection as standard, but cars destined for the USA were fitted with twin Stromberg carburettors and were designated TR250. In the latter guise, almost 8,500 examples were produced before the advent of the TR6.

1970 Triumph TR6, 2498cc, overhead-valve 6-cylinder engine, 4-speed manual gearbox with overdrive, servo-assisted front disc/rear drum brakes, rack-and-pinion steering.
£7,700–9,200 / €11,400–13,600 / $13,600–16,200 ≯ CGC
Launched in 1968, the TR6 replaced the TR250/TR5 models and proved a strong seller on both sides of the Atlantic. Its low-slung, Kamm-tailed styling was underpinned by a strong cruciform chassis boasting all-round, independent coil-sprung suspension.

► **1971 Triumph TR6,** 2498cc, overhead-valve 6-cylinder engine, 4-speed manual gearbox, stainless steel exhaust system, hood and hardtop, finished in red, black leather interior.
£6,200–7,400 / €9,200–11,000 / $10,900–13,000 ≯ CGC

1971 Triumph Herald 13/60 Convertible, 1300cc, overhead-valve 4-cylinder engine, 4-speed manual gearbox, front disc brakes, finished in yellow, black hood, tan interior, 1 family ownership from new, 60,000 miles recorded.
£1,900–2,250 / €2,800–3,350 / $3,350–3,950 ≯ B(Kn)

1971 Triumph Vitesse 2 Litre Mk II Convertible, 1998cc, overhead-valve 6-cylinder engine, 4-speed manual gearbox, finished in brown, tan interior, excellent condition.
£3,900–4,700 / €5,800–7,000 / $6,900–8,300 ≯ BRIT
The Vitesse arrived in 1962, taking its name from a famous pre-war Triumph and being powered by a sleeved-down version of the Standard Vanguard six-cylinder engine. During 1966, the engine was enlarged to 2 litres, further improving performance. This car dates from the final year of production.

1972 Triumph Stag, 2998cc, V8 engine, 4-speed manual gearbox with overdrive, rust-proofed from new, finished in dark green, black interior, 2 owners from new, fewer than 25,000 miles recorded, unrestored.
£7,600–9,100 / €11,200–13,500 / $13,400–16,000 ≯ B(Kn)

1973 Triumph Stag, 2997cc, original V8 engine, automatic transmission, finished in dark blue, black interior, 1 owner for 22 years.
£2,650–3,200 / €3,900–4,700 / $4,650–5,600 ≯ BARO

1973 Triumph GT6 Mk III, 1998cc, 6-cylinder engine, twin Stromberg carburettors, 104bhp, 4-speed manual gearbox.
£7,000–8,000 / €10,400–11,800 / $12,300–14,100 ≯ B(Kn)
In all, 13,042 GT6 Mk IIIs were made between 1970 and 1973.

◀ **1973 Triumph Stag,** fitted 3.5 litre Rover V8 engine, recent cylinder head overhaul, good condition.
£4,350–5,200 / €6,400–7,700 / $7,700–9,200 ➶ BARO

1973 Triumph Toledo Four-Door Saloon, 1296cc, overhead-valve 4-cylinder engine, finished in pale blue, black interior, 3 owners from new.
£400–480 / €590–710 / $700–840 ➶ BRIT

1973 Triumph TR6, 2498cc, 6-cylinder engine, 4-speed manual gearbox, finished in blue, black hood, black vinyl interior, 1 owner from new.
£4,350–5,200 / €6,400–7,700 / $7,700–9,200 ➶ CGC
Production of the TR6 ran from late 1968 to 1974.

▶ **1973 Triumph TR6,** 2498cc, overhead-valve 6-cylinder engine, fuel injection, 125bhp, converted to unleaded fuel, 4-speed manual gearbox with overdrive, fully restored, concours condition.
£9,200–11,000 / €13,600–16,300
$16,200–19,400 ➶ CGC

1973 Triumph TR6, 2498cc, overhead-valve 6-cylinder engine, 4-speed manual gearbox, finished in red, black interior.
£9,500–11,400 / €14,100–16,900 / $16,700–20,100 ➶ H&H
Such was the popularity of the Karmann styled TR6, particularly in its export market, that 94,619 were built from 1968 to 1976. The TR6 was the first of the TRs to have headlights positioned at the corners, the tail being redesigned with wrap-around rear lamps. Until 1973, the European TRs were fitted with 150bhp engines; subsequently, the power output was reduced to 124bhp.

▶ **1975 Triumph Stag,** 2997cc, V8 engine, 4-speed manual gearbox with overdrive, finished in green, stored for last 5 years, in need of recommissioning.
£1,450–1,700 / €2,150–2,500 / $2,550–3,000 ➶ BARO

1975 Triumph TR6, 2498cc, 6-cylinder engine,
4-speed manual gearbox, alloy wheels, left-hand drive,
mechanics overhauled, new hood, seats, carpets,
door panels and bumpers.
£6,300–7,500 / €9,300–11,100 / $11,100–13,200 ⌖ BJ

1980 Triumph TR7, 1998cc, inclined overhead-camshaft
4-cylinder engine, 105bhp, 5-speed manual gearbox,
finished in black, beige interior, 67,000 miles recorded.
£1,800–2,150 / €2,650–3,200 / $3,150–3,800 ⌖ H&H

▶ **1981 Triumph Dolomite Sprint,** 1998cc, overhead-
camshaft 16-valve 4-cylinder engine, 127bhp, top speed
115mph, 57,000 miles recorded, near concours condition.
£3,300–3,950 / €4,900–5,800 / $5,800–6,900 ⌖ H&H
This car dates from the last year of production. In all,
22,941 Sprint models were built.

1980 Triumph Dolomite 1500SE, 1493cc, 4-cylinder
engine, 4-speed manual gearbox, finished in black with
silver side stripes, blue/grey velour upholstery,
£1,200–1,400 / €1,800–2,050 / $2,100–2,450 ⌖ BRIT

1981 Triumph TR8 Convertible, 3528cc, V8 engine, 135bhp, top speed 121mph, finished in gold, tan velour interior.
£5,300–6,300 / €7,800–9,300 / $9,300–11,100 ⌖ H&H
This car is a genuine, factory-built, right-hand drive TR8. In all, 2,722 TR8s, most of which had left-hand drive,
were constructed.

Turner *(British 1950–66)*

Turner sports cars were designed and built by Jack Turner, around 700 being constructed between 1950 and 1966, when production ended.

They ranged from the A30/803 two-seater sports model of the mid-1950s to the Formula 2 cars of the early 1960s. Some were powered by the all-Turner, 2-litre, twin-cam engine. A feature of all Turners (apart from the GT) was a simple, but strong, ladder chassis constructed from large-diameter steel tubes. The bodies of all Turners produced between 1955 and 1966 comprised a GRP outer skin over a sheet-metal inner structure with aluminium doors that sat above the chassis. Independent front suspension and rack-and-pinion steering were based on BMC components for most models up to the early 1960s, being superseded and complemented by Triumph Herald/Spitfire units. The BMC rear axle was suspended by multi-leaf, transverse torsion bars and located by twin lower trailing arms with single or twin upper links, side-to-side location being provided by a panhard rod. Power came from a variety of engines, including the BMC A-series, Ford 997–1500cc and Coventry-Climax FWA/FWE.

1960 Turner Sports Mk I, 948cc, BMC 4-cylinder engine, 4-speed manual gearbox, finished in yellow, black interior, 1 of 18 built.
£7,200–8,000 / €10,700–11,800 / $12,700–14,100 🚗 Tur
The Sports Mk I was built in 1959 to 1960; a total of 18 cars were produced, 17 with BMC engine, one with a 1216cc Climax FWE unit.

1962 Turner Sports Mk II, 948cc, BMC 4-cylinder engine, 4-speed manual gearbox, finished in dark green, matching interior.
£7,200–8,000 / €10,700–11,800 / $12,700–14,100 🚗 Tur

TVR *(British 1949–)*

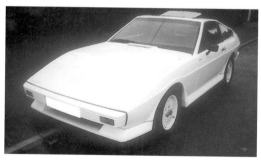

1982 TVR Tasmin Coupé, 2792cc, Ford V6 engine, automatic transmission, finished in white, black interior, fewer than 67,000 miles recorded.
£1,950–2,300 / €2,900–3,400 / $3,450–4,000 🔨 H&H
The name TVR was derived from the christian name of Trevor Wilkinson, who built the first cars and set up the first of many companies involved in the TVR story in Blackpool during 1949.

1986 TVR 420SEAC, 4235cc, V8 engine, recently refurbished.
£7,000–8,400 / €10,400–12,4200 $12,300–14,800 🔨 BARO
Based on the Tasmin, the 420/450SEAC models were the highest-performance TVRs of their era. Only 40 420SEACs were built.

TVR Model	ENGINE cc/cyl	DATES	CONDITION		
			1	2	3
Grantura I	1172/4	1957–62	£5,000	£3,000	£2,000
Grantura II	1558/4	1957–62	£5,500	£3,000	£2,000
Grantura III/1800S	1798/4	1963–67	£6,000	£3,000	£2,200
Tuscan V8	4727/8	1967–70	£12,000	£7,000	£6,000
Vixen S2/3	1599/4	1968–72	£5,000	£3,000	£1,500
3000M	2994/6	1972–79	£7,000	£4,000	£3,000
Taimar	2994/6	1977–79	£7,500	£5,000	£3,500

Cross Reference
See Colour Review (pages 145–152)

◄ **1995 TVR Chimera**, 3952cc, V8 engine, finished in metallic red, cream leather interior, concours condition.
£13,900–16,600 / € 20,600–24,600
$24,500–29,200 ✦ COYS

Vanden Plas *(British 1959–75)*

VANDEN PLAS Model	ENGINE cc/cyl	DATES	CONDITION 1	2	3
3 Litre I–II	2912/6	1959–64	£5,000	£3,000	£1,000
4 Litre R	3909/6	1964–67	£4,000	£2,500	£700
1100 Princess	1098/4	1964–67	£2,000	£1,000	£500
1300 Princess	1275/4	1967–74	£2,200	£1,500	£500

Vauxhall *(British 1903)*

A known continuous history can add value to and enhance the enjoyment of a car.

▶ **1925 Vauxhall 30/98 OE Fast Light Tourer**, 4.5 litres, side-valve 4-cylinder engine, 90bhp, top speed 85mph, Velox 4-seater body, 1 owner for 40 years.
£77,000–92,000 / € 114,600–136,000
$136,000–162,000 ✦ COYS

◄ **1966 Vauxhall Viva HA90 De Luxe**, 1057cc, overhead-valve 4-cylinder engine, 4-speed manual gearbox, finished in red, cream interior, fewer than 67,000 miles recorded, excellent condition.
£950–1,100 / € 1,400–1,650
$1,650–1,950 ✦ H&H
Owned by General Motors, Vauxhall entered the highly competitive UK small-car market in 1963 with the Viva. Essentially, the original series was a British version of the German Opel Kadett.

▶ **1991 Vauxhall Lotus Carlton**, 3615cc, 24-valve 6-cylinder engine, 2 turbochargers, 377bhp, 6-speed manual gearbox, top speed 187mph, 0–60mph in 4.9 seconds, finished in metallic dark green, green interior, 1 of 284 right-hand-drive examples built.
£10,700–12,800 / € 15,800–18,900
$18,800–22,500 ✦ H&H
At the time of its launch in 1990, the Vauxhall Lotus Carlton was the fastest production saloon that money could buy. Besides its high power, its bodyshell had been given a serious make-over, with vents, skirts, front dam, rear spoiler and 17in (43.2cm) alloy wheels.

VAUXHALL Model	ENGINE cc/cyl	DATES	CONDITION 1	2	3
D/OD	3969/4	1914–26	£35,000	£24,000	£18,000
E/OE	4224/4	1919–28	£80,000+	£60,000+	£35,000
Eighty	3317/6	1931–33	£10,000	£8,000	£5,000
Cadet	2048/6	1931–33	£7,000	£5,000	£3,000
Lt Six	1531/6	1934–38	£5,000	£4,000	£1,500
14	1781/6	1934–39	£4,000	£3,000	£1,500
25	3215/6	1937–39	£5,000	£4,000	£1,500
10	1203/4	1938–39	£4,000	£3,000	£1,500
Wyvern LIX	1500/4	1948–51	£2,000	£1,000	£500
Velox LIP	2200/6	1948–51	£2,000	£1,000	£500
Wyvern EIX	1500/4	1951–57	£2,000	£1,320	£400
Velox EIPV	2200/6	1951–57	£3,000	£1,650	£400
Cresta EIPC	2200/6	1954–57	£3,000	£1,650	£400
Velox/Cresta PAS/PAD	2262/6	1957–59	£2,850	£1,300	£300
Velox/Cresta PASY/PADY	2262/6	1959–60	£2,700	£1,500	£300
Velox/Cresta PASX/PADX	2651/6	1960–62	£2,700	£1,300	£300
Velox/Cresta PASX/PADX Est	2651/6	1960–62	£2,700	£1,300	£300
Velox/Cresta PB	2651/6	1962–65	£1,600	£800	£100
Velox/Cresta PB Est	2651/6	1962–65	£1,600	£800	£100
Cresta/Deluxe PC	3294/6	1964–72	£1,500	£800	£100
Cresta PC Est	3294/6	1964–72	£1,500	£800	£100
Viscount	3294/6	1964–72	£1,700	£900	£100
Victor I–II	1507/4	1957–61	£2,000	£1,000	£250
Victor I–II Est	1507/4	1957–61	£2,100	£1,100	£300
Victor FB	1507/4	1961–64	£1,500	£900	£200
Victor FB Est	1507/4	1961–64	£1,600	£1,000	£300
VX4/90	1507/4	1961–64	£2,000	£900	£150
Victor FC101	1594/4	1964–67	£1,600	£900	£150
Victor FC101 Est	1594/4	1964–67	£1,800	£1,000	£200
101 VX4/90	1594/4	1964–67	£2,000	£1,500	£250
VX4/90	1975/4	1969–71	£1,000	£600	£100
Ventora I/II	3294/6	1968–71	£1,000	£375	£100
Viva HA	1057/4	1963–66	£1,000	£350	£100
Viva SL90	1159/4	1966–70	£1,000	£350	£100
Viva Brabham	1159/4	1967–70	£2,000	£1,000	£800
Viva	1600/4	1968–70	£500	£350	£100
Viva Est	1159/4	1967–70	£500	£400	£100

Volkswagen (*German 1936–*)

► 1969 Volkswagen D26 Type E Microbus De Luxe, 1584cc, air-cooled overhead-valve 4-cylinder engine, left-hand drive, laminated windscreen, heated rear window, sealed-beam headlamps, 1 owner from new, fewer than 4,000 miles recorded.
£12,000–14,400
€17,800–21,300
$21,100–25,300
⋏ B(Kn)

The Volkswagen Type 2 and its derivatives enjoyed an even longer period in production than the famous Beetle. The original was conceived in the late 1940s by a Dutch Volkswagen agent, Ben Pon, who drew up plans for a van based on the Beetle floorpan and running gear. Known as the Type 2 (the Beetle saloon being Type 1), it arrived in 1950, offering a bewildering variety of models that catered for an enormous range of commercial and domestic activities. The original retained the Beetle's rear-mounted, 1200cc, air-cooled engine and four-speed gearbox, with suitable ratios to cope with the van's greater weight. Engines grew in size and power, while handling and comfort improved steadily. The first major revision occurred in 1968, by which time almost two million had been sold worldwide. The replacement, also called Type 2, was an entirely new vehicle, being larger and roomier than before, but still rear-engined. Power units grew in size from 1600cc to 2 litres before production ceased in 1978 with the introduction of the third generation.

VOLKSWAGEN Model	ENGINE cc/cyl	DATES	CONDITION 1	2	3
Beetle (split rear screen)	1131/4	1945–53	£5,000	£3,500	£2,000
Beetle (oval rear screen)	1192/4	1953–57	£4,000	£2,000	£1,000
Beetle (slope headlamps)	1192/4	1957–68	£2,500	£1,000	£600
Beetle DHC	1192/4	1954–60	£6,000	£4,500	£2,000
Beetle 1500	1493/4	1966–70	£3,000	£2,000	£1,000
Beetle 1302 LS	1600/4	1970–72	£2,500	£1,850	£850
Beetle 1303 S	1600/4	1972–79	£3,000	£2,000	£1,500
1500 Variant/1600	1493/ 1584/4	1961–73	£2,000	£1,500	£650
1500/1600	1493/ 1584/4	1961–73	£3,500	£2,000	£800
Karmann Ghia/I	1192/4	1955–59	£5,000	£3,000	£1,000
Karmann Ghia/I DHC	1192/4	1957–59	£8,000	£5,000	£2,500
Karmann Ghia/I	1192/4	1960–74	£5,500	£3,000	£1,800
Karmann Ghia/I DHC	1192/4	1960–74	£7,000	£4,500	£2,000
Karmann Ghia/3	1493/4	1962–69	£4,000	£2,500	£1,250

1970 Volkswagen Beetle 1600, 1584cc, air-cooled overhead-valve 4-cylinder engine, 4-speed manual gearbox, left-hand drive, finished in red and cream, black interior, roof rack, excellent condition.
£3,500–4,200 / €5,200–6,200 / $6,200–7,400 ⚒ BJ

1971 Volkswagen Karmann Ghia Cabriolet, 1200cc, air-cooled overhead-valve 4-cylinder engine, 4-speed manual gearbox, alloy wheels, finished in magenta, black hood, black interior, excellent condition.
£4,100–4,900 / €6,100–7,300 / $7,200–8,600 ⚒ B(Kn)
Launched in 1955 in 1200cc form, the Kharman Ghia was based on a modified export Beetle floorpan. It kept abreast of mainstream Beetle developments, gaining an all-synchromesh gearbox and progressively larger and more powerful engines. This example was one of the last to be built.

1974 Volkswagen K70LS, 1807cc, 4-cylinder engine, finished in blue, light brown interior, 1 of only 5 LS models known to exist in the UK.
£720–800 / €1,050–1,200
$1,250–1,400 🚗 KR

▶ **1975 Volkswagen Beetle 1600,** 1584cc, air-cooled overhead-valve 4-cylinder engine, 4-speed manual gearbox, top speed 84mph, restored at a cost of £20,000 / 29,600 / $35,000 1998–2001, EMPI-style alloy wheels, concours condition.
£2,400–2,850 / €3,550–4,200
$4,200–5,000 ⚒ CGC

Volvo *(Swedish 1926–)*

1960 Volvo PV544 B16, 1598cc, 4-cylinder engine,
twin SU carburettors, new suspension.
£2,700–3,000 / €4,000–4,450 / $4,750–5,300 ⊞ AMA
The first Volvo car appeared in 1926, production
beginning in 1927. It was the post-WWII era,
however, that saw the marque reaching a wider
audience. Initially, this was with the PV444 and
PV544, which earned respect for their solid build,
excellent roadholding and international rallying
success. In 1966, the model B18 became available
with a 1780cc engine.

◄ **1964 Volvo 121S Amazon Estate,** 1986cc, 4-cylinder
engine, finished in green, black interior, 2 owners from new,
74,000 miles recorded, in need of some reconditioning.
£700–840 / €1,050–1,250 / $1,250–1,500 ↗ BARO

► **1967 Volvo 121 Amazon Four-
Door Saloon,** 1780cc, 4-cylinder
engine, twin SU carburettors,
front disc brakes, new suspension,
engine rebuilt.
**£5,400–6,000 / €8,000–8,900
$9,500–10,600** ⊞ AMA

VOLVO Model	ENGINE cc/cyl	DATES	CONDITION		
			1	2	3
PV444	1800/4	1958–67	£4,000+	£1,750	£800
PV544	1800/4	1962–64	£4,000	£1,750	£800
120 (B16)	1583/4	1956–59	£3,000	£1,000	£300
121	1708/4	1960–67	£4,500	£1,500	£350
122S	1780/4	1960–67	£4,500	£1,500	£250
131	1780/4	1962–69	£4,000	£1,500	£350
221/222	1780/4	1962–69	£2,500	£1,500	£300
123GT	1986/4	1967–69	£3,000	£2,500	£750
P1800	1986/4	1960–70	£5,500	£2,500	£1,000
P1800E	1986/4	1970–71	£6,000	£3,000	£1,000
P1800ES	1986/4	1971–73	£4,800	£3,000	£1,000

Whitney *(American 1896–98)*

1896 Whitney Two-Cylinder Steam Runabout, chain drive to rear wheels, leaf-spring front and rear suspension, wire wheels.
£42,000–50,000 / €62,000–74,000
$74,000–88,000 ➹ B(Kn)

In 1887, William Mason commissioned George Eli Whitney to design a small engine for carriage use. Widely known as the Mason engine, Whitney's design was the American motor industry's first production engine. Whitney built his own steam carriage in 1896, selling it to a New York jeweller called Charles Gibson, who claimed the car was his own. Whitney sued and won, then began work on improved versions of the steam carriage. Eventually, he formed a partnership with George B. Upham, a lawyer. Whitney continued with his work while Upham applied for over 300 patents relating to his efforts.

Willys *(American 1908–63)*

◀ **1929 Willys-Overland 30hp Whippet,** 4-cylinder engine, 3-speed manual gearbox, completely restored 1997, finished in maroon and black, maroon interior, concours condition.
£5,200–6,200 / €7,700–9,200
$9,200–11,000 ➹ BB(S)

Wolseley *(British 1896–1975)*

◀ **1927 Wolseley E4 11/22 Tourer,** 1260cc, overhead-camshaft 4-cylinder engine, worm drive and rear transaxle, engine rebuilt, finished in dark blue, dark blue leather upholstery.
£8,900–10,700 / €13,200–15,800
$15,700–18,800 ➹ CGC

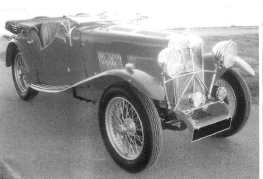

1932 Wolseley Hornet Special, coachwork by Keville, Davis & March, 1271cc, 6-cylinder overhead-camshaft engine, restored early 1990s, concours winner.
£7,200–8,000 / €10,700–11,800 / $12,700–14,100 🚗 WHS

1934 Wolseley Hornet Special, coachwork by Holbrook, 1271cc, overhead-camshaft 6-cylinder engine, engine-turned aluminium dashboard.
£15,700–17,500 / €23,200–25,900
$27,600–31,000 🚗 WHS

Condition guide

1. A vehicle in top class condition but not 'concours d'elegance standard', either fully restored or in very good original condition.
2. A good, clean, roadworthy vehicle, both mechanically and bodily sound.
3. A runner, but in need of attention, probably both to bodywork and mechanics. Must have current MoT.

WOLSELEY (Veteran & Vintage) Model	ENGINE cc/cyl	DATES	CONDITION 1	2	3
10	987/2	1909–16	£16,000	£12,500	£9,000
CZ (30hp)	2887/4	1909	£18,000	£13,000	£9,000
15hp & A9	2614/4	1920–27	£12,000	£10,000	£8,000
20 & C8	3921/				
	3862/6	1920–27	£11,000	£8,000	£6,000
E4 (10.5hp)	1267/				
	1542/4	1925–30	£6,000	£4,000	£3,000
E6, Viper & 16hp	2025/6	1927–34	£15,000	£12,000	£8,000
E8M	2700/8	1928–31	£18,000	£15,000	£12,000
Hornet	1271/4	1931–35	£10,000	£8,000	£4,500
Hornet Special	1271/				
	1604/6	1933–36	£12,000	£8,000	£5,000
Wasp	1069/4	1936	£7,000	£5,000	£3,500
Hornet	1378/6	1936	£8,000	£6,000	£4,000
21/60 & 21hp	2677/				
	2916/6	1932–39	£11,000	£6,000	£4,000
25	3485/6	1936–39	£8,500	£5,500	£4,000
12/48	1547/4	1937–39	£5,000	£3,000	£2,000
14/56	1818/6	1937–39	£6,000	£4,000	£2,000
18/80	2322/6	1938–39	£7,500	£5,500	£4,000

Early Wolseley cars are well made and very British, and those with coachbuilt bodies command a premium of at least 25%.

1934 Wolseley Hornet Special 2+2 Daytona, coachwork by Eustace Watkins, 1271cc, overhead-camshaft 6-cylinder engine, restored 2002, concours winner, excellent condition.
£18,000–20,000 / €26,600–29,900
$32,000–36,000 🚗 WHS

1934 Wolseley Hornet Special Drophead Coupé, coachwork by Tickford, 1271cc, overhead-camshaft 6-cylinder engine, twin SU carburettors, floor-change gearbox, wooden dashboard, wire wheels, finished in British Racing green, green leather interior.
£22,500–25,000 / €33,200–37,000 / $40,000–44,000 🚗 WHS

1937 Wolseley 14/56 Saloon, 1816cc, rebuilt 6-cylinder engine, brakes relined, new kingpins, finished in dark green, black interior.
£4,000–4,800 / €5,900–7,100 / $7,000–8,400 ✈ BRIT

1938 Wolseley 18/80 Four-Door Saloon, 2322cc, 6-cylinder engine, 4-speed manual gearbox, finished in black, brown leather interior, older restoration, good condition.
£4,150–5,000 / €6,100–7,400 / $7,300–8,800 ✈ CGC

WOLSELEY Model	ENGINE cc/cyl	DATES	CONDITION 1	2	3
8	918/4	1939–48	£3,000	£2,000	£1,000
10	1140/4	1939–48	£3,500	£2,000	£1,000
12/48	1548/4	1939–48	£4,000	£2,000	£1,250
14/60	1818/6	1946–48	£4,500	£2,500	£1,500
18/85	2321/6	1946–48	£6,000	£3,000	£2,000
25	3485/6	1946–48	£7,000	£4,000	£2,500
4/50	1476/4	1948–53	£2,500	£1,000	£450
6/80	2215/6	1948–54	£3,000	£1,500	£750
4/44	1250/4	1952–56	£2,500	£1,250	£750
15/50	1489/4	1956–58	£1,850	£850	£500
1500	1489/4	1958–65	£2,500	£1,000	£500
15/60	1489/4	1958–61	£2,000	£700	£400
16/60	1622/4	1961–71	£1,800	£800	£400
6/90	2639/6	1954–57	£2,500	£1,000	£500
6/99	2912/6	1959–61	£3,000	£1,500	£750
6/110 MK I/II	2912/6	1961–68	£2,000	£1,000	£500
Hornet (Mini)	848/4	1961–70	£1,500	£750	£400
1300	1275/4	1967–74	£1,250	£750	£400
18/85	1798/4	1967–72	£1,000	£500	£250

Police & Military Vehicles

1938 Tempo G1200 All-Terrain Vehicle, 1196cc, two 598cc twin-cylinder 2-stroke engines, each producing 19bhp, 4-speed Hermes gearbox for each engine, choice of 2-wheel (1 engine) or 4-wheel (both engines) drive, mechanical drum brakes, top speed 42mph.
£6,900–8,200 / €10,200–12,100 $12,100–14,400 ✗ B(Kn)
Around 20 examples of the G1200 were built for the German Army between 1936 and 1939, but the VW Kübelwagen was chosen for mass-production. This example was sent as a demonstration vehicle to Argentina in 1939, but no export orders were forthcoming.

1959 MG MGA Police Car, 1588cc, 4-cylinder engine, correct police accessories, finished in white, red and white interior, concours condition.
£14,900–17,900 / €22,100–26,500 / $26,600–32,000 ✗ B(Kn)
This car was one of 50 supplied to the Lancashire police force, the cars being driven exclusively by women officers. MGAs used by police were basically to 1600 De Luxe/Twin Cam specification, with drum rear brakes instead of discs and extended battery carriers for the additional electrical equipment.

1960 MG MGA 1600 Police Car, 1588cc, 4-cylinder engine, 4-speed manual gearbox, period police equipment.
£10,900–13,100 / €16,100–19,400 / $19,200–23,100 ✗ B(Kn)

1965 Austin Gypsy, 2199cc, overhead-valve 4-cylinder engine, 4-speed manual gearbox, 4-wheel drive, fewer than 2,000 miles from new.
£4,150–5,000 / €6,100–7,300 $7,300–8,700 ✗ CGC
Originally registered to the Home Office, this vehicle was kept in storage for use following a nuclear war.

Racing & Rallying

c1909 Benz Two-Seater 60hp Raceabout, 8 litres, fully restored to 1919 race specification, concours condition.
£35,000–42,000 / €52,000–62,000 / $62,000–74,000 ⚲ B(Kn)
In 1885, Karl Benz designed and built the first working motor car powered by an internal-combustion engine. This particular racing two-seater spent most of its life in Argentina.

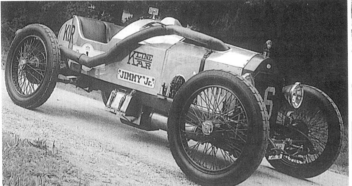

c1914 Kline-Duesenberg 'Jimmy Junior', 4900cc, Duesenberg 16-valve 4-cylinder engine, 3-speed gearbox, semi-elliptic leaf springs, rear wheel brakes, fully restored late 1980s, new aluminium body, original bodywork included, concours winner.
£137,000–165,000 / €203,000–244,000 / $241,000–290,000 ⚲ B(Kn)
James Kline built his first car in 1900. Subsequently, he went into partnership with Samuel Baily and Joseph Carroll, forming the BCK Motor Company to build the Kline car in 1910. To publicize the new car, Kline built two dirt-track racing specials, named 'Jimmy' and 'Jimmy Junior' after the designer and his son. They were raced initially with Kline engines, but in 1914, Kline obtained a Duesenberg four-cylinder racing engine for 'Jimmy Junior'. Thus equipped, the car won as many as 19 races between 1914 and 1919, mostly on dirt and board tracks on the US East Coast.

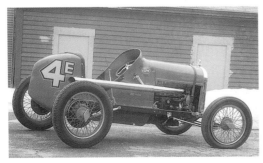

◄ **1919 Ford Model T Frontenac Special,** Ford Model T engine bottom end, Frontenac top end including double overhead camshafts, 2 Winfield carburettors, torsion-bar suspension.
£13,100–15,700 / €19,400–23,200
$23,100–27,600 ⚲ BB(S)
Many people built Model T Ford racing cars, but the most well-known was the Frontenac. The man behind this venture was Swiss born racing driver Louis Chevrolet. He was backed by Billie Durant of General Motors fame, but the partnership ended when Chevrolet's ideas went in a different direction to Durant's. By 1916, Chevrolet was in Indianapolis building Frontenac racing cars and speed equipment for Model T Fords.

► **c1923 Wolseley Model Ten Two-Seater,** 1261cc, overhead-camshaft 4-cylinder engine, Reece camshaft profiled to original pattern, twin SU carburettors, high-compression pistons, restored over 14 years.
£12,900–15,500 / €19,100–22,900
$22,700–27,300 ⚞ B(Kn)
This car was driven by George Newman in the Brooklands 200-mile race of 1923.

c1930s Austin 7 Single-Seater, 750cc, completely restored, rebuilt tuned 4-cylinder engine with big valves and dual valve springs, taper-bored ports, full-race camshaft, Speedex alloy cylinder head, large-capacity sump, 4-speed manual gearbox.
£4,100–4,900 / €6,100–7,300
$7,200–8,600 ⚞ H&H

1931 Invicta S-Type Low-Chassis Tourer, 4500cc, Meadows engine, 115bhp, wire wheels, top speed 100mph, 1 of 77 built, excellent condition.
£238,000–285,000 / €352,000–422,000 / $419,000–502,000 ⚞ COYS

◄ **1933 Alvis Firefly Tourer,** coachwork by Cross & Ellis, 1645cc, overhead-valve engine, 4-speed pre-selector gearbox, good bodywork and mechanics, hand painted, original interior.
£14,200–17,100 / €21,000–25,300
$25,000–30,000 ⚞ H&H
The Firefly arrived in 1932, having been developed from the earlier 12/50 and 12/60 series. It was available with a choice of 1496 or 1645cc engines, and conventional or pre-selector gearboxes.

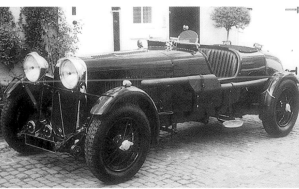

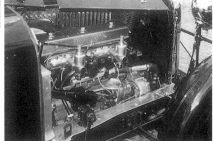

1934 Lagonda M45 Le Mans Replica, coachwork by GP Panelcraft, 4500cc, built to resemble a Fox & Nicholl team car, finished in dark green, black interior, near concours condition.
£74,000–89,000 / €110,000–132,000 / $130,000–156,000 ⚞ COYS

The price paid for a car can vary according to the country in which it was sold. To discover where the car sold, cross reference the code at the end of each caption with the Key to Illustrations on page 251.

1936 AC 16/80 Sports/Racing Two-Seater, 2000cc, rebuilt 1960s, recently restored, in need of recommissioning.
£16,700–20,000 / €24,700–29,600
$29,400–35,000 ⚲ COYS

c1935 Austin 7 Racing Special, 747cc, engine rebuilt with new Phoenix crankshaft and bearings, remetalled con-rods, racing pistons, skimmed alloy head and oversize valves, finished in blue, black interior, excellent condition.
£6,000–7,200 / €8,900–10,700 / $10,600–12,700 ⚲ H&H

▶ **1946 CUERL Single-Seater,** 248cc, Velocette air-cooled overhead-valve single-cylinder motorcycle engine, Amal carburettor, BTH magneto, chain drive, 4-wheel independent suspension, in need of restoration.
£1,600–1,900 / €2,350–2,800 / $2,800–3,350 ⚲ CGC
CUERL stood for Cambridge University Engineering Research Laboratories.

1950 Jaguar XK120 Roadster, 3442cc, rebuilt mid-1990s, original Protheroe 6-cylinder engine overhauled, full synchromesh overdrive gearbox, Koni shock absorbers, Harvey Bailey anti-roll bar, polyurethane bush kit, uprated disc brakes all-round.
£36,000–43,000 / €53,000–63,000 / $63,000–75,000 ⚲ COYS
This car is one of the best-known racing XK120s, having been campaigned throughout the 1950s and 1960s by J. Mays and Duncan Bray, and prepared by 'Dick' Protheroe.

1954 Arnolt Bristol Bolide Roadster, 1998cc, 6-cylinder engine, recently restored, race-prepared, painted to resemble an Arnolt Sebring racer.
£44,000–53,000 / €65,000–78,000 / $78,000–93,000 ⚲ B(Kn)

1954 Connaught ALSR, 1484cc, 115bhp, magnesium wheels, integral hub/brake drum assemblies.
£100,000–120,000 / €148,000–178,000 / $176,000–211,000 ↗ CGC
Continental Cars was formed in 1946, being run by Rodney Clarke and Mike Olivers. Their first racer was the Connaught L3, which debuted at Silverstone in mid-1949 and was immediately successful. From this came a whole family of sports/racing cars. This particular car has a glittering race history, having been driven by Stirling Moss, Les Leston and Archie Scott-Brown. During 1954, it had placings and victories at Goodwood, Castle Combe, Silverstone, Davidstowe, Crystal Palace, Aintree and Montlhéry; it broke the lap record at Brands Hatch. In 1955, it was even more successful, with victories at Oulton Park, Goodwood, Ipsley, Brands Hatch, Chaterhall and Silverstone.

◄ **1954 Lotus Mk VIII-MG Sports/Racing Two-Seater,**
1250cc, MG 4-cylinder engine, original-style aluminium body by GP Panelcraft fitted 1992, Buckler 4.3:1 torque-tube rear axle fitted 2001.
£17,200–20,700 / €25,500–30,000
$30,000–36,000 ↗ B(Kn)
This car is believed to have been built by Colin Chapman's business partner, Nigel Allen.

1955 Tojeiro-MG Sports/Racing Two-Seater, 1250cc, MG 4-cylinder engine, 4-speed close-ratio gearbox.
£49,000–59,000 / €73,000–87,000 / $87,000–104,000 ↗ COYS

1956 Cooper-Climax Type 39 'Bobtail' Sports/Racing Two-Seater, 1.5 litres, Coventry-Climax overhead-camshaft 4-cylinder engine, SU carburettors, newly manufactured Citroën ERSA gearbox and later-type gear-change linkage, transaxle with limited-slip differential, finished in British Racing green.
£47,000–57,000 / €70,000–84,000 / $83,000–100,000 ↗ B(Kn)

1956 RGS-MG Sports/Racing Car, 1600cc, tuned MGA
4-cylinder engine, 4-speed gearbox, tubular chassis,
Morris-derived front suspension, MG Magnette rear axle,
restored early 1990s.
**£13,000–15,500 / €19,200–22,900
$22,900–27,300 ↗ B(Kn)**

c1956 Renault 4CV Racing Saloon, 1565cc, rear-mounted
4-cylinder engine from a Renault 12 Gordini, uprated brakes
and suspension, single racing seat with harness, full roll cage.
£2,400–2,900 / €3,600–4,300 / $4,300–5,100 ↗ BRIT

1957 Mercury Turnpike Cruiser Convertible, 368cu.in, V8 engine, Sam Hanks' signature on door, finished in yellow,
black top, black interior.
£22,200–26,600 / €33,000–39,000 / $39,000–46,000 ↗ BB(S)
This car was the official Indianapolis 500 pace car in 1957, when the event was won by Sam Hanks. It was
presented to him after the race.

1958 Austin A35, built to re-create a Speedwell
A35 for historic saloon car racing, 1380cc,
4-cylinder engine, twin SU carburettors, 4-speed
straight-cut close-ratio gearbox, 2-piece
competition halfshafts, locked differential.
**£12,000–14,400 / €17,800–21,300
$21,200–25,300 ↗ H&H**

1958 Cooper-Climax Type 45 Single-Seater, completely restored
1990s, original 1.5 litre engine replaced by 2 litre Coventry-Climax FF
4-cylinder unit, ex-Jack Brabham and Stirling Moss.
£60,000–72,000 / €89,000–107,000 / $109,000–127,000 ↗ B(Kn)

▶ **c1958 Lister-Jaguar Replica,**
3.8 litres, Jaguar 6-cylinder engine,
dry-sump lubrication, forged pistons,
Carillo con-rods, correct alloy centre-
peg wheels, near concours condition.
**£52,000–62,000 / €77,000–92,000
$92,000–109,000 ↗ COYS**

1958 Lotus Eleven S2 Le Mans, 1460cc, Coventry-Climax 4-cylinder engine, de Dion rear axle, 4-wheel disc brakes, finished in British Racing green.
£42,000–50,000 / €62,000–74,000 / $74,000–88,000 ⚒ COYS

1959 Stanquellini Formula Junior Single-Seater, 1100cc, race-prepared Fiat 4-cylinder engine, twin Weber 38D carburettors, close-ratio gearbox, restored, new brakes, shock absorbers, ATL 8 gallon (36.4 litre) fuel cell, water pump and radiator expansion tank.
£20,900–25,100 / €31,000–37,000 $37,000–44,000 ⚒ BB(S)

1959 Sunbeam Rapier Mk II Ex-Works Rally Car, 1600cc, 4-cylinder engine, 4-speed gearbox, spot lamps, roll cage.
£17,000–20,400 / €25,200–30,000 $29,900–36,000 ⚒ H&H

Restored values

The cost of a professional restoration will have an influence on, but no direct relation to, a car's market value. A restored car can have a market value lower than the cost of its restoration.

1960 Aston Martin DB4 GT Competition, 3670cc, double-overhead-camshaft 6-cylinder engine, twin-plug conversion, 331bhp.
£330,000–396,000 / €488,000–586,000 / $581,000–697,000 ⚒ B(Kn)

1960 Sunbeam Rapier Mk III Ex-Works, 1494cc, 4-cylinder engine, 100bhp, originally driven by Peter Harper and Ricardo Rodriguez
£14,700–17,600 / €21,800–26,000 / $25,900–31,000 ✗ CGC

◄ **1960 Riley 1.5 Rally Car,** 1489cc, 4-cylinder engine, high-lift camshaft, twin SU HS6 carburettors, converted to unleaded fuel, roll cage, competition seats, full harnesses, Ponti magnifier, trip meter, reading light, stop watches, near concours condition.
£3,200–3,850 / €4,750–5,700 / $5,600–6,700 ✗ H&H

1960 Turner Climax Mk I, 1149cc, 4-cylinder engine, 4-speed gearbox, hardtop, master cylinders and brake calipers overhauled.
£14,000–16,800 / €20,700–24,900
$24,600–29,600 ✗ H&H
This Turner was one of the best known club racers of the early 1960s. It has spent its entire life as a racing car and is affectionaly known as 'Tatty' following a remark made by a commentator at its first race meeting, when it was unpainted. It holds the lap record for its class at the Goodwood circuit.

1961 Lotus-Ford Formula Junior Single-Seater, 1598cc, Ford 105E-based 4-cylinder engine, Hewland Mark V transaxle, engine overhauled.
£25,300–30,000 / €37,000–44,000
$45,000–53,000 ✗ B(Kn)

◄ **1962 Austin-Healey 3000 Mk II BT7 Rally Car,** 2912cc, 6-cylinder engine, overdrive gearbox, engine and gearbox rebuilt, fast road camshaft, triple carburettors, new side-exit exhaust, wire wheels, works-type hardtop, left-hand drive, Halda Twinmaster Speedpilot, roll cage.
£24,100–29,000
€36,000–43,000
$43,000–51,000 ✗ B(Kn)

Colour Review

1959 MGA EX182 Le Mans Replica, 1489cc, overhead-valve 4-cylinder engine, independent coil-sprung wishbone front suspension, left-hand drive, fully converted to racing specification.
£11,100–13,300 / €16,400–19,700 / $19,500–23,400 ⚲ BB(S)

1960 Warwick GT Saloon, 3500cc, Buick V8 engine, 4-speed manual gearbox, alloy wheels, fibreglass body.
£6,900–8,300 / €10,200–12,300
$12,100–14,600 ⚲ COYS
The Peerless GT and Warwick GT were developed by engine tuner and specialist builder Bernie Rodger. The Peerless was introduced in 1958 as a low-volume, low-cost sports/GT, using a Triumph TR3 engine and running gear in a steel spaceframe chassis with a fibreglass body. It was followed in late 1960 by the Warwick GT. This particular example was the sixth of 25 cars built, and it was used as the works car, being raced by Bernie Rodger throughout 1961 and 1962. In late 1961, its 2 litre Triumph engine was replaced by a 2.2 litre Bristol unit, which eventually gave way to a 3.5 litre Buick V8.

c1960 Mini Cooper S Works Replica Rally Car, 1000cc, tuned engine, roll cage, spot lights, navigation equipment, ready for competition, good condition.
£18,000–20,000/ €26,600–29.600
$31,000–35,000 🚗 MINI

◄ 1961 Austin-Healey 3000 Mk II 2+2, 2912cc, race tuned 6-cylinder engine, triple 2in SU carburettors, Cosworth pistons, larger valves, competition valve springs and caps, Denis Welsh camshaft and followers, competition timing chain and tensioner, uprated oil pump, new pressure-relief valve, fully rebuilt on new chassis.
£18,000–21,600 / €26,600–32,000
$32,000–38,000 ⚲ H&H

► 1964 Mini Cooper S Mk I, 1293cc, Swiftune Engineering engine, close-ratio 4-speed gearbox, competition clutch, adjustable suspension, internally routed brake lines, full roll cage, 5-point harness, plumbed-in fire extinguisher, rally intercom, heated windscreen.
£10,900–13,000 / €16,100–19,200
$19,400–22,900 ⚲ B(Kn)
This Cooper S has been modified to resemble the 1964 Monte Carlo Rally winning works car.

c1970 Crossle 9S Sports Racer, 1998cc, Opel Lotus 4-cylinder engine, original factory specification, excellent condition.
£16,600–19,800 / €24,400–29,300
$29,000–35,000 ✗ H&H
John Crossle's first creation was a Ford Special, which he completed in 1957. In the following year, the Crossle Car Company became by far the longest established Irish racing car manufacturer. Although the company made forays into senior formulae, with Formula Atlantic/B, F3, F2 and even F5000 chassis, Crossle shrewdly concentrated on more realistic markets, most of them employing Ford power. More than 40 Formula Ford 16s were sold. Crossle sports racers helped to establish the marque on the Continent. In 1966, the company built five 9S models with rear-mounted Ford Lotus twin-cam motor and Hewland transmission in a spaceframe chassis, with stressed aluminium and fibreglass bodywork.

1971 Ford Mustang Convertible Competition, 4949cc, V8 engine, 3-speed C4 automatic transmission, engine rebuilt and tuned, quick-shift transmission upgrade, locking differential, fuel capacity increased to 36 gallons, multipoint roll cage.
£4,000–4,800 / €5,900–7,100 / $7,000–8,400 ✗ H&H

1984 Audi Sport Quattro Group B Rally Car, 2144cc, 5-cylinder engine, turbocharger, stainless steel exhaust, permanent 4-wheel drive, alloy wheels, left-hand drive, 6 Hella spot lamps, Kevlar body panels, full body kit and rear spoiler, 1 of only 20 short-wheelbase works cars prepared for competition, completely restored, engine rebuilt 1999, only 300 miles recorded since.
£97,000–116,000 / €143,000–171,000 / $170,000–204,000 ✗ H&H
This car was driven by ex-World Rally Champions Hannu Mikkola and Arnè Hertz during 1984–85.

1991 Formula Renault Single-Seater, 1721cc, 4-cylinder engine, 5-speed close-ratio gearbox, Renault livery, very low mileage, original, unrestored.
£8,500–10,200 / €12,600–15,100 / $15,000–18,000 ✗ B(Mu)
This car was used by Renault Germany for display purposes during 1991–93. Subsequently, it was raced by historic racer Erwin Derichs.

Gamy, 'Tour de France 1913, 1er Van Den Born sur "Aries"', coloured lithograph, published by Mabileau & Co, Paris, 1913, 17¾ x 35½in (45 x 90cm).
£150–180 / €220–260 / $260–320 ↗ NSal

A BP advertisement, 'The New BP puts New Life in Your Car', taken from *The Graphic*, 1929, mounted, 18¼ x 13½in (46.5 x 34.5cm).
£35–40/ €50–60 $60–70 ↗ CGC

A Bugatti poster, 'Bugatti Automobiles, Autorails', with printed signature 'R. Geri', 1930s, 38¼ x 23¼in (97 x 59cm).
£190–220 / €280–330 $330–390 ↗ BR

British Empire Trophy Race, a poster advertising the first ever British Racing Drivers Club race at Donington Park, 1936, framed, 30 x 12in (76 x 30.5cm).
£310–350 / €460–520 $550–620 ⊞ MURR

◄ Abarth World Championship Exhaust Systems, an advertising poster, designed by Andrea Rossini, 1950s, 39 x 26¾in (99 x 68cm).
£200–240 / €300–360 / $350–420 ↗ B(Kn)

12hrs of Sebring, an advertising poster, 1963, 28¾ x 19¾in (73 x 50cm).
£460–550 / €680–810 $810–970 ↗ B(Kn)

Les Grands Prix de France, Rouen, an advertising poster, 1966, framed and glazed, 25½ x 16½in 65 x 42cm).
£50–60 / €75–90 $90–105 ↗ B(Kn)

An Exide advertising poster, c1925, framed, 33in (84cm) wide.
£220–250 / €330–370 / $390–440 ⊞ JUN

Second Annual International George Vanderbilt Cup, a poster for the 'World's Richest Road Race', 1930s, some foxing and fading, framed.
£1,100–1,300 / €1,650–1,900 / $1,950–2,300 ↗ BB(S)

Aintree RAC British Grand Prix, an advertising poster, 1950s.
£450–540 / €670–800 $790–950 ↗ BB(S)

Jaguar, a poster celebrating performance at the 1954 Le Mans endurance race, with details of the manufacturer's achievements in previous years, 1954, 42¼ x 30¼in (107.5 x 77cm).
£900–1,050 / €1,350–1,550 $1,600–1,850 ↗ B(Kn)

Two light bulbs, c1900, larger 4in (10cm) high.
£11–15 / €16–22
$19–26 each ⊞ JUN

Labatt's 50 Grand Prix of Canada, a signed advertising poster, signatures include Jackie Stewart, Jean-Pierre Beltoise, Emerson Fittipaldi, Tim Schenken and Clay Regazzoni, 1972, 31½ x 21¾in (80 x 55cm).
£170–200 / €250–300
$300–350 ⚒ B(Kn)

Fangio, a film advertising poster, 1979, laid to linen, excellent condition, framed, 55¼ x 37¼in (140 x 95cm).
£1,150–1,350 / €1,700–2,000
$2,000–2,400 ⚒ B(Kn)

▶ **A ceramic advertising wall plate,** inscribed 'Pirelli' on a Hispano-Moresque pattern ground, impressed marks, Moroccan, early 20thC, 11¾in (30cm) diam.
£70–80 / €105–120
$125–140 ⚒ SWO

A Pascall sweets tin, depicting a vintage car scene, 1910–20, 10in (25.5cm) wide.
£100–120 / €150–180
$175–210 ⊞ MURR

◀ **A nickel-plated car pin cushion,** 1920s, 4in (10cm) wide.
£25–30
€35–45
$45–55 each
⊞ JUN

A Wilkinsons Motor Engineers brass ashtray, 1920s, 5in (12.5cm) square.
£45–50 / €65–75 / $80–90 ⊞ MURR

A set of six copper and brass petrol measures, by Gaskell & Chambers, Birmingham, measures from ½ to 5 gallons, engraved 'Rye District County of East Sussex', 1920s.
£2,500–3,000 / €3,700–4,450
$4,400–5,300
⚒ BR

◀ **A Redex lubricant can,** with curled spout and pump lever, 1930s, 7½in (19cm) high
£40–45
€60–65
$70–80 ⊞ MURR

A Meccano model car, 1930s, 11in (28cm) wide.
£55–65 / €80–95 / $95–115 ⊞ JUN

◀ **An MG blotter,** including stamp and pad, 1930s, 8in (20.5cm) wide.
£120–140
€180–210
$210–250
⊞ MURR

▶ **A Bugatti Type 57 brochure,** two-sided, illustrated, full colour, 1939, very good condition.
£100–120 / €150–180
$175–210 ➶ B(Kn)

A Rolls-Royce/Bentley glass ashtray, inscribed 'JB' for Jack Barclay, 1940s, 5in (12.5cm) square.
£30–35 / €45–50 / $55–65 ⊞ MURR

Two Rootes promotional sales guides and three brochures, the guides for the 1949 Humber Super Snipe and Hillman Minx, both spiral bound with full-colour illustrations, the brochures for the 1949 Humber Snipe and Hawk, and the Hillman Station Wagon, 1940s–50s.
£40–45 / €60–65 / $70–80 ➶ H&H

A Victory jigsaw puzzle, 'Seaside Traffic', 1950s, 11in (28cm) wide.
£11–15 / €16–22 / $19–26 each ⊞ JUN

A pair of chrome and leather goggles, by Climax, with glass lenses, c1950, 7in ((18cm) wide.
£30–35 / €45–50 / $55–65 each ⊞ JUN

Austin-Healey sales brochures, for the 100, 3000 and Sprite models, 1950s–60s.
£130–155 / €190–220 / $230–270 ➶ H&H

▶ **An Avery Hardoll Shell petrol pump,** reproduction globe, c1960, 72in (183cm) high.
£600–680 / €890–1,000
$1,050–1,200 ⊞ JUN

A Caravan Club car badge, 1950s, 4in (10cm) high.
£11–15 / €16–22
$19–26 ⊞ JUN

An enamelled and chrome-plated
Junior Car Club badge, 1930s,
3½in (9cm) high.
**£220–250 / € 330–370
$390–440 ⊞ MURR**

A London Motor Club badge, for the 1956 London Rally, 3in (7.5cm) wide.
£15–20 / € 20–30 / $25–35 ⊞ JUN

A cloth Motor Oil badge, c1920, 5in (12.5cm) wide.
£15–20 / € 20–30 / $25–35 ⊞ JUN

An enamelled and chrome-plated
RAC car badge, 1950s,
3in (7.5cm) wide.
£25–30 / € 35–45 / $45–55 ⊞ JUN

An enamelled silver **Rolls-Royce
School of Instruction cap badge,**
the reverse stamped '308', c1920.
**£410–490 / € 610–730
$720–860 ⚲ B(Kn)**

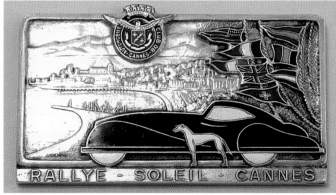

A Drago silver-plated bronze Rallye Soleil Cannes plaque, French, c1938,
3½in (9cm) wide.
**£270–300 / € 400–440
$480–530 ⊞ AU**

▶ **A silver-plated bronze caricature
mascot,** by Vernon March and
Elkington, 1907, 5in (12.5cm) high.
**£1,000–1,150 / € 1,500–1,700
$1,750–2,000 ⊞ AU**

A chrome bird mascot, with flapping wings,
c1920, 11in (28cm) wide.
£175–195 / € 260–290 / $300–340 ⊞ JUN

A bronze eagle mascot, 1930s, 15in (38cm) wide.
£1,800–2,000 / €2,650–2,950
$3,150–3,500 ⊞ AU
This mascot was fitted to parade vehicles of
the German Third Reich.

**A plated brass policeman
mascot,** marked, 1922,
5½in (13cm) high.
£250–300 / €370–440
$440–530 ⚒ CGC

A cold-painted bronze robin mascot,
by A.E.L., c1928, 5in (12.5cm) high.
£580–650 / €860–960
$1,000–1,150 ⊞ AU

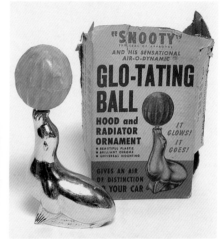

A 1/12-scale model of a Ferrari 553 Squalo, as driven by Mike
Hawthorn in the 1954 Spanish Grand Prix, removable engine cover,
replicated engine, 1970s, in Perspex display case.
£1,350–1,600 / €2,000–2,350 / $2,400–2,800 ⚒ B(Mon)

A chrome Snooty Glo-tating mascot, 1950s,
6in (15cm) high, with original packaging.
£105–120 / €155–180 / $185–210 ⊞ JUN

A scratchbuilt model of a Ferrari 250TR, sheet metal
and alloy body, 1 of only 2 made, 1970s, on a wooden
base, with incised signature plaque.
£10,000–12,000 / €14,800–17,800
$17,600–21,100 ⚒ B(Mon)

**A 1/12-scale handbuilt model of a 1970 Ferrari 5125
Longtail,** as driven by Hughes De Fierlant and Alistair Walker
to 5th place at Le Mans, 1970, in a Perspex display case.
£1,000–1,200 / €1,500–1,800 / $1,750–2,100 ⚒ B(Kn)

A tin Wakefield Castrol XXL sign,
1928, 20in (51cm) high.
£220–250 / €330–370
$390–440 ⊞ MURR

A Shell tanker sign, 1938, 36in (91.5cm) wide.
£300–350 / €440–520 / $530–620 ⊞ MURR

A Brooklands official race card, 1933, 8 x 5in (20.5 x 12.5cm).
£65–75 / €95–110 / $115–130 ✗ VS

◀ A Brooklands 500 Miles Race programme, 48 pages, 1933, 8 x 5in (20.5 x 12.5cm).
£110–130 / €165–190 $195–230 ✗ VS

A George Vanderbilt Cup race programme, 1936, with lapel pin.
£110–130 / €165–190 $195–230 ✗ BB(S)

A metal plate, commemorating Graham Hill's 1965 World Championship, 1965, French, 8in (20.5cm) diam.
£30–35 / €45–50 / $55–60 ✗ VS

◀ Graham Hill, *Life at the Limit*, signed by the author, 1972, 9 x 4in (23 x 10cm).
£180–210 / €270–310 $320–370 ✗ VS

A collection of Auto Union- and Mercedes-related signed photographs and postcards, signatures include Manfred von Brauchitsch, Karl Kling, Hans Stuck, Rudolf Hasse, Tazio Nuvolari, Hermann Lang, Richard Seaman, H.P. Müller and Hans Hermann, 1930s.
£1,250–1,500 / €1,850–2,200 $2,200–2,650 ✗ B(Mu)

◀ Arturo Merzario, a signed photograph, 1979, 4 x 6in (10 x 15cm).
£15–20 €20–30 $25–35 ⊞ RaA

Jochen Rindt, a black and white photograph, signed by the photographer, 1960s, framed and glazed, 11½ x 19¾in (29 x 50cm).
£80–95 / €120–140 / $140–165 ✗ CGC

Tiff Nedell, a signed photograph, 1980, 4 x 6in (10 x 15cm).
£11–15 / €16–22 / $19–26 ⊞ RaA

1962 Brabham BT4 Single-Seater, 2495cc,
Coventry-Climax 4-cylinder engine, space-frame chassis,
outboard coil-spring/damper units all-round,
last of 3 examples built.
£100,000–120,000 / €148,000–178,000
$176,000–211,000 ✗ H&H

◀ **1963 Alfa Romeo Giulia Spider,** 1600cc,
rebuilt double-overhead-camshaft 4-cylinder engine,
forged pistons, reground crank, ported and polished
cylinder head, Jim Evans race/rally camshafts, twin Weber
carburettors, tubular exhaust manifold, front disc brakes,
aluminium fuel tank, stripped interior.
£6,000–7,200 / €8,900–10,700
$10,600–12,700 ✗ H&H

1963 Austin-Healey 3000 Mk II, 2963cc, tuned 6-cylinder engine, triple Weber 45DCOE carburettors, straight-cut Tulip
competition gearbox, finished in silver-blue, white works hardtop.
£26,400–32,000 / €39,000–46,000 / $46,000–55,000 ✗ B(Kn)

▶ **1963 Morris Mini Cooper Rally Car,** 997cc,
4-cylinder engine, Stage 2 cylinder head,
'fast road' camshaft, oil cooler, 2 electric fuel
pumps, 2 fuel tanks, Minilite alloy wheels,
Spax adjustable dampers, negative-camber
bottom arms, sump guard, Cibié headlights,
Lucas foglamps, reversing light, fire extinguisher,
works-style dashboard, fly-off handbrake,
full harnesses, roll cage, map light,
fluorescent interior light, digital stopwatch.
£4,800–5,700 / €7,100–8,400
$8,400–10,000 ✗ H&H

◀ **1964 Cooper T72 Single-Seater,** 1000cc, Ford MAE 4-cylinder engine, rebuilt Hewland gearbox, restored.
£17,700–21,200 / €26,200–31,000
$31,000–37,000 ⋟ COYS

1964 Ford Cortina Lotus Mk I, 1560cc, double-overhead-camshaft 4-cylinder engine, Weber carburettors, 4-speed gearbox, finished in red and gold, 1 owner since 1967, ex-Alan Mann Racing.
£60,000–73,000 / €92,000–108,000 / $107,000–128,000 ⋟ B(Kn)
Team Lotus cars ran in the usual Cortina Lotus livery of white with green flashes, whereas the Alan Mann cars were red with gold flashes. This car was campaigned by Sir John Whitmore and fellow team members during the fiercely contested European Touring Car Championships of 1964, 1965 and 1966.

1964 MGB Roadster Rally Car, 1800cc, 4-cylinder engine, rebuilt 1990, Weber 45 DCOE carburettor, B & G cylinder head, 770 rally camshaft, 130bhp, competition-specification overdrive gearbox, 4.5:1 differential, wire wheels, grooved brake discs.
£10,000–12,000 / €14,800–17,800
$17,600–21,100 ⋟ H&H

1964 Vauxhall VX 4/90 Works Replica Rally Car, 1507cc, 4-cylinder engine, 4-speed manual gearbox, fully restored to Vauxhall rallying specification.
£3,100–3,700 / €4,600–5,500
$5,500–6,500 ⋟ BRIT

▶ **1965 Austin-Healey 3000 Mk III Rally Car,** 2992cc, 6-cylinder engine, 200bhp, straight-cut gearbox with Tulip ratios, limited-slip differential, competition springs and shock absorbers, wire wheels, long-range foam-filled fuel tank, spot lamps, finished in red, black interior, roll cage, intercom, excellent condition.
£31,000–37,000
€46,000–55,000
$55,000–65,000 ⋟ H&H

1965 Brabham BT8 Sports/Racer, 2700cc,
Coventry-Climax 4-cylinder engine, dry-sump lubrication,
Weber carburettors, Hewland 5-speed gearbox,
1 of 12 examples built, ex-Bill Kay/Peter Revson.
**£102,000–122,000 / € 151,000–181,000
$180,000–215,000** ✗ H&H

1966 Alfa Romeo GTA Competizione, 1570cc,
double-overhead-camshaft 4-cylinder engine, twin-plug
ignition, 2 fuel pumps, 5-speed gearbox, aluminium body,
'barn discovery', in need of restoration.
**£20,500–24,600 / € 30,000–36,000
$36,000–43,000** ✗ COYS
The GTA was a development of the GT Junior.
The letters 'GTA' stood for Gran Turismo Allegerata
(Grand Touring Lightweight). These cars were built in
Stradale (road-going) or Competizione (competition)
versions. The former produced 115bhp, and the
latter 170bhp.

1967 Volvo 123GT Rally Car, 1780cc, 4-cylinder engine,
4-speed manual gearbox, sump guard, finished in red and
white, beige interior, Retrotrip mileage recorder, rally seats,
full safety harnesses.
£2,650–3,150 / € 3,900–4,650 / $4,650–5,500 ✗ H&H

1968 Morris Mini Rally Car, 1275 GT engine with
capacity increased to 1380cc, sump guard, roll cage,
bucket seats, plumbed-in fire extinguisher.
£3,650–4,400 / € 5,400–6,500 / $6,400–7,700 ✗ H&H

1970 British Leyland Ex-Works Mini 4WD, 1293cc,
overhead-valve 4-cylinder engine, 124bhp, 4-speed
gearbox, 4-wheel drive, restored 1999, finished in blue and
white, black interior.
**£15,000–18,000 / € 22,300–26,600
$26,500–32,000** ✗ H&H
This one-off four-wheel-drive Mini was built by
BL's Special Tuning division specifically to win the
televised Lydden Rallycross event. It was assembled in
less than two weeks and won its debut race at
Lydden. The four-wheel-drive components were taken
from a Mini-based experimental military vehicle
known as the Ant. They were fitted into a Mini
Clubman bodyshell, which had more under-bonnet
space to accommodate the crossflow aluminium head
and four Amal carburettors of the ultimate 1293cc
Cooper S 'eight-porter'.

▶ **1970 Porsche 911E,** 2341cc, air-cooled flat-6 engine,
5-speed gearbox, 4-wheel disc brakes, stainless steel brake
pipes, modified and lowered suspension, front and rear
anti-roll bars, racing fuel cell, fully padded roll-cage.
**£9,400–11,300 / € 13,900–16,700
$16,600–19,900** ✗ H&H

1970 Chevrolet Camaro, 5 litres, V8 engine, 500bhp,
Azev 17in alloy wheels, AP racing brake calipers,
uprated suspension, straight-through twin-exhaust
system with balance pipes and Joe Ellis silencers.
**£8,800–10,500 / € 13,000–15,500
$15,500–18,500** ✗ COYS
This car built to compete in the Trueseal Challenge series.

1973 Saab 96 Rally Car, 1815cc, V4 engine, 145bhp, 2 trip meters, 3 spare wheels, set of studded winter tyres.
£4,050–4,850 / €6,000–7,200 / $7,100–8,500 ✗ H&H

1975 Lancia Stratos HF Group 4 Rally Car,
2418cc, V6 engine, 230bhp, 5-speed manual
gearbox, 4-wheel disc brakes.
£70,000–84,000 / €104,000–124,000
$123,000–148,000 ✗ B(Kn)

1975 Morris Mini Rally Car, full competition
specification, 1330cc, special crank, Omega
pistons, high-lift camshaft, ported head with
large valves, roller rockers, high-performance
cam followers, Aldon distributor, Lumenition
ignition, ultra-light flywheel, Maniflow manifolds,
Jack Knight dog box transmission, Tranex limited-
slip differential, GKN driveshafts.
£4,000–4,800 / €5,900–7,100
$7,000–8,400 ✗ H&H

▶ **1983 Laser Formula Ford Single-Seater,**
1600cc, Burton Ford 4-cylinder engine, Hewland
5-speed close-ratio gearbox, fibreglass body.
£2,600–3,100 / €3,850–4,600
$4,600–5,500 ✗ H&H

1986 Ford RS200 Evo Rally Car, 2137cc, double-overhead-camshaft all-aluminium 16-valve 4-cylinder engine, Bosch Motronic electronic engine management, turbocharger with aftercooler, 640bhp, X-Trac gearbox, ex-Stig Blomqvist/Martin Stanche.
£79,000–95,000 / €117,000–140,000
$139,000–167,000 ➤ B(Kn)

1987 Lola-Cosworth T87/00 CART Single-Seater, 2650cc, Cosworth DFX engine, turbocharger, 670bhp.
£16,500–19,800 / €24,400–29,300
$29,100–35,000 ➤ COYS

1988 Peugeot 205 Rally Car, 1294cc, 4-cylinder engine, sump guard, 5-speed gearbox, fuel tank guard, full roll cage, plumbed-in fire extinguisher, bucket seats, left-hand drive.
£1,800–2,150 / €2,650–3,150 / $3,150–3,750 ➤ H&H
This car is one of a limited edition produced by the French manufacturer specifically to gain FIA homologation for national and international rallying.

1989 Ford Cosworth Ex-Works Group N Rally Car, 5 litres, Terry Hoyle built engine with RS500 cylinder block, uprated turbocharger, fuel injection, engine management system and gearbox.
£18,400–22,100 / €27,500–33,000
$33,000–39,000 ➤ B(Kn)
This three-door Sierra Cosworth was built by R.E.D. for the Ford Motor Company and was driven by Roger Clarke to third place in the 1989 Tour of Britain Rally.

1989 Lotus Formula 1 Type 101-4 Single-Seater, rebuilt as a show car, no engine, painted to represent Ayrton Senna's 1987 Lotus 99T.
£12,600–15,200 / €18,700–22,500
$22,500–26,800 ➤ B(Kn)

1991 Porsche 962 Kremer CK6 Group C Sports/Racing Car, ex-Le Mans.
£180,000–216,000
€266,000–320,000
$317,000–380,000 ➤ H&H

► 1994 Van Dieman Formula Renault Single-Seater, 1700cc, Renault 4-cylinder engine, fuel injection, space-frame, trailer and assorted spares.
£3,700–4,500 / €5,500–6,500
$6,500–7,800 ➤ CGC

Replica, Kit & Reproduction Cars

1886/1986 Benz Patent Motorwagon Centenary Replica, 984cc, single-cylinder engine, 0.9bhp, excellent condition.
£3,450–4,150 / €5,100–6,100 / $6,100–7,300 ✗ B(Kn)

1934/1936 Riley 9hp Special, built late 1980s,1097cc, tuned 1934 Riley 9hp engine with lightened flywheel, skimmed head, enlarged ports and dual valve springs, Brooklands oil pump, twin SU carburettors, 4-branch exhaust, shortened and tapered 1936 Kestrel chassis.
£6,300–7,600 / €9,300–11,200 / $11,200–13,400 ✗ CGC

> A known continuous history can add value to and enhance the enjoyment of a car.

▶ **1955 Jaguar XK140 Four-Seater Tourer,** 3.4 litres, 6-cylinder XK140 engine, overdrive gearbox, finished in red.
£5,400–6,400 / €8,000–9,500 / $9,500–11,300 ✗ H&H
This XK140 was rebodied during the early 1980s with vintage-style tourer coachwork. The original Jaguar chassis was reconditioned at the same time and extended by some 12in (30.5cm).

1932 Ford Roadster Hot Rod, 265cu.in, Chevrolet Corvette overhead-valve V8 engine, 4-barrel carburettor, 1940 Ford 3-speed manual gearbox with 24-tooth Lincoln Zephyr gears, 1940 Ford rear axle, Z'd chassis, body channelled over the chassis, finished in metallic green, concours condition.
£109,000–131,000 / €161,000–194,000 $192,000–231,000 ✗ BB(S)
This Ford 'Deuce' roadster was turned into a hot rod in the late 1950s. It has appeared in several films and TV programmes, notably the 'Ozzie and Harriet' show, in which is was driven by Ricky Nelson.

1999 Mercedes Benz 300SLR Replica, 2.8 litres, based on Mercedes-Benz 280SL, 1 of only 4 built.
£78,000–94,000 / €115,000–138,000 / $137,000–165,000 ✗ COYS
This 300SLR replica was built by Proteus Cars in 1999. The double-skinned aluminium body required no fewer than 17 major pieces of equipment to produce and took over six months to complete.

◄ **1990s Ferrari Daytona Spyder Replica,** 5343cc, Jaguar V12 engine, 5-speed manual gearbox, correct 5-spoke alloy wheels, finished in red, beige leather interior.
£11,800–14,200 / € 17,500–21,000
$20,800–25,000 ⚒ BRIT

▶ **1978 Ferrari 250 GTO Replica,** 2565cc, Datsun 6-cylinder engine, 150bhp, 5-speed gearbox, front disc/rear drum brakes, wire wheels, wood-rimmed steering wheel, finished in red, tan leather upholstery, 900 miles recorded since completion.
£20,000–24,000
€ 29,600–35,000
$35,000–42,000 ⚒ CGC
This car is based on a 1978 Datsun 260Z.

◄ **1990s GP Porsche RSK 60 Replica,** 1493cc, Volkswagen air-cooled 4-cylinder engine, racing camshaft, 2 twin-choke Dell'Orto carburettors, oil cooler, tuned exhaust, period wheels, finished in silver, 3,600 kilometres recorded.
£8,600–10,300
€ 12,700–15,200
$15,100–18,100 ⚒ H&H
This car was the GP demonstrator.

1985 Jaguar D-Type Replica, 3781cc, Jaguar 6-cylinder engine, finished in blue, grey interior.
£18,000–21,600 / € 26,600–32,000
$32,000–38,000 ⚒ COYS

1990s Ram Jaguar D-Type Replica, 3781cc, Jaguar 6-cylinder engine, triple SU carburettors, 4-speed gearbox with overdrive, finished in green, green interior, 1 owner from new.
£12,800–15,300 / € 18,900–22,600
$22,500–26,900 ⚒ H&H

◄ **c1967 AC Cobra Replica,** 3500cc, MGB V8 engine, 5-speed manual gearbox, stainless steel exhaust, MGB braking and cooling systems, Spax adjustable shock absorbers, built at a cost of £17,000 / € 25,000 / $30,000.
£7,500–9,000 / € 11,100–13,300
$13,200–15,800 ⚒ COYS

◀ 1972/1987 BRA AC Cobra 427 Replica, new 350cu.in Chevrolet V8 engine fitted 1999, 300bhp, 5-speed manual gearbox, finished in red, black Connolly leather interior.
£16,400–19,700
€ 24,300–29,200
$29,200–35,000 ⚒ B(Kn)
This right-hand-drive Cobra 427 replica was first registered in 1972, but not completed until 1987. It is one of 30 built by BRA before manufacture was transferred to Germany.

▶ 1972/1991 Teal Bugatti Type 35 Replica, 1798cc, Morris 4-cylinder engine, 4-speed manual gearbox, finished in blue, blue interior, fewer than 16,000 miles recorded.
£6,000–7,200
€ 8,900–10,700
$10,600–12,700 ⚒ H&H
The car was based on a 1972 Morris Marina donor vehicle.

◀ 1973 Jaguar D-Type Replica, 4.2 litres, Jaguar 6-cylinder engine, 4-speed manual gearbox with overdrive, original D-style steering wheel, period instruments, GRP body, finished in British Racing green.
£15,500–18,600 / € 22,900–27,500
$27,500–33,000 ⚒ H&H

1973 Steadman Jaguar SS100 Replica, 4.2 litres, Jaguar 6-cylinder engine, Borg Warner automatic transmission, finished in red, black leather interior, fewer than 2,000 miles recorded.
£9,300–11,100 / € 13,800–16,400
$16,400–19,500 ⚒ BARO

Auction prices

Miller's only includes cars declared sold. Our guide prices take into account the buyer's premium, VAT on the premium, and the extent of any published catalogue information relating to condition and provenance. Cars sold at auction are identified by the ⚒ icon; full details of the auction house can be found on page 251.

1973 Mini Cooper S Replica, 1071cc, tuned 4-cylinder engine, 4-speed gearbox, alloy wheels, quick-release bonnet, finished in British Racing green and white, 1 owner since 1975, near concours condition.
£10,500–12,600 / € 15,500–18,600
$18,500–22,200 🚗 MINI

c1973 Mini Innocenti Cooper Replica, 1380cc, tuned 4-cylinder engine, uprated suspension and brakes.
£1,800–2,150 / €2,700–3,200 / $3,200–3,800 ✗ CGC

1975 Dutton B-Type Roadster, 2 litres, Ford 4-cylinder engine, 4-speed gearbox, Triumph running gear, Lotus-style coil spring/damper units, spare set of wheels.
£1,950–2,350 / €2,900–3,500 / $3,450–4,150 ✗ BB(S)

◀ **1975 Gazelle Mercedes-Benz Roadster Replica,** 2.3 litres, 4-cylinder engine, wire wheels, wooden dashboard, finished in white, black leather interior, 1 of only 10 built, concours condition.
£8,600–10,300 / €12,700–15,200 / $15,100–18,100 ✗ BJ
This car was built for the actor Robert Crawford.

1980s Kougar Roadster, 3.8 litres, Jaguar 6-cylinder engine, road/race camshaft, triple SU carburettors, free-flow exhaust, Jaguar 4-speed close-ratio gearbox with overdrive, 4-wheel disc brakes, GRP bodywork, finished in red, black leather interior.
£10,300–12,400 / €15,200–18,200 $18,100–21,800 ✗ B(Kn)

◀ **1990 Dax Cobra Turbo,** 2 litres, Ford Cosworth double-overhead-camshaft engine, turbocharger, 400bhp, 0–60mph in 5.74 seconds, finished in red, black leather interior.
£14,100–16,900 / €20,900–25,000 $24,800–29,700 ✗ COYS

▶ **1994 Dax Ford GT40 Replica,** 5 litres, Ford V8 engine, fully balanced crankshaft, polished and gas-flowed cylinder heads, stainless steel valves, Holley carburettors, Peugeot 5-speed gearbox, 0–60mph in 5 seconds, top speed 165mph, c1,000 miles recorded, concours condition.
£23,000–27,600 €34,000–40,000 $40,000–48,000 ✗ B(Kn)

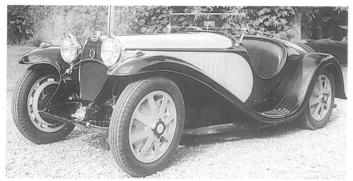

◀ **1995 Bugatti Type 55 Replica,** 2.3 litres, new reproduction chassis, many original Bugatti parts used including front axle, radiator, Scintilla magneto, starter and generator, correct pattern gearbox and clutch housing, aluminium body, finished in black and yellow, concours condition.
£176,000–211,000 €260,000–312,000 $310,000–371,000 ✗ B(Kn)

1995 Ferrari 500 Mondial Replica, 2000cc, Alfa Romeo double-overhead-camshaft 4-cylinder engine, Dell'Orto carburettors, Alfa Romeo gearbox, GRP body, de Dion suspension, 4-wheel disc brakes.
£21,000–25,200 / €31,000–37,000 / $37,000–44,000 ⚡ CGC

1996 HMC Austin-Healey 3000 Replica, 3.9 litres, Rover V8 engine, 5-speed manual gearbox, chromed wire wheels, GRP body, walnut dashboard, finished in British Racing green, beige leather upholstery.
£13,800–16,600 / €20,500–24,600
$24,300–29,200 ⚡ B(Kn)

Restored values

The cost of a professional restoration will have an influence on, but no direct relation to, a car's market value. A restored car can have a market value lower than the cost of its restoration.

1998 Pilgrim Sumo Mk III AC Cobra Replica, 5.7 litres, Chevrolet V8 engine, Rover 5-speed manual gearbox, 4-wheel disc brakes, fewer than 5,000 miles recorded.
£16,100–19,300 / €23,800–28,600
$28,300–34,000 ⚡ CGC
Introduced in 1987, the Pilgrim Sumo was based on Ford running gear and soon became the best-selling kit Cobra replica. Bowing to customer pressure for a version that could accommodate large-displacement American V8 engines, Pilgrim launched the Mk III Sumo in 1993.

1997 Ultima Spyder Mk IV, 5.7 litres, Chevrolet V8 engine, 0-60mph in 3.8 seconds, top speed 156mph, built at a cost of over £57,000 / €84,000 / $100,000, 8,000 miles recorded.
£27,000–32,000 / €40,000–47,000
$48,000–56,000 ⚡ B(Kn)

Restoration Projects

1916/23 Morris Cowley 11.9hp Sliding-Door Saloon,
coachwork by Bowden Tyseley, 1550cc, 4-cylinder engine,
Brolt lighting, calormeter, double-twist bulb horn,
electric klaxon, all 1916/23 specification apart from later SU
carburettor and Lucas magneto.
£4,850–5,800 / €7,200–8,600 / $8,500–10,200 ➹ B(Kn)

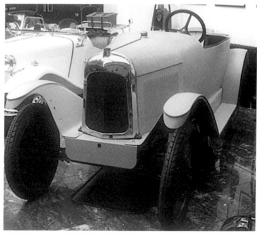

1925 Citroën C3 5CV Trefle, 856cc, side-valve 4-cylinder
engine, partly restored, some parts missing.
£2,300–2,750 / €3,400–4,050 / $4,050–4,850 ➹ B(Kn)

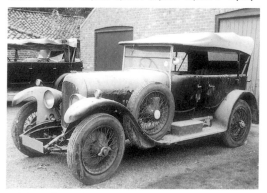

1926 Bentley 3 Litre Tourer, coachwork by Vanden Plas,
2996cc, 4-cylinder engine, unused for 31 years.
£51,000–61,000 / €75,000–90,000
$91,000–109,000 ➹ CGC

1926 Morris Cowley Two-Seater with Dickey, 1550cc,
4-cylinder engine, Smiths speedometer and clock,
Lucas dash light, visible-level fuel guage, dry stored for
over 30 years.
£6,800–8,200 / €10,100–12,100
$12,000–14,400 ➹ CGC
Introduced in 1913, the basic 'bull-nose' Morris design
lasted until 1926, by which time its variants accounted
for an impressive 45 per cent of the UK sales market.

> **Cross Reference**
> See Colour Review (pages 217–224)

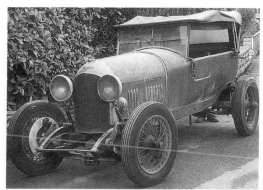

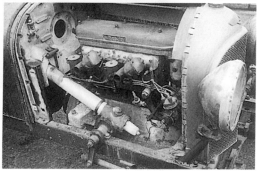

1927 Bentley 3 Litre Short-Chassis Speed model,
2996cc, 4-cylinder engine, 1 owner for 40 years.
£53,000–64,000 / €78,000–93,000
$93,000–112,000 ➹ COYS

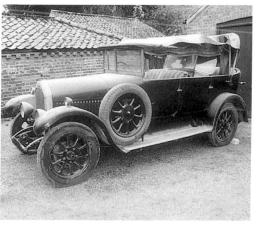

1928 Humber 14/40 Tourer, 2050cc, 4-cylinder engine.
£13,600–16,300 / €20,300–24,100
$23,900–28,700 ➹ CGC

◀ **1928 Rolls-Royce Phantom I Limousine,** coachwork by Windovers, 7668cc, overhead-valve 6-cylinder engine, unused for last 15 years.
£26,000–31,000 / €37,000–46,000
$46,000–55,000 ✗ H&H

1929 Rolls-Royce Phantom II, 7668cc, 6-cylinder engine, in need of complete restoration, engine free, fewer than 65,000 miles recorded.
£10,200–12,200 / €15,100–17,900
$18,000–21,500 ✗ H&H

◀ **1930 Daimler 20/70 Saloon,** 2648cc, dismantled 6-cylinder engine, some parts missing, in need of complete restoration.
£550–660 / €810–970 / $970–1,150 ✗ H&H

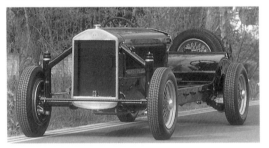

c1930 Lancia Dilambda Rolling Chassis, 3960cc, V8 engine, partly restored, some parts missing including bodywork.
£16,100–19,300 / €23,800–28,600
$28,300–34,000 ✗ B(Kn)
Only 1,884 Dilambdas were built before production ceased in 1935.

◀ **1931 Bentley 4¼ Litre Tourer,** 4398cc, 4-cylinder engine, 'barn discovery', complete, 1 owner for 35 years.
£97,000–116,000 / €144,000–171,000
$171,000–204,000 ✗ H&H

1931 Duesenberg Model J Rolling Chassis, 420cu.in, partially restored, rebuilt 8-cylinder engine, new radiator and brass surround, wire wheels, fuel tanks, stainless steel exhaust, bodywork missing.
£44,000–53,000 / €65,000–78,000 / $78,000–93,000 ✗ BB(S)

1931 Lagonda 3 Litre Tourer, 2931cc, overhead-valve 6-cylinder engine, converted from sports saloon to tourer 1950s, 'barn find', last used 1960s.
£22,600–27,100 / €34,000–40,000 **/ $40,000–48,000** ⚹ H&H

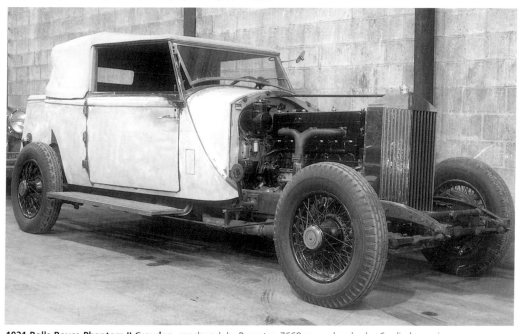

1931 Rolls-Royce Phantom II Croydon, coachwork by Brewster, 7668cc, overhead-valve 6-cylinder engine, left-hand drive, partially restored, engine rebuilt, unpainted aluminium body panels, rust-free steel wings.
£41,000–49,000 / €61,000–73,000 **/ $72,000–86,000** ⚹ BB(S)
This Phantom II is an American-built example.

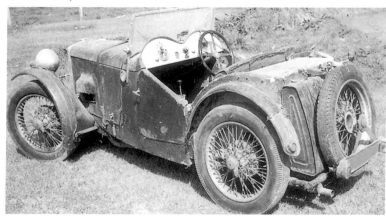

▶ 1933 MG J2, original engine replaced by Ford side-valve 4-cylinder unit, brakes converted to hydraulic operation, 1 family ownership since 1959.
£9,500–11,400
€14,100–16,900
$16,700–20,100 ⚹ CGC

1934 Rolls-Royce 20/25 Limousine, coachwork by Harper, 3669cc, engine overhauled and ready for reassembly, 1 family ownership since 1966.
£11,700–14,000 / €17,300–20,700 $20,600–24,600 ✗ B(Kn)

▶ **1935 Rolls-Royce 20/25 Saloon,** 3669cc, 6-cylinder engine, original Lucas lights, centre spotlamp, driver's spotlight, 'barn discovery'.
£6,000–7,200 / €8,900–10,700 $10,600–12,700 ✗ H&H

◀ **1934 Lanchester 18 Drophead Coupé,** coachwork by Martin Walter, 2504cc, unused since 1968, in need of complete restoration.
£2,400–2,900 / €3,600–4,300 / $4,300–5,100 ✗ BRIT

1934 Morris Cowley Four-Door Saloon, 1938cc, 6-cylinder engine, 4-speed manual gearbox, 2 owners from new, fewer than 86,000 miles recorded, in need of minor attention to electrics and brakes.
£3,500–4,200 / €5,200–6,200 / $6,200–7,400 ✗ BWL

◀ **1936 Railton Straight 8 Raneleigh Saloon,** 4 litres, engine partly dismantled, interior in need of attention, 1 family ownership since 1961.
£1,900–2,300 / €2,800–3,350 / $3,350–4,000 ✗ CGC

1937 Austin 7 Ruby Saloon, 747cc, 4-cylinder engine, unused for 17 years, in need of extensive work.
£430–520 / €640–770 / $770–920 ✗ BRIT

◀ **1937 Aston Martin 15/98 Sports Tourer,** 1939cc, 4-cylinder engine, last used 1965, dry stored, in need of complete restoration.
£28,500–34,000 / €42,000–50,000 $50,000–60,000 ✗ H&H

1937 Daimler 4½ Litre Limousine, coachwork by Hooper, 4624cc, 8-cylinder engine, all period features intact, sliding division, working blinds, 'barn discovery', unused since 1960s.
£7,900–9,500 / €11,700–14,000 / $13,900–16,700 ⚒ H&H

1937 Rolls-Royce 25/30 Limousine, coachwork by Windovers, 4257cc, 6-cylinder engine, stored for c40 years, running, in need of complete restoration.
£7,900–8,700 / €11,700–12,900 / $13,900–15,300 ⊞ RCC

◄ **1938 Austin Seven Cambridge Special,** 747cc, 4 cylinder engine, Cambridge alloy cylinder head, all-aluminium body, rear-mounted slab fuel tank, split front axle for independent suspension, wheels rebuilt with 15in (38.1cm) rims, in need of considerable work.
£1,200–1,450 / €1,800–2,150 / $2,100–2,500 ⚒ CGC

1939 Morris 12/4 Four-Door Saloon, dry stored for 30 years, engine running, little rust apart from on door rocker panels, mechanics recently recommissioned.
£900–1,100 / €1,350–1,600 / $1,600–1,900 ⚒ CGC

◄ **1950 Morgan 4/4,** 1267cc, 4-cylinder engine, 1 owner from new, unused since early 1970s.
£6,200–7,400 / €9,200–11,000 / $10,900–13,000 ⚒ BRIT

◀ **c1951 JP500 Mk 1 Single-Seater,** missing many parts, including drive-train, wheels, brakes and interior, in need of complete restoration.
£2,500–3,050 / €3,700–4,400 / $4,500–5,400 ⚒ CGC
The JP500 had a ladder frame with twin tubes on each side and transverse-leaf-spring suspension. The bodywork was in aluminium, while customers could choose from a variety of engines, although this was usually a Norton, JAP or Vincent. A total of 33 Formula 3 JP500s were sold during 1950–54. Few have survived.

The price paid for a car can vary according to the country in which it was sold. To discover where the car sold, cross reference the code at the end of each caption with the Key to Illustrations on page 251.

▶ **1961 Morris Oxford Series VI,** 1622cc, 4-cylinder engine.
£3,000–3,600 / €4,450–5,300 $5,300–6,300 ⚒ BRIT
This car was owned originally by Lady Clementine Churchill.

1962 Alfa Romeo 2000 Sprint Coupé, unused for 10 years, in need of complete restoration.
£200–240 / €300–360 / $350–420 ⚒ H&H

1967 MGB Roadster, 1798cc, 4-cylinder engine, finished in red, red leather interior, dry stored for 8 years, ideal restoration project.
£1,200–1,450 / €1,800–2,150 / $2,150–2,550 ⚒ CGC

1969 Morris Minor 1000, 1098cc, 4-cylinder engine, 4-speed manual gearbox, suitable for restoration or spares.
£85–100 / €125–150 / $150–180 ⚒ CGC

1969 Morris Minor Convertible, 1098cc, engine runs, in need of considerable cosmetic and some mechanical attention.
£840–1,000 / €1,250–1,500 / $1,500–1,800 ⚒ CGC

◀ **1973 Lamborghini Espada,** 3929cc, V12 engine, interior partially stripped, side body trim mouldings missing, engine rebuilt at a cost of over £20,000 / €29,600 / $35,000, engine and gearbox in need of fitting.
£8,000–9,600 / €11,800–14,200 / $14,100–16,900 ⚒ COYS

Taxis

1935 Austin 12/4 Taxi, 1861cc, side-valve 4-cylinder engine, completely restored 1995, converted to unleaded fuel, finished in dark blue and black, navy blue leather interior.
£14,400–17,200 / €21,300–25,500 / $25,300–30,000 ↗ B(Kn)

1937 Austin 12/4 Taxi, 1861cc, side-valve 4-cylinder engine, 27bhp, completely restored late 1990s.
£19,000–22,800 / €28,500–34,000 / $34,000–40,000 ↗ B(Kn)

1937 Austin 12/4 Taxi, 1861cc, side-valve 4-cylinder engine, completely restored, converted to unleaded fuel, excellent condition.
£22,200–26,700 / €33,000–30,000 / $40,000–47,000 ↗ CGC
This particular taxi was used in the film 'Carry On Cabby'.

1953 Morris Oxford SIII Nuffield Taxi, 1802cc, overhead-valve 4-cylinder engine, completely restored, gearbox and clutch overhauled.
£4,500–5,400 / €6,700–8,000
$7,900–9,500 ↗ H&H

Children's Cars

◀ **1950s Austin J40 Junior Joy Pedal Car,** pressed-steel construction, dummy engine with spark plugs, battery-operated lights and horn, unrestored.
£720–800
€1,050–1,250
$1,200–1,400
🚗 PCCC

1950s Austin-Healey Pedal Car, electric motor, restored 1970s for use as a fairground car.
£340–380 / €500–560 / $600–670 ⊞ BAJ

▶ **Bugatti Type 35 Grand Prix Pedal Car,** by Elantec-Eureka, built 1997–98
£2,350–2,600
€3,500–3,850
$4,150–4,600
🚗 PCCC

1920s Lyons Brothers Fiat Racer Pedal Car, fully restored.
£220–250 / €330–370 / $390–440 🚗 PCCC
Lyons Brothers later became Tri-ang Toys.

Bugatti 55 child's car, 170cc, air-cooled Honda 4-stroke 3 bhp engine, 12-volt batttery, one-piece body on a steel chassis, rubber pneumatic tyres, twin chromed working headlamps, finished in black and yellow, built in 1989.
£10,000–12,000 / €14,800–17,700
$17,600–21,000 🔨 COYS

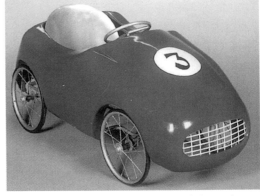

c1940 Ferrari pedal car, steel body and tubular steel frame, finished in red.
£960–1,150 / €1,450–1,700 / $1,700–2,000 🔨 B(Ge)

Ferrari 500 F2 Pietro Zani child's car, rear-mounted Minarelli two-stroke petrol engine, built to ⅓ scale, fibreglass body, aluminium chassis, chromed wire wheels and matching spinners, pneumatic tyres, finished in Rosso livery.
£10,000–12,000 / €14,800–17,700
$17,600–21,000 ⚒ COYS

c1950 Tri-ang Brooklands pedal car, finished in green.
£760–850 / €1,100–1,250 / $1,350–1,500 ⊞ JUN

1960s Tri-ang Ford-Style Fire Truck Pedal Car, pressed-steel construction, restored, original chrome wheels painted white.
£220–250 / €330–370 / $390–440 🚗 PCCC

Panhard-Levassor Tourer Child's Car, by Elantec-Eureka, built 1997–98.
£2,300–2,600 / €3,500–3,850 / $4,150–4,600 🚗 PCCC

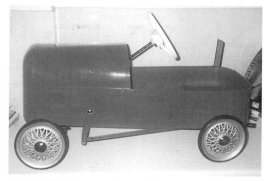

1950s/1960s Tri-ang Duke Pedal Car, all-metal construction apart from plastic steering wheel.
£135–150 / €200–220 / $230–260 🚗 PCCC

1950s/1960s Tri-ang Royal Prince Pedal Car,
metal construction, plastic steering wheel.
£135–150 / €200–220 / $230–260 🚗 PCCC

Automobile Art

Brockbank, set of 17 cartoons, each framed and glazed, initialled 'RB', 1970.
£1,150–1,350 / €1,700–2,000
$2,000–2,400 ⚹ **B(Kn)**
These cartoons were used as chapter title illustrations in *The Dashboard Revolution* published by Smith Industries in 1970.

Bowyer, an original painting depicting a racing car at speed, framed and signed, c1910, 18 x 22in (45.5 x 56cm).
£360–430 / €530–620 / $630–760 ⚹ **BB(S)**

Dexter Brown, 24 Heures du Mans, watercolour and gouache on paper, depicting Mike Hawthorn in the Jaguar D-Type, signed, 1955, 28 x 20in (71 x 51cm), mounted, framed and glazed.
£2,100–2,500 / €3,100–3,700
$3,700–4,400 ⚹ **B(Kn)**

▶ **Coton, Paris to Madrid,** pen, ink and watercolour wash, signed and titled, mounted, 1903, 15 x 20¾in (38 x 52.5cm).
£360–430
€530–640
$630–760
⚹ **B(Kn)**

◀ **F. Gordon Crosby, The 24 Hour Touring Car Race at Le Mans,** charcoal, monochrome wash, inscribed 'how the armed searchlight lorries will be used to illuminate the course', mounted, framed and glazed, signed, 1923, 14¼ x 20in (36 x 51cm).
£4,000–4,800 / €5,900–7,100
$7,000–8,400 ⚹ **B(Kn)**
This is believed to be the first illustration of the event in 1923. Crosby inscribed it using the future tense, which suggests that he completed it during a practice race before the actual event took place.

▶ **Brian Hatton, BRM P160 F1 Racing Car,** cut-away illustration for *The Motor*, watercolour and gouache with pen and ink lining, on artist's board, 1971, 15¾ x 24½in (40 x 62cm), mounted, framed and glazed.
£280–330 / €410–490
$490–580 ⚹ **B(Kn)**

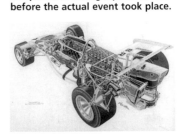

Carlo Demand, Paris to Madrid, Race of Death, preliminary mixed-media sketch on paper, 1903, 12in (30.5cm) square, mounted, framed and glazed.
£410–490 / €610–730 / $720–860 ⚹ **B(Kn)**

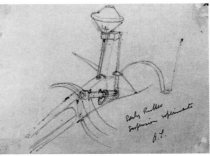

◀ **Alec Issigonis, Early Rubber Suspension Refinements,** pen and ink on paper, initialled, 1950s, 8½ x 12in (21.5 x 30.5cm).
£460–550
€680–810
$810–970
⚹ **B(Kn)**

Posters

Daily Telegraph Sports Car Race, Aintree, an advertising poster depicting an Aston Martin DBS and DB2, c1950s.
£460–550 / €680–810
$810–970 ⚬ BB(S)

Carrera de Automoviles, an original advertising poster, 1950s,
23¼ x 15¾in (59 x 40cm).
£230–270 / €340–400
$400–480 ⚬ B(Mu)

Mercedes-Benz poster, celebrating first and second place in the 1955 Italian Grand Prix, depicting a W196 Streamliner, 1955, 22¾ x 33½in (85 x 58cm).
£155–185 / €230–270
$270–330 ⚬ H&H

BARC Brands Hatch, an advertising poster, c1965.
£45–50 / €65–75 / $80–90 ⚬ CGC

24 Heures du Mans, an advertising poster, 1966, 22¾ x 15¾in (58 x 40cm).
£115–135 / €170–200
$200–240 ⚬ B(Mu)

BRSCC/Castrol F3 Races, Brands Hatch, an advertising poster, late 1960s, together with another poster for Silverstone Formula Ford Races, 1970s.
£60–70 / €90–105
$105–125 ⚬ CGC

Cross Reference
See Colour Review
(pages 217–224)

◄ **McQueen Drives Porsche,**
an advertising poster, monochrome with coloured lettering, small repair, printed in Germany, 1970, 40 x 30in (105.5 x 76cm).
£1,700–2,000 / €2,500–2,950
$3,000–3,500 ⚬ B(Kn)

Uniflo Trophy Meeting, Silverstone,
an advertising poster, 1971.
£40–45 / €60–70 / $70–80 ⚬ CGC

Automobilia

Armstrong Tires, an advertising sign, with painted raised wooden letters, slight damage, American, early 20thC, 24 x 216in (61 x 548.5cm).
£450–540 / € 670–800 / $800–960 ⚒ BB(S)

Le Petit Journal, a set of 4 colour supplement prints, 1901–1904, 11¾ x 10½in (30 x 26.5cm).
£100–120 / € 150–180
$175–210 ⚒ CGC

Two white-metal pincushions, in the shape of early motor cars, 1910, longest 5in (12.5cm) long.
£50–60 / € 75–90 / $90–105 ⊞ JUN

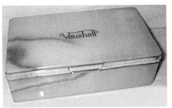

A Vauxhall white marble and silver cigar box, London 1919, 7in (18cm) wide.
£300–360 / € 440–530
$530–630 ⚒ H&H

An Alfa Romeo catalogue, for the Coupé, Limousine, Runabout, RM, 4-cylinder Sport, Cabriolet RL, RL Saloon, Torpedo and 6-cylinder Grand Sport, loose staple, French text, 1924.
£690–820 / € 1,000–1,200
$1,200–1,450 ⚒ B(Kn)

Ford Times Monthly, dealership booklets, with coloured plates, 1924–25, 9 x 6in (23 x 15cm).
£45–50 / € 65–75
$80–90 each ⊞ MURR

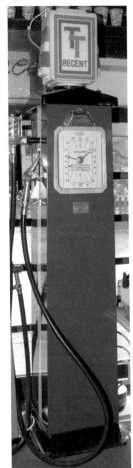

A Gilbert petrol pump, reproduction globe, c1930, 108in (274.5cm) high.
£900–1,000
€ 1,350–1,500
$1,600–1,750 ⊞ JUN

A silver-plated cigarette dispenser, in the shape of an early saloon car, 1930s, 8in (20.5cm) long.
£180–200 / € 270–300 / $320–350 ⊞ JUN

A Jaguar leather notepad and calendar, 1930s, 11 x 7in (28 x 18cm).
£160–180 / € 240–270
$280–320 ⊞ MSh

A Cord wooden model car, given as a showroom gift, 1930s, 11in (28cm).
£60–70 / € 90–105 / $105–125 ⊞ DRJ

A Smiths dashboard clock, brass mounting, 1930s, 2½in (6.5cm) diam.
£180–200 / € 270–300
$320–350 ⊞ CARS

An Avery Hardoll petrol pump, with reproduction globe, 1930s, 85in (216cm) high.
£950–1,050
€1,400–1,550
$1,650–1,850 ⊞ JUN

Collection of motor racing programmes and photographs, including official Grand Prix and other Nürburgring literature, German, 1930s.
£1,250–1,500 / €1,850–2,200
$2,200–2,650 ✗ B(Mu)

A dinner menu, for a banquet in honour of Sir Malcolm Campbell, the cover with embossed monochrome portrait, with a Bluebird technical illustration pull-out, 1935.
£115–135 / €170–200 / $200–240 ✗ B(Kn)

A pair of Lucas P100L chrome headlamps, slight damage, 1 with Lucas badge missing, 1930s.
£195–230 / €290–340
$340–400 ✗ BB(S)

◄ *The Autocar* **London Show Review issue,** 1954, 12 x 8¼in (30.5 x 21cm).
£3–7 / €4–10
$6–12 ⊞ RTT

A collection of books, leaflets and maps, relating to car maintenance and accessories, 1950s.
£10–14 / €14–20 / $18–24 ✗ CGC

Redex, a tin advertising sign, 1950s, together with a cardboard display stand for Drecosol Upholstery Cleaner and an Esso promotional magic painting book.
£100–120 / €150–180
$175–210 ✗ CGC

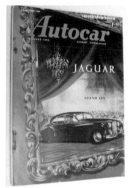

1994 Porsche 904 Race Engine, 2 litre, double-overhead-camshaft engine, 180bhp, complete with exhibition stand.
£31,000–37,000
€46,000–55,000
$55,000–65,000 ✗ B(Mon)

► **A GRP Castrol clock,** in the form of an oil-bottle top, painted with 1934 World Record design, battery movement, some wear, 41in (104cm) diam.
£430–510 / €640–750
$760–900 ✗ B(Kn)

A signed letter from Enzo Ferrari, inviting a friend to dine at the Cavallino Restaurant, mounted, framed and glazed, 1960–70, 6¼ x 7½in (16 x 19cm).
£460–550 / €680–810
$810–970 ✗ B(Kn)

Badges

A brass AA member's badge, with markings, 1906–07, 6in (15cm) high.
£240–290 / €360–430
$420–510 ♠ H&H

◀ A nickel and enamel Brooklands Automobile Racing Club 130mph badge, by Spencer & Co, marked, 1935.
£4,600–5,500
€6,800–8,100
$8,100–9,700 ♠ B(Kn)
During 28 seasons of racing at Brooklands, only 16 drivers received 130mph badges. Charles Brackenbury won this example in 1935.

A Brooklands Automobile Racing Club member's badge and guest brooch, decorated in vitreous enamels, 1907.
£135–150 / €200–220
$230–260 🚗 BARCC

A Brooklands Automobile Racing Club member's badge and guest brooch, decorated in vitreous enamels, 1932.
£220–250 / €330–370
$390–440 🚗 BARCC

A Brooklands Automobile Racing Club member's badge and two guest brooches, decorated in vitreous enamels, 1936.
£220–250 / €330–370
$390–440 🚗 BARCC

◀ A nickel and enamel Guild of Master Motorists member's badge, by Spencer & Co, in original box with gilt lettering, marked 'Captain George Eyston', 1938.
£1,700–2,000
€2,500–2,950
$3,000–3,500
♠ B(Kn)

Models

A 1/12-scale resin and alloy model of an Aston Martin DBR/1, painted to represent the 1959 Le Mans winning car, in a glazed case and mounted on a wooden base, 1950s.
£920–1,100 / €1,350–1,600
$1,600–1,900 ♠ B(Kn)

A 1/2.5-scale model of an 1886 Daimler Motorwagon, c1935, 38in (96.5cm) long.
£1,700–2,000
€2,500–2,950
$3,000–3,500 ♠ B(Kn)

A 1/8-scale clockwork model of a 1922 Miller Indianapolis racing car, tinplate body, clockwork-powered front-wheel drive, nickel-plated brightwork.
£630–750 / €930–1,100
$1,100–1,300 ♠ B(Kn)

Books

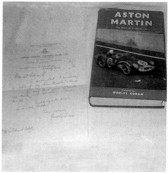

British Racing Cars,
1929–30, 8½ x 5½in
(21.5 x 14cm).
**£520–580 / €770–860
$920–1,000 ⊞ MURR**

Laurence Pomeroy, *The Grand Prix Car,*
volumes 1 and 2, volume 2 with damaged dust
jacket, 1954–55.
**£280–330 / €410–490
$490–580 ➹ H&H**

**Dudley Coram, *Aston Martin – the
Story of a Sports Car,*** including
original colour plate, signed, c1960s,
together with a signed letter from the
author enclosing the book.
**£520–620 / €770–920
$920–1,100 ➹ H&H**

Motor Racing Memorabilia

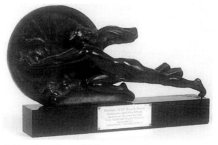

**A Vanden Plas British 1,000 Miles Race
trophy,** with plaque engraved 'Won by Car
No. 10 A.W. Fox (Talbot 3), Driver A. O. S.
Saunders Davies', signed 'A. Gennarelly', L. N. J.
L. foundry marks, Paris, 1932, 24in (61cm) long.
**£2,000–2,400 / €3,250–3,550
$3,850–4,200 ➹ B(Kn)**

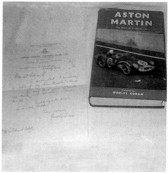

A James Hunt Bell Star helmet,
restored to Hunt's traditional colours,
visor, with Bell cloth bag, 1976.
**£2,000–2,400 / €3,250–3,550
$3,850–4,200 ➹ B(Kn)**

**A World's Mile
Straightaway Record
trophy,** by Wallace Bros,
Connecticut, awarded to
Malcolm Campbell,
the nickled-silver body
with embossed foliate
decoration and hand-
chased inscription,
AAA sanction No. 1944,
1928, 22½in (57cm) high.
**£3,000–3,600
€4,450–5,300
$5,300–6,300 ➹ B(Kn)**

◄ **A Marlboro McLaren MP4-6 nose-
cone panel,** carbon-fibre composite,
decorated with Marlboro, Honda, Tag
Heuer, Shell, Goodyear and McLaren
logos, the underside hand-written
'Test Team MP4-6-01 No 2', 1991.
**£1,400–1,650 / €2,050–2,450
$2,450–2,900 ➹ B(Kn)**

► **A McLaren pit board,**
with applied Marlboro,
Goodyear and Shell logos,
1980s, 44 x 20in (112 x 51cm).
**£270–320 / €400–470
$480–560 ➹ B(Kn)**

Prices

The price ranges quoted in this book reflect the average price a
purchaser might expect to pay for a similar item. The price will vary
according to the condition, rarity, size, popularity, provenance,
colour and restoration of the item, and this must be taken into
account when assessing values. Don't forget that if you are selling it
is quite likely that you will be offered less than the price range.

A Momo steering wheel, on a display
base, engraved plaque 'Nigel Mansell
3rd GP of Brazil 21.3.82 JPS 91', 1991.
**£630–750 / €1,100–3,550
$1,100–1,300 ➹ B(Kn)**

Photographs

A black and white still of Steve McQueen, taken from the film 'Le Mans', mounted, framed and glazed, c1970.
£100–120 / €150–180 $175–210 ✗ CGC

Klemantaski, a photograph of nine Bugattis, taken outside Continental Autos in Send, Surrey, 1930s, 24 x 36in (61 x 91.5cm).
£120–140 / €180–210 / $210–250 ✗ CGC

A signed photograph of Jackie Ickx, 1976, 4 x 6in (10 x 15cm).
£11–15 / €17–22 / $20–26 ⊞ RaA

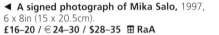

◀ **A signed photograph of Mika Salo,** 1997, 6 x 8in (15 x 20.5cm).
£16–20 / €24–30 / $28–35 ⊞ RaA

A commemorative album of the Argentinian Grand Prix, belonging to Mike Hawthorn, including 25 black-and-white photographs with signatures and inscriptions, rexine cord-bound covers, 1953, together with a press photograph commemorating Eva Peron's visit to the Autodromo Mar del Plate.
£4,600–5,500 / €6,800–8,100 $8,100–9,700 ✗ B(Kn)

A photograph of the start of the Le Mans 24-hour Race, depicting Corvettes, E-Types and Ferraris, c1960, 18 x 24in (45.5 x 61cm).
£30–35 / €45–50 / $55–65 ✗ CGC

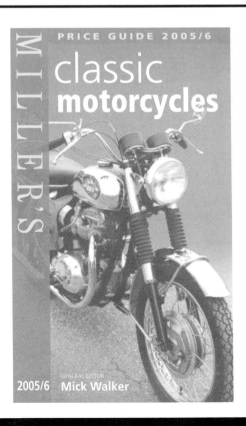

Key to Illustrations

Each illustration and descriptive caption is accompanied by a letter code. By referring to the following list of Auctioneers (denoted by ⚒), dealers (⊞), Clubs, Museums and Trusts (🚗), the source of any item may be immediately determined. Inclusion in this edition no way constitutes or implies a contract or binding offer on the part of any of our contributors to supply or sell the goods illustrated, or similar articles, at the prices stated. Advertisers in this year's directory are denoted by †.

If you require a valuation, it is advisable to check whether the dealer or specialist will carry out this service and if there is a charge. Please mention *Miller's* when making an enquiry. A valuation by telephone is not possible. Most dealers are willing to help you with your enquiry; however, they are very busy people and consideration of the above points would be welcomed.

AMA ⊞ Amazon Cars, Top Road,
Wingfield, Suffolk IP21 5QT
Tel: 01379 388400
sales@amazoncars.co.uk

AU ⊞ Auto Suggestion
Tel: 01428 751397

B(Ge) ⚒ Bonhams, 7 Av. Pictet-de-Rochemont,
1207 Geneva, Switzerland
Tel: (0) 22 300 3160

B(Kn) ⚒† Bonhams, Montpelier Street,
Knightsbridge, London SW7 1HH
Tel: 020 7393 3900
www.bonhams.com

B(Mon) ⚒ Bonhams, Le Beau Rivage,
9 Avenue d'Ostende,
Monte Carlo MC 98000, Monaco
Tel: +41 (0)22 300 3160

B(Mu) ⚒ Bonhams GmbH, Widenmayerstr. 4,
80538 Munich, Germany
Tel: +41 (0)22 300 3160

BAJ ⊞ Beaulieu Autojumble,
Beaulieu, Hampshire

BARCC 🚗 Brooklands Automobilia & Regalia
Collectors' Club, The (B.A.R.C.C.),
Hon. Sec. G. G. Weiner,
4-4a Chapel Terrace Mews,
Kemp Town, Brighton,
East Sussex BN2 1HU
Tel: 01273 601960
Mobile: 07890 836734
www.barcc.co.uk
www.brmmbrmm.co.uk
www.brooklands-automobilia-regalia-
collectors-club.co.uk

BARO ⚒† Barons (Auctioneers) Ltd,
Quayside House, 23 St. Johns Street,
Hythe, Southampton,
Hampshire SO45 6BZ
Tel: 023 8084 0081/8084 7164
info@barons-auctions.com
www.barons-auctions.com

BB(S) ⚒ Bonhams & Butterfields,
220 San Bruno Avenue,
San Francisco CA 94103,
U.S.A. Tel: 415 861 7500

BJ ⚒ Barrett-Jackson Auction Company, LLC,
3020 N Scottsdale Road,
Scottsdale, Arizona, U.S.A.
Tel: 480-421-6694
www.barrett-jackson.com

BLE ⊞ Ivor Bleaney, PO Box 60,
Salisbury, Wiltshire SP5 2DH
Tel: 01794 390895

BR See DN(BR)

BRIT ⚒ British Car Auctions Ltd,
Classic & Historic Automobile Division,
Auction Centre, Blackbushe Airport,
Blackwater, Camberley,
Surrey GU17 9LG
Tel: 01252 878555

BWL ⚒ Brightwells Fine Art, The Fine Art Saleroom,
Easters Court, Leominster,
Herefordshire HR6 0DE
Tel: 01568 611122
fineart@brightwells.com
www.brightwells.com

CARS ⊞† C.A.R.S. (Classic Automobilia & Regalia
Specialists), 4-4a Chapel Terrace Mews,
Kemp Town, Brighton,
East Sussex BN2 1HU
Tel: 01273 60 1960/622722
or 07890 836734
cars@kemptown-brighton.freeserve.co.uk
www.brmmbrmm.com/barcc
www.carsofbrighton.co.uk
www.brmmbrmm.com/pedalcars
www.brooklandsbadges.com
www.brooklands-automobilia-regalia-
collectors-club.co.uk

CGC ⚒† Cheffins, Vintage Car Department,
8 Hill Street, Saffron Walden, Essex
CB10 1JD Tel: 01799 513131
vintage@cheffins.co.uk
www.cheffins.co.uk

COYS ⚒ Coys of Kensington, 2/4 Queens Gate
Mews, London SW7 5QJ
Tel: 020 7584 7444

DN(BR) ⚒ Dreweatt Neate, formerly Bracketts Fine
Art Auctioneers, The Auction Hall,
The Pantiles, Tunbridge Wells,
Kent TN2 5QL Tel: 01892 544500
tunbridgewells@dnfa.com
www.dnfa.com/tunbridgewells

DRJ ⊞ The Motorhouse, DS & RG Johnson,
Thorton Hall, Thorton,
Buckinghamshire MK17 0HB
Tel: 01280 812280

FHD ⊞† F. H. Douglass, 1a South Ealing Road,
Ealing, London W5 4QT
Tel: 020 8567 0570

H&H ⚒† H & H Classic Auctions Ltd,
Whitegate Farm, Hatton Lane,
Hatton, Warrington, Cheshire WA4 4BZ
Tel: 01925 730630
www.classic-auctions.co.uk

HLR 🚗 Historic Lotus Register, Victor Thomas
(Registrar), Badgers Farm, Short Green,
Winfarthing, Norfolk IP22 2EE

HUMB 🚗 The Humber Register 1896 to 1932, R.N. Arman, Northbrook Cottage, 175 York Road, Broadstone, Dorset BH18 8ES Tel: 01202 695937 thearmans@tiscali.co.uk

IMP 🚗 Imp Club, Richard Sozanski (PR/Events Sec), 19 Chesford Grove, Stratford-on-Avon, Warwickshire CV37 9LS Tel: 01789 298093

JNic 🔧 John Nicholson, The Auction Rooms, Longfield, Midhurst Road, Fernhurst, Surrey GU27 3HA Tel: 01428 653727

JUN ⊞† Junktion, The Old Railway Station, New Bolingbroke, Boston, Lincolnshire PE22 7LB Tel: 01205 480068/480087 or 07836 345491

KR 🚗 K70 Register, SAE to: Mr Bood, 25 Cedar Grove, Penn Fields, Wolverhampton WV3 7EB Tel: 01902 566623

MINI 🚗 Mini Cooper Register, Cliff Porter (General Secretary), PO Box 1275, Farnham, Surrey GU10 4XD Tel: 020 8925 4086 secretary@minicooper.org

MSh ⊞ Manfred Schotten, 109 High Street, Burford, Oxfordshire OX18 4RG Tel: 01993 822302 www.antiques@schotten.com

MURR ⊞ Murrays' Antiques & Collectables Tel: 01202 823870

NSal 🔧 Netherhampton Salerooms, Salisbury Auction Centre, Netherhampton, Salisbury, Wiltshire SP2 8RH Tel: 01722 340 041

PCCC 🚗 Pedal Car Collectors' Club (P.C.C.C.), A. P. Gayler (Secretary), 4/4a Chapel Terrace Mews, Kemp Town, Brighton, East Sussex BN2 1HU Tel: 01273 601960 www.brmmbrmm.com/pedalcars

PM ⊞ Pollard's Motorcycles, The Garage, Clarence Street, Dinnington, Sheffield, South Yorkshire S31 7HA Tel: 01909 563310

RaA ⊞ Race Art, 33 Westgate Street, Southery, Norfolk PE38 0PA Tel: 01366 377069 or 07876 548160 simon@race-art.com www.race-art.com

RCC ⊞† Real Car Co Ltd, Coed y Parc, Bethesda, Gwynedd LL57 4YS Tel: 01248 602649 mail@realcar.co.uk www.realcar.co.uk

RTT ⊞ Rin Tin Tin, 34 North Road, Brighton, East Sussex BN1 1YB Tel: 01273 672424 rick@rintintin.freeserve.co.uk

SBR 🚗 Star, Starling, Stuart and Briton Register, D E A Evans, New Wood Lodge, 2A Hyperion Rd, Stourton, Stourbridge, West Midlands DY7 6SB Tel: 01384 374329 www.localhistory.scit.wlv.ac.uk/museum /transport/cars/starregister/starreg00

SWO 🔧 Sworders, 14 Cambridge Road, Stansted Mountfitchet, Essex CM24 8BZ Tel: 01279 817778 auctions@sworder.co.uk www.sworder.co.uk

Tur 🚗 Turner Register, Russell Filby, 5 Claremont Gardens, Nailsea, Bristol, North Somerset, BS48 2HY Tel: 01275 791569 turnersportscars@blueyonder.co.uk www.turnersportscars.com

UMC ⊞† Unicorn Motor Company, Brian R. Chant M.I.M.I., Station Road, Stalbridge, Dorset DT10 2RH Tel: 01963 363353 www.unicornmotor.com

VS 🔧 T. Vennett-Smith, 11 Nottingham Road, Gotham, Nottinghamshire NG11 0HE Tel: 0115 983 0541 info@vennett-smith.com www.vennett-smith.com

WHS 🚗 Wolseley Hornet Special Club 1930–35, Wolseley Hornet, Sports & Specials, Chris Hyde, Lyme Cottage, 5 Orchard Lane, Winterborne Kingston, Dorset DT11 9BF whsc.sec@btinternet.com www.whsc.co.uk

Index to Advertisers

Glossary

We have attempted to define some of the terms that you will come across in this book. If there are any terms or technical expressions that you would like explained or you feel should be included in future, please let us know.

Aero screen A small, curved windscreen fitted to the scuttle of a sports car in place of the standard full-width screen. Used in competition to reduce wind resistance. Normally fitted in pairs, one each in front of the driver and passenger.

All-weather A term used to describe a vehicle with a more sophisticated folding hood than the normal Cape hood fitted to a touring vehicle. The sides were fitted with metal frames and transparent material, in some cases glass.

Barchetta Italian for 'little boat', an all-enveloping open sports bodywork.

Berline *See* **Sedanca de Ville**.

Boost The amount of pressure applied by a supercharger or turbocharger.

Boxer Engine configuration with horizontally-opposed cylinders.

Brake A term dating from the days of horse-drawn vehicles. Originally the seating was fore and aft, the passengers facing inwards.

Brake horsepower (bhp) This is the amount of power produced by an engine, measured at the flywheel (*See* **Horsepower**).

Cabriolet The term Cabriolet applies to a vehicle with a hood that can be closed, folded half-way or folded right back. A Cabriolet can be distinguished from a Landaulette because the front of the hood reaches the top of the windscreen, whereas on a Landaulette, it only covers the rear half of the car.

Chain drive A transmission system in which the wheels are attached to a sprocket, driven by a chain from an engine-powered sprocket, usually on the output side of a gearbox.

Chassis A framework to which the car body, engine, gearbox, and axles are attached.

Chummy An open-top, two-door body style, usually with a single door on each side, two seats in the front and one at the rear.

Cloverleaf A three-seater, open body style, usually with a single door on each side, two seats in the front and one at the rear.

Concours Concours d'Elegance is a competition in which cars are judged by their condition. Concours has become a byword for a vehicle in excellent condition.

Cone clutch A clutch in which both driving and driven faces form a cone.

Connollising Leather treatment produced by British firm Connolly to rejuvenate and restore suppleness to old and dry leather.

Convertible A general term (post-war) for any car with a folding soft top.

Continental A car specifically designed for high-speed touring, usually on the Continent. Rolls-Royce and Bentley almost exclusively used this term during the 1930s and post-WWII.

Coupé In the early Vintage and Edwardian period, Coupé was only applied to what is now termed a Half Limousine or Doctor's Coupé, which was a two-door two-seater. The term is now usually prefixed by Drophead or Fixed-Head.

Cubic capacity The volume of an engine obtained by multiplying the area of the bore by the stroke. Engine capacity is given in cubic centimetres (cc) in Europe and cubic inches (cu.in) in the USA. 1 cubic inch equals 16.38cc (1 litre = 61.02cu.in).

de Ville A style of coachwork in which the driver/chauffeur occupies an open driving position, and the passengers a closed compartment – thus, Coupé de Ville or Sedanca de Ville. In America, these vehicles are known as Town Cars.

Dickey seat A passenger seat, usually for two people, contained in the boot of the car and without a folding hood (the boot lid forms the backrest). See **Rumble seat**.

Doctor's coupé A fixed or drophead coupé without a dickey seat, the passenger seat being slightly staggered back from the driver's to accommodate the famous doctor's bag.

Dog cart A form of horse-drawn vehicle originally designed for transporting beaters and their dogs to a shoot (the dogs were contained in louvred boxes under the seats; the louvres were kept for decoration long after the practice of carrying dogs in this way had ceased).

Dos-à-dos Literally back-to-back, i.e. the passenger seating arrangement.

Double-duck Double-layered fabric used in construction of folding convertible tops.

Drophead coupé Originally a two-door two-seater with a folding roof.

Dry sump A method of lubricating engines in which the oil is contained in a separate reservoir rather than in a sump at the bottom of the cylinder block. Usually, two oil pumps are used, one to remove oil from the engine to the reservoir, the other to pump it back to the engine.

Fender American term used to describe the wing of a car.

F-head An engine design in which the inlet valve is in the cylinder head, while the exhaust valve is in the cylinder block. Also referred to as inlet-over-exhaust.

Fixed-head coupé A coupé with a solid fixed roof.

Golfer's coupé Usually an open two-seater with a square-doored locker behind the driver's seat to accommodate golf clubs.

Hansom As with the famous horse-drawn cab, an enclosed two-seater with the driver out in the elements, either behind or in front of the passenger compartment.

Homologation To qualify for entry into some race series, the rules can require that a minimum number of road-going production versions of the race car are built. These are generally known as 'homologation specials'.

Hood American term used to describe the bonnet of a car.

Horsepower (hp) The unit of measurement of engine power – one horsepower represents the energy expended in raising 33,000lb by one foot in 60 seconds.

Landau An open town carriage for four people with a folding hood at each end, which would meet in the middle when erected.

Landaulette A horse-drawn Landaulette carried two people and was built much like a coupé. The roof line of a Landaulette is always angular, in contrast to a Cabriolet, and the folding hood is very often made of patent leather. A true Landaulette only opens over the rear compartment and not over the front seat at all. (Also Landaulet.)

L-head An engine design in which the inlet and exhaust valves are contained within the cylinder block. *See* **Sidevalve**.

Limousine French in origin and used to describe a closed car equipped with occasional seats and a division between the rear and driver's compartments.

Monobloc engine An engine with all its cylinders cast in a single block.

Monocoque A method of constructing a car without a separate chassis, structural strength being provided by the arrangement of the stressed panels. Most modern, mass-produced cars are built in this way.

Monoposto Single-seater (Italian).

Nitrided Used to describe engine components, particularly crankshafts, that have been specially hardened to withstand the stresses of racing or other high-performance applications.

OHC Overhead camshaft, either single (SOHC) or double (DOHC).

OHV Overhead valves.

Phaeton A term dating back to the days of horse-drawn vehicles and used to describe an open body, sometimes with a dickey or rumble seat for the groom at the rear. It was an owner/driver carriage and designed to be pulled by four horses. A term often misused during the Veteran period, but still in common use, particularly in the USA.

Post Vintage Thoroughbred (PVT) A British term created by the Vintage Sports Car Club (VSCC) to describe selected models made in the vintage tradition between 1931 and 1942.

Roadster A two-seater, open sporting vehicle, the hood of which is removed completely rather than being folded down, as on a drophead coupé. Early versions without side windows.

Roi des Belges A luxurious open touring car with elaborately contoured seat backs, named after King Leopold II of Belgium. The term is sometimes incorrectly used to describe general touring cars.

Rotary engine A unique form of car engine in which the cylinders, pistons and crankshaft of the normal reciprocating engine are replaced by a triangular rotor that rotates about an eccentric shaft within a special waisted chamber. One or more rotor/chamber assemblies may be used. On the whole, the engine has a third of the number of parts of a comparable reciprocating engine. The engine was designed by Dr Felix Wankel and has been used in a range of sports cars by Mazda.

RPM Engine revolutions per minute.

Rumble seat An American term for a folding seat for two passengers, used to increase the carrying capacity of a standard two-passenger car. *See* **Dickey seat**.

Runabout A low-powered, lightweight, open two-seater from the 1900s.

Saloon A two- or four-door car with four or more seats and a fixed roof.

Sedan *See* **Saloon**.

Sedanca de Ville A limousine body with an open driving compartment that can be covered with a folding or sliding roof section, known in America as a Town Car.

Side-valve Used to describe an engine in which the valves are located in the cylinder block rather than the head.

Sociable A cyclecar term used to describe the side-by-side seating of the driver and passenger.

Spider/Spyder An open two-seater sports car, sometimes a 2+2 (with two small occasional seats behind the two front seats).

Station wagon American term for an estate car.

Supercharger An engine-driven pump for forcing the fuel/air mixture into the cylinders to gain extra power.

Surrey An early 20thC open four-seater with a fringed canopy. A term from the days of horse-drawn vehicles.

Stanhope A single-seat, two-wheeled horse-drawn carriage with a hood. Later, a four-wheeled, two-seater, sometimes with an underfloor engine.

Stroke The distance an engine's piston moves up-and-down within its cylinder. The stroke is invariably measured in millimetres, although in the USA, inches may be used.

Superleggera Italian for 'super lightweight' and used to describe a method of construction devised by Touring of Milan, whereby an aluminium skin was attached to a framework of steel tubes to produce a light, yet strong, structure. One of the best-known proponents of this method was Aston Martin, which employed Superleggera construction in some of its DB series cars.

Tandem A cyclecar term used to describe the fore-and-aft seating of the driver and passenger.

Targa A coupé fitted with a removable central roof section.

Tonneau A rear-entrance tonneau is a four-seater to which access is provided through a centrally-placed rear door. A detachable tonneau meant that the rear seats could be removed to make a two-seater. Today, 'tonneau' usually refers to a waterproof cover that can be fitted over the cockpit of an open car when the roof is detached.

Torpedo An open tourer that has coachwork with an unbroken line from the bonnet to the rear of the body.

Tourer An open four- or five-seater with three or four doors, a folding hood (with or without sidescreens) and seats flush with the body sides. This body style began to appear in about 1910 and, initially, was known as a torpedo (*see above*), but by 1920, the word 'tourer' was being used instead – except in France, where 'torpedo' continued in use until the 1930s.

Turbocharger An exhaust-gas-driven pump for forcing the air/fuel mixture into the engine's cylinders to produce extra power.

Unitary construction Used to describe a vehicle without a separate chassis, structural strength being provided by the arrangement of the stressed panels. *See* **Monocoque**.

Veteran All vehicles manufactured before 31 December 1918; only cars built before 31 March 1904 are eligible for the London to Brighton Commemorative Run.

Victoria Generally an American term for a two- or four-seater with a very large folding hood. If a four-seater, the hood would only cover the rear seats. In some cases, applied to a saloon with a 'bustle' back.

Vintage Any vehicle manufactured between the end of the veteran period and 31 December 1930. *See* **Post Vintage Thoroughbred**.

Vis-à-vis Face-to-face; an open car in which the passengers sit opposite each other.

Voiturette A French term used to describe a very light car, originally coined by Léon Bollée.

Wagonette A large car for six or more passengers, in which the rear seats face each other. Entrance is at the rear, and the vehicle is usually open.

Waxoyled Used to describe a vehicle in which the underside has been treated with Waxoyl, a proprietary oil and wax spray that protects against moisture.

Weymann A system of body construction employing Rexine fabric panels over a Kapok filling to prevent noise and provide insulation.

Wheelbase The distance between the centres of the front and rear wheels of a vehicle.

Directory of Car Clubs

If you would like your Club to be included in the next edition, or have a change of address or telephone number, please inform us by 31 May 2006.

105E Anglia Owners Club, Middlesex Group, 9 Evelyn Avenue, Ruislip, Middlesex HA4 8AR

1958 Cadillac Owners Association, PO Box 850029, Braintree, Maine, U.S.A.

2CVGB Deux Chevaux Club of GB, PO Box 602, Crick, Northampton NN6 7UW

750 Motor Club Ltd, Worth Farm, Little Horsted, West Sussex TN22 5TT

A C Owners Club, P S Tyler Hopwoods House, Sewards End, Saffron Walden, Essex CB10 2LE

A40 Farina Club, Membership Secretary, 2 Ivy Cottages, Fullers Vale, Headley Down, Bordon, Hampshire GU35 8NR

ABC Owners Club, D A Hales, The Hedgerows, Sutton St Nicholas, Hereford HR1 3BU

Alexis Racing and Trials Car Register, Duncan Rabagliati, 4 Wool Road, Wimbledon, London SW20 0HW

Alfa Romeo 1900 Register, Peter Marshall, Mariners, Courtlands Avenue, Esher, Surrey KT10 9HZ

Alfa Romeo Owners Club, Michael Lindsay, 97 High Street, Linton, Cambridgeshire CB1 6JT

Alfa Romeo Section (VSCC Ltd), Allan & Angela Cherrett, Old Forge, Quarr, Nr Gillingham, Dorset SP8 5PA

Allante Owners' Association, 140 Vintage Way #456, Navato CA, U.S.A.

Allard Owners Club, Miss P Hulse, 1 Dalmeny Avenue, Tufnell Park, London N7

Alvis Owners Club, 1 Forge Cottages, Little Bayham, Lamberhurst, Kent TN3 8BB

Alvis Register Ltd, Mr J Willis, The Vinery, Wanborough Hill, Nr Guildford, Surrey GU3 2JR Tel/Fax: 01483 810308

AMC Rambler Club, 2645 Ashton Road, Cleveland Heights, Ohio 44118, U.S.A. www.amcrc.com

American Auto Club UK, 11 Wych Elm, Colchester, Essex CO2 8PR Tel: 01206 564404

American Motors Owners Association Inc., Don P. Loper, 1615 Purvis Avenue, Janesville WI 53545, U.S.A. www.amotional.com

Amilcar Salmson Register, RAF King, Apple House, Wildmoor Lane, Sherfield on Lodden, Hampshire RG27 0HA

Antique Automobile Club of America, 501 W. Governor Road, PO Box 417, Hershey PA 17033, U.S.A.

Anchorage Corvette Association, P.O. Box 211802, Anchorage, Alaska 99521, U.S.A. www.alaskacorvette.com

Armstrong Siddeley Owners Club Ltd, Peter Sheppard, 57 Berberry Close, Bournville, Birmingham, West Midlands B30 1TB

Associated Ford of the Fifties, PO Box 33063, Portland OR, U.S.A.

Association of American Car Clubs UK, PO Box 2222, Braintree, Essex CM7 9TW Tel/Fax: 01376 552478 www.motorvatinusa.org.uk

Association of British Volkswagen Clubs, Dept PC, 76 Eastfield Road, Burnham, Buckinghamshire SL1 7PF www.abvwc.org.uk

Association of Healey Owners, Roger Crouch, Slades Paddock, East Coker, Nr Yeovil, Somerset BA22 9JY

Association of Old Vehicle Clubs in Northern Ireland Ltd, Secretary Trevor Mitchell, 38 Ballymaconnell Road, Bangor, Co. Down, Northern Ireland BT20 5PS secretary@aovc.co.uk www.aovc.co.uk

Association of Singer Car Owners, Anne Page, 39 Oakfield, Rickmansworth, Hertfordshire WD3 2LR

Aston Martin Owners Club Ltd, Drayton St Leonard, Wallingford, Oxfordshire OX10 7BG Tel: 01865 400400 hqstaff@amoc.org

ATCO Car Owners Club, British Lawnmower Museum, 106-114 Shakespeare Street, Southport, Lancashire PR8 5AJ Tel: 01704 501336 atcocar@lawnmowerworld.co.uk www.lawnmowerworld.co.uk

Atlas Register, 38 Ridgeway, Southwell, Nottinghamshire NG25 0DJ

Austin 3 Litre Owners Club, 33 Westholme Road, Ipswich, Suffolk IP1 4HH n.kidby@virgin.net

Austin A30-35 Owners Club, Membership Secretary Tracey Dracup www.austin-club.com membershipsecretary@austin-club.com

Austin Atlantic Owners Club, Membership Secretary Lee Marshall, Wildwood, 21 Cornflower Close, Stamford, Lincolnshire PE9 2WL

Austin Big 7 Register, R E Taylor, 101 Derby Road, Chellaston, Derbyshire DE73 1SB

Austin Cambridge/Westminster Car Club, Arthur Swann, 21 Alexander Terrace, Corsham, Wiltshire SN13 0BW

Austin Counties Car Club, Martin Pickard, 10 George Street, Bedworth, Warwickshire CV12 8EB

Austin Eight Register, Ian Pinniger, 3 La Grange Martin, St Martin, Jersey, Channel Islands JE3 6JB

Austin Gipsy Register 1958-1968, Mike Gilbert, 24 Green Close, Rixon, Sturminster Newton, Dorset DT10 1BJ Tel: 07966605024 gipsymick@aol.com www.austingipsy.co.uk

Austin Healey Club, Colleen Holmes, REF MP, 4 Saxby Street, Leicester LE2 0ND Tel: 0116 254411 www.austin-healey-club.com

Austin J40 Pedal Car Club, Mary Rowlands, 21 Forest Close, Lickey End, Bromsgrove, Worcestershire B60 1JU

Austin Maxi Club, Mrs C J Jackson, 27 Queen Street, Bardney, Lincolnshire LN3 5XF

Austin Seven Mulliner Register, Mike Tebbett, Little Wyche, Walwyn Road, Upper Colwall, Nr Malvern, Worcestershire WR13 6PL

Austin Seven Van Register 1923-29, NB Baldry, 32 Wentworth Crescent, Maidenhead, Berkshire SL6 4RW

Austin Sheerline & Princess Club, Ian Coombes, 44 Vermeer Crescent, Shoeburyness, Essex S53 9TJ

Austin Swallow Register, GL Walker, School House, Rectory Road, Great Haseley, Oxfordshire OX44 7JP

Austin Taxi Club, A. Thomas, 52 Foss Avenue, Waddon, Croydon, Surrey CR0 4EU

Austin Ten Drivers Club Ltd, 10-28hp Austin vehicles 1931–1939, Mike Bevan, 98 Heage Road, Ripley, Derbyshire DE5 3GH Tel/Fax: 01773 749891 mike.bevan@btinternet.com www.austintendriversclub.com

Battery Vehicle Society, Keith Roberts, 29 Ambergate Drive, North Pentwyn, Cardiff, Wales CF2 7AX

Bentley Drivers Club, 16 Chearsley Road, Long Crendon, Aylesbury, Buckinghamshire HP18 9AW

Berkeley Enthusiasts Club, Phil James, 55 Main Street, Sutton Bonington, Loughborough, Leicestershire LE12 5PE

Biggin Hill Car Club with XJ Register of JDC, Peter Adams, Jasmine House, Jasmine Grove, London SE20 8JY

BMC J2/152 Register, 10 Sunnyside Cottages, Woodford, Kettering, Northamptonshire NN14 4HX

BMW Drivers Club, Sue Hicks, Bavaria House, PO Box 8, Dereham, Norfolk NR19 1TF

Bond Owners Club, Stan Cornock, 42 Beaufort Avenue, Hodge Hill, Birmingham, West Midlands B34 6AE

Borgward Drivers Club, Mr D.C. Farr, 19 Highfield Road, Kettering, Northamptonshire NN15 6HR

Brabham Register, Ed Walker, The Old Bull, 5 Woodmancote, Dursley, Gloucestershire GL11 4AF

Bristol Austin Seven Club, 1 Silsbury Hill Cottages, West Kennett, Marlborough, Wiltshire SN8 1QH

Bristol Microcar Club, 123 Queens Road, Bishopsworth, Bristol, Gloucestershire BS13 8QB

Bristol Owners Club, Kevin Jones, 27 Henry Road, Oxford OX2 0DG Tel: 01865 791466 memsec@boc.net

British Ambulance Society, Roger Leonard (General Sec), 21 Victoria Road, Horley, Surrey RH6 9BN Tel: 01293 776636 BASocHQ@aol.com www.b-a-s.org.uk

British Automobile Racing Club, Thruxton Circuit, Andover, Hampshire SP11 8PN Tel: 01264 882200 info@barc.net www.barc.net

British Columbia Corvette Club, PO Box 80508, Burnaby BC V5H 3X9, Canada www.bccorvetteclub.ca

British Hotchkiss Society, Hon Sec Michael J Edwards, Yew Cottage, Old Boars Hill, Oxford OX1 5JJ

British Saab Enthusiasts, Mr M Hodges, 75 Upper Road, Poole, Dorset BH12 3EN

British Salmson Owners Club, John Maddison, 8 Bartestree Close, Matchborough, East Redditch, Worcestershire B98 0AZ

British Saloon Car Club of Canada, 1404 Baldwin Street, Burlington, Ontario L7S 1K3, Canada

Brooklands Automobilia & Regalia Collectors' Club, Hon Sec G.G. Weiner, 4/4a Capel Terrace Mews, Chapel Terrace, Kemp Town, Brighton, East Sussex BN2 1HU Tel: 01273 601960 www.barcc.co.uk www.brooklands-automobilia-regalia-collectors-club.co.uk

Brough Superior Club, Justin Wand (Secretary), Flint Cottage, St Paul's Walden, Hitchin, Hertfordshire SG4 8ON

BSA Front Wheel Drive Club, Membership Secretary Barry Baker, 164 Cottimore Lane, Walton-on-Thames, Surrey KT12 2BL

Bugatti Owners Club Ltd, Sue Ward, Prescott Hill, Gotherington, Cheltenham, Gloucestershire GL52 9RD Tel: 01242 673136 club@bugatti.co.uk www.bugatti.co.uk/club

Buick Club of America, PO Box 360775, Columbus, Ohio 43236, U.S.A. www.buickclub.org

Buick Club UK, PO Box 2222, Braintree, Essex CM7 9TW www.buickclub.co.uk

Buick GS Club of America, 625 Pine Point Circle, Valdosta, Georgia 31602, U.S.A.

'53-'54 Buick Skylark Club, 51 Statesville Quarry Rd, Lafayette, New Jersey 07848, U.S.A.

Buick Street Rod Association, 824 Kay Cir, Chattanooga, Tennessee 37421, U.S.A. www.buickrods.org

C A Bedford Owners Club, GW Seller, 7 Grasmere Road, Benfleet, Essex SS7 3HF

California Sports Car Club, 9534 S. Painter Avenue, Whittier CA90605, U.S.A.

Camaro Firebird Car Club of Dallas/Fort Worth, P.O. Box 645, Allen, Texas 75013, U.S.A. www.cfcc-dfw.org

Cambridge-Oxford Owners Club, 32 Reservoir Road, Southgate, London N14 4BG

Cape Cod Classics, PO Box 615, South Yarmouth, Massachusetts MA02664-0615, U.S.A.

Capri Club International, 18 Arden Business Centre, Arden Road, Alcester, Warwickshire B49 6HW

Capri Club International, North London Branch, 12 Chalton Road, Edmonton, London N9 8EG

Capri Drivers Association, Mrs Moira Farrelly (Secretary), 9 Lyndhurst Road, Coulsdon, Surrey CR5 3HT

Caprock Classic Car Club, PO Box 53352, Lubbock, Texas TX 79453-5335, U.S.A.

Carolina C3 Corvettes, 1501 S. Blount St, Raleigh NC, U.S.A.

Citroen Car Club, P O Box 348, Steyning, West Sussex BN44 3XN Tel: 07000 248 258 members@citroencarclub.org.uk www.citroencarclub.org.uk

Citroen Traction Owners Club, Mr M. Holmes, 35 Mays Avenue, Nottingham NG4 1AS Tel: 0870 012 2002

Clan Owners Club, Chris Clay, 48 Valley Road, Littleover, Derbyshire DE23 6HS

The Classic Camper Club, PO Box 3, Amlwch, Anglesey LL68 9ZE

The Classic Car Club of America, Inc., 1645 Des Plaines, River Road, Suite 7A, Des Plaines IL 60018-2206, U.S.A.

Classic Chevrolet Club, PO Box 2222, Braintree, Essex CM7 9TW www.chevyclub.co.uk

Classic Hearse Register, Paul Harris, 121 St Mary's Crescent, Basildon, Essex SS13 2AS

Classic Z Register, Jon Newlyn, 11 Lawday Link, Upper Hale, Farnham, Surrey GU9 0BS

Club Alpine Renault UK Ltd, 1 Bloomfield Close, Wombourne, Wolverhampton, West Midlands WV5 8HQ

Club Lotus, Lotus Lodge, P O Box 8, Dereham, Norfolk NR19 1TF

Club Peugeot UK, Peter Vaughan, 41 Hazelwood Drive, Bourne, Lincolnshire PE10 9SZ

Club Peugeot UK, Club Regs 504 Cab/Coupe, Beacon View, Forester Road, Soberton Heath, Southampton, Hampshire SO32 3QG

Clyno Club & Register, Red Hall, 105 Shilton Road, Barwell, Leicestershire LE9 8BP

Commercial Vehicle and Road Transport Club, Steven Wimbush, 8 Tachbrook Road, Uxbridge, Middlesex UB8 2QS

Connaught Register, Duncan Rabagliati, 4 Wool Road, Wimbledon, London SW20 0HW

Contemporary Historical Vehicle Association, PO Box 98, Tecumesh, Kansas KS 66542-0098 U.S.A.

The Corvair Society of America, PO Box 607, Lemont IL 60439, U.S.A.

Corvette Club of America, P.O. Box 9879, Bowling Green, Kentucky 42102, U.S.A. www.corvetteclubofamerica.com

International Society Corvette Owners, P.O. Box 740614, Orange City, Florida 32774, U.S.A.

National Corvette Owners Association, 900S Washington St #G-13, Falls Church, Virginia 22046, U.S.A. www.ncoa-vettes.com

53-54-55 Corvette Registry, 856 Iron City Hill Rd, Belle Vernon, Pennsylvania 15012, U.S.A.

Cougar Club of America, Barrie S Dixon, 11 Dean Close, Partington, Greater Manchester M31 4BQ Tel: 0161 775 0820 membership@cougarclub.org www.cougarclub.org

Crayford Convertible Car Club, 58 Geriant Road, Downham, Bromley, Kent BR1 5DX Tel: 020 8461 1805

Crossley Register, Malcolm Jenner, Willow Cottage, Lexham Road, Great Dunham, Kings Lynn, Norfolk PE32 2LS Tel: 01328 701240

Crown Victoria Association, P.O. Box 6, Bryan, Ohio 43506, U.S.A. www.clubs.hemmings.com/crownvictoria/

DAF Owners Club, SK Bidwell (Club Sec), 56 Ridgedale Road, Bolsover, Chesterfield, Derbyshire S44 6TX

Daimler and Lanchester Owners Club, PO Box 276, Sittingbourne, Kent ME9 7GA

Datsun Owners Club, Jon Rodwell, 26 Langton Park, Wroughton, Wiltshire SN4 0QN Tel: 01793 845271

De Tomaso Drivers Club, Philip Stebbings, Founder & Club Secretary, Flint Barn, Malthouse Lane, Ashington, West Sussex RH20 3BU Tel/Fax: 01903 893870

Delage Section of the VSCC Ltd, Peter Jacobs (Secretary), Clouds' Reach, The Scop, Almondsbury, Bristol, Gloucestershire BS32 4DU

Delahaye Club GB, A F Harrison, 34 Marine Parade, Hythe, Kent CT21 6AN

Dellow Register, Douglas Temple, Design Group, 4 Roumelia Lane, Bournemouth, Dorset BH5 1EU

Delorean Owners Club, Hon Sec Mr Chris Parnham, 14 Quarndon Heights, Allestree, Derby DE22 2XN

Diva Register, Steve Pethybridge, 8 Wait End Road, Waterlooville, Hampshire PO7 7DD Tel: 023 9225 1485 pandhlr@hotmail.com

DKW Owners Club GB, David Simon, Aurelia, Garlogie, Skene, Westhill, Aberdeenshire AB32 6RX, Scotland Tel: 01224 743429

Droop Snoot Group, 41 Horsham Avenue, Finchley, London N12 9BG

Dunsfold Land Rover Collection, Dunsfold, Surrey GU8 4NP Tel: 01483 200567 www.dunsfoldcollection.co.uk

Dutton Owners Club, Rob Powell, 20 Burford Road, Baswich, Stafford ST17 0BT

Early Ford V8 Club, 12 Fairholme Gardens, Cranham, Upminster, Essex RM14 1HJ www.earlyfordV8.co.uk

Early Ford V8 Club of America, P.O. Box 2122, Livermore, California 94577, U.S.A. www.earlyfordv8.org

East Anglia Fighting Group, 206 Colchester Road, Lawford, Nr Manningtree, Essex

Elva Owners Club, 8 Liverpool Terrace, Worthing, West Sussex BN11 1TA Tel/Fax: 01903 823710 roger.dunbar@elva.com www.elva.com

Enfield & District Veteran Vehicle Trust, Whitewebbs Museum, Whitewebbs Road, Enfield, Middlesex EN2 9HW Tel: 020 8367 1898 Fax: 020 8363 1904 museum@whitewebbs.fsnet.co.uk www.whitewebbsmuseum.co.uk

ERA Club, Guy Spollon, Arden Grange, Tanworth-in-Arden, Warwickshire B94 5AE

F and FB Victor Owners Club, Wayne Parkhouse, 5 Farnell Road, Staines, Middlesex TW18 4HT

F-Victor Owners Club, Alan Victor Pope, 34 Hawkesbury Drive, Mill Lane, Calcot, Reading, Berkshire RG3 5ZR

Fabulous Fifties Ford Club of America, Inc., Phoenix, Arizona 85355, U.S.A. www.clubs.hemmings.com/fabfifty

Facel Vega Car Club, Secretary Mr M. Green, 17 Stanley Road, Lymington, Hampshire SO41 3SJ

Fairthorpe Sports Car Club, Tony Hill, 9 Lynhurst Crescent, Uxbridge, Middlesex UB10 9EF Tel: 01895 256799 www.fairthorpescc.co.uk

Fallbrook Vintage Car Club, PO Box 714, Fallbrook CA, U.S.A. Tel: 760-723-5324 www.fallbrookvintagecarclub.com

Ferrari Club of GB, Betty Mathias, 7 Swan Close, Blake Down, Kidderminster, Worcestershire DY10 3JT

Ferrari Owners Club, 35 Market Place, Snettisham, Kings Lynn, Norfolk PE31 7LR Tel: 01485 544500 ever.focuk@btinternet.com www.ferrariownersclub.co.uk

Fiat 130 Owners Club, Michael Reid, 28 Warwick Mansions, Cromwell Crescent, London SW5 9QR

Fiat 500 Club, Membership Sec Janet Westcott, 33 Lionel Avenue, Wendover, Aylesbury, Buckinghamshire HP22 6LP

Fiat Motor Club (GB), Hon. Membership Sec Mrs S. Robins, 118 Brookland Road, Langport, Somerset TA10 9TH

Fiat Osca Register, Mr M Elliott, 36 Maypole Drive, Chigwell, Essex IG7 6DE

Fiesta Club of GB, S. Church, 145 Chapel Lane, Farnborough, Hampshire GU14 9BN

Fifty's Automobile Club of America, Bill Schmoll, 1114 Furman Drive, Linwood, New Jersey NJ 08221, U.S.A.

Fire Service Preservation Group, Andrew Scott, 50 Old Slade Lane, Iver, Buckinghamshire SL0 9DR www.firespg.freeserve.co.uk

Five Hundred Owners Club Association, David Docherty, 'Oakley', 68 Upton Park, Chester CH2 1DQ

Ford 105E Owners Club, Sally Harris, 30 Gower Road, Sedgley, Dudley, West Midlands DY3 3PN

Ford Avo Owners Club, D. Hensley, 11 Sycamore Drive, Patchway, Bristol, Gloucestershire BS12 5DH

Ford Capri Enthusiasts Register, Glyn Watson, 7 Louis Avenue, Bury, Lancashire BL9 5EQ

Ford Classic and Capri Owners Club, 1 Verney Close, Covingham, Swindon, Wiltshire SN3 5EF

Ford Corsair Owners Club, Mrs E Checkley, 4 Bexley Close, Hailsham, East Sussex BN27 1NH Tel: 01323 840655

Ford Cortina Mk II and 1600E Owners' Club Limited, Dave Johnson, 16 Woodlands Close, Sarisbury Green, Southampton, Hampshire SO31 7AQ Tel: 01395 276701 davejohnson@ford-cortina-1600e-club.org.uk www.ford-cortina-1600e-club.org.uk

Ford Cortina Owners Club, Mr D. Eastwood (Chairman), 52 Woodfield, Bamber Bridge, Preston, Lancashire PR5 8ED Tel/Fax: 01772 627004

Ford Escort 1300E Owners Club, Robert Watt, 65 Lindley Road, Walton on Thames, Surrey KT12 3EZ

Ford Executive Owners Register, Maureen Long, 22 Warwick Green, Bulkington, Bedworth, Warwickshire CV12 9RA

Ford Mk II Independent O.C. International, B. & J. Enticknap, 173 Sparrow Farm Drive, Feltham, Middlesex TW14 0DG Tel: 020 8384 3559

Ford Mk IV Zephyr & Zodiac Owners Club, Richard Cordle, 29 Ruskin Drive, Worcester Park, Surrey KT4 8LG

Ford Model "T" Ford Register of GB, Mrs Julia Armer, 3 Strong Close, Keighley, Yorkshire BD21 4JT

Ford Sidevalve Owners Club, Membership Secretary, 30 Earls Close, Bishopstoke, Eastleigh, Hampshire SO50 8HY

Ford Y&C Model Register, Bob Wilkinson, 9 Brambleside, Thrapston, Northamptonshire NN14 4PY

Frazer-Nash Section of the VSCC, Mrs J Blake, Daisy Head Farm, South Street, Caulcott, Bicester, Oxfordshire OX6 3NE

Friends of The British Commercial Vehicle, c/o BCVM, King Street, Leyland, Preston, Lancashire PR5 1LE

The Gentry Register, Barbara Reynolds (General secretary), Barn Close Cottage, Cromford Road, Woodlinkin, Nottinghamshire NG16 4HD

Gilbern Owners Club, Alan Smith, Hunters Hill, Church Lane, Peppard Common, Oxon RG9 5JL

Gordon Keeble Owners Club, Ann Knott, Westminster Road, Helmdon, Brackley, Northamptonshire NN13 5QB

Great Autos of Yesteryear, PO Box 4, Yorba Linda, California CA 93666-1314, U.S.A.

Guernsey Motorcycle & Car Club, c/o Graham Rumens, Glenesk, Sandy Hook, St Sampsons, Guernsey GY2 4ER, Channel Islands

Gwynne & Albert Register, Mr I.H. Walker, 8 Baines Lane, Datchworth, Knebworth, Hertfordshire SG3 6RA Tel: 01438 812041 updraught@btinternet.com

Heinkel Trojan Owners and Enthusiasts Club, Y Luty, Carisbrooke, Wood End Lane, Fillongley, Coventry, Warwickshire CV7 8DF

Heinz 57 Register, Secretary Barry Priestman, 58 Geriant Road, Downham, Bromley, Kent BR1 5DX

Hermon Enthusiasts Club, 6 Westleton Way, Felixstowe, Suffolk IP11 8YG

Hillman, Commer & Karrier Club, A Freakes, Capri House, Walton-on-Thames, Surrey KT12 2LY

Historic Caravan Club, Secretary Barbara Bissell, 29 Linnet Close, Lodgefield Park, Halesowen, West Midlands B62 8TW Bbissechcc@aol.com www.hcclub.co.uk

Historic Commercial Vehicle Society HCVS Ltd, Michael Banfield, Iden Grange, Cranbrook Road, Staplehurst, Kent TN12 0ET Tel: 01580 892929 hcvs@btinternet.com

Historic Grand Prix Cars Association, 106 Gifford Street, London N1 0DF Tel: +44(0)20 7697 3097 Fax: +44(0)20 7609 8124 contact@hgpca.net www.hgpca.com

Historic Lotus Register, Registrar Victor Thomas, Badgers Farm, Short Green, Winfarthing, Norfolk IP22 2EE

Historic Rally Car Register RAC, Martin Jubb, 38 Longfield Road, Bristol, Gloucestershire BS7 9AG

Historic Sports Car Club, Cold Harbour, Kington Langley, Wiltshire SN15 5LY

Historic Volkswagen Club, Rod Sleigh, 28 Longnor Road, Brooklands, Telford, Shropshire TF1 3NY

Horseless Carriage Club of America, 128 S. Cypress St, Orange, California CA93666-1314, U.S.A.

HRG Association, Hon Sec Peter Mitchell, 12 First Avenue, Felpham, West Sussex PO22 7LG hrgsec@btopenworld.com

The Hudson-Essex-Terraplane Club, Inc., P.O. Box 8412, Wichita, Kansas 67208, U.S.A. www.classiccar.com/clubs/hudson

Post-Vintage Humber Car Club, Stephen Lewis, 42 Uplands Avenue, High Salvington, Worthing, West Sussex BN13 3AE Tel: 01903 694924 steve.g.lewis@ic24.net www.pvhcc.fsnet.co.uk

The Humber Register 1896 to 1932, R.N. Arman, Northbrook Cottage, 175 York Road, Broadstone, Dorset BH18 8ES Tel: 01202 695937 thearmans@tiscali.co.uk

Imp Club, Richard Sozanski (PR/Events sec), 19 Chesford Grove, Stratford-on-Avon, Warwickshire CV37 9LS Tel/Fax: 01789 298093

Invicta Military Vehicle Preservation Society, North Thames Branch, Tim Wood, 22 Victoria Avenue, Grays, Essex RM16 2RP

Isetta Owners Club, 19 Towcester Road, Old Stratford, Milton Keynes, Buckinghamshire MK19 6AH

Jaguar and Daimler Owners Club, Secretary Malcolm Pugh, 130/132 Bordesley Green, Birmingham, West Midlands B9 4SU Tel: 0121 773 1861 jaguaranddaimlerowners@blueyonder.co.uk www.stiffsteiffs.pwp.blueyonder.co.uk/jdoc.htm

Jaguar Car Club, R Pugh, 19 Eldorado Crescent, Cheltenham, Gloucestershire GL50 2PY

Jaguar Drivers Club, JDC Jaguar House, 18 Stuart Street, Luton, Bedfordshire LU1 2SL Tel: 01582 419332 jaguar-drivers-club@lineone.net www.jaguardriver.co.uk

Jaguar Enthusiasts Club, 176 Whittington Way, Pinner, Middlesex HA5 5JY

Jensen Owners' Club, Membership Secretary Keith Andrews, 2 Westgate, Fulshaw Park, Wilmslow, Cheshire SK9 1QQ

Jowett Car Club, Secretary Mary Young, 15 Second Avenue, Chelmsford, Essex CM1 4ET Tel: 01245 256944

JU 250 Register, Stuart Cooke, 34 Thorncliffe Drive, Darwen, Lancashire BB3 3QA

Junior Zagato Register, Kenfield Hall, Petham, Nr Canterbury, Kent CT4 5RN

Jupiter Owners Auto Club, Steve Keil, 16 Empress Avenue, Woodford Green, Essex IG8 9EA

K70 Register, SAE to: Mr Bood, 25 Cedar Grove, Penn Fields, Wolverhampton WV3 7EB Tel: 01902 566623

Karmann Ghia Owners Club (GB), Peter/Lynn Skinner (Membership Secretary), Rowan House, Harvington Lane, Norton, Nr Evesham, Worcestershire WR11 4TN

Kieft Racing and Sports Car Club, Duncan Rabagliati, 4 Wool Road, Wimbledon, London SW20 0HW

Lagonda Club, Colin Bugler (Hon Secretary), Wintney House, London Road, Hartley Wintney, Hook, Hampshire RG27 8RN

Land Rover Register (1947-1951), Membership Secretary, High House, Ladbrooke, Leamington Spa, Warwickshire CV33 0BT

Land Rover Series 3 Owners Club Ltd, 23 Deidre Avenue, Wickford, Essex SS12 0AX

Land Rover Series One Club, David Bowyer, East Foldhay, Zeal Monachorum, Crediton, Devon EX17 6DH

Land Rover Series Two Club Ltd, Laurence Mitchell Esq., PO Box 251, Barnsley S70 5YN

Landcrab Owners Club International Ltd, 5 Rolston Avenue, Huntington, York YO31 9JD

Lea Francis Owners Club, R Sawers, French's, High Street, Long Wittenham, Abingdon, Oxfordshire OX14 4QQ

Lincoln-Zephyr Owners Club, Colin Spong, 22 New North Road, Hainault, Ilford, Essex IG6 2XG

London Bus Preservation Trust, Cobham Bus Museum, Redhill Road, Cobham, Surrey KT11 1EF Tel: 01932 868665 www.lbpt.org

London Vintage Taxi Association, Steve Dimmock, 51 Ferndale Crescent, Cowley, Uxbridge, Middlesex UB8 2AY

Lotus Cortina Register, Andy Morrell, 64 The Queens Drive, Chorleywood, Rickmansworth, Hertfordshire WD3 2LT Tel: 01923 776219

Lotus Drivers Club, Lee Barton, 15 Pleasant Way, Leamington Spa, Warwickshire CV32 5XA

Lotus Seven Club, PO Box 777, Haywards Heath RH16 2YA

Manta A Series Register, Mark Kinnon, 112 Northwood Avenue, Purley, Surrey CR8 2EQ mail@mantaclub.org www.mantaclub.org

Marcos Owners Club, 62 Culverley Road, Catford, London SE6 2LA

Marendaz Special Car Register, John Shaw, 107 Old Bath Road, Cheltenham, Gloucestershire GL53 7DA

Marina/Ital Drivers' Club, Mr J G Lawson, 12 Nithsdale Road, Liverpool L15 5AX

Maserati Club, Michael Miles, The Paddock, Old Salisbury Road, Abbotts Ann, Andover, Hampshire SP11 7NT

Masters Club, Barry Knight, 2 Ranmore Avenue, East Croydon, Surrey CR0 5QA

Matra Enthusiasts Club (MEC), 19 Abbotsbury, Orton Goldhay, Peterborough, Cambridgeshire PE2 5PS

The Mechanical Horse Club, The Secretary, 2 The Poplars, Horsham, East Sussex RH13 5RH

Mercedes-Benz Owners Association, Upper Birchetts House, Langton Road, Langton Green, Tunbridge Wells, Kent TN3 0EG

Mercedes-Benz Owners Club, Northern Ireland Area, Trevor Mitchell, 38 Ballymaconell Road, Bangor, Co. Down, Northern Ireland BT20 5PS

Messerschmitt Owners Club, Mrs Eileen Hallam, Birches, Ashmores Lane, Rusper, West Sussex RH12 4PS

Metropolitan Owners Club, Tinkers Green, Nutbourne Common, Pulborough, West Sussex RH20 2HB Tel/Fax: 01798 813713 metclubuk@aol.com

MG Car Club Ltd, Kimber House, PO Box 251, Abingdon, Oxon OX14 IFF

MG Owners Club, Octagon House, Swavesey, Cambridgeshire CB4 5QZ

MG 'Y' Type Register, Mr J G Lawson, 12 Nithsdale Road, Liverpool L15 5AX

Midas Owners Club, c/o Steve Evans, No 8 Mill Road, Holyhead, Anglesey LL65 2TA

Midget & Sprite Club, Nigel Williams, 15 Foxcote, Kingswood, Bristol, Gloucestershire BS15 2TX

Military Vehicle Trust, PO Box 6, Fleet, Hampshire GU52 6GE

The Mini Cooper Club, Mary Fowler, 59 Giraud Street, Poplar, London E14 6EE Tel: 020 7515 7173 info@minicooperclub.org.uk www.minicooperclub.com

Mini Cooper Register, General Secretary Cliff Porter, PO Box 1275, Farnham, Surrey GU10 4XD Tel/Fax: 0208 925 4086 secretary@minicooper.org

Mini Marcos Owners Club, Roger Garland, 28 Meadow Road, Claines, Worcester WR3 7PP Tel: 01905 458533 rog@minimarcos.plus.com

Mini Moke Club, Paul Beard, 13 Ashdene Close, Hartlebury, Herefordshire DY11 7TN

Mini Owners Club, 15 Birchwood Road, Lichfield, Staffordshire WS14 9UN

Mini Seven Racing Club, Mick Jackson, 345 Clay Lane, S. Yardley, Birmingham, West Midlands B26 1ES

MK I Consul, Zephyr and Zodiac Club, 180 Gypsy Road, Welling, Kent DA16 1JQ

Mk I Cortina Owners Club, A. Raymond, 35 Wilton Drive, Trowbridge, Wiltshire BA14 0PU Fax: 01225 350096

Mk II Consul, Zephyr and Zodiac Club, Del Rawlins, Bryn Gwyn Farm, Carmel, Cearnafon, Gwynedd LL54 7AP

The Mk II Cortina Owners Club Limited trading as The Ford Cortina Mk II Owners Club, Company Secretary Mrs K. Sirett, 12 Le Brun Square, Carlton in Lindrick, Worksop, Nottinghamshire S81 9LW

Mk II Granada Owners Club, Paul Farrer, 58 Jevington Way, Lee, London SE12 9NQ

Model A Ford Club of Great Britain, Mr S. J. Shepherd, 32 Portland Street, Clifton, Bristol, Gloucestershire BS8 4JB

Morgan +4 Club, c/o 11423 Gradwell, Lakewood CA, U.S.A.

Morgan Sports Car Club Limited, 'The Mogs', 7 Woodland Grove, Gornal Wood, Dudley, West Midlands DY3 2XB Tel: +44(0)1384 254480 Fax: +44(0)1384 254474 membership@mscc.uk.com

Morgan Three-Wheeler Club Ltd, Secretary Dennis Plater, Holbrooks, Thoby Lane, Mountnessing, Brentwood, Essex CM15 0TA Tel: 01277 352867 www.mtwc.co.uk

Morris 12 Club, D Hedge Crossways, Potton Road, Hilton, Huntingdon, Cambridgeshire PE18 9NG

Morris Cowley and Oxford Club, Derek Andrews, 202 Chantry Gardens, Southwick, Trowbridge, Wiltshire BA14 9QX Tel: 01225 766800

Morris Marina Owners Club, Nigel Butler, Llys-Aled, 63 Junction Road, Stourbridge, West Midlands DY8 4YJ

Morris Minor Owners Club, Jane White, 127-129 Green Lane, Derby DE1 1RZ

Morris Minor Owners Club, N. Ireland Branch, Secretary Mrs Joanne Jeffery, 116 Oakdale, Ballygowan, Newtownards, Co. Down, Northern Ireland BT23 5TT

Morris Register, Roger Bird, PO Box 47, Woking, Surrey GU22 8WE Tel: 0845 458 2545 secretary@morrisregister.co.uk www.morrisregister.co.uk

Moss Owners Club, David Pegler, Pinewood, Weston Lane, Bath, Somerset BA1 4AG

Motorvatin' USA American Car Club, T. Lynn, PO Box 2222, Braintree, Essex CM7 6TW www.motorvatinusa.org.uk

Mustang Club of America, 3588 Highway 138, PMB 365, Stockbridge GA 30281, U.S.A.

Mustang Club of Argentina, Defensa1215 - Haedo, Buenos Aires 1706, Argentina www.mustang-club.com.ar

Naylor Car Club, Mrs F. R. Taylor (Registrar), 21 Anglesey Place, Great Barton, Bury St Edmunds, Suffolk IP31 2TW Tel: 01284 787539 freda.naylorcarclub@btinternet.com www.naylorcarclub.org.uk

Nobel Register, Mike Ayriss, 29 Oak Drive, Syston, Leicester LE7 2PX Tel Home: 0116 2608221 Work: 0116 2601749 michael.ayriss@virgin.net

Norfolk Military Vehicle Group, Fakenham Road, Stanhoe, King's Lynn, Norfolk PE31 8PX Tel: 01485 518052

North East Club for Pre War Austins, Hon Sec John Ashbridge, 6 College View, Monkwray, Whitehaven, Cumbria CA28 9PH Tel: 01946 67640 john@johnandcarolyn.freeserve.co.uk www.necpwa.demon.co.uk

North Thames Military Vehicle Preservation Society, 22 Victoria Avenue, Grays, Essex RM16 2RP

Northern California Corvette Association, 119 Marlow Drive, Oakland CA, U.S.A.

Nova Owners Club, Ray Nicholls, 19 Bute Avenue, Hathershaw, Oldham, Lancashire OL8 2AQ

NSU Owners Club, Nutleigh, Rabies Heath Road, Bletchingley, Surrey RH1 4LX Tel: (00 44) 01883 744431 Fax: (00 44) 01883 742437 nsuoc@btinternet.com

Old Bean Society, PP Cole, 165 Denbigh Drive, Hately Heath, West Bromwich, West Midlands B71 2SP

Opel GT UK Owners Club, Dean Hayes, 11 Thrale Way, Parkwood, Rainham, Kent ME8 9LX

Opel Vauxhall Drivers Club, The Old Mill, Dereham, Norfolk NR20 5RT

Packards of Oregon, P.O. Box 42127, Portland, Oregon 97242, U.S.A.

Panhard et Levassor Club GB, Martin McLarence, 18 Dovedale Road, Offerton, Stockport, Cheshire SK2 5DY

Panther Enthusiasts Club UK, George Newell (Secretary), 91 Fleet Road, Cove, Farnborough, Hampshire GU14 9RE george@pantherclub.co.uk www.pantherclub.co.uk

Pedal Car Collectors' Club (P.C.C.C.), Secretary A. P. Gayler, 4/4a Chapel Terrace Mews, Kemp Town, Brighton, East Sussex BN2 1HU Tel/Fax: 01273 601960 www.brmmbrmm.com/pedalcars

Piper (Sports and Racing Car) Club, Clive Davies, Pipers Oak, Lopham Rd, East Harling, Norfolk NR16 2PE

Porsche Club Great Britain, Robin Walker, c/o Cornbury House, Cotswold Business Village, London Road, Moreton-in-Marsh, Gloucestershire GL56 0JQ

Post Office Vehicle Club, John Targett, 3 Tallowood, Lower Charlton, Shepton Mallett, Somerset BA4 5QN Tel: 01749 345494

Post War Thoroughbred Car Club, 87 London Street, Chertsey, Surrey KT16 8AN

Potteries Vintage and Classic Car Club, B Theobald, 78 Reeves Avenue, Cross Heath, Newcastle ST5 9LA

Pre 1940 Triumph Owners Club, Jon Quiney, 2 Duncroft Close, Reigate, Surrey RH2 9DE

Pre 67 Ford Owners Club, Alastair Cuninghame, 13 Drum Brae Gardens, Edinburgh EH12 8SY, Scotland

Pre-50 American Auto Club, Alan Murphy,
41 Eastham Rake, Wirral, Merseyside L62 9AN

Pre-War Austin Seven Club Ltd, Stephen Jones, 1 The Fold,
Doncaster Road, Whitley, Nr Goole, Yorkshire DN14 0HZ

Quad Cities Antique Ford Club, 1314 LeClaire St, Davenport,
Iowa 52803, U.S.A. www.clubs/hemmings.com/qcafc

Railton Owners Club, Barrie McKenzie, Fairmiles,
Barnes Hall Road, Burncross, Sheffied, Yorkshire S35 1RF

Range Rover Register, Chris Tomley, Cwm/Cochen,
Bettws, Newtown, Powys SY16 3LQ, Wales

The Rapier Register, DCH Williams, Smithy, Tregynon,
Newtown, Powys SY16 3EH, Wales

Rear Engine Renault Club, R Woodall, 346 Crewe Road,
Cresty, Crewe, Cheshire CW2 5AD

Register of Unusual Micro-Cars, Jean Hammond, School
House Farm, Hawkenbury, Staplehurst, Kent TN12 0EB

Reliant Kitten Register, Brian Marshall,
16 Glendee Gardens, Renfrew PA4 0AL

Reliant Owners Club, National Secretary Ian Gibson,
57 Church Road, Newton Abbot, Devon TQ12 1AN
Tel: 01626 201491

Reliant Sabre and Scimitar Owner's Club Ltd, P.O. Box 67,
Teddington, Middlesex TW11 8QR Tel: 0208 977 6625
rssoc@btconnect.com wwwscimitarweb.com

Renault Freres Club, Secretary Mrs Pam Mills,
54 High Street, Durrington, Salisbury, Wiltshire SP4 8AQ

Renault Owners Club, J. Henderson, 24 Long Meadow,
Mansfield Woodhouse, Mansfield, Nottinghamshire NG19 9QW

Riley MC Ltd, J. Hall, Treelands, 127 Penn Road,
Wolverhampton WV3 0DU

The Riley Register, Pre-1940 Cars, J A Clarke,
56 Cheltenham Road, Bishops Cleeve, Cheltenham,
Gloucestershire GL52 8LY

Riley RM Club, Mrs J. Morris, Y Fachell, Ruthin Road,
Gwernymynydd CH7 5LQ, North Wales

Riviera Owners Association, P.O. Box 27412, Ralston,
Nebraska 68127, U.S.A. www.rivowners.org

Ro80 Club GB, Mr Alec Coutts, 46 Molivers Lane,
Bromham, Bedfordshire MK43 8LD

Rochdale Owners Club, Alaric Spendlove, 24 North Street,
Ashburton, Devon TQ13 7QH Tel: 01364 654419

Rolls-Royce Enthusiasts' Club, Peter Baines,
The Hunt House, Paulerspury, Northamptonshire NN12 7NA
Tel: 01327 811788 admin@rrec.org.uk www.rrec.co.uk

Ronart Drivers Club, Simon Sutton (Membership
Secretary), Orchard Cottage, Allan Lane, Fritchley,
Belper, Derbyshire DE56 2FX

Rover P4 Drivers Guild, Colin Blowers, 32 Arundel Road,
Luton, Bedfordshire LU4 8DY Tel: 01582 572499
www.roverp4.com

Rover P5 Owners Club, Geoff Moorshead, 13 Glen Avenue,
Ashford, Middlesex TW15 2JE Tel/Fax: 01784 258166

Rover P6 Owners Club, M Jones, 48 Upper Aughton
Road, Birkdale, Southport PR8 5NH

Rover Sports Register, Cliff Evans, 8 Hilary Close,
Great Boughton, Chester CH3 5QP

Royal Automobile Club, PO Box 700, Bristol,
Gloucestershire BS99 1RB

Saab Owners Club of GB Ltd, Membership Secretary
J Chamberlin, PO Box 250, Carlisle CA2 7YB

Scimitar Drivers Club International, Steve Lloyd,
45 Kingshill Park, Dursley, Gloucestershire GL11 4DG

Scootacar Register, Stephen Boyd, Pamanste,
18 Holman Close, Aylsham, Norwich, Norfolk NR11 6DD
Tel: 01263 733861 scootacar@btinternet.com
www.scootacar.org

Simca Owners Register, David Chapman,
18 Cavendish Gardens, Redhill, Surrey RH1 4AQ

Singer Owners Club, Secretary Martyn Wray, 11 Ermine Rise,
Great Casterton, Stamford, Lincolnshire PE9 4AJ
Tel: 01780 762740 martyn@singeroc.free-online.co.uk
www.singerownersclub.co.uk

Small Ford Club, 115 Woodland Gardens, Isleworth,
Middlesex TW7 6LU

Solent Austin Seven Club Ltd, F Claxton,
185 Warsash Road, Warsash, Hampshire SO31 9JE

South Devon Commercial Vehicle Club, Bob Gale,
Avonwick Station, Diptford, Totnes, Devon TQ9 7LU

South Hants Model Auto Club, C Derbyshire, 21 Aintree
Road, Calmore, Southampton, Hampshire SO40 2TL

South Wales Austin Seven Club, Mr H Morgan,
'Glynteg', 90 Ammanford Road, Llandybie, Ammanford
SA18 2JY, Wales

Spartan Owners Club, Steve Andrews, 28 Ashford Drive,
Ravenhead, Nottinghamshire NG15 9DE

Split Screen Van Club, Mike & Sue Mundy, The Homestead,
Valebridge Road, Burgess Hill, West Sussex RH15 0RT

Sporting Escort Owners Club, 26 Huntingdon Crescent,
Off Madresfield Drive, Halesowen, West Midlands B63 3DJ

Stag Owners Club, c/o The Old Rectory, Aslacton,
Norfolk NR15 2JN Tel: 01379 677362 www.stag.org.uk

Standard Motor Club, Tony Pingriff (Membership Secretary),
57 Main Road, Meriden, Coventry, West Midlands CV7 0LP

Star, Starling, Stuart and Briton Register, D E A Evans,
New Wood Lodge, 2A Hyperion Rd, Stourton, Stourbridge,
West Midlands DY7 6SB Tel: 01384 374329
www.localhistory.scit.wlv.ac.uk/museum/transport/cars/starr
egister/starreg00

Steel City Thunderbird Club, 129 Palm Drive, Alabaster,
Alabama 35007, U.S.A. www.geocities.com/steelcitytbirds

Sunbeam Alpine Owners Club, Pauline Leese,
53 Wood Street, Mow Cop, Stoke-on-Trent ST7 3PF

Sunbeam Rapier Owners Club, Ruth Kingston, Wayside,
Depmore Lane, Kingsley, Nr Warrington, Cheshire WA6 6UD

Sunbeam Talbot Alpine Register, Memebership
Secretary Derek Cook, 47 Crescent Wood Road,
Sydenham, London SE26 6SA

Sunbeam Talbot Darracq Register, R Lawson,
West Emlett Cottage, Black Dog, Crediton, Devon EX17 4QB

Sunbeam Tiger Owners Club, Brian Postle, Beechwood,
8 Villa Real Estate, Consett, Co Durham DH8 6BJ

The Swift Club, Hon Secretary Graham Birchmore,
7 Tamworth Road, Bedford MK41 8QU

Tame Valley Vintage and Classic Car Club Limited,
Mrs S Ogden, 13 Valley New Road, Royton, Oldham,
Lancashire OL2 6BP tvvccc.co.uk

Tornado Register, Dave Malins, 31 Blandford Avenue,
Luton, Bedfordshire LU2 7AY Tel: 01582 495351
TornadoRegistrar@aol.com
www.astruc.s.easynet.co.uk/tornado_register

Toyota Enthusiasts Club, c/o Secretary/Treasurer
Billy Wells, 28 Park Road, Feltham, Middlesex TW13 6PW

TR Drivers Club, Bryan Harber, 19 Irene Road,
Orpington, Kent BR6 0HA

TR Register, 1B Hawksworth, Southmead Industrial Estate,
Didcot, Oxon OX11 7HR

Trident Car Club, David Rowlinson, 23 Matlock Crescent,
Cheam, Sutton, Surrey SM3 9SS Tel: 020 8644 9029
www.tridentcarclub.fsnet.co.uk

Triumph 2000/2500/2.5 Register, Carole Hathaway,
70 Green Road, Headington, Oxford OX3 8LA
Tel: 01865 750778 Fax: 01865 744938
carole.hathaway@tesco.net www.t2000register.co.uk

Club Triumph, John & Bridget Snook, 2 Brook Way, Christchurch, Dorset BH23 4HA Tel/Fax: 01425 274193 enquiries@club.triumph.org.uk www.club.triumph.org.uk

Club Triumph Eastern, Andrew Fisher (Advertising Officer), 39 Maltings Road, Great Baddow, Chelmsford, Essex CM2 8HQ www.club.triumph.org.uk

Triumph Dolomite Club, 39 Mill Lane, Upper Arncott, Bicester, Oxfordshire OX6 0PB

Triumph Mayflower Club, John Oaker, 19 Broadway North, Walsall, West Midlands WS1 2QG

Triumph Razoredge Owners Club, Stewart Langton, 62 Seaward Avenue, Barton-on-Sea, Hampshire BH25 7HP

Triumph Roadster Club, G. Windibank, 'Gwynyol', Chyvogue Meadow, Perranwell Station, Truro, Cornwall TR3 7JP

Triumph Spitfire Club, Mr Cor Gent, Anemoon 41, 7483 AC Haaksbergen, The Netherlands

Triumph Sporting Owners Club, G R King, 16 Windsor Road, Hazel Grove, Stockport, Cheshire SK7 4SW

Detroit Triumph Sportscar Cub, 39148 Boston, Sterling Heights, Michigan 48313, U.S.A. www.detroittriumph.org

Triumph Stag Register, M. Wattam, 18 Hazel Close, Highcliffe, Dorset BH23 4PS

Trojan Owners Club, President Derrick Graham, Troylands, St Johns, Earlswood Common, Redhill, Surrey RH1 6QF Troylands@aol.com.uk

Turner Register, Russell Filby, 5 Claremont Gardens, Nailsea, Bristol, North Somerset BS48 2HY Tel: 01275 791569 turnersportscars@blueyonder.co.uk www.turnersportscars.com

TVR Car Club, c/o David Gerald, TVR Sports Cars, The Green, Inkberrow, Worcester WR7 4JF

United States Army Vehicle Club, Dave Boocock, 31 Valley View Close, Bogthorn, Oakworth Rd, Keighley, Yorkshire BD22 7LZ

United States Army Vehicle Club, Simon Johnson, 7 Carter Fold, Mellor, Lancashire BB2 7ER

Unloved Soviet Socialist Register, Julian Nowill, Earlsland House, Bradninch, Exeter, Devon EX5 4QP

Vanden Plas Owners Club, Hon Sec Mrs M Hill, 33 Rectory Lane, Houghton Conquest, Bedfordshire MK45 3LD

Vanguard 1&2 Owners Club, R Jones, The Villa, The Down, Alviston BS12 2TQ

Vauxhall Convertible Car Club, Mr P. Scrivener, 124 North Cray Road, Bexley, Kent DA5 3NA

Vauxhall Owners Club 1903–1957, Roy Childers (Membership Secretary), 31 Greenbanks, Melbourn, Nr Royston, Cambridgeshire SG8 6AS

Vauxhall PA/PB/PC/E Owners Club, G Lonsdale, 77 Pilling Lane, Preesall, Lancashire FY6 0HB

Vauxhall Viva OC, Adrian Miller, The Thatches, Snetterton North End, Snetterton, Norwich, Norfolk NR16 2LD

Vauxhall VX4/90 Drivers Club(FD/FE 1972-1978), c/o 1 Milverton Drive, Uttoxeter, Staffordshire ST14 7RE

Vectis Historic Vehicle Club, Nigel Offer, 10 Paddock Drive, Bembridge, Isle of Wight PO35 5TL

Ventura County Chevys, PO Box 309, Camarillo CA 93011, U.S.A.

Veteran Car Club Of Great Britain, Jessamine Court, 15 High Street, Ashwell, Baldock, Hertfordshire SG7 5NL

Vintage Austin Register, Hon Sec Frank Smith, The Briars, Four Lane Ends, Oakerthorpe, Alfreton, Derbyshire DE55 7LH

Vintage Sports-Car Club Ltd, The Secretary, The Old Post Office, West Street, Chipping Norton, Oxon OX7 5EL Tel: 01608 644777 info@vscc.co.uk www.vscc.co.uk

Volkswagen '50-67' Transporter Club, Peter Nicholson, 11 Lowton Road, Lytham St Annes, Lancashire FY8 3JD

Volkswagen Cabriolet Owners Club (GB), Mr I. Alcock, 12 Overlea Avenue, De Ganwy, Gwynedd LL31 9TH, N Wales

Volkswagen Owners Club (GB), PO Box 7, Burntwood, Walsall, West Midlands WS7 2SB

Volvo Enthusiasts Club, Kevin Price, 4 Goonbell, St Agnes, Cornwall TR5 0PH

Vulcan Register, D Hales, The Hedgerows, Sutton St Nicholas, Herefordshire HR1 3BU

VW Type 3 and 4 Club, Jane Terry, Pear Tree Bungalow, Exted, Elham, Canterbury, Kent CT4 6YG

Wartburg Owners Club, Bernard Trevena, 55 Spiceall Estate, Compton, Guildford, Surrey GU3 1

West Coast Classics, 4606 N.E. 112th Ave, Vancouver WA, U.S.A.

Wolseley 6/80 and Morris Oxford MO Club, Dave Robinson, 6 Kings Drive, Wigston, Leicestershire LE8 1AG Tel: 0116 212 9972 davro49smo@ntlworld.com

Wolseley Hornet Special Club 1930-1935 Wolseley Hornet, Sports & Specials, Chris Hyde, Lyme Cottage, 5 Orchard Lane, Winterborne Kingston, Dorset DT11 9BF whsc.sec@btinternet.com www.whsc.co.uk

Wolseley Register, M. Stanley (Chairman), 1 Flashgate, Higher Ramsgreave Road, Ramsgreave, Nr Blackburn, Lancashire BB1 9DH

XR Owners Club, PO Box 47, Loughborough, Leicestershire LE11 1XS

Yankee Jeep Club, 8 Chew Brook Drive, Greenfield, Saddleworth, Lancashire OL3 7PD

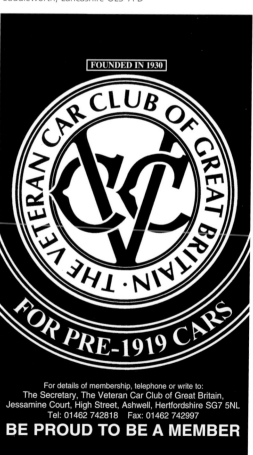

Directory of Auctioneers

Auction Team Koln, Postfach 50 11 19, 50971 Koln, Germany Tel: 00 49 0221 38 70 49 auction@breker.com

Barons (Auctioneers) Ltd, Quayside House, 23 St. Johns Street, Hythe, Southampton, Hampshire SO45 6BZ Tel: 023 8084 0081/8084 7164 info@barons-auctions.com www.barons-auctions.com

Barrett-Jackson Auction Company, LLC., 3020 N Scottsdale Road, Scottsdale, Arizona, U.S.A. Tel: 480-421-6694 www.barrett-jackson.com

Bonhams, London Tel: 020 7629 6602 www.bonhams.com

Bonhams & Butterfields, 220 San Bruno Avenue, San Francisco, CA 94103, U.S.A. Tel: 415 861 7500

Brightwells Fine Art, The Fine Art Saleroom, Easters Court, Leominster, Herefordshire HR6 0DE Tel: 01568 611122 fineart@brightwells.com www.brightwells.com

British Car Auctions Ltd, Classic & Historic Automobile Division, Auction Centre, Blackbushe Airport, Blackwater, Camberley, Surrey GU17 9LG Tel: 01252 878555

Mervyn Carey, Twysden Cottage, Scullsgate, Benenden, Cranbrook, Kent TN17 4LD Tel: 01580 240283

Central Motor Auctions Plc, Central House, Pontefract Road, Rothwell, Leeds, Yorkshire LS26 0JE Tel: 0113 282 0707

Cheffins, 8 Hill Street, Saffron Walden, Essex CB10 1JD Tel: 01799 513131 vintage@cheffins.co.uk www.cheffins.co.uk

Christie's, 8 King Street, St James's, London SW1Y 6QT Tel: 020 839 9060 www.christies.com

Classic Automobile Auctions B.V., Goethestrasse 10, 6000 Frankfurt 1, Germany Tel: 010 49 69 28666/8

Coys of Kensington, 2/4 Queens Gate Mews, London SW7 5QJ Tel: 020 7584 7444

DDM Auction Rooms, Old Courts Road, Brigg, Lincolnshire DN20 8JD Tel: 01652 650172 www.ddmauctionrooms.co.uk

Doyle New York, 175 East 87th Street, New York 10128, U.S.A. Tel: 212 427 2730 info@doylenewyork.com www.doylenewyork.com

Evans & Partridge, Agriculture House, High Street, Stockbridge, Hampshire SO20 6HF Tel: 01264 810702

Thomas Wm Gaze & Son, Diss Auction Rooms, Roydon Road, Diss, Norfolk IP22 4LN Tel: 01379 650306 sales@dissauctionrooms.co.uk www.twgaze.com

Goodmans in association with Bonhams, 7 Anderson Street, Double Bay, Sydney NSW 2028, Australia Tel: +61 (0) 9327 7311 info@goodmans.com.au

Gorringes Inc Julian Dawson, 56 High Street, Lewes, East Sussex BN7 2PD Tel: 01273 478221 www.gorringes.co.uk

Greens (UK) Ltd, Worcestershire Tel: 01684 575902

H & H Classic Auctions Ltd, Whitegate Farm, Hatton Lane, Hatton, Warrington, Cheshire WA4 4BZ Tel: 01925 730630 www.classic-auctions.co.uk

Andrew Hartley, Victoria Hall Salerooms, Little Lane, Ilkley, Yorkshire LS29 8EA Tel: 01943 816363 info@andrewhartleyfinearts.co.uk www.andrewhartleyfinearts.co.uk

Kidson Trigg, Estate Office, Friars Farm, Sevenhampton, Highworth, Swindon, Wiltshire SN6 7PZ Tel: 01793 861000

Kruse International, PO Box 190, 5400 County Road 11A, Auburn, Indiana 46706, U.S.A. Tel: 219 925 5600

Lambert & Foster, 77 Commercial Road, Paddock Wood, Kent TN12 6DR Tel: 01892 832325

Lawrences Auctioneers Limited, Norfolk House, 80 High Street, Bletchingley, Surrey RH1 4PA Tel: 01883 743323 www.lawrencesbletchingley.co.uk

Thomas Mawer & Son, Dunston House, Portland Street, Lincoln LN5 7NN Tel: 01522 524984 mawer.thos@lineone.net

Paul McInnis Inc Auction Gallery, Route 88, 356 Exeter Road, Hampton Falls, New Hampshire, U.S.A. Tel: 603 778 8989

Mealy's, Chatsworth Street, Castle Comer, Co Kilkenny, Republic of Ireland Tel: 00 353 564 441 229 www.mealys.com

Mecum Collector Car Auctioneers, P.O. Box 422, Marengo, Illinois 60152-0422, U.S.A. Tel: 815 568 8888 www.mecumauction.com

Morphets of Harrogate, 6 Albert Street, Harrogate, Yorkshire HG1 1JL Tel: 01423 530030

Neales, 192 Mansfield Road, Nottingham NG1 3HU Tel: 0115 962 4141 fineart@neales-auctions.com www.neales-auctions.com

John Nicholson, The Auction Rooms, Longfield, Midhurst Road, Fernhurst, Surrey GU27 3HA Tel: 01428 653727

Onslow's Auctions Ltd, The Coach House, Manor Road, Stourpaine, Dorset DT8 8TQ Tel: 01258 488838

Palm Springs Auction Inc., DBA Palm Springs Exotic Car Auctions, 244 N. Indian Canyon Drive, Palm Springs, California 92262, USA Tel: 760 320 3290 www.classic-carauction.com

Palmer Snell, 65 Cheap Street, Sherborne, Dorset DT9 3BA Tel: 01935 812218

J.R. Parkinson Son & Hamer Auctions, The Auction Rooms, Rochdale Road (Kershaw Street), Bury, Lancashire BL9 7HH Tel: 0161 761 1612/761 7372

RM Auctions, Inc., 9300 Wilshire Boulevard, Suite 550, Beverley Hills CA 90212, U.S.A. Tel: 310 246 9880 www.rmauctions.com

R M Classic Cars, One Classic Car Drive, Ontario NOP 1AO, Canada Tel: 519 352 4575 www.rmclassiccars.com

Rogers Jones & Co, The Saleroom, 33 Abergele Road, Colwyn Bay, Wales LL29 7RU Tel: 01492 532176 www.rogersjones.co.uk

RTS Auctions Ltd, Unit 1 Alston Road, Hellesden Park Industrial Estate, Norwich, Norfolk NR6 5OS Tel: 01603 418200

Silver Collector Car Auctions, E204 Spokane, Washington 99207, U.S.A. Tel: 509 326 4485

Sotheby's, 34-35 New Bond Street, London W1A 2AA Tel: 020 7293 5000 www.sothebys.com

Sotheby's, 1334 York Avenue at 72nd St, New York 10021, U.S.A. Tel: 212 606 7000 www.sothebys.com

Spectrum Auction Company, California, U.S.A Tel: 818 999 0832 www.spectrumauctions.com

Tennants, 34 Montpellier Parade, Harrogate, Yorkshire HG1 2TG Tel: 01423 531661 enquiry@tennants-ltd.co.uk www.tennants.co.uk

'The Auction', 3535 Las Vegas Boulevard, South Las Vegas, Nevada 89101, U.S.A. Tel: 702 794 3174

Thimbleby & Shorland, 31 Great Knollys Street, Reading, Berkshire RG1 7HU Tel: 0118 9508611

Wealden Auction Galleries, Desmond Judd, 23 Hendly Drive, Cranbrook, Kent TN17 3DY Tel: 01580 714522

Wellers Auctioneers, 70/70a Guildford Street, Chertsey, Surrey KT16 9BB Tel: 01932 568678

World Classic Auction & Exposition Co, 3600 Blackhawk Plaza Circle, Danville, California 94506, U.S.A.

Directory of Museums

BEDFORDSHIRE
Shuttleworth Collection,
Old Warden Park, Biggleswade SG18 9EA
Tel: 01767 627288 enquiries@shuttleworth.org
www.shuttleworth.org
A collection of vintage aircraft plus cars, motorcycles and horsedrawn carriages from c1880 to 1945. Open daily except Christmas to New Year week, April to Oct 10am–5pm, Nov to March 10am–4pm.

Stondon Transport Museum,
Station Road, Lower Stondon, Henlow SG16 6JN
Tel: 01462 850339 info@transportmuseum.co.uk
www.transportmuseum.co.uk
Large private collection with over 400 exhibits, covering 100 years of motoring. Open daily 10am–5pm.

CHESHIRE
Mouldsworth Motor Museum,
Smithy Lane, Mouldsworth CW3 8AR Tel: 01928 731781
Collection of over 60 vintage, classic and sport cars, motorcycles and early bicycles housed in 1930s Art Deco building. Open Sundays Noon–5pm and Bank Holiday weekends, also Weds July and August.

CORNWALL
Automobilia Motor Museum,
The Old Mill, St Stephen, St Austell PL26 7RX
Tel: 01726 823092 www.3m.co.uk/automobilia
Over 50 vehicles and associated automobilia. Autojumble and vintage and classic vehicles purchased and for sale. Open daily April, May and October 10am–4pm, closed Sats early and late season, June to September 10am–6pm.

CUMBRIA
Cars of the Stars Motor Museum,
Standish Street, Keswick CA12 5LS Tel: 017687 73757
cotsmm@aol.com www.carsofthestars.com
World famous museum of vehicles from film and television. Open Feb half term for 2 weeks 7 days 10am–5pm, 1 week prior to Easter until Dec 7 days 10am–5pm, Dec until Christmas weekends only 10am–5pm.

Lakeland Motor Museum,
Holker Hall, Cark-in-Cartmel, Grange-over-Sands LA11 7PL
Tel: 015395 58509 www.lakelandmotormuseum.co.uk
Extensive collection of cars, motorcycles, tractors, cycles, pedal cars and engines plus rare motoring automobilia. Also the Campbell Legend Bluebird Exhibition featuring videos, photographs and scale models of the cars and boats used by Sir Malcolm Campbell and his son Donald Campbell. Open daily 1st March 10.30am–4.45pm.

Western Lakes Motor Museum,
The Maltings, Brewery Lane, Cockermouth Tel: 01900 824448
Located in Jennings Castle Brewery beneath the walls of Cockermouth Castle. Some 45 cars and 17 motorcycles from Vintage to Formula 3.

DERBYSHIRE
The Donington Grand Prix Collection,
Donington Park, Castle Donington DE74 2RP
Tel: 01332 811027 enquiries@doningtoncollection.co.uk
www.doningtoncollection.com
World's largest collection of Grand Prix racing cars, tracing their history from the early 1900s to the present day. Open daily 10am–5pm except during Christmas period.

GLOUCESTERSHIRE
Bristol Industrial Museum,
Princes Wharf, Wapping Road, Bristol BS1 4RN
Tel: 0117 925 1470
www.bristol-city.gov.uk/museums
A collection of land transport with a particular Bristol twist, including motorcycles and cars. Open all year, Sat–Wed 10am–5pm.

The Bugatti Trust,
Prescott Hill, Gotherington,
Cheltenham GL52 9RD
Tel: 01242 677201
www.bugatti.co.uk/trust
An exhibition telling the Bugatti story. Open Mon to Fri 10.30am–3.30pm and during Hill Climb Events and at other times by arrangement.

Cotswold Motoring Museum & Toy Collection,
Old Mill, Bourton-on-the-Water,
Nr Cheltenham GL54 2BY Tel: 01451 821 255
www.csma.uk.com
Collection of cars, motorcycles and caravans. Also large collection of enamel signs, garage equipment and automobilia. This is the home of the Brough Superior Company and of "Brum", the small open 1920's car that has a television series. Open 11th Feb to 31 Oct, 10am–6pm.

GREATER MANCHESTER
Manchester Museum of Transport,
Boyle Street, Cheetham M8 8UW
Tel: 0161 205 2122
www.gmts.co.uk
Collection of over 80 restored vintage buses and other vehicles. Open Wed, Sat, Sun and Public Holidays Nov to Feb 10am–4pm, March to Oct 10am–5pm.

HAMPSHIRE
National Motor Museum,
Brockenhurst, Beaulieu SO42 7ZN
Tel: 01590 612345
www.beaulieu.co.uk/motormuseum
Collection comprising 250 vehicles from some of the earliest examples of motoring to legendary World Record Breakers like Bluebird and Golden Arrow. Open daily except Christmas Day, May to Sept 10am–6pm, Oct to April 10am–5pm.

HUMBERSIDE
Hull Museum of Transport,
Hull City Museums & Art Galleries, Monument Buildings, Queen Victoria Square, Hull HU1 3RA Tel: 01482 613902
museums@hullcc.gov.uk
www.hullcc.gov.uk/museums
Collection of 50 vehicles covering over 200 years of land transport. Open daily Mon to Sat 10am–5pm, Sunday 1.30pm–4.30pm.

ISLE OF MAN
Manx Motor Museum,
Crosby Isle of Man Tel: 01624 851236
History of the motor car illustrated mainly by unusual cars. Open May 21st to Sept 11th 10am–5pm

KENT
C.M. Booth Collection of Historic Vehicles,
Falstaff Antiques, 63-67 High Street, Rolvenden
TN17 4LP Tel: 01580 241234
A private museum consisting mainly of Morgan three-wheelers but also some motorbikes. A most interesting collection plus memorabilia all to be found at the rear of the Antique shop. Open all year Mon to Sat, 10am–5.30pm.

Canterbury Motor Museum,
11 Cogans Terrace, Canterbury CT1 3SJ Tel: 01227 451718
Interesting collection of veteran and vintage cars and motorcycles, as well as memorabilia. Open any day by appt.

Dover Transport Museum,
Willingdon Road, White Cliffs Business Park, Whitfield, Dover CT16 2HJ Tel: 01304 822409/01303 248999
www.dovertransportmuseum.homestead.com
General transport museum with an emphasis on East Kent. Road vehicles of all types and related displays, including a working model tramway and model railway. Contact for new opening times.

Ramsgate Motor Museum,
West Cliff Hall, Ramsgate CT11 9JX
Tel: 01843 581948 or 01268 785002
A private collection of 65 classic cars dating from 1900–70, 70 motorcycles, 30 bicycles plus memorabilia including 200 petrol globes. Open Easter to October, 10.30am–5.30pm.

LANCASHIRE
British Commercial Vehicle Museum,
King Street, Leyland, Nr Preston PR25 2LE Tel: 01772 451011
A unique display of 60 historic commercial vehicles and buses spanning a century of truck and bus building, with appropriate memorabilia. Open 10am–5pm April to Sept Sun, Tues, Wed & Thurs, October Sundays only, Nov to March closed, open Bank Holiday Mondays.

The British Lawnmower Museum,
106–114 Shakespeare Street, Southport PR8 5AJ
Tel: 01704 501336 help@lawnmowerworld.co.uk
www.lawnmowerworld.co.uk
Engines and garden machinery. Also the head office of the ATCO Car Owners Club with one of the best 1939 ATCO cars and memorabilia on display to the general public. Open all year 9am–5.30pm except Sundays and Bank Holidays.

LONDON
London Transport Museum,
Covent Garden Piazza WC2E 7BB
Tel: 020 7565 7299/020 7379 6344
www.ltmuseum.co.uk
Displays of vehicles telling the story of London and it's transport history since the early 1800s. Open daily 10am–6pm Fridays 11am–6pm, closed 24, 25, 26 Dec.

MIDDLESEX
Whitewebbs Museum of Transport,
Whitewebbs Road, Enfield EN2 9HW
Tel: 020 8367 1898
museum@whitewebbs.fsnet.co.uk
www.whitewebbsmuseum.co.uk
A varied collection of cars, light commercials, motorcycles and bicycles. Open Tuesdays Noon–4pm, last Sunday in month 10am–4pm.

NORFOLK
Caister Castle Car Collection,
Caister-on-Sea, Nr Great Yarmouth Tel: 01572 787251
Private collection of cars and motorcycles dating back to 1893. Open daily mid May to September 10am–4.30pm, closed Saturdays.

NORTHERN IRELAND
Ulster Folk & Transport Museum,
Cultra, Holywood, Co. Down BT18 0EU
Tel: 028 90 428 428
www.nidex.com/uftm
Unique collection of wheeled vehicles, ranging from cycles and motorcycles to trams, buses and cars. Open daily except a few days at Christmas.

SCOTLAND
Grampian Transport Museum,
Alford, Aberdeenshire AB33 8AE Tel: 019755 62292
info@gtm.org.uk www.gtm.org.uk
Displays and working exhibits tracing the history of travel and transport in the locality. Open daily from April to Oct, 10am–5pm, October until 4pm.

Moray Motor Museum,
Bridge Street, Elgin IV30 2DE Tel: 01343 544933
Interesting collection of cars and motorcycles plus memorabilia and diecast models.
Open daily April to Oct, 11am–5pm.

Myreton Motor Museum,
Aberlady, East Lothian EH32 0PZ
Tel: 01875 870288/853117
Collection of over 50 cars, motorcycles, commercial vehicles and WWII military vehicles. Also collection of period advertising, posters and enamel signs.

National Museum of Scotland,
The Granton Centre, 242 West Granton Road, Edinburgh EH1 1JF Tel: 0131 551 4106
Small display of engines and complete machines includes the world's first 4 cylinder motorcycle, an 1895 Holden. Tours available, book in advance.

Transport Museum,
Kelvin Hall, 1 Bunhouse Road, Glasgow G3 8DP
Tel: 0141 287 720
Museum covering road, rail and sea. Replica 1938 city street and reconstructed Glasgow Underground Station. Open daily 10am–5pm Mon, Thurs & Sat, 11am–5pm Fri & Sun.

SHROPSHIRE
Midland Motor Museum,
Stanmore Hall, Stourbridge Road, Bridgnorth WV15 6DT
Tel: 01746 762992
Collection of cars and motorcycles dating from 1920s–80s. Open daily 10.30am–5pm.

SOMERSET
Haynes Motor Museum,
Sparkford, Yeovil BA22 7LH
Tel: 01963 440804
mike@haynesmotormuseum.co.uk
www.haynesmotormuseum.com
Haynes Publishing Company museum with collection of vintage, veteran and classic cars and motorcycles. Some 250 cars and 50 motorcycles. Open daily Mar to Oct 9.30am–5.30pm, Nov to Feb 10am–4.30pm, closed Christmas and New Years Days.

SUFFOLK
East Anglia Transport Museum,
Chapel Road, Carlton, Coleville, Lowestoft NR33 8BL Tel: 01502 518459
enquiries@eatm.org.uk www.eatm.org.uk
Wide range of preserved vehicles on display including cars, battery vehicles, trams and trolleybuses. Contact for opening hours.

Ipswich Transport Museum,
Old Trolleybus Depot, Cobham Road, Ipswich IP3 9JD Tel: 01473 715666
www.ipswichtransportmuseum.co.uk
Collection of road transport items either made or used in and around Ipswich, also a substantial archive of documents, photographs, etc. Contact for opening times.

SURREY
Brooklands Museum Trust Limited,
Brooklands Road, Weybridge KT13 0QN Tel: 01932 857381
info@brooklandsmuseum.com
www.brooklandsmuseum.com
Motorsport and Aviation museum including historic racing cars and aircraft. About 20 motorcycles pre WWII. Open Mon to Sun & Bank Holidays 10am–5pm

Dunsfold Land Rover Trust and Museum,
Dunsfold Land Rovers, Alfold Road, Dunsfold GU8 4NP
Tel: 01483 200568
www.landroverclub.net/Club/HTML/Dunsfold_trust.htm
Collection based only on Land Rovers. Contact for viewing days.

EAST SUSSEX
Bentley Wild Fowl and Motor Museum,
Halland, Nr Lewes BN8 5AF Tel: 01825 840573
www.bentley.org.uk
Collection of veteran, Edwardian and vintage cars and motorcycles. Contact for opening times.

Foulkes-Halbard of Filching,
Filching Manor, Filching, Wannock, Polegate BN26 5QA
Tel: 01323 487838/487124
About 100 cars dating from 1893 to 1993, also 30 motorcycles including American pre 1940's bikes ex Steve McQueen. Open by appointment only, Easter to Oct, Thurs to Sun.

TYNE & WEAR
Newburn Hall Motor Museum,
Townfield Gardens, Newburn, Newcastle upon Tyne
NE15 8PY Tel: 0191 264 2977
Family motoring from the 1920s to the present day,
with 50 vehicles on display. Open all year round except
Mondays and Christmas Day, 10am–6pm.

WALES
Anglesey Transport & Agriculture Museum,
Tacla Taid, Tyddyn Pwrpas, Newborough,
Anglesey Tel: 01248 440344
Display of 23 cars, 11 tractors, 20 motorcycles and
commercial vehicles. All with Anglesey connection.

Llangollen Motor Museum,
Pentre Felin, Llangollen LL20 8EE
Tel: 01978 860324
Cars, motorcycles, model vehicles, signs and tools and
parts. Open March to Oct, Tues to Sundays, 10am–5pm.

Madog Car & Motorcycle Museum,
Madog Street West, Porthmadog, Gwynedd LL49 9DF
Tel: 07789 063030
Restored collection of British cars and motorcycles.
Also memorabilia.
Open Whitsun to Oct Mon to Friday, 10am–5pm.

WARWICKSHIRE
Coventry Transport Museum,
Millennium Place, Hales Street, Coventry CV1 1PN
Tel: 024 7683 2425 museum@transport-museum.com
www.transport-museum.com
Large collection of British Road Transport with over 230
cars and commercial vehicles, 250 cycles and 90 motorcycles.
Open all year round except Christmas Eve, Day and Boxing
Day, 10am–5pm

Heritage Motor Centre,
Banbury Road, Gaydon CV35 0BJ Tel: 01926 641188
www.heritage.org.uk
The Heritage Motor Centre is home to the British Motor
Industry Heritage Trust which maintains a collection of 200
vehicles on display, charting the British car industry from the
turn of the century to the present day. Open daily 10am–5pm.

WEST MIDLANDS
Aston Manor Road Transport Museum,
208-216 Witton Lane, Aston, Birmingham B6 6QE
Tel: 0121 322 2298
This former tram depot houses a collection of buses,
trucks and tramcars in an authentic setting. Open most
Sat/Sun & Bank Holiday Monday 11am–5pm

The Birmingham & Midland Museum of Transport,
Chapel Lane, Wythall, Birmingham B47 6JX
Tel: 01564 826471
www.bammot.org.uk
Over 80 buses and coaches including the biggest collection
of Midland Red vehicles, plus vehicles from the former
Birmingham, West Bromwich, Walsall and Wolverhampton
Corporations & West Midlands PTE. Also collection of
Bristol vehicles, London Transport RT, RF, RM and RCL
buses. Commercial vehicles and fire engines, also battery-
electric vehicle display. Open every weekend between
Easter and the last Sunday in October.

Black Country Living Museum,
Tipton Road, Dudley DY1 4SQ Tel: 0121 557 9643
www.bclm.co.uk
Open 1st March to 31st October daily 10am–5pm,
Nov to Feb Weds to Sun only 10am–4pm

WILTSHIRE
Atwell-Wilson Motor Museum,
Stockley Lane, Calne SN11 0NF Tel: 01249 813119
www.atwell-wilson.org www.atwell-museum.freeuk.com
Collection or cars, lorries, motorcycles, mopeds, pushbikes
and a large selection of vehicle manuals, archive material
and motoring memorabilia. Open Sun to Thurs 11am–4pm.

YORKSHIRE
Bradford Industrial Museum,
Moorside Road, Bradford BD2 3HP Tel: 01274 435 900
paula.walsh@bradford.gov.uk
General industrial museum including many engineering
items, Jowett cars, Panther and Scott motorcycles, a steam
roller and Bradford's last tram. Open Tues to Sat 10am–5pm,
Sun Noon–5pm, closed Mon except Bank Holidays.

Skopos Motor Museum,
Alexandra Mills, Alexandra Road,
Batley WF17 6JA Tel: 01924 444423
Over 70 vintage, veteran and classic vehicles.
Open wed to Sun 10.30am–4.30pm.

NEW ZEALAND
Te Puke Vintage Auto Barn,
Te Puke, Tepuke-Rotorua Highway Tel: 64 07 573 6547
www.vintagecars.nzhere.com
Over 90 vintage and classic vehicles. Phone for opening times.

REPUBLIC OF IRELAND
Kilgarvan Motor Museum,
KIlgarvan, Co. Kerry Tel: 353 64 85346
Family run museum with vintage and classic cars plus
automobilia. Open 7 days all year round 9.30am–7pm.

U.S.A.
Larz Anderson Auto Museum,
15 Newton Street, Brookline,
Massachusetts 02445 Tel: 617 522 6547
www.mot.org
One of America's oldest collection of automobiles.
Open Tues to Sun 10am–5pm, open Bank Holiday
Mondays, closed Thanksgiving, Christmas and New Year's
Day. Closed to the public April 26 to May 11.

Auburn-Cord-Duesenberg Museum,
1600 South Wayne Street, Auburn,
Indiana IN 46706 Tel: 260 925 1444
www.acdmuseum.org
Collection of at least 100 vehicles and artifacts, with an
emphasis on Auburn, Cord and Duesenberg cars, in the
original Art Deco building that was used by the Auburn
Automobile Company. Open daily 9am–5pm, closed
Thanksgiving, Christmas and New Year's Day.

Automotive Hall of Fame,
21400 Oakwood Boulevard, Dearborn,
Michigan MI48124 Tel: 313 240 4000
www.automotivehalloffame.org
Open Nov to April daily 9am–5pm, closed Mondays and
some holidays.

Bellm's Cars & Music,
500 N. Tamiami Trail, Sarasota, Florida
Tel: 941 355 6228
Eclectic collection of cars, antiques and music, some dating
back to early 1700s. Phone for details.

Blackhawk Museum,
3700 Blackhawk Plaza Circle, Danville, California 94506
Tel: 925 736 2277
www.blackhawkauto.org
Open Wed to Sun 10am–5pm and most holidays except
Thanksgiving, Christmas and New Year's Day.

Otis Chandler Museum of Transportation,
1421 Emerson Ave, Oxnard CA 93033
Tel: 805 486 5929
www.chandlerwheels.com
Over 100 motorcycles, automobiles including 1930s
American cars. Contact for opening times.

Chevyland USA Auto Museum,
Elm Creek, Nebraska 68836
Tel: (308) 856 4208
chevylandusa@nebi.com
Dozens of restored Chevys. Open Memorial Day to Labor
Day 8am–5pm, by appointment rest of the year.

Corvette American Museum,
Cooperstown, New York 13326 Tel: (607) 547 4135

Fagan's Antique & Classic Automobile Museum,
162nd Street & Clairmont Avenue, Markham,
Illinois IL 60426 Tel: 312 331 3380

Henry Ford Museum & Greenfield Village,
20900 Oakwood Blvd, Dearborn,
Michigan 48124-4088
Tel: 313 982 6100/313 271 2455
www.hfmgv.org
World-renowned exhibition describing the history of the
automobile in America. Open 7 days 9.30am–5pm,
closed Thanksgiving and Christmas Days.

Hall of Fame & Classic Car Museum,
PO Box 240, 1 Speedway Drive, Weedsport NY 12166
Tel: 315 834 6606
Classic cars, historic race cars, racing memorabilia and a full
color racing pictorial exhibit. Open April to Labor Day Mon
to Sat 10am–5pm Sun 12 Noon–7pm, Sept to Dec Mon to
Fri 10am–5pm Sat & Sun 11am–4pm.

Imperial Palace Auto Collection
Imperial Palace Hotel & Casino, 3535
Las Vegas Blvd South, Las Vegas, Nevada 89109
Tel: (702) 794 3174

Indianapolis Motor Speedway, Hall of Fame Museum,
4790 West 16th Street, Indianapolis, Indiana 46222
Tel: 317 484 6747

J.E.M. Classic Car Museum,
R.D.#1, Box 120C, Andreas, Pennsylvania 18211
Tel: (717) 368 3554

Justice Brothers Racing Museum,
2734 East Huntington Drive, Duarte,
California 91010 Tel: 626 359 9174
mail@justicebrothers.com
www.justicebrothers.com/jb6.html

Louisville Automobile Museum,
737 South Third Street, Louisville, Kentucky 40202-2150
Tel: (502) 568 2277

Memoryville, USA. Autos of Yesteryear,
Route 63 North, Rolla, Missouri 65401
Tel: (314) 364 1810

S. Ray Miller Foundation, Inc.,
Antique & Classic Auto Museum,
2130 Middlebury St, Elkhart, Indiana 46516
Tel: 219 522 0539

National Automotive & Truck Museum
of the United States, Inc.,
1000 Gordon M. Buehrig Place, Box 686, Auburn,
Indiana 46706-686 Tel: 219 235 9714

National Corvette Museum,
350 Corvette Drive, Bowling Green, KY 42101
Tel: US TOLL FREE: 1-800-53-VETTE
www.corvettemuseum.com

Owls Head Transportation Museum,
PO Box 277, Route 73, Owls Head,
Maine 04854 Tel: 207 594 4418
info@ohtm.org www.ohtm.org
Antiques, classic and special interest auto, motorcycles,
aircraft, engines, bicycles and related vehicles. Open daily
except for Thanksgiving, Christmas, New Year's Day and
the first non-Easter Sunday of each April, April to October
10am–5pm, November to March 10am–4pm.

Packard Museum (W.D. Packard Music Hall),
1703 Mahoning Ave, NW Warren, Ohio 44483
Tel: (216) 395 8442

Shelby American Collection,
5020 Chaparral Court, PO Box 19228, Boulder,
Colorado Tel: 303 516 9565

Silver Springs Antique Car Collection,
State Road 40, Ocala, Florida 32670 Tel: (904) 236 2121

Studebaker National Museum,
525 S Main Street, South Bend, Indiana 46601
Tel: 219 235 9714

David Taylor Classic Car Museum,
918 Mechanic, Galveston Island, Texas 77550
Tel: 409 765 6590

Toyota Museum,
1901 South Western Avenue, Torrance, California 90509
Tel: (213) 618 4000

Wells Auto Museum,
Rt 1, PO Box 496, Wells, Maine 04090
Tel: (207) 646 9064

Bibliography

Baldwin, Nick; Georgano, G. N.; Sedgwick, Michael;
and Laban, Brian; *The World Guide to Automobiles*,
Guild Publishing, London, 1987

Colin Chapman Lotus Engineering,
Osprey, 1993.

Flammang, James M; *Standard Catalog of Imported Cars*,
Krause Publications Inc, 1992.

Georgano, G. N.; ed: *Encyclopedia of Sports Cars*,
Bison Books, 1985.

Georgano, Nick; *Military Vehicles of World War II*,
Osprey 1994.

Harding, Anthony; Allport, Warren; Hodges, David;
Davenport, John; *The Guinness Book of the Car*,
Guinness Superlatives Ltd, 1987

Hay, Michael; *Bentley Factory Cars*,
Osprey, 1993.

Hough, Richard; *A History of the World's Sports Cars*,
Allen & Unwin, 1961.

Isaac, Rowan; *Morgan*, Osprey, 1994.

McComb, F. Wilson; *MG by McComb*,
Osprey, 1978.

Nye, Doug; *Autocourse History of the Grand Prix Car
1966–1991*, Hazleton Publishing, 1992.

Posthumus, Cyril, and Hodges, David;
Classic Sportscars, Ivy Leaf, 1991.

Robson, Graham; *Classic and Sportscar A–Z of Cars of
the 1970s*, Bay View Books, 1990.

Sedgwick, Michael; Gillies, Mark;
Classic and Sportscar A–Z of Cars of the 1930s,
Bay View Books, 1989.

Sedgwick, Michael, Gillies, Mark;
Classic and Sportscar A–Z of Cars 1945–70,
Bay View Books, 1990.

Sieff, Theo; *Mercedes-Benz*, Gallery Books, 1989.

Vanderveen, Bart; *Historic Military Vehicles Directory*,
After the Battle Publications, 1989.

Willson, Quentin; Selby David, *The Ultimate Classic
Car Book*, Dorling Kindersley, 1995.

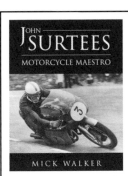
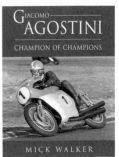

Index

Italic Page numbers denote colour pages, **bold** numbers refer to information and pointer boxes